Implementing Sustainable Development

Implementing Sustainable Development

Integrated Assessment and Participatory Decision-making Processes

Edited by

Hussein Abaza

Chief, Economics and Trade Branch, Division of Technology, Industry and Economics, United Nations Environment Programme, International Environment House, Geneva, Switzerland

Andrea Baranzini

Senior Lecturer, University of Geneva, Lecturer, Swiss Federal Institute of Technology, Lausanne, and Co-Principal Investigator, Swiss National Centre of Competence in Research 'Climate', Switzerland

THE WORK IS PUBLISHED FOR AND ON BEHALF OF UNEP

Edward Elgar

Cheltenham, UK • Northampton, MA, USA

Published by
Edward Elgar Publishing Limited
Glensanda House
Montpellier Parade
Cheltenham
Glos GL50 1UA
UK

Edward Elgar Publishing, Inc.
136 West Street
Suite 202
Northampton
Massachusetts 01060
USA

A catalogue record for this book
is available from the British Library

Library of Congress Cataloguing in Publication Data

Implementing sustainable development: integrated assessment and participatory decision-making processes/edited by Hussein Abaza, Andrea Baranzini; published for and on behalf of UNEP.
p. cm.
Includes bibliographical references and index.
1. Sustainable development. 2. Economic development—Environmental aspects. I. Abaza, Hussein. II. Baranzini, Andrea. III. United Nations Environment Programme.
HC79.E5 I51115 2002
338.9'27—dc21
2002019540

ISBN 1 84064 913 5

Typeset by Manton Typesetters, Louth, Lincolnshire, UK.

Printed and bound in Great Britain by Bookcraft (Bath) Ltd.

Contents

Contributors

Hussein Abaza, *United Nations Environment Programme, Geneva.*
Andrea Baranzini, *University of Geneva, Geneva and Swiss Federal Institute of Technology, Lausanne.*
Dave Biggs, *Envision Sustainability Tools Inc., Vancouver.*
Judith Bradbury, *Pacific Northwest National Laboratory, California.*
Stewart J. Cohen, *Environment Canada and University of British Columbia, Vancouver.*
Silvio O. Funtowicz, *European Commission Joint Research Centre, Ispra.*
Juan Martinez-Alier, *Universitat Autonoma de Barcelona, Bellaterra.*
Giuseppe Munda, *Universitat Autonoma de Barcelona, Bellaterra.*
Claudia E. Natenzon, *Universidad de Buenos Aires, Buenos Aires.*
Maryam Niamir-Fuller, *United Nations Development Programme, New York.*
Martin O'Connor, *Université de Versailles Saint-Quentin-en-Yvelines, Guyancourt.*
Héctor A. Poggiese, *Facultad Latinoamericana de Ciencias Sociales – Sede Argentina, Buenos Aires.*
Jerry Ravetz, *The Research Methods Consultancy Ltd, London.*
Steve Rayner, *Columbia University, New York.*
Emiko Kawakami de Resende, *Centro de Pesquisa Agropecuaria do Pantanal, Corumbá.*
John B. Robinson, *University of British Columbia, Vancouver.*
Dale S. Rothman, *Maastricht University, Maastricht.*
Jan Rotmans, *Maastricht University, Maastricht.*
Matthias Ruth, *University of Maryland, College Park.*
Sylvia S. Tognetti, *US World Wildlife Fund, Washington, DC.*
Marjolein B.A. van Asselt, *Maastricht University, Maastricht.*
Jeroen C.J.M. van den Bergh, *Free University, Amsterdam.*
Maria J. Willumsen, *Florida International University, Miami.*

Preface

Decision makers increasingly seek to design environmental and development policies that will support sustainable development. To support these efforts, practical tools to formulate sustainable development policies and clear methods to assess their acceptability and effectiveness are urgently needed. This book contributes to meeting these needs by presenting both analytical and empirical aspects of decision-making processes that can support the design, implementation and assessment of sustainable development policies.

Sustainable development decisions are particularly complex and uncertain, and have varied implications for different stakeholders. The decision-making process is thus very often confronted by conflicting objectives and contrasting perspectives and interests. Even after a participatory process is able to define a common set of policy objectives agreed to by all stakeholders, the choice of the analytical methodologies, technical assumptions, and scale and time dimensions used to formulate these policies are themselves not neutral. Recognizing this, the chapters of this book present and discuss methods for integrating environmental and social sciences to support participatory policy design, implementation and assessment processes. The methods are applied, richly illustrated and discussed with reference to several case studies from various regions of the world. Although chapters have distinct focuses – some more methodological and others more empirical – they all contribute to a clearer understanding of the way sustainable development is perceived and assessed by society.

This volume brings together twelve studies which originated from a joint project of the United Nations Environment Programme (UNEP), Economics and Trade Branch, Division of Technology, Industry and Economics and the Scientific Committee on Problems of the Environment (SCOPE) of the International Council of Scientific Unions. The book is divided into three parts. Part I describes various methodological approaches to policy design and their implications for decision-making processes; Part II explores possible ways for stakeholders to be included in complex environmental management problems; and Part III presents issues and case studies on modelling aspects of integrated policy assessment.

In contrast to other publications and approaches, which usually treat sustainable development from the point of view of a single discipline, this publication is interdisciplinary, emphasizing how the integration of a wide set of disciplines and stakeholder perspectives into the policy-making process can help better understand sustainable development policies. In each chapter there is also a willingness to make explicit all of the assumptions and conflicting values implied in sustainable development decisions. Finally, proposed methodologies are policy-oriented and fully compatible with decision-making practices.

H.A.
A.B.

Acknowledgements

Much of the material presented in this book originated from a joint project of the Scientific Committee on Problems of the Environment (SCOPE) and the United Nations Environment Programme (UNEP). The concept for this project was initially proposed by Hussein Abaza from the Economics and Trade Branch of UNEP's Division of Technology, Industry and Economics. The project aimed to synthesize and assess the implications of new economic tools developed in the field of ecological economics for integrated assessment and policy planning at global and regional levels. During this project, there were a number of activities, seminars and regional workshops, also attended by some of the contributors to the present book.

This book would thus not have been possible without the active involvement, efforts and enthusiasm of the many people who participated in the SCOPE/UNEP project. In particular, we should like to thank Professor Robert Costanza, who chaired the Scientific Advisory Committee, Sylvia Tognetti (Project Officer), who also developed the project in consultation with many of the participants, and who conceived, assembled and produced a first version of this book, and Lisa Speckhardt, who provided editorial assistance in initial stages. Silvio Funtowicz was particularly helpful in the initial phase of project development, in identifying important issues that might be addressed, and existing research efforts that might have otherwise been overlooked. Professor Bedrich Moldan, Professor Ted Munn, Professor Richard Norgaard and other, anonymous, referees provided valuable comments and suggestions on previous versions of some of the papers.

Several meetings and regional workshops organized within the SCOPE/UNEP project also contributed to the publication of this book. In particular, we are grateful to Peter May and Marilia Pastuk, from PRO-ECO (the Programme in Ecological Economics and Agrarian Policies of the Univesidade Federal Rural do Rio de Janeiro) who organized seminars and planning meetings in Campo Grande and Cuiabá, together with the project officer. In Campo Grande the meeting was hosted by SODEPAN (The Society for the Defense of the Pantanal) with the assistance of Edson Cardoso (former director of SODEPAN), UCDB (the Dom Bosco Catholic University) and the Fundação Pantanal, which is part of the Environment Ministry of Mato Grosso do Sul. The seminar in Cuiabá was hosted by Ecotropica. Participants included representatives from regional research institutions and non-governmental organizations, including the Centro de Pesquisa Agropecuária do Pantanal (EMBRAPA/CPAP) and the Federal Universities of Mato Grosso do Sul. The first regional workshop was held in the Pantanal region of Brazil, and included the presentations of papers on individual methods in the context of case studies. The aim of the workshop was to review computational questions, integrating ecological and economic theory and models, time- and space-scale issues, and interactions among the different stakeholders. The second regional workshop focusing on modelling aspects was held in Boston, USA. As a case study, special attention was given to land management by the US army, which also sponsored the workshop, through the US Army Environmental Policy Institute.

We should also like to thank Véronique Plocq-Fichelet, SCOPE Executive Director, J.M. Melillo, SCOPE Executive Committee President, and Professor Philippe Bourdeau, SCOPE Past President for their active involvement during this project.

Introduction

Hussein Abaza and Andrea Baranzini

This book is devoted to sustainable development, with special reference to its implications in terms of policy implementation and assessment. As development can only be sustainable if it considers its environmental, social and economic implications, this book therefore relies on the common understanding that implementation of sustainable development must be approached by establishing a bridge between the environmental and social sciences. Although the chapters have different focuses, some more methodological, others more empirical, they all possess profound implications in the way sustainability is understood and assessed. In different ways, they also indicate that the black box of modelling and integrated assessment should be revealed in order to increase transparency, interdisciplinarity and meaningful participation of all the stakeholders in the decision-making process.

Sustainable development definitely entered the political agenda following the report by the World Commission on Development and the Environment (WCED, 1987). The often quoted definition given by the WCED is that 'sustainable development is development that meets the needs of the present without compromising the ability of future generations to meet their needs' (ibid., p. 43). Sustainable development is the foundation of Agenda 21 and of the Rio Declaration on Environment and Development. Since then, it has become the guiding principle of environmental and development policies. However, at the present time, there is no clear and common understanding of the real implications of sustainable development or ways to develop methods for addressing and assessing sustainability – be it at the local and project level or at the global level. There is, nevertheless, some general agreement on some key dimensions of sustainable development.

The concept of sustainability is usually grounded on three criteria, biophysical (or environmental), social (or ethical) and economic. As pointed out by Daly (1987), these three criteria may be interpreted as defining three filters in deciding respectively what is (physically) possible; what is possible and (socially) desirable; and finally what is possible, desirable and (economically) feasible. Assessing sustainability is thus by definition an interdisciplinary effort. This argument is reinforced by the focus of sustainable development on meeting people's needs and thus increasing their welfare. Of course, welfare has very different components, such as produced goods and services, income and wealth distribution, leisure time, employment security, health, freedom, and environmental goods and services (see Hueting, 1990). Therefore development should not only imply a quantitative increase in economic goods and services, as production growth may be in conflict with other elements that contribute to welfare, such as in diminished environmental services resulting from pollution and degradation of natural resources.

Another important dimension introduced by sustainable development is the long-term setting in which projects and policies have to be assessed. On the one hand, quantitative increases in produced economic goods that are material- and energy-intensive cannot be sustained indefinitely, because our material world is a finite one. On the other hand, sustainability explicitly emphasizes the welfare interdependence between generations (see Faucheux *et al.*, 1996). In this context, sustainability is also related to the debate on governance and participatory approaches. In particular, to avoid the constraints of current choices impinging on the freedom of future generations institutions should preferably be designed so as to impose social controls combined with a minimal sacrifice of personal freedom. Discussions on institutional changes have sometime split the debate between advocates of state intervention and supporters of free market mechanisms, and strengthened the widespread conflict between individualism and collectivism, and between a market-oriented and a civil society (cf. Bürgenmeier, 1999).

Part I of this volume is concerned with the methodological implications of sustainability and with the resulting ramifications for decision-making processes. Confronted by the fundamental issues implied by sustainable development, an analysis of environmental problems from the perspective of natural sciences alone is indeed insufficient and often inadequate. These issues are actually closely related to conflicting values and stem from the failure of institutions to control access to resources, which includes their exploitation and distribution. As a consequence, as Judith Bradbury and Steve Rayner point out in Chapter 1, social scientists have increasingly been included in the integrated assessment of policies. However, the authors observe that social sciences have mainly provided highly aggregated data that are compatible within the framework already established by the natural sciences. This chapter thus argues that it is essential to incorporate data that provide further insights into human behaviour and motivations, and the associated ethical and distributive implications. In other words, Bradbury and Rayner assert that the basis of disagreement about policy issues affecting the relationship between human activities and the ecosystems is societal rather than technical. The chapter then explores research into technical controversies related to nuclear waste and chemical weapons disposal in the United States to demonstrate the necessity of addressing issues pertaining to the meaning of proposed policies to those affected.

Martin O'Connor explores this argument further in Chapter 2. Although the author also supports the argument that sustainability demands more than just a descriptive (for example, resource inventory) type of analysis, he adopts a different starting point. Indeed, O'Connor stresses that a central question raised by sustainability is how to reconcile preoccupations with the future with those of the present. In other words, policies for ecological, social and economic sustainability involve choices for the redistribution through time of economic opportunities and of access to services and benefits provided by the biophysical environment. The chapter discusses the guiding concepts that might be appropriate for informed decision making as the scope of concern widens to the ecosystems of the planet and the long term. In that context, the response of conventional economics has been to extend cost–benefit analysis across time, through the valuation of environmental damages and of economy–environment trade-offs through time, using the discounting procedure. However, high uncertainties, the irreversibility of many impacts and the divergences of opinion about the basis for resolving questions of fairness imply that the cost–benefit optimizing approach may not be sufficient as a guide for decision making. Using examples of water resources and forests, the chapter thus develops the theme of the distribution of sustainability, placing an emphasis on managing and investing in the reproduction, transformation and renewal of the habitats that are our life-support systems. Valuation for sustainability means the appraisal of options whose effect is to sustain a given form or way of life, and this is inseparable from the question of the communities of interest to be sustained.

The environment as an area of conflict between competing values and interests, and the different groups and communities that represent them, is also highlighted by Silvio Funtowicz, Juan Martinez-Alier, Giuseppe Munda and Jerry Ravetz (Chapter 3). Those authors use 'post-normal science' to build a bridge between complex systems and environmental policy. This approach focuses on aspects of problem solving that tend to be neglected in traditional accounts of scientific practice, namely uncertainty and value loading. It also provides a coherent explanation of the need for greater participation in science-policy processes. Using that approach, and given that welfare is a multidimensional concept, they question the assumption of value commensurability used by conventional economics in the context of conflict resolution. Instead, the authors use multicriteria evaluation as a tool for conflict management, given its ability to address problems marked by various conflicting evaluations. In particular, multicriteria evaluation techniques can help provide more insight into the nature of the conflicts and into ways to arrive at political compromises, thereby increasing the transparency of the choice processes. Examples of land use conflicts in The Netherlands and of water management issues in Italy illustrate how conflictual policy issues can be opened up for resolution with multicriteria evaluation. The authors also discuss how multicriteria evaluation may address macroeconomic issues, in relation to green national accounting and physical indices of sustainability.

Chapter 4, by Jan Rotmans and Marjolein van Asselt, is also concerned with the multidimensionality and interdisciplinary tasks related to sustainable development. The chapter provides a survey of current and past practices in integrated assessment (IA), focusing on modelling, scenario development and participatory methods. In order to improve the credibility of integrated assessment as an approach for complex issues, the authors also develop a code of good practice and quality criteria. The framework for quality assessment is based on a distinction between analytical quality, methodological quality and usability. In addition, Rotmans and van Asselt further appraise integrated assessment practices by critically assessing an existing IA model, TARGETS ('Tool to Assess Regional and Global Environmental and health Targets for Sustainability'). The TARGETS project can be considered as a scientific assessment of global change taking into account plural social and cultural objectives. The model enables evaluation of a number of environmental, social and economic consequences of several human activities simultaneously. The reflexive assessment upon the TARGETS project (which both authors have led) and the identification of gaps in knowledge are used for setting an agenda for future developments in integrated assessment. The areas pointed out for future research include the development of scientific methods for participatory processes; protocols for integrated uncertainty management, aggregation and disaggregation; and elaboration of the link between different spatial and temporal scales to identify the role of individuals and institutions, and their systems of governance. Some of these issues are explored further in Part II and Part III.

The contributions in Part I show that sustainable development decisions are particularly complex and uncertain, and have different implications for people. The decision-making process is very often confronted by conflicting social objectives and contrasting stakeholders' perspectives and interests. The choice of analytical methodologies, technical assumptions and scale and time dimensions are not neutral and are themselves policy decisions, which should not be taken without consideration of the people and interests involved. However, much research is still needed on participatory approaches and how models could be linked to stakeholders' perspectives. Part II of this book is thus devoted to the exploration of possible ways in which stakeholders may be included in complex environmental management problems.

Chapter 5, by Emiko Kawakami de Resende and Sylvia Tognetti, focuses on the implications for decision making of using information derived from different approaches. It also analyses the potential consequences of the proposed Paraguay–Paraná waterway ('Hidrovia') project, giving special attention to the conservation of biodiversity in the Pantanal. They argue that attempts to analyse costs and benefits of the project depend on how the problem is defined and are based on questionable and often arbitrary assumptions, which are in turn influenced by the interests and perspectives that have a voice in the decision-making process. Insufficient data and the complexity of the Pantanal ecosystem suggest limits to precise predictions of the impacts of the Hidrovia project. In addition, the project has the potential for large-scale irreversible impacts at the local and regional level. The authors contend that this kind of complex problem is beyond the capacities of existing institutions, and that it may be impossible to capture it in a technical framework and by standard valuation methods. Therefore they suggest an adaptive approach to valuation which provides stakeholders with opportunities for mutual learning, to reframe the problem in a broader context including the indirect effects of the Hidrovia project, to reconsider their values based on new information, and to engage in a process of negotiation and conflict resolution regarding what is to be sustained. The results of this process can then provide a set of criteria for evaluating the success of development efforts and for identifying trade-offs. Valuation thus becomes an institutional problem of access to the decision-making process. In this chapter, the value of the participatory process is also discussed with reference to other water development projects.

The relationship between increased public participation in the decision-making process and democracy is explored further by Claudia Natenzon and Héctor Poggiese in Chapter 6. These authors propose a methodology for participatory planning and co-management for application to critical situations in Latin America. This methodology involves formulation of public policies, elaboration of development projects that consolidate the democratic process, and consideration of environmentally sustainable interventions. Its main features are analysed in one of the cases to which it was applied, the Development Plan of Province Zudañez in Bolivia. The project was initiated by a non-governmental organization which originally directed its actions towards rural development and, more specifically, towards the improvement of peasant agricultural production. However, it was realized that modernization of agricultural techniques was not possible without considering basic structural issues affecting the population, such as education, health, nutrition and cultural values. In addition, it was necessary to address political issues both within the local community and in its relation to other levels of public management. In other words, in this context it was necessary to develop a strategy for collaboration which included finding the common ground between traditionally opposed actors possessing distinct perceptions of reality and different cultural backgrounds. The methodology proposed by Natenzon and Poggiese involves the actors in a continuous process of modelling the reality that they want to transform and generating conditions conducive to the emergence of new social actors. It involves two working tools, referred to as the 'methodological cycle' and the 'logical sequence'. The authors' final objective is to show the existence of tested methods for the collaborative construction of the future.

In the context of climate change, Chapter 7, by Stewart Cohen, focuses on collaboration between various stakeholders and the scientific community. The starting point for Cohen is that research and the current discussion on climate change are focused on uncertainties in climate projections and calculation of mitigation options (that is, how to reduce greenhouse gas emissions). Consequently, most integrated assessment efforts have been directed at the mitigation component and comparatively less information is provided on the benefits of impacts avoided, including adaptation options. However, the author points out that the problem of climate change is really about the potential effects on ecosystems, resources and the societies that depend on them. These effects will be unique to each region and country, depending on their vulnerabilities and adaptive capacities. Cohen argues that the narrow dimensions of the current debate on climate change may be a consequence of the lack of attention given to the needs of stakeholders who may be affected by the impacts of climate change. The purpose of this chapter is thus to explore a more holistic approach to integrated assessment of climate change impacts and adaptation which can complement continental/global-scale integrated assessment modelling efforts that largely focus on emissions limitation. This approach includes stakeholder participation in the formation of research questions, the generation of new information, and the discussion on results and recommendations. It is suggested that a broad 'scientists–stakeholder collaborative' could be a useful framework for an IA of climate change impacts on regions and countries, which would include modelling and non-modelling approaches, and incorporate institutional and stakeholder issues that do not readily lend themselves to economic analyses. The collaborative process can also help in capacity building, providing the foundation for creating a common property institution that focuses on climate change stewardship. The discussion is highlighted by a case study from Canada (the Mackenzie Basin Impact Study), which explores the regional impacts of climate change by involving both scientists and stakeholders.

Starting from a different perspective, Chapter 8 presents a possible way to involve users in models that are conceived as an aid to decision-making processes. In this chapter, Dale Rothman, John Robinson and Dave Biggs discuss how the relationship between indicators, models of sustainability and users has been approached in the development of QUEST ('Quite Useful Ecosystem Scenario Tool'). QUEST is a microcomputer-based scenario generation and evaluation system which is intended to encourage thinking about sustainability in a regional context. It is being applied in different contexts in Canada, Latin America, Europe and Asia. Through QUEST, an individual user or a group of users can explore different possible future scenarios in terms of their social, economic and environmental characteristics and consequences. Recognizing that much of the value of models is also the learning that takes place during their construction, QUEST is intended to allow the users to actually construct and evaluate scenarios based on their own needs. These scenarios and consequences can be actively created by users in the form of a computer game. The objective is to acquaint users with the complex realities of the decision-making process, specifically the uncertainties involved, the necessary trade-offs and the role of subjective values.

Part III of the volume presents issues and case studies that are more related to the modelling aspect of integrated assessment. In Chapter 9, Jeroen van den Bergh surveys the spatial and temporal aspects of integrated environmental–economic modelling from the perspective of formal modelling and evaluation in a sustainable development policy context. To clarify this context, the author presents an overview of different perspectives on sustainable development, along with the corresponding modelling implications. Several ecological–economic models are then presented and compared, and the possibilities of integration discussed. Van den Bergh examines the relevance of thermodynamics for integrated models and its implications, for example in relation to specification of production functions and substitution possibilities. Observing that the spatial dimension of sustainable development has received less attention than the global context, the author discusses some of the main advantages of performing integrated studies at the regional level. This forms the basis for a critical discussion of a very aggregated indicator, the 'ecological footprint'. Since sustainable development is inherently dynamic, van den Bergh then considers various types and aspects of dynamic integrated models. Compared with neoclassical models, the two most important differential characteristics of evolutionary models are non-determinism and non-average behaviour. It is argued that standard growth theory may be interpreted as dealing with a rather short-term horizon and a stable economic regime characterized by a set of homogeneous firms, whereas evolutionary theory is concerned with a longer time frame in which diversity has an essential impact. In this sense, the author suggests that the two fields are rather complementary. An additional dimension analysed by van den Bergh is related to dynamic and spatial indicators, which may be generated by integrated models. The issue of aggregation, discounting and uncertainty in this context is emphasized. To illustrate how some of those ideas can be operationalized, the chapter presents two examples. The first integrates elements from growth theory with a multisectoral economic structure and a materials flow model, based on dynamic mass balance production functions. The model allows for an analysis of limits to growth and sustainable development through numerical simulations of scenarios. The second example refers to the Sporades, an island region in Greece. It is a systems modelling study linking dynamic and spatial models into one comprehensive model. Scenario analysis and multicriteria evaluation are used to examine which policy options aimed at sustainable regional development are the most attractive.

Non-average behaviour and variability, spatial heterogeneity, time and dynamics, and indicators are also at the heart of Chapter 10, by Maryam Niamir-Fuller. This chapter reviews some of the theoretical background and points out some guidelines for monitoring and evaluating ecosystem function, structure and health in arid and semi-arid environments. The objective is to translate theoretical advances in ecological theory into appropriate policies and development activities. The discussion concentrates on African drylands, where development interventions in the last three decades have often been labelled failures. Such failures were often related to inappropriate paradigms used by scientists and development workers on the relationship between man and the environment. Anthropological work in the last decades, together with a greater understanding of non-equilibrium systems, has helped to improve appreciation of the way pastoral systems function, in order to understand the relationships between long-term and short-term strategies, and avoid an underestimation of their true economic value, for example in terms of production. This chapter shows some of the theoretical and practical differences between equilibrium and non-equilibrium systems, and draws implications for better monitoring and evaluation. Non-equilibrium ecological theory recognizes three characteristics of arid ecosystems: ecological variability, unpredictability and resilience. As a consequence, indicators that track variability (that is, range as opposed to average) appear more appropriate in capturing the complexity and uncertainty of arid lands. In addition, non-equilibrium systems require more frequent measurement, more sampling to cover space variability, more reliance on ground measures rather than on remote sensing, and more emphasis on monitoring soil and climatic factors, rather than on vegetation. The additional costs implied by this approach can be reduced through a decentralized system, which includes the local land users and their organizations. Non-equilibrium theory also maintains that the mobility of traditional extensive grazing systems in Africa was the key factor in ensuring ecological sustainability, since it is a mechanism which adapts to the variability and unpredictability of the ecosystem. In this context, appropriate social indicators of the viability of pastoral production and livelihood systems must consider several interrelated factors, ranging from production parameters to land tenure security. Niamir-Fuller thus shows that sustainable development in arid systems requires fundamental changes in the way the system is evaluated and monitored. The variability and uncertainty in arid systems requires modification of research networks, monitoring programmes and the process of indicator selection. Management-oriented decision-making and monitoring programmes need to be decentralized and participatory in order to account for the inherent variability in time, and heterogeneity in space and scale.

In Chapter 11, Maria Willumsen is concerned with possible trade-offs between alternative growth strategies and environmental degradation, more specifically the interactions between production activities and deforestation in the Eastern Amazon region of Brazil (the Carajás Region). This region has experienced rapid growth and settlement over the last three decades, particularly after the discovery of a large deposit of strategic minerals. This growth process has been followed by significant depletion of natural resources, in particular deforestation. Exploration of the region's iron ore mines for export and the emergence of the pig iron industry – which relies on charcoal as an energy source – have been held responsible for the high level of deforestation. However, environmental assessments focused mainly on the direct effects of the growth process, and did not extend beyond the immediate project area. Other studies pointed out the role of infrastructures, population, subsidies and property rights, but Willumsen argues that they contained little formal analysis of the determinants of deforestation. Therefore the methodology presented in this chapter is designed to overcome the limitations of previous studies by capturing a wide range of interactions among different economic sectors and between these sectors and other aspects of society, including the environment. Willumsen develops an input–output (I–O) model representing the basic economic interactions between sectors, and between the broader Carajás Region and the more immediately affected Carajás area. The structure of the model is relatively simple and designed to allow a clear exposition of the existing relationship between production and environmental degradation. It explicitly integrates socioeconomic information with technical aspects of production and the environment, and is able to generate an integrated account of the effects of production and deforestation. Simulation results show that, contrary to common belief, the impact of industrial production (including the pig iron industry) on deforestation has been indirect and not significant at this stage. In fact, the study points out that the major impacts are due to agriculture and livestock. Willumsen argues that I–O models offer a flexible framework that is useful for visualizing complex interactions and are thus an interesting tool to support decision-making processes.

Another example of an applied integrated assessment model is given by Matthias Ruth in Chapter 12. This chapter shows how to model and analyse energy use and carbon emissions through a dynamic computer model which explicitly incorporates the expertise of decision makers in industry and government agencies. Many industries are in a situation that requires rapid adjustments to changes in their markets for inputs and outputs, and to the policy environment in which they operate. The necessary investments to make these changes are typically large, and the consequences of the decisions are often felt for decades. Adjustments in one part of the industry may require and trigger adjustments elsewhere. The resulting dynamics of the industrial system are highly complex. To understand these dynamics requires detailed knowledge of the industry, and simultaneously, of the aggregate behaviour that results from changes in each individual part of the industry in their relationship to the factor and product markets. The development of a dynamic computer model can help put the individual pieces together and provide insight into the likely responses of the aggregate system. The dynamic computer model can also facilitate dialogue among scientists, engineers, modellers, the integrated assessment community and decision makers in industry and policy. Generating and maintaining such dialogue requires that adequate emphasis be placed on the modelling process, rather than solely on the results of a model. Using these premises, Ruth develops a dynamic model of the USA iron and steel industry, using the graphical programming language STELLA, a transparent modelling approach that facilitated dialogue among stakeholders. Several actors and types of information were used at various levels of modelling. The author establishes a baseline for likely future energy use and emissions based on time-series analysis of the industry. Engineering-based forecasts and different assumptions on climate change policies defined alternative scenarios. The model is used to investigate which segments within the industry would be most responsive to climate policies. In addition, climate change policies are prioritized on the basis of their effectiveness in reducing carbon emissions. The results obtained by Ruth show that the dynamics that describe technology change and fuel choice are fundamental in assessing market-based climate policies in the US iron and steel industry. The effectiveness of policies depends on the technical details of the production process and on past technology lock-in.

REFERENCES

Bürgenmeier, B. (1999), 'Environment protection: Towards a socio-economic policy design', in M. O'Connor and C. Spash (eds), *Valuation and the Environment. Theory, Method and Practice*, Cheltenham, UK and Northampton, MA, USA: Edward Elgar, pp. 73–86.

Daly, H.E. (1987), 'Filters against folly in environmental economics: The impossible, the undesirable and the uneconomic', in G. Pillet (ed.), *Environmental Economics – The Analysis of a Major Interface*, Geneva: R. Leimgruber, pp. 1–10.

Faucheux S., D. Pearce and J. Proops (eds) (1996), *Models of Sustainable Development*, Cheltenham, UK and Brookfield, US: Edward Elgar.
Hueting, R. (1990), 'The Brundtland Report: A matter of conflicting goals', *Ecological Economics*, **2** (2), 109–17.
WCED (1987), *Our Common Future*, Oxford: Oxford University Press.

PART I

Methodological Issues towards Integrative Analysis

1. Reconciling the irreconcilable

Judith Bradbury and Steve Rayner

INTRODUCTION

Leading thinkers in both the natural and social sciences are increasingly recognizing that the basis of disagreement about science policy issues affecting the relationship between human activities and the ecosystems on which humans depend is societal rather than technical. This recognition, however, is not accompanied by agreement on how to proceed. Developing such agreement thus presents a major challenge, since lack of a clear strategy for addressing the social and economic driving forces of environmental degradation constitutes the greatest barrier to achieving the goal of sustainable development.

Our thesis is that ecological economic assessment requires integration of two styles of social science, if such assessment is to be truly integrated. We present this thesis in four primary sections. First, we examine the status of integrated assessment to identify the full scope of social science data that should be included. We distinguish between two types or styles of social science (which we term *descriptive* and *interpretive* approaches) and point to the omission of interpretive social science from integrated assessment. Second, we draw on research that we and others have conducted over the past two decades to illustrate the need to include interpretive as well as descriptive data in addressing policy issues that are fundamentally social in nature. Following an examination of seemingly irreconcilable difficulties in attempts to link the two styles of social science, we conclude with some recommendations for possible approaches to the problem.

INTEGRATING THE SOCIAL INTO INTEGRATED ASSESSMENT

Substantial progress in integrated ecological economic assessment has been made over the past few decades. Scientists from a variety of disciplines have developed 'end-to-end' models capable of addressing multiple perturbations and of calculating the full cycle of the relationship between human activities and the ecosystem. Social scientists have increasingly been drawn into the modelling work in an attempt to assist in understanding human response and inform wise decision making in the context of human-induced change.

To date, the social sciences have provided primarily highly aggregated data that are compatible with the framework already established by the natural sciences; for example, data on human activities leading to gas emissions that are compatible with the stocks and flows emphasis of modelling and the instrumental nature of the enterprise. However, data that provide insight into the way in which the affected people view, and are likely to respond to, potential changes, or that give ethical guidance on issues related to the distributive, equity issues that arise, are conspicuous by their absence. We would argue that incorporating such data is essential if we are to develop truly integrated assessment, and that purely descriptive data – whether from the natural or the social sciences – fail to address the heart of the policy problem.

Two Styles of Social Science

Since C.P. Snow's classic essay on the two cultures, we have become accustomed to the idea of a major fault line that separates the natural from the social sciences. It is our belief, however, that the most significant fault does not, in fact, fall between the natural and the social sciences. Rather, the significant intellectual rupture falls right in the middle of the social sciences, one side of which blends seamlessly with natural science while the other ultimately merges with the humanities. Understanding the nature and implications of this rupture sheds light on the dilemma (and possible solutions to this dilemma) we face in integrated assessment.

An examination of the social sciences reveals the uneasy coexistence of two distinctive approaches of the natural sciences and the humanities: the *descriptive* approach of the natural sciences and the *interpretive* approach of the humanities. (In this context, *descriptive* does not imply a contrast with *normative*; both terms have both positive and normative aspects.) These approaches have their roots in the respective philosophical traditions of Hume's empiricism and the idealism of Kant. The descriptive tradition in social science derives from the empirical philosophy underlying natural science descriptions, specifically Newtonian science that is based on the belief that the mind learns everything from what is evident to the senses. The interpretive tradition derives from philosophical discussions about the way human beings acquire knowledge and form (and are formed into) social structures. Although the interpretive tradition can be traced back to classical Greece, the modern interpretist tradition derives from Immanuel Kant's disagreement with the radical empiricist claims of David Hume that all knowledge derives from sensory experience, insisting instead that reason was itself a capacity of the human mind that shaped experience.

The term 'descriptive' refers to the development and analysis of mass-balance descriptions of social systems that use inventories and accounting systems for the stocks and flows of people, money, raw materials, pollutants and so. This approach is typical of economics and demography as well as of much of American quantitative sociology and political science. The approach is entirely compatible with the natural sciences; it relies on the ability to count and measure and is epistemologically realist, adopting Ricardo's dismissal of the role of human intention. The results of descriptive social science investigations are able to draw on the legitimacy of the natural science by mirroring the 'scientific method' and the thermodynamic paradigm. Counting and measuring provide insight into the scope and severity of a problem or locate probable causes among many candidates. Descriptive analysis can compare various pathways from the standpoint of economic efficiency. Its simplifying assumptions and equations can lay out large problems and render them more tractable. And, finally, because description deals primarily with tangibles, it provides a basis for control; for example, counting tons of fossil fuel used can provide a basis for a tax scheme that will limit the number of tons burned.

The term 'interpretive' refers to the analysis of the values, meaning and motivation of human agents. Social scientists in this school focus on the nature of experience and the structure of perceptions: the meaning that human agents create in social interactions on which they build their understanding of their world and through which they seek to act on it. The interpretive method is epistemologically nominalist, emphasizing that no standpoint exists outside of history or of society from which either can be independently observed. All organized knowledge, by definition, depends upon socially construed conventions for its organization.

One of the primary foci of the interpretive method is understanding how humans draw meaning out of the data presented to them, emphasizing the sociocultural and institutional processes involved. The systematic study of such processes yields understanding that can help us make critical choices, knowing what assumptions, values and decision elements underlie those choices.

The descriptive approach has been incorporated easily into the framework for integrated economic ecological assessment established by the natural sciences. Indeed, the conceptual and methodological approaches of modelling the demographic and macroeconomic systems are essentially indistinguishable from those employed to model changes in ecosystems. Interpretive data are less easily integrated – and, indeed, to date have not been integrated – into such assessments. Our thesis is that integrating both descriptive and interpretive data is essential to the solution of what are ultimately ethical issues.

THE LIMITATIONS OF A DESCRIPTIVE APPROACH

As we have discussed, descriptive, aggregated data on human activities play an important role in integrated assessment, helping define the scope of the problem at hand and identifying possible impacts that can be used to inform the stakeholder debate. Additional tools are needed, however, to deal with societal values and with social processes and institutional issues.

For example, the descriptive approach, which has played an important role in policy analysis that serves an instrumental use of 'speaking truth to power', is less well suited to assisting with the critical task of problem structuring, that is, ensuring that all of the dimensions of the policy problem are taken into account. These dimensions include consideration of the political aspects of decision making, in particular the need to take into account the range of public as well as expert views, if socially viable policies, that is, policies that are regarded as legitimate by those affected by them, are to be developed. The dimensions also include consideration of ethical issues involved in choosing among different political options or in evaluating differing views on critical issues that arise in ecological assessment. Examples include species loss, habitat degradation, declines in human health and loss of human lives, and the distribution of potential impacts among affected populations.

Insights from Cultural Theory

Over the past two decades, cultural theorists have made substantial contributions to our understanding of the underlying issues involved in policy decisions concerning technological risk and uncertainty. Their work also lays the conceptual foundation for understanding and addressing the fundamentally social nature of policy decisions that similarly involve issues of relationships between human activities and the ecosystem on which humans depend.

Building on work in the sociology of science, cultural theorists have emphasized the social processes of knowledge production and utilization and the inherently value-embedded nature of all knowledge, including scientific knowledge. They have pointed out that knowledge is *socially constructed*: that ideas about the world stem from human experience and that this experience differs among groups with different value systems and forms of organization. Wynne, for example, points to the conditional nature of knowledge, arguing that validity is dependent on conditions embedded in a particular knowledge model being fulfilled in actuality and that the experts' trust in supporting social institutions (which is not necessarily shared by the public) is key to understanding disputes about assessments of technological risk or potential impacts on the environment (Wynne, 1992). He emphasizes also that uncertainties and conflict arise not simply from the physical consequences of technological (or environmental) change but also from uncertainty over potential social changes and relationships. He argues that interaction among groups with different perspectives is a prerequisite to the development of socially viable policy; further, he views social interaction as a process of shaping identities and values as opposed to a process solely concerned with achieving instrumental goals (Wynne, 1982).

Douglas and Wildavsky (1982), Douglas (1985), Rayner (1984), Thompson (1982) and Schwartz and Thompson (1992) identify different forms of social organization and underlying value systems that, in Schwartz and Thompson's words, constitute a 'consistent package of biases', or differing political cultures by which humans interpret and respond to the world. A key aspect of these differing political or institutional cultures is that they display differing preferences for methods as well as solutions to policy problems (Rayner, 1984).

Funtowicz and Ravetz (1985) argue that the traditional view of science as the provider of 'simple' factual information is inadequate for addressing policy problems involving high decision stakes and high uncertainty. As the appropriate model of science for the latter types of problems, they recommend 'total environmental assessment', where inquiry takes the form of a dialogue among different perspectives. Ecological economic assessment and modelling similarly deals with problems that are inherently complex and involve high decision stakes and high uncertainty. Four of the cultural theorists' conclusions concerning issues of technological risk and uncertainty are especially pertinent to the current discussion about assessment of risks or potential impacts to the environment and affected populations.

First, these problems are not simply technical but also involve decisions that affect social relationships and associated discussion and/or conflict over the level, acceptability and distribution of impacts. As pinpointed by Rayner and Cantor (1987) in their discussion of the acceptability of risk, the essential policy question is ethical: 'How *fair* is safe enough?' Second, it is not possible to make a clear distinction between the facts of descriptive or technical analysis and the value-laden process of implementation. The 'facts' derived from descriptive analyses are inherently value-laden and, in turn, values are ultimately justified by what people construct as being the facts about the real world. Different groups, or political cultures, have differing combinations of facts and values and differing preferences for both solutions and methods. Third, since facts cannot be clearly distinguished from values, outcomes cannot be determined on the basis of purely technical or descriptive data, but must be negotiated among these alternative cultural perspectives. And finally, the process of interaction is not solely instrumental but has intrinsic value as an enterprise in which humans jointly create values and the nature of social reality.

Insights from Research

Our own and others' research into a variety of technical controversies confirms the insights of cultural theorists and illustrates problems that typically and increasingly occur in attempts to exclude the interpretive dimension from policy. We emphasize that our viewpoint is not that descriptive analyses are unnecessary; indeed, they are an essential part of the debate. The problems that we discuss arise in situations where the descriptive analyses *structure* rather than *serve* the policy debate.

The research demonstrates that the basis for disagreement on policy issues involving high decision stakes and a high degree of uncertainty is social rather than technical and that a focus on improved technical or descriptive analysis serves to polarize rather than resolve controversy. It also demonstrates that differences among the various parties to a policy debate extend beyond differences over preferred outcomes and technical solutions; frequently, these differences represent different political cultures – fundamental differences in world views or rationalities that affect the way people interpret and frame the issues. Failure to acknowledge the legitimacy of differing viewpoints and to engage representatives of these viewpoints in meaningful discussion and negotiation about the issues that concern them contributes to escalating controversy and the inability of governmental agencies to build the necessary societal consensus to implement policy effectively.

Early research

Nelkin's early case study research demonstrated both the distributive, equity issues that arise in ostensibly technical disputes and also the limitations of technical expertise in bringing about solutions (Nelkin, 1979). The case studies, which were analysed to emphasize and clarify the political dimensions of technical decisions, showed that, 'while many of the debates were about technical questions, in the end they involve political choices from among competing social values' (ibid., p. 14). Further, the debates among technical experts polarized rather than solved the controversy by 'calling attention to areas of technical ambiguity and to the limited ability to predict and control risks' (ibid., p. 16). Socolow, reflecting on the controversy surrounding construction of a proposed dam on the Delaware River, similarly reported that technical studies were clearly inadequate in resolving the issues at stake. His conclusion was that the public debate, which focused purely on the technical issues, was 'cloaked in a formality that excludes a large part of what people most care about' (Socolow, 1976, p. 2).

Wynne's analyses of controversy expand this early work to demonstrate the logical nature of the differing rationalities, or perspectives, revealed in public debates. For example, his analysis of the Windscale Inquiry, which was held in Britain in 1977 to investigate plans to build a thermal oxide reprocessing plant for spent nuclear fuel, demonstrates the need to acknowledge the rationality and address the arguments advanced by the very different frames of reference of the parties to the debate. For supporters, who constituted the 'dominant rationality', the issue was framed as one of 'rational and objective discussion' by which 'emotional arguments can be reduced to an objective and intelligent level' (Wynne, 1982, p. 165). For opponents, however, the issue was one of belief in the impartiality of the social institutions responsible for managing the nuclear technology. Further expansion of the technology was opposed on the grounds that these institutions could not be trusted. The opponents' frame of reference was, in actuality, no less rational than that of the supporters, if one defines rationality as a 'self-conscious process of using reasoned argument to make and defend advocative claims' (Dunn, 1981), yet their views were characterized as factually wrong or irrational.

Our own research

Research that we have conducted on nuclear waste and chemical weapons disposal confirms these findings in the literature. Although conducted several years apart and for different agencies and policy issues, the findings were strikingly similar.

The nuclear waste controversy Passage of the US Nuclear Waste Policy Act of 1982 followed many years of controversy and criticism of the Department of Energy's focus on technical issues and lack of recognition of the political and social implications of nuclear technology and nuclear waste disposal. The Act established a process for siting a radioactive waste repository that, for the first time, formally recognized a consultative role for states and Indian tribes in selecting three potential candidate sites for detailed technical consideration. This provision was designed to address issues related to lack of public acceptance that had been a major contributor to the controversy over where and how to deal with nuclear waste.

Research conducted by one of the authors four years after the Act's passage found that senior managers most frequently cited lack of public acceptance as the most significant barrier to successful policy implementation. Nevertheless, the research confirmed a pattern that had first been noted by Hewlett prior to passage of the Act of giving 'lip service … to the importance of non-technical factors … and almost nothing … invested in the analysis or evaluation of these factors' (Hewlett, 1978, p. 1).

Despite recognition that the problems of repository siting were as much social as technical, the agency limited the extent of discussion on social issues in its environmental documentation. Adhering to an artificial separation between facts and values that paralleled the descriptive/interpretive divide, agency personnel divided social and economic phenomena into 'admissible' and 'inadmissible' categories. Descriptive data such as the number of workers moving into a community or the need for additional schoolrooms were deemed admissible; interpretive data such as the quality of education, changes in the general quality of life or concerns about risk were excluded on the grounds that they were speculative and could not be shown, a priori, to bear a close causal relationship to construction of the proposed facility.

In a similar manner, the agency limited stakeholder participation to formal provision of information and opportunities for comment. The research showed that participation and communication were viewed instrumentally as a way in which information from the agency is a commodity (input) causing change (response) in a passive, public recipient. This approach denied the importance of meanings that are attributed to the physical symbols of communication and the role of all participants (agency and expert participants as well as stakeholders) in the creative negotiation of meaning and solutions.

The agency thus failed to address and engage the various stakeholders in a meaningful debate about the issues that were of concern to them. They failed to recognize the role of their own values in selecting the issues deemed critical for analysis and placed a priority on production of technical and descriptive social analyses. Yet, given the inherent uncertainty of disposing of a waste that would remain radioactive for thousands of years, technical analyses could not prove the feasibility of the project to the critics' satisfaction. And descriptive social analyses could not discuss the meaning of change to affected populations and address their concerns about equity, risk bearing and changes in quality of life. This failure to address the full scope of the problem – both its descriptive and interpretive dimensions – was a key factor that undermined the legitimacy of the programme and resulted in a major revision of the Act (Bradbury, 1989).

The chemical weapons controversy Our research into the US chemical demilitarization programme provides a final example of the limitations and resulting problems of overreliance on technical analysis in disputes with a social basis. Despite completion of required environmental documentation, the army's plans for on-site incineration of the nation's stockpile of chemical weapons have encountered extensive delay and escalating costs that have been widely regarded as attributable to public opposition. The research, conducted by Battelle for the US army (Bradbury *et al.* 1994), was designed to identify and analyse the nature of the concerns of nearby communities about the risks of incineration and other technologies for disposing of the nation's stockpile of chemical weapons, currently stored at eight sites in the continental United States. Three research findings are of particular significance to the current discussion.

A first key finding was that production of additional technical analyses in response to issues raised in the Draft Environmental Impact Statement failed to resolve citizens' concerns and aid in effective policy implementation. Our study confirmed the claims of the cultural theories of risk that conflict is not only about risk but also about a number of broader issues that have been hidden by the almost exclusive focus on technical risk assessment. Despite differences in views about the army's plans, residents' arguments were strikingly similar in structure – in the broad scope of concerns and the basic reasoning used to support, oppose or express uncertainty about the programme.

Specifically, residents' concerns were much broader than the narrow definition of the problem in terms of concerns about technology that the research had been commissioned to address. Essentially, the army's failure to address this broad scope of concerns had contributed to their inability to implement their preferred technology. Residents' concerns incorporated four interrelated dimensions that we have characterized as an *acceptability diamond.*

1. The substantive decision: how was the technology selected, the schedule established and the programme designed?
2. The decision-making process: who is making the decision? Is it fair? Has the public been given an opportunity for involvement?
3. Relationships: how do people feel that the army has treated them? Has the army demonstrated in previous actions that the well-being of the community is a factor in its decisions or that it will be a factor influencing future decisions?
4. Accountability: can the public trust the organizations that have responsibility for ensuring safety? Will these institutions ensure that the technology performs as planned? Who will be responsible if anything goes wrong? Will the community be informed?

A second finding was the existence of differing political cultures, both among groups of residents and between the army and residents overall. Among residents, for example, views on incineration were typically associated with fundamentally different views of how the decision process should be structured, of relationships between the army and the community, and trust in the institutions responsible for ensuring safety. Supporters of incineration were more likely to agree that it was 'the army's decision to make'; to believe that the army's presence had been and continued to be an advantage (both economically and socially) to the community; and to trust the institutional arrangements in place for ensuring safety. Opponents, in contrast, were more likely to complain that 'this is not the way decisions should be made', and that the army should have placed a priority on building consensus for their programmes; that the army had demonstrated that it could not be trusted to act in the interests of the community; and that governmental institutions, in general, were unwilling to take responsibility for their actions and could not be relied on to regulate the army's activities.

Our third finding was the existence of an even more marked difference between the structure of the army's views and those of citizens. Whereas residents considered a broad range of factors in assessing the acceptability of incineration, Army personnel focused very narrowly – and almost exclusively – on technical aspects of the decision. They defined the policy problem and their scope of responsibility as one of ensuring that technical analyses were appropriate and compartmentalized community concerns into two categories, a technical category and a personal/political category. They considered issues in the technical category as legitimate and were prepared to address them through additional studies and analyses. Other issues were deemed illegitimate; that is, the programme was not able, and should not try, to address them. As with the Department of Energy in its selection of the issues deemed important for analysis, the army asserted the primacy of its own value system, effectively denying the legitimacy of residents' concerns and the need to address the meaning of proposed policies to those who would be most affected by them.

Residents' belief that the army was denying that their concerns were legitimate issues for discussion and that no-one was responsible for the welfare of their communities contributed to an even greater level of concern about incineration. In this situation, constructive debate and the associated legitimacy on which to implement policy were entirely lacking.

Summary

Our review of the experience of these policy disputes serves as a warning to the development of integrated assessment. A frequent criticism of descriptive analyses is that they fail to address the meaning of proposed policies to affected groups. As a result, resolution of the policy problem becomes more difficult: opponents continuously raise new technical issues that cannot be answered definitively and people's perception that no-one is responsible for addressing the ethical and social issues of concern to them exacerbates the overall level of concern and the difficulty of implementing policy. The research also shows the existence of differing cultures or rationalities – including those of the experts and implementing agencies – that typically underlie the policy debates, and the need to address these differences by engaging all of the participants in constructive, civilized debate. It is critical, therefore, that in developing an approach to integrated economic ecological assessment we place a priority on developing ways to incorporate both descriptive and interpretive social science approaches.

AN IRRECONCILABLE PROBLEM?

Linking together interpretive and descriptive approaches poses a major challenge. The gap between the two approaches, however, is more than one of using different data; rather, it raises fundamental issues of what kinds and sorts of knowledge we value as analysts.

Ingold argues that the differences between the descriptive and interpretive approaches is one of kind. Present-day inquiry favours detached observation. The interpretive approach is based on an 'altogether different *mode* of apprehension', one based on an active perceptual engagement with the components of the dwelt-in world, in the practical business of life, rather than on the detached interested observation of a world apart (Ingold, 1993, pp. 40–41). Ingold illustrates this point by tracing the change in the standpoint of human inquiry from the Enlightenment to the present. Thus, in 1564, Maffei's *Scala Naturale* shows the scholar at the centre of the environment consisting of fourteen concentric spheres envisaged to form a giant stairway, the ascent of which, step by step, affords more comprehensive knowledge of the world through experience within it. Modern satellite imagery, in contrast, shows the scholar as an observer viewing the world from without rather than from within.

The scholar-as-observer mode versus the scholar-as-experiencer mode, on which the two social science approaches rest, raises several key issues that must be addressed in a truly integrated assessment. These seemingly irreconcilable issues include those of scale, treatment of human values and values in science, and normative imperatives for decision makers.

Scale

The descriptive approach derives much of its strength from simplifying assumptions about complex behaviours. It tends to assume homogeneity (or at least a tendency to homogeneity) of human responses to price signals. It therefore seeks high levels of aggregation in its analyses. In contrast, the interpretive approach emphasizes complexity and variation in human motivation and tends to produce highly disaggregated analyses.

As a result of their different approaches to aggregation, the two kinds of social science tend to be comfortable at different extremes of scale. The descriptive approach tends towards large-scale analyses. The nation state is often accepted quite unquestioningly as the appropriate level for analysis. The interpretive approach, on the other hand, tends to focus on the local scale of face-to-face discourse. Here, the human individual is often regarded as being the natural, self-evident unit of analysis. It is often difficult to demonstrate the relevance of social science at this scale to the global-level research agendas of the descriptive sciences, although, as these scholars emphasize, in the last analysis, the activities that drive ecological impacts are always local and whatever impacts of ecological change affect human populations will be experienced at the local level.

The issue, however, is not merely the assertion of the importance of local-level analysis. As a result of the polarization of descriptive and interpretive methods, the social sciences are shaped like an hourglass, demonstrating that theories, methods and data are undeveloped at the meso scale between the individual and nation state. Neither approach, alone, is adequate. At the global level, the nation state or firm is often treated as if it were an individual writ large, with a unitary intelligence and decision-making capacity. Similarly, the local level assumes that the behaviour of individuals reflects that of the national population in proportion to their numbers. Neither approach is based on a theory of micro–macro scale articulation and both are essentially descriptive, macromodelling approaches.

Treatment of Values

At the human level, ecological issues are ultimately ethical issues involving human choice. They are decisions about equity, what is fair in our relationships with each other, and about natural ethics, what is right with respect to our relationship with nature. The descriptive approach, however, can provide no guidance in understanding human choice in social change. Following in Ricardo's footsteps, it assumes continuity of human preferences and consistency of human behaviour over time. Because a vast array of human behaviour is effectively compressed into drivers and responses, the descriptive approach encourages adoption of behaviourist kinds of explanations for the actions of social systems and the individuals within them. Hence policy prescriptions based solely on the descriptive paradigm are inevitably limited to instrumental tinkering with technology and prices.

Human choice also raises a methodological problem for the construction and operation of descriptive social science. Unlike a billiard ball shot across a table, a human being has the ability to make conscious decisions about the directions in which he or she is moving and at what speed. Science, whether natural or social, is conducted by humans and is thus itself subject to human choice. Thus the treatment of values involves more than addressing the values of affected populations; it involves also consideration of the researcher's or proponent's values. As demonstrated in our research findings, the agencies and experts who advised them chose what to study and what to ignore, what methods to use in their analysis and what criteria to apply in determining the validity of the data they gathered.

In making these choices, we therefore inevitably make value judgments. However, when the value-based assumptions embedded in theory or model disappear into the background, they come to be seen as 'natural' and are uncritically accepted. Yet excluding human agency from applied social science research is itself a powerful and constraining assertion of the researcher's own choice upon society.

Utility and Rights-based Approaches to Decision Making

The descriptive and interpretive approaches respectively embody quite different normative imperatives for decision makers. The tendency of the descriptive paradigm towards high levels of aggregation gives rise to a top-down approach to decision making. The quantitative aspect of the paradigm leads to an essentially utilitarian perspective on decision making: the practice of inventorying the stocks and flows of goods and bads creates the conditions for a decision framework based on a technique for calculating societal happiness measured by their distribution.

It is but a short step to turn the possibility of such a means for calculating what would contribute to the greatest happiness of the greatest number into the imperative that one should pursue that goal. Further, the solution which provides the greatest happiness of the greatest number also must be an efficient solution, since any departure from efficiency, also by definition, reduces the amount of good available for distribution. Thus efficiency becomes not merely a technical issue, or an indication of rational behaviour within utilitarianism, but is also an intrinsically moral imperative that arises from the descriptive paradigm itself. By the same process, decision-maker awareness of alternative ethical considerations becomes systematically attenuated. The imperative to provide for societal good at the highest level of aggregation provides no guidance for securing the happiness of minorities and individuals.

In contrast, the tendency of the interpretive tradition to focus on the individual rather than the nation state directs the attention of scholars working in that paradigm to the particular circumstances of decision making rather than the aggregative outcome. Thus the insights of the interpretive paradigm are more likely to be of interest to those who espouse libertarian or egalitarian ethics, emphasizing the rights of the individual or the minority in the face of majority preferences.

Increasing insight into the diversity of motives, values and preferences of individuals actually tends to frustrate utilitarian social accountancy, which depends on dissipating such distinctions in the process of aggregation. It is hardly surprising, therefore, that the insights of the interpretive paradigm are not merely considered irrelevant to, but actually have to be excluded from, utilitarian decision making in order to preserve the rationality and legitimacy of the utility principle.

Hence the distinction between the two social science paradigms is not merely a scholarly distinction of mere academic interest. It actually lies at the heart of the current crisis of governance that pervades the local, national and global communities: the tension between interdependence and independence; between pursuit of the greatest happiness of the greatest number and the assertion of individual, local, or ethnic rights that ought not to be violated even at the expense of the aggregate good. Whereas Kant's principle that every person is to be regarded as an end in himself is generally recognized as a form of the doctrine of human rights, Bentham dismissed the concept of rights as 'plain nonsense' (Russell, 1946, p. 742).

SOME SUGGESTIONS FOR RECONCILING THE IRRECONCILABLE

As we have argued, an integrated ecological economic assessment requires integration of descriptive and interpretive social science approaches. Such integration involves bringing together both modes of research – the scholar-as-observer mode and the scholar-as-experiencer mode – in addition to the data supplied by each mode. The goal of bringing together the two approaches is to achieve a more complete analysis and to facilitate collaboration among the different perspectives of participants affected by the policy decision.

A key contribution of interpretive social science in the current context is its introduction of *reflexivity* into the research and policy-making process. By reflexivity, we mean the self-conscious examination of implicit assumptions, awareness of human agency and examination of whether or not the assumptions embedded in the approach actually match the policy context in which the knowledge is being used; that is, explicit recognition of the *conditional* nature of knowledge. In the descriptive approach, assumptions may be laid out but are typically unquestioned within the research study. By making these assumptions explicit, the researcher has an opportunity to question them, rather than taking them as a given.

Increased opportunities for the productive exercise of reflexivity require collaboration in both research and policy making. In research, scientists could adopt either a multidisciplinary or an interdisciplinary approach. In the former, scientists from various fields work together on a problem that has been defined within the framework of one particular discipline. In the latter, people from different fields work together on a problem that they have defined together in such a way that it cannot be defined from within any single discipline. This type of environment can be especially conducive to reflexivity in providing an opportunity to challenge definitions and assumptions that are taken for granted within a particular discipline. In effect, it provides opportunity for a dialogue among differing disciplinary rationalities.

In policy, Robinson (1982, 1988, 1992a, 1992b) proposes adoption of a model of mutual learning systems among researchers, policy makers and the public, using modelling tools to explore alternative futures rather than to try to predict the future. Key elements of this model include the explicit recognition that policy questions are not essentially questions of fact but of value, and that both the descriptive perspective and the 'actor-system' perspective are needed to provide a usefully integrated approach to policy questions. Again, the use of reflexivity in this context would allow a critical assessment of the varying rationalities of stakeholders to the debate.

The Toulmin method of argumentation (Toulmin, 1978; Toulmin *et al.*, 1979) offers a useful tool to enhance understanding of the rationalities of the various parties to a policy debate. This tool, which was used by the authors in the research related to the chemical demilitarization programme, provides a systematic way to display, for public review, the train or structure of reasoning of the stakeholders. It demonstrates the primary viewpoints and the nature of the reasons and evidence used to support those viewpoints, ultimately providing a sounder basis for negotiation of differences.

Adoption of such approaches within the context of a scoping process such as that envisioned in the US National Environmental Policy Act could effectively transform the current mode of conducting integrated ecological economic assessment. Initiating a discussion at an early phase of the process provides the opportunity for structuring the policy problem in a manner that reflects various perspectives on the scope of the issues to be analysed. It also reduces the likelihood that policy makers will have made irreversible commitments to a particular decision prior to considering their own goals, values and perceptions of the issues in relation to those of others. Subsequent discussions could be continued, as needed, as part of the learning process envisaged by Robinson. Such interactions have intrinsic value as a process of joint creation of meaning and of building consensus and legitimacy for controversial decisions.

Reforming the relationship between science research and policy making would make space for the useful research that exists within interpretive science. It would make space also for alternative world-views of less industrialized peoples who have challenged modernity and supported environmentalism as based on an integrated perception of humans and nature, placing emphasis on issues of justice, equity, institutions of governance and property rights. In this way, the science and policy community would then include needs, wants and beliefs in their data sets alongside measurements and statistics. Policy agreements would explicitly include social organization data and cultural assumptions as well as market and consumption data, to make them more implementable and effective.

REFERENCES

Bradbury, J.A. (1989), *The Use of Social Science Knowledge in Implementing the Nuclear Waste Policy Act*, PhD dissertation, Graduate School of Public and International Affairs, University of Pittsburgh, Pittsburgh, Pennsylvania.

Bradbury, J.A., K.M. Branch, J.H. Heerwagen and E. Liebow (1994), *Community Viewpoints of the Chemical Stockpile Disposal Program*, Washington, DC: Battelle, Pacific Northwest National Laboratories.

Douglas, M. (1985), *Risk Analysis According to the Social Sciences*, New York: Russell Sage Foundation.

Douglas, M. and A. Wildavsky (1982), *Risk and Culture*, Berkeley, California: University of California Press.

Dunn, W.N. (1981), *Public Policy Analysis: An Introduction*, Englewood Cliffs, New Jersey: Prentice-Hall.

Funtowicz, S.O. and J.R. Ravetz (1985), 'Three types of risk assessment: a methodological analysis', in V.T. Covello, J.L. Mumpower, P. M. Stallen and V.R.R. Uppuluri (eds), *Environmental Impact Assessment, Technology Assessment, and Risk Analysis*, New York: Springer-Verlag, pp. 831–48.

Hewlett, R.G. (1978), *Federal Policy for the Disposal of Highly Radioactive Wastes from Commercial Nuclear Power Plants*, (DOE/MA-0153), Washington, DC: U.S. Department of Energy.

Ingold, T. (1993), 'Globes and spheres: the topology of environmentalism', in K. Milton (ed.), *The View from Anthropology*, London: Routledge.

Nelkin, D. (1979), *Controversy: Politics of Technical Decisions*, Beverly Hills, California: Sage.

Rayner, S. (1984), 'Disagreeing about risk: The institutional cultures of risk management', in S.G. Hadden (ed.), *Risk Analysis, Institutions, and Public Policy*, Port Washington, New York: Associated Faculty Press, pp. 150–68.

Rayner, S and R. Cantor (1987), 'How fair is safe enough? The cultural approach to technology choice', *Risk Analysis*, **7** (1), 3–9.

Robinson, J.B. (1982), 'Apples and horned toads: on the framework-determined nature of the energy debate', *Policy Sciences*, **15**, 23–45.

Robinson, J.B. (1988), 'Unlearning and backcasting: rethinking some of the questions we ask about the future', *Technological Forecasting and Social Change*, **33**, 325–38.

Robinson, J.B. (1992a), 'Of maps and territories: the use and abuse of socioeconomic modeling in support of decision making', *Technological Forecasting and Social Change*, **42**, 147–64.

Robinson, J.B. (1992b), 'Risks, predictions and other optical illusions: rethinking the use of science in social decision making', *Policy Sciences*, **25**, 237–54.
Russell, B. (1946), *History of Western Philosophy*, London: George Allen and Unwin.
Schwartz, M. and M. Thompson (1992), *Divided We Stand*, Philadelphia, Pennsylvania: University of Pennsylvania Press.
Socolow, R.H. (1976), 'Failures of discourse', in H.A. Fieveson, F.W. Sinden and R.H. Socolow (eds), *Boundaries of Analysis*, Cambridge, Massachussets: Macmillan, pp. 9–40.
Thompson, M. (1982), 'Among the Energy Tribes: The Anthropology of the Current Energy Debate', working paper 82-59, International Institute for Applied Systems Analysis, Laxenburg, Austria.
Toulmin, S. (1978), *The Uses of Argument*, Cambridge: Cambridge University Press.
Toulmin, S., R. Reike and A. Janik (1979), *An Introduction to Reasoning*, New York: MacMillan.
Wynne, B. (1982), 'Rationality and Ritual: The Windscale Inquiry and Nuclear Decisions in Britain', British Society for the History of Science, Chalfont St Giles, England.
Wynne, B. (1992), 'Risk and social learning', in S. Krimsky and D. Golding (eds), *Social Theories of Risk*, Westport, Connecticut: Praeger, pp. 275–397.

2. Reframing environmental valuation: reasoning about resource use and the redistribution of sustainability

Martin O'Connor

INTRODUCTION

Since its inception as a separate discipline at the beginning of the industrial age, economics has focused primarily on mechanisms of production and exchange of commodities (that is, produced capital and consumption goods). This commodity production activity was represented as drawing upon an *external (environmental) domain* – the land and water and, more generally, nature – that furnished energy, raw materials and waste disposal services. Subsequently, it was admitted that there were 'environmental costs' associated with the economic commodity production. The question from an optimizing point of view became to know whether the economic benefits outweighed the environmental costs.

The comparison of alternative uses of environmental assets, and the assessment of risks and impairment of habitat conditions due to pollutants and ecosystem disruption, pose difficulties of high uncertainties, the irreversibility of many effects, and (thus) long time-scales. Concern with economic, ecological and social sustainability brings the 'long-term future' into confrontation with the considerations of the present. How should we seek to reconcile preoccupations with the future with those of the present? The response of established economic valuation methodology has been to extend conventional cost–benefit analysis also across time, through the attempted quantification of environmental damages and of economy–environment trade-offs through time with 'discounting'. Yet this practice does *not* reconcile future interests with the present; it simply discounts future values. Conversely, the less the future is discounted, the more weighty in the cost–benefit scales become the imponderables of uncertainties about longer-term change. Given the distributional conflicts between present and future, and the ethical and culturally based disagreements between existing interested parties, the cost–benefit 'optimizing' approach becomes fairly useless as a guide for decision making.

The suggestion of this chapter is that, if we want to provide decision support while we enlarge our scope of concern to the ecosystems of the planet and the long term, we should adopt a different perspective. One option is the representation of 'sustainable development' as a symbiosis between economic production and ecological (re)production. This implies an emphasis on *managing and investing in* the reproduction, transformation and renewal of the terrestrial habitats that are not just raw materials sources but veritable life-support systems that underpin the overly analysed commodity production systems. These are also habitats in the sense of being the places of life, invested with social and community significance, or meanings. So valuation for sustainability cannot be separated from the idea of actions whose effect is *to sustain this or that form of life, way of life – in the cultural as well as ecological–economic sense.*

Early sections of the chapter retrace some of the (insurmountable) difficulties encountered in attempts at the application of cost–benefit analysis as a decision aid for large-scale and long-term environmental problems. Subsequent sections give an outline of a different approach to environmental valuation, centred upon the notion of the *distribution of sustainability* (see also O'Connor and Martinez-Alier, 1997; O'Connor, 1997b). Policies for economic, ecological and social sustainability involve choices for the redistribution through time of economic opportunity and of access to services and benefits provided by the biophysical environment. Out of the range of possible economic and ecological trajectories, there are choices to be made about which environmental features and functions, which ecosystems and habitats and which spectra of economic opportunities, might be sustained – and for whom. Choices are also made about the distribution of hazards and environmental 'bads', the 'disservices' deriving from poisoned or disrupted life-support systems. Sustainability of what and for whom; at the expense of what and of whom? This is the *problématique* of value.

ECONOMY, ENVIRONMENT AND VALUE

If essential natural resources such as water, biodiversity and land (and not only energy) are depletable, and if essential environmental services can be irreversibly impaired through pollution or ecosystem change, present-day economic activity can have very high intertemporal opportunity costs. The existence of such irreversibilities implies a possible conflict between short-run performance (GNP growth) and long-run prospects for (a) economic output and hence consumption levels and (b) the sustaining of the cycles of resource renewal and the environmental life-support functions that underpin economic activity. In this context it is not possible to regard commodity output indicators such as GDP growth as reliable signposts pointing in the direction of long-run economic progress. There are two dimensions to this. First, the pursuit of rapid (economic) output growth as a short-term objective may impair the economic welfare prospects of future generations. Second, since economic value cannot increase without limit and even short-term growth in value of economic output can have a durable impact on environmental quality, it is no longer satisfactory to confine valuation attention to the produced goods and services alone, while ignoring 'ecological' determinants of well-being.

In recent years, a wide range of approaches have been devised with a view to ensuring that the various categories of environmental change (deterioration, depletion, damage and so on) are 'taken properly into account'. Often the demand for taking the environment into account is for valuation in monetary terms. This allows environmental impacts and protection questions to be formulated as optimal resource use problems through the extension of traditional cost–benefit analysis techniques. However, for reasons such as uncertainty, distributional concerns and diversity of ethical positions, the difficulty or inappropriateness of monetary valuation becomes clear. In such cases there is a need for decision support techniques that do not depend exclusively on monetary valuation, such as multicriteria and deliberative methods (see Holland *et al.*, 1996; O'Connor, 1997a, 2002; Faucheux and O'Connor, 1998; Brouwer *et al.*, 1999).

MONETARY VALUATION OF ENVIRONMENTAL DAMAGE

The reason usually put forward for monetary valuation of environmental benefits and damages is to provide a common and understandable measure through which different objectives can be traded off. Placing money figures on environmental damage gives a quantification of the scale of adverse effects, and of the investment and adjustments that might be needed to restore damaged environments and avoid further damages. In conventional economic terms, the *internalization of the environment* in evaluation practices requires (a) developing ways of estimating in monetary terms the 'opportunity costs' associated with alternative uses of economic and environmental resources, which means placing monetary values on environmental goods and services (and also environmental 'bads'), and (b) choosing the course of action that is judged to be the 'best' for the society. This sort of approach depends on a combination of analytical and normative premises. First, the act of 'costing' environmental damage is taken to mean finding a way of comparing environmental with non-environmental goods in monetary terms. We refer to this as *the assumption of monetary commensurability*. Second, the monetization of environmental costs and benefits provides the basis for maximizing the 'balance' of benefits over costs for the society, by applying *the criterion of Pareto-improvement* for policy and project selection decisions. (Note: a state of affairs is called *Pareto-efficient* if, and only if, under the defined constraints on opportunities and actions, all the opportunities for improving the welfare of some individual(s) without lowering that of any other(s) have been exhausted. A policy is said to offer a *potential Pareto improvement* if those who gain from the policy could fully compensate the losers and still be better off.)

The underlying principle of environmental cost–benefit analysis is that, although we cannot introduce all ecological goods and services into actual markets, it is nevertheless possible to extrapolate in various ways from actual market transactions so as to get an estimate in money terms of the value of some environmental good, or the cost of some environmental harm. Environmental good or damage may, for instance, be assessed in terms of its impact (direct or indirect) on the production of goods having a market price (such as impacts of water pollution on agricultural production), or it may be assessed on the basis of substitute or complementary goods that do have a price (see, for example, Hanley and Spash, 1993; Jakobsson and Dragun, 1996). In brief:

- *Cost-of-response methods* look at actual expenditures incurred in environmental protection or in abating or repairing damage or for access to comparable amenities. There are two sorts of reasons for such expenditures. The first is that there is a benefit obtained directly by the person or agency taking the protection, abatement or repair action. The second is the existence of an obligation to pay in relation to damages for which the party is in some way held responsible: for example, versions of the polluter pays principle (PPP) imposing tax, restoration or damage compensation payments.
- *Revealed-preference methods* seek to value individuals' preferences for environmental goods through inference from their behaviour in actual markets. The two main categories of such methods are (1) the travel cost method, which uses the costs that are incurred by visitors to a site as a proxy to calculate the recreation value they place upon that site, and (2) the hedonic pricing method, which employs a proxy good in the market to estimate individuals' willingness to pay for environmental goods and to avoid environmental damage. The most widely used proxy good is property: property values reflect many different attributes, both non-environmental (for example, room numbers and sizes, proximity to work and recreation) and environmental (such as noise levels from road and airports, the surrounding landscapes).

- *Expressed-preference methods*, notably contingent valuation (CVM), seek by means of questionnaires to present people with hypothetical situations, with the aim of eliciting statements about what they would be willing to pay for preserving a specified environmental feature or the compensation that they would find acceptable in the case of its loss.

All of these methods have distinctive limitations (see O'Connor, 1997a, 1997b; O'Connor and Spash, 1999). Many of the difficulties stem from the fact that the 'goods' or 'damages' in question are being treated, rather implausibly, as analogous to goods and services produced for real exchange in markets. In effect, the conventional approach is to consider the physical environment as comprising *stocks of natural capital* which furnish *environmental goods and services*; that is, primary energy and other natural resources, waste assimilation services, recreational amenities, and life-support functions. Given that natural capital is limited, there are constraints on availability and trade-offs between different uses. So valuation of these natural capital stocks and the flows of benefits obtainable from them (or reductions in flows due to pollution or other degradation) may be attempted through making estimates of *shadow prices reflecting opportunity costs*, along the same lines as opportunity costs for produced commodities and economic capital goods bought and sold in markets.

THE (IMPOSSIBLE) QUANTIFICATION OF OPPORTUNITY COSTS

The necessary conditions for establishing monetary commensurability in this sense are very restrictive. Strictly speaking, the 'opportunity costs' of this or that use (or non-use) of an environmental resource are quantifiable only within a tightly formalized modelling perspective which defines the set of interdependent production–consumption–conservation and other possibilities for the ecological–economic system and for the time frame in question. The preferred modelling framework for many valuation economists is 'general equilibrium'. By this is meant, broadly, a situation where a defined set of processes, actors and exchanges are in a compatible relation to each other, subject to the various laws and constraints, and to the behavioural rules presumed to govern them. For many, the reference point more particularly is the idea of an equilibrium between 'supply' and 'demand' for a good in a market. Here the price that a buyer is willing to pay represents, by hypothesis, the value of the marginal unit of that good by comparison with other goods available in other markets. In a similar general sense, one seeks to identify, construct or 'reveal' relative prices of environmental as well as economic goods and services that represent the opportunity costs of their production and use in the society.

The adoption of this opportunity-cost analytical framework is explicit or implicit in most 'applied' valuation studies. So it is exceedingly important to understand not only the assumptions that underpin the habitual practices of searching for a 'willingness to pay' or a measure of a 'trade-off' in monetary terms, but also the interpretation of this measure as an opportunity cost for the society. The latter is what allows application of 'optimization' concepts and, thence, normative application of cost–benefit analysis.

The presumption behind most monetary valuation work is of a (theoretical) reference state with a 'Pareto-efficient' resource allocation. This is called 'first best'. The specific problem under investigation, such as polluted water or destroyed wetlands or devastated butterfly ecosystems, is then considered as an 'externality', that is, a deviation from this 'first best'. Through estimation of a marginal damage curve and/or of a 'demand curve' for the environmental good/service in question, the basis can be given for 'correction' of this local deviation, thus obtaining the 'first best'. If given an explicit model representation, this 'first best' would most often be an equilibrium satisfying the rule of *maximum net present value of economic output* (henceforth NPV-max) or, as a variation along the same principle, *maximum present value of utility* (henceforth PVU-max). Examples include the modelling of economic costs and benefits of different technological choices for energy supply and for the abatement of carbon dioxide (and other) emissions thought to be contributing to climate change (for critical appraisals of features of some typical models of 'optimal abatement' of CO_2 and their results, see among others, Funtowicz and Ravetz, 1994; Howarth, 2001; Spash, 1994a, 1994b). A typical feature is the reliance on mathematical constrained maximization techniques to define an 'optimal abatement' trajectory for the economy in question; in most cases this is net present value maximization with a positive time discount rate.

Such model solutions are often interpreted, in policy advice contexts, as proxies (or intertemporal analogues) for a 'perfect competition' general equilibrium having 'first best' Pareto-efficiency properties. It is true that in theory – under certain fairly standard and, as it happens, highly unrealistic analytical assumptions – one can establish that a PVU-max solution is characterized by a set of (shadow) equilibrium relative prices for all economic and environmental goods and services (present and future), *these prices including the interest rates from period to period*, that correctly 'signal' the relative marginal productivities and the relative marginal utilities, hence the opportunity costs, *including intertemporal opportunity costs*, on all margins. But in reality we are always a very long way from a heavenly first best situation like that. There are, indeed, many reasons why this approach to environmental valuation raises more imponderables than it resolves.

For argument's sake, let us, momentarily, accept the proposition of monetary commensurability. It must still be noted (see Martinez-Alier and O'Connor, 1996) that the results obtained for environmental and economic goods/services, and damages valuations – and hence estimates about 'optimal' levels of environmental resource use, conservation, degradation and so on – can depend very strongly on the values of model parameters chosen, such as elasticities of substitution between different forms of natural and produced capital, relative factor importance, consumer preferences and social rules for intertemporal distribution of purchasing power: the sociopolitical dimensions of entitlements and 'property rights'. Take the simple case of defining prices to guide an 'intertemporally efficient' use of a depletable environmental resource. Recent work has shown that, for standard growth-with-natural capital models, at least four qualitatively different sorts of PVU-maximizing time paths are obtainable, depending on initial stock levels and the specification of the social discount rate (Asheim, 1994; Pezzey, 1997; Pezzey and Withagen, 1998; Faucheux *et al.*, 1997):

- monotonic decrease in utility over time: non-sustained;
- increase of utility for a while, then a turning point with monotonic decline thereafter: non-sustained;
- exactly constant utility through time: sustained economic activity;
- monotonic increase in utility: more than sustainability.

The models in question are highly unrealistic, but they serve to illustrate a logical point. If the analyst knows what the model parameters are, it is possible to infer from current-period price and quantity information (a) whether or not the economy is on an 'efficient' path and (b) whether or not this efficient path provides for non-decreasing utility through time. But it is impossible to deduce from current-period price–quantity information what the model parameters are. Thus, as Norgaard (1990) pointed out, little can reliably be inferred from measurements of current prices, economic outputs and environmental changes as to the potential for a sustainable economic output, nor as to the conformity or divergence of present economic activity compared with sustainability requirements. In order to get out of this situation, the analyst has to be able to answer the question: which model is the 'right' one for value estimation purposes? What functional forms and parameter settings are plausible? In this regard, first, there is much scientific uncertainty, and it is difficult in any case to reduce the complexity of biophysical cycles and ecological processes from local to planetary scale, as required for sharp mathematical specification of 'intertemporal production possibility frontiers'. Second, within any chosen model there will be valuation indeterminacies associated with the sensitivity of the equilibrium relative prices (measuring the opportunity costs) to the distribution of property rights and prevailing power structures. Third, there are enormous problems with empirical measurements of all the relevant ecosystem and social variables, even if the theoretical specifications were resolved. These include the difficulty of achieving complete inventories of all significant environmental damages in the short and long term.

All of this adds up to the difficulty – partly theoretical, partly empirical – of estimating in any meaningful way the intertemporal opportunity costs associated with complex environmental functions. These obstacles to applying the monetary valuation methods are intrinsic to the nature of the problems being addressed. They arise, in fact, directly from the attempt to transpose traditional economic valuation methodology into an arena for which it was not originally devised, and where it may not be able to be applied in a meaningful way, namely: extension spatially and materially to the non-produced and largely non-commodified natural environment; and extension temporally to the long term of ecological change and sustainability concerns.

Ecosystems are not markets, and the biosphere processes do not necessarily unfold 'harmoniously' in accordance with coherent governing principles. If the biophysical milieu is treated as 'exogenous' relative to a commodity production system, then, under certain conventions, a system of prices can be defined for the opportunity costs between different economic commodities. But once environmental changes are admitted as significant, this analytical convenience breaks down. The biosphere evolves, locally and globally, under the influence of forces that are largely independent of human action; and at the same time it is subject to uncontrolled (and increasingly severe) perturbation as a 'side-effect' of human economic activity. The complex habitats that furnish life-support functions for human and other species cannot be produced in factories. So restoration of ecosystems that are damaged or altered through economic activity or pollution is often impossible. Ecosystem change and biosphere dynamics are *not controllable* by human intervention in the same way that commodity production processes are (Godard, 1984; Peet, 1992; Norgaard, 1994; O'Connor, 1989, 1994; Funtowicz and O'Connor, 1999). For all these reasons, the provision of many environmental services, and also of harmful effects, is characterized by incommensurabilities and by time-irreversibilities. Ecological harms include the risks and burdens falling on people as a result of pollution or exploitation: for example, disturbed or degraded ecosystems, interruptions to ecological life-support cycles, carcinogenic substances and toxic substances in workplaces and in homes, and loss of food production capacity. The unplanned 'side-effects' on ecological distribution will, in many cases, fully emerge only over long periods of time and across large distances. The interested parties may be extremely diffuse (for example, people suffering from health problems induced or aggravated by urban pollution or carcinogenic substances), or hypothetical in character (future generations that may be affected by climate change and accumulation of toxic wastes). It is hard to see how 'optimization' can meaningfully be carried out by setting the statistical losses due to chemical carcinogen wastes stocked dangerously in Tahiti against the 'probabilities' of flood damage in Bangladesh.

VALUATION AND FAIRNESS FOR THE LONG TERM

While mathematical formalism can lend an aura of quantification – and hence of a superior(?) 'rationality' – to the evaluation procedure, these are situations where precise quantification is quite impossible. First, it is impossible to quantify all the roles played by the environment as a source of livelihood, as a place of perception and physical activity, and as a site for waste disposal. Second, long-term ecological effects of many economic decisions are non-quantifiable, and in any case will depend on actions subsequently taken, interwoven with side-effects of other past actions. Consequently, the optimization approach that, implicitly or explicitly, most cost–benefit analysis defends is unlikely to produce decision support information which commands scientific or political consensus. Underlying disagreements on scientific, political and ethical matters may end up reframed in the arcane language of modelling, but without being resolved at all.

The 'NPV-optimization' and 'expected value' procedures are grounded on the hypothesis of making 'trade-offs' between, *inter alia*, the present generation's economic welfare and the possible exposure of future generations to unlivable damages. This sort of 'substitutability' assumption is not only difficult to quantify, it is open to objections on justice grounds. In effect, discounting combined with NPV-optimizing appears to provide a rationale for displacing environmental damage onto the most vulnerable groups – poorer people first of all, since the money value able to be placed upon damage by/for poorer people based on 'willingness to pay' or money-income losses will (*ceteris paribus*) be less than the valuations by/for richer people; and future generations subsequently, because damages felt in the future will be evaluated as smaller than the same dollar value of current damage consumption. This offloading is ethically questionable. As many commentators have pointed out, it is one thing to be impatient yourself, that is, to have a preference for consumption desires to be satisfied now rather than later. This relates to what is 'optimal' for me or you, a consumer making choices with a given budget constraint. It does not resolve the question of what is or might be fair or unfair between generations (Holland *et al.*, 1996).

Thus, apart from scientific uncertainties about economic and ecological evolutions, there are also irreducible social obstacles to specification of opportunity costs in monetary terms, linked, for example, to notions of rights to life or property for other people or other species; to people's individual and collective sense of the sacred; or to natural or built features that are paramount matters of local identity. When people express, for example, a love of particular scenery or preferences for a world with wolves and whales rather than one without wolves and whales, they are affirming the goodness of a certain order of things, which is quite different from their need to buy milk or bread. They are signalling a sort of affection or caring, and perhaps also a desire that *society as a whole* should take more proper account of it.

The problem of the 'long term' is at the heart of sustainability concerns. It is true that, in this context, decisions must be formulated with a view to 'keeping options open for the future'. Yet while there are benefits and burdens to be assessed, little is gained from complicated discussions about public and market interest rates, social and private preferences, risks and portfolio choices. In the context of sustainability goals, the best way out of these analytical convolutions is simply to emphasize that the basic issues refer not to criteria for optimization but rather to the intertemporal distribution of benefits and costs, including exposure to different sorts of environmental changes and hazards. In practice, the best way to deal with 'discounting' questions is to formulate explicitly the intertemporal performance goals (social and economic distribution, ecosystem protection, biodiversity, and so on) and then to assess the compatibility of policy alternatives with these goals.

SUSTAINABILITY AS A GUIDING PRINCIPLE FOR VALUATION WORK

Making attempts to put money values on stocks of natural capital, on environmental life-support functions and on damages that are spread over time, and whose significance is sometimes as much ethical as biophysical, is often quite an artificial process. Monetary valuation of damages to environmental functions will, for this reason, often find little consensus for policy support. On the contrary, conflicts of opinion and interest will arise, and compromises (or else solutions using force) will have to be found involving the exercise of judgment in the face of unclear consequences and differing principles (Holland, 1997; Foster *et al.*, 2002).

It is not, in fact, necessary to base 'valuation' studies on speculative propositions about the money value of environmental assets and damages. On the contrary, a more modest (and, perhaps, also more robust) approach is to confine monetary aspects of valuation to the question of economic resources that must be committed in order to meet specified hazards or categories of damage or to ensure the maintenance of specified dimensions of environmental quality (Brouwer *et al.*, 1996, 1999; O'Connor and Ryan, 1999). The logic of valuation would then be as follows: *first make the proposition to sustain/conserve the forms of life or environmental features in question* (for example, avoid the production of toxic wastes, preserve a designated forest system, or the biological diversity, or other features of nature), *and then investigate what commitments this does or might entail* (O'Connor and Martinez-Alier, 1997).

This is an example of the employment of 'sustainability' consciously as a guiding principle for action (individual and collective) aimed at influencing systems dynamics on various scales (cf. Schütz, 2000). Once sustainability has been announced as the guiding principle, it is important to appreciate the variety of forms that the commitment to sustainability may take, and indeed would have to take. Consider any given sustainability objective, say a river's flow or a lake or a human settlement or a bird-rich ecosystem: the question 'how much is it worth?' may first be answered by making explicit the nature of the choices as to what forms of life are sustained and what other sustainability possibilities are forgone. But many different scales and units of analysis are involved.

Looked at this way, it is easy to acknowledge that the identification of a commercial or tangible economic interest does not exhaust the inquiry into value. People in their different cultural settings articulate their sense of value about nature in multilayered ways (O'Connor, 1998, 2000). The significance of nature, and of built environments, is embodied in a person's or a community's way of life, in their institutions and taboos, in their principles and precepts of right conduct, their habits and forms of cooperation. Very often, explicit value statements about the environment emerge only when these principles are compromised or ways of life are threatened: 'value', then, is associated with social processes of controversy and conflict. So 'valuation' should be taken broadly to refer to *people's notions of what matters for the future, and why.* Moreover, the persons or communities involved are faced not only with decisions regarding protection and damage, but with the distribution of different kinds of damage and benefits, and with conflicts between the avoidance of environmental damage and various other social, economic and cultural objectives (Martinez-Alier, 1991, 1995). Many of the adverse consequences of current environmental activity will also fall upon future generations and this raises ethical issues about our responsibilities to them.

These choices for the 'distribution of sustainability' often cannot be quantified, or can only be partly quantified (often only in non-monetary and somewhat speculative terms). Nonetheless, we emphasize, these arbitrations and compromises over survival, expansion and disappearance of different forms of life, economies, ethical and aesthetic sensibilities, constitute real resource management choices. As such they can quite properly be seen as embodying statements of relative valuation. This is not the same valuation logic as is conveyed in, for example, the notion of 'ecologically right prices' or in the proposals for creating legal rights to carbon dioxide emissions or to biological diversity, and then organizing a market in these rights so as to encourage an 'optimal use' of these resources. The first of these notions glosses over the question: sustaining of what and for whom? The second is related to the ideology of 'wealth maximization', meaning maximization of 'present value' based on some existing structure of market power, purchasing power and control, which (as previously discussed) has nothing in particular to do with sustainability.

VALUATION AS CHOICE AMONGST DIFFERENT POSSIBILITIES OF (SOCIO-ECOLOGICAL) SOLIDARITY

In defining options for sustainability, policy makers must compare options across the different values and objectives that inform our choices: economic, aesthetic, social justice, cultural, recreational and so on. Many of these considerations cannot be made commensurate with each other (O'Neill, 1993; Munda, 1995; O'Connor, 2002). Resource requirements and effects of alternative courses of action may be comparable in a number of different ways, but often this information cannot easily be brought into a single unit of measure, and even where a common unit is possible (such as energy flow units) this may not be decisive for judging between alternatives. An evaluative procedure would seek, from this point of view, to structure the problem for the decision maker in the sense of presenting the information about the different objectives and the various bases for comparisons in a systematic way.

Representation of 'sustainable development' as a symbiosis between economic production and ecological (re)production (cf. Faucheux and O'Connor, 1998) implies emphasis on managing and investing in the reproduction, transformation and renewal of the terrestrial habitats that are not just raw materials sources but veritable life-support systems that underpin commodity production systems. These are also habitats in the sense of being the places of life, invested with social and community significance, or meanings. So valuation for sustainability cannot be separated from the idea of actions whose effect is *to sustain this or that form of life, way of life, in the cultural as well as ecological–economic sense*.

The view of sustainable development as a process based on cycles of renewal and regeneration, a symbiosis of ecological and economic reproduction, is already found in the concept of *ecodevelopment*, expounded in the early 1970s by some international agencies, at first with reference mainly to rural development projects in the Third World. At that time it joined a large array of concepts and terminologies proposing an 'alternative' development, whose common feature was rejection of the dominant views of development couched in terms of rapid GNP growth, throughput of resources and technological modernization. More specifically, as Ignacy Sachs wrote (1980, p. 37):

> Ecodevelopment is a development of peoples through themselves utilizing to the best the natural resources, adapting to an environment which they transform without destroying it. […] Development in its entirety has to be impregnated, motivated, underpinned by the research of a dynamic equilibrium between the life process and the collective activities of human groups planted in their particular place and time.

Emphasis is on 'the cultural contributions of the peoples concerned' in the effort to 'transform the various elements of their environment into useful resources' (Sachs, 1984, pp. 28–30). In effect, systems concepts from ecology, such as cycles and functional harmonization, were transposed to the social and organizational domain. In biophysical terms, ecodevelopment aims at achieving a lasting symbiosis between humanity and the earth; at the social level the search is for a harmonization of relationships based on cooperation at local and international levels to achieve economic equity.

This picture is good as far as it goes, but in order to allow resource management decisions to be framed incisively we must add a further dimension, that of conflict resolution or choices regarding *which sustainability and for whom*. The simple invocation of 'symbiosis' or 'sustainability' as a reference concept does not serve as a decision criterion. It does not, for example, guarantee the conservation of specified productive or reproductive potentialities of any particular society or ecosystem. Nor does it assure the sustaining of all the particular interests, communities or ecologies thus given hope. So we must introduce explicitly the idea of human actions, and policy choices more particularly, as involving *decisions about the distribution of sustainability:* which interests and forms of life will be sustained, and which ones left behind, relinquished, destroyed or left to rot?

Take the example of flowing water resources, as in a river (cf. McCully, 1996). The watershed defines a 'natural' unit of ecosystem analysis; the flow patterns are woven into the habitats of hillside, swamp, riverbank and aquatic species; but the water may also be considered as a valuable input for industrial, agricultural and urban consumption. Who 'owns' the water? If water flow is diverted for irrigation, for factory use, for power plant cooling or for urban drinking supply purposes (for example), or if the continuity of flow is interrupted through dams, reservoirs and other forms of storage, these 'natural' forms of life may be put at risk. Dyke and dam systems can stabilize minor floods (yet may not be able to master the '100 year' ones), but salmon (for example) cannot swim upstream beyond a dam, and so the upper river ecosystems are species-impoverished (which may have repercussions for recreational and aesthetic attraction). There is also the problem of water given away. Water that has been 'used' for economic purposes may be allowed to flow back into 'natural' systems in a dirtied or 'polluted' condition; this also can menace the viability of life forms and can pose problems for human health. Finally, nature herself gives water away. Rivers are not always docile systems, and (for example) floods can damage or destroy the 'natural' habitats as well as the built human habitats that have been constructed over time.

The decisions regarding management of flowing water systems can thus be understood as a problem of the distribution of sustainability; and the regulation of access to water and the control of water quality can be posed in terms of distinct (yet often interdependent) 'needs for sustainability' and of the vulnerabilities of the different habitats and forms of life to changes, controlled or uncontrolled, in the terms of access and quality (Funtowicz and O'Connor, 1999; Allal and O'Connor, 1999).

Sustainability of the set of sectors and proprietors making up the watershed together (and also, by extension, linked further afield) means that the sectors that are mutually interdependent for their water flows must operate (*de facto* or by design) in solidarity with each other. If some users accumulate water stocks or flow volumes at the expense of others, or some users maintain their activity while dumping their toxic wastes and unwanted refuse into waters flowing on to other populations and habitats, we could speak of an 'uneven distribution of the conditions for sustainability'. So lived sustainability implies a *logic of reciprocation* expressed on material and social planes. Distributed sustainability means affirming the richness of diversity, and accepting the obligations and inconveniences alongside the pleasures of coexistence with others considered as friends and members of the extended community (human and non-human life).

How may the various candidates for sustainability – for example, terrestrial and aquatic ecosystems in 'natural' or human-modified form, agricultural systems, and rural and urban communities in their physical settings – be assessed in relation to each other? We are forced to acknowledge incommensurabilities. In a typical watershed management situation the maintenance of (say) bird populations and riverbank rural economies through flood management assuring year-round flows would serve different communities of interest from those served by (say) damming and piping the water for urban supply.

From a decision making and policy assessment point of view, there are both advantages and disadvantages in sacrificing the ideal of full commensurability of valuations. The approach being suggested here emphasizes the need to present information for discussion and decision-making procedures in ways that will not yield a unique ranking of options but that make explicit the sorts of social choices and ecological and economic trade-offs that might be involved. The disadvantage is the greater complexity in the way of framing decision problems. The advantage is the richer appreciation of the significance to different communities of interest of the choices to be made. Choices about sustainability goals and priorities are unavoidable. The way they are made can vary from acts of straight violence to patient efforts at accommodation of distinct interests. Where compromise or reconciliation is sought after, the decision process has to involve an iterative collective process of analysis, debates, negotiations, trade-offs and compromises, with the aim of ending up with a solution that is satisfactory in terms of economic, social and ecological imperatives. Thus the selection of spaces and species to be protected, pollutants to be curbed, and more generally the 'social demand' for this or that level of environmental functions to be 'sustained' emerges from a choice process that is essentially collective and sociopolitical rather than technical in nature (O'Connor, 2002).

BIOPHYSICAL SUSTENANCE AND CULTURAL VITALITY

As Richard Norgaard (1988, 1994) suggests in his coevolutionary perspective on sustainability, the questions of coexistence and coevolution can usefully be considered along several different spatial, as well as temporal, scales: from specific 'local' communities and territories, through nation states, regions and trade blocs, to the global level. At each scale, one can consider the community or system for itself, and also its exchanges and coevolution with other systems and communities, asking: 'Will the resource base, environment, technologies and culture evolve over time in a mutually reinforcing manner? .... Will [the resource users] destroy the local resource base and environment or, just as bad, the local people and their cultural system?' (Norgaard, 1988, p. 607).

These characterizations address the sustainability of the interactions between people and their environments over time. They refer particularly to 'the sustainability of the interactions between regions and cultural systems' (ibid., p. 607); that is, to exchange and reciprocal transformation as a cultural as well as material process. A coevolution, if it occurs, is a biophysical symbiosis; but it is not simply the biophysical coexistence. The crucial questions of autonomy and vitality are located on the symbolic planes as well as the biophysical planes. Economic autonomy refers not just to indigenous sources of natural wealth, it also means, in cultural terms, the experience and action of being part of a meaningful and creative social process. This raises the questions: in what ways does a person feel part of a community, and in what ways do their choices and actions depend on their sense of being part of a community?

With colleagues, we have studied the case of small forest pockets in agricultural France, in the Gâtinais region some 100 kilometres south of Paris (Héron, 1996; Héron and O'Connor, 1999; Noël *et al.*, 2000). There are many small such 'forest islands' *(îlots boisés)* in France, which have been the object of a number of recent studies (carried out by several different research teams) looking at various ecological, economic and social dimensions (see also Dubien, 1993; de la Gorce, 1994). This is a relatively simple situation: at least the woodland itself has boundaries that are clearly defined, although the forces acting in and on this woodland are perhaps less easy to define.

Our approach was one that sought to place the emphasis on a whole 'socioecological system' as a *unité de valeur*. The focus was on obtaining a picture of the local economy–community–ecosystem features, but implicitly this 'unit of analysis' is embedded in the larger fabric of French society, agricultural practice and patrimonies. In part, the analysis meant documenting the *human appreciation of the richness of the forest life forms.* For example, studies have identified an 'economic' value of the wood as fuel and (to a lesser degree) as timber, and perhaps also of the food items to be found in the forest; no doubt the hunt may be said to be a recreational value (perhaps quantifiable in terms of other opportunities forgone and the travel costs involved). Yet all these 'non-market values' and the labours of wood-lot tending and other maintenance are inseparable from the tissue of a *customary way of life.* The men, women and children who walk and ride horses and who search for the mushrooms, daffodils and berries probably do not make a 'rational' use of their time: they talk and they play. The investments of time, thought and effort in wood-lot maintenance, trail clearing and replanting would be unlikely to take place on an individualistic basis: they depend for meaning and justification on the membership *(appartenance)* of each person to the social groups and networks that constitute this way of life. So notwithstanding the clear 'private' dimensions of the wood-lot property as an exploitable resource, we are presented with a wealth-held-in-common: this is the significance (value) of the forest to the members of the community. It is a 'value as a whole' and it is not easy to see how it could be made divisible. The tending of the forest is a sort of metaphor for the maintaining of human community; and the one and the other are vulnerable to decline, death or decay (Boisvert *et al.*, 1998).

Indeed, in view of aging and the diminishing economic vigour of the community of interested local users and owners, the 'organic' maintenance of the woodland may be at risk. Suppose that a demand were expressed to have an external agency assume responsibility for maintaining the woodland as an amenity value. Can it be expected that a new generation of users, not having the same sorts of communal roots, would be willing to pay money (through, for example, local or national taxes, or access fees) in scale equivalent to the embodied-time willingness to pay of the traditional communal owners? Quite possibly not. The economists' standard explanation might then be that the population's tastes would have changed (and in fact, it would also be that the population itself has changed). This explanation could be true, yet is it the most useful one? Another form of explanation would be that the forest–community symbiosis as a *structure of lived and shared meaning* (and a form of local economic life) has not been sustained. This second form of explanation is possibly no 'more' true than the first, but it may be a more useful one for helping to decide about rural and regional development and nature conservation policies.

CONCLUDING REMARKS

The concepts and arguments presented briefly here can, we would suggest, fruitfully be applied as a framework for identifying the dimensions of choice for many sorts of ecosystem and 'renewable natural capital' management problems. For any ecosystem, environmental function or category of natural resource, the process of identification of alternative uses and their benefits and costs is made inseparable from the question of the *distinct (but often interdependent) communities of interest to be, or not to be, sustained.*

This reframing involves more than just a descriptive (resource inventory) type of analysis. It involves a distinctive and self-conscious reframing of the 'normative' as well as 'positive' dimensions of valuation theory and its reasons. In part, the argument of this chapter is a revisitation, and an extension to new terrains, of the old quarrel of welfare economics concerning the inseparability of allocative (efficiency) and distributional (equity) goals (see Samuels, 1992; also Martinez-Alier and O'Connor, 1996). First, we insist that the further concerns of environmental policy extend to the 'long-term' future, the more intertemporal distributional considerations will predominate, in theory and in reality, over allocative efficiency in policy formulation and appraisal. Second, we insist that the further concerns for environmental 'values' extend into the domains of aesthetic and cultural as well as economic appreciation of natural cycles and systems, the more difficult it becomes to apply (or justify) the assumptions of value commensurability and substitutability that underlie conventional economic valuation methodology. For both these reasons, it is necessary to frame decision-making ideals in terms such as compromise and fairness – acceptability and judgment over what Warren Samuels (1992) describes as the necessary and socially instituted 'distribution of sacrifice' – distinguishing this sharply from the more familiar 'optimization' and its close cousin 'best balance'.

The nature of the choices inherent in the setting of ecological, social and economic sustainability goals cannot be expressed satisfactorily in such terms as 'optimal choice', nor can the pursuit of sustainability goals be guided by market-based valuations. The reasons for this are simple. Optimal choice requires, at some level or other, the application of a single principle for ordering, judging and ranking what is right and 'best'. But 'sustainability' in its general social–economic–ecological acceptance signals a requirement to accommodate a multiplicity of different ordering principles, and its realization will depend on cherishing the richness of *living with and living in nature* with its great variety of life forms. Market-type valuations are based on a logic of *rational exploitation of an external domain* (the 'free gifts and services of nature'), and on a similarly utilitarian attitude towards others as fellow economic agents (producers, traders and consumers, and police, reconciled contractually in a general equilibrium). But valuation for sustainability as framed in this chapter starts from, and seeks to affirm, an experience of intersubjectivity and symbiosis, deeper and more complex than a rational contractual form (O'Connor, 1996, 1999, 2000).

The fundamental normative orientations are thus established along two axes: firstly, when a sustainability 'goal' is initially expressed, from which point of view feasibility and opportunity costs can be explored; secondly, when attention is given to the question of how to reconcile this goal with the diverse sustainability concerns expressed by others. In short, a sustainability commitment, even if affirmed individually, must find collective expression and be accommodated with other parties' concerns. In situations of indeterminacy and conflict (which are most often the case), many different sustainability commitments might be identified and explored. Difficult choices and compromises will have to be made. This is the matter of the distribution of sustainability; these are not the sorts of choices that may be determined on allocative efficiency grounds. If there is to be any alternative to endemic war on various scales of a small planet, these are choices that must be made on a basis of purposefulness and compassion, acknowledging the grief of those whose principles, sentiments and interests are not respected, and sharing empathetically in this pain.

ACKNOWLEDGEMENTS

Thanks to C3ED colleagues Christophe Héron, Jessy Tsang and Jean-François Noël whose empirical research work has provided direct stimulus to the arguments constructed here. In part, the work on valuation theory and practice was supported by the DG-XII of the European Commission under contracts ENV4-CT94-0363 (the GREENSTAMP project) and ENV4-CT96-0226 for the project 'Social Processes for Environmental Valuation: Procedures and Institutions for Social Valuations of Natural Capital in Environmental Conservation and Sustainability Policy', known as The VALSE project. My acknowledgements to colleagues from several countries who worked on these (and other) collaborative projects; also to Andy Dragun, Joan Martinez-Alier, Silvio Funtowicz, Ariel Salleh, Sylvie Faucheux and other comrades in arms.

REFERENCES

Allal, S. and M. O'Connor (1999), 'Water resource distribution and security in the Jordan–Israel–Palestinian peace process', in S.C. Lonergan (ed.), *Environmental Change, Adaptation, and Security*, Dordrecht: Kluwer, pp. 109–29.

Asheim, G.B. (1994), 'Net national product as an indicator of sustainability', *Scandanavian Journal of Economics*, **96**, 257–65.

Boisvert, V., J.-F. Noël and J. Tsang-King-Sang (1998), 'Le bois Bouchereau : résultats d'une enquête auprès des propriétaires', *Rapport de recherche du C3ED*, UVSQ, Paris, May.

Brouwer, R., M. O'Connor and W. Radermacher (1996), 'Defining cost effective responses to environmental deterioration in a periodic accounting system', in *Proceedings of the Third Meeting of the London Group on Natural Resource and Environmental Accounting* (held at Stockholm, 28–31 May 1996), Stockholm: Statistics Sweden, pp. 397–422.

Brouwer, R., M. O'Connor and W. Radermacher (1999), 'Greened national statistical and modelling procedures: the GREENSTAMP approach to the calculation of environmentally adjusted national income figures', *International Journal of Sustainable Development*, **2**, 7–31.

de la Gorce, L. (1994), 'Homme/Biodiversité: l'impact des coupes forestières sur la richesse floristique d'un îlot boisé en plaine de grande culture', unpublished research essay (*maîtrise*), UFR de Géographie, Université de Paris I, France.

Dubien, I. (1993), 'Devenir des Ilots Boisés du Gâtinais Nord Occidental', unpublished research essay (*mémoire de DEA*), UFR d'Economie, , Université de Paris I, France.

Faucheux, S. and M. O'Connor (eds) (1998), *Valuation for Sustainable Development: Methods and Policy Indicators*, Cheltenham, UK and Lyme, NH, US: Edward Elgar.

Faucheux, S., E. Muir and M. O'Connor (1997), 'Neoclassical theory of natural capital and "weak" indicators for sustainability', *Land Economics*, **73**, 528–52.

Foster J., A. Holland, M. Jacobs, G. Munda, M. O'Connor and J. O'Neill (2002), 'Multi-criteria and deliberative procedures for environmental evaluation', in M. O'Connor and V. Meite (eds), *Environmental Evaluation*, Cheltenham, UK and Northampton, MA, USA: Edward Elgar.

Funtowicz, S.O. and M. O'Connor (1999), 'The passage from entropy to thermodynamic indeterminacy: a social and science epistemology for sustainability', in K. Mayumi and J. Gowdy (eds), *Bioeconomics and Sustainability: Essays in Honour of Nicholas Georgescu-Roegen*, Cheltenham, UK and Northampton, MA, USA: Edward Elgar, pp. 257–86.

Funtowicz, S. and J. Ravetz, J. (1994), 'The worth of a songbird: ecological economics as a post-normal science', *Ecological Economics*, **10**, 197–207.

Godard, O. (1984), 'Autonomie socio-économique et externalisation de l'environnement: la théorie néoclassique mise en perspective', *Economie Appliquée*, **37**, 315–45.

Hanley, N. and C.L. Spash (1993), *Cost–Benefit Analysis and the Environment*, Aldershot, UK and Brookfield, US: Edward Elgar.

Héron, C. (1996), 'La représentation systémique de l'Ilot Boisé: Vers une mise en evidence de la valeur sociale', *Cahiers du C3ED*, Université de Versailles St-Quentin-en-Yvelines, France.

Héron, C. and M. O'Connor (1999), 'Forest value and the distribution of sustainability: valuation concepts and methodology in application to forest islands in agricultural zones in France', in Roper C.S. and A. Park (eds), *The Living Forest, Non-market Benefits of Forestry*, London: The Stationery Office, pp. 99–107.

Holland, A. (1997), 'The foundations of environmental decision-making'. *International Journal of Environment and Pollution*, **7**, 483–96.

Holland, A., M. O'Connor and J. O'Neill (1996), 'Costing environmental damage: a critical survey of current theory and practice and recommendations for policy implementation', report for the Directorate General for Research, STOA programme, European Parliament, Guyancourt: C3ED, Université de Versailles St-Quentin-en-Yvelines, France, April.

Howarth, R.B. (2001), 'Intertemporal social choice and climate stabilization', *International Journal of Environment and Pollution*, **15**(4), 386–405.

Jakobsson, K.M. and A.K. Dragun (1996), *Contingent Valuation and Endangered Species: Methodological Issues and Applications*, Cheltenham, UK and Brookfield, US: Edward Elgar.

Martinez-Alier, J. (1991), 'Environmental policy and distributional conflicts', in R. Costanza (ed.), *Ecological Economics: The Science and Management of Sustainability*, New York: Columbia University Press, pp. 118–36.

Martinez-Alier, J. (1995), 'Political ecology, distributional conflicts, and economic incommensurability', *New Left Review*, **211**, 70–88.

Martinez-Alier, J. and M. O'Connor (1996), 'Economic and ecological distribution conflicts', in R. Costanza, O.Segura and J. Martinez-Alier (eds), *Getting Down to Earth: Practical Applications of Ecological Economics*, Washington, DC: Island Press, pp. 153–84.

McCully, P. (1996), *Silenced Rivers: The Ecology and Politics of Large Dams*, London: Zed Books.

Munda, G. (1995), *Multicriteria Evaluation in a Fuzzy Environment: Theory and Applications in Ecological Economics*, Berlin: Physica-Verlag.

Noël J.-F., M. O'Connor and J. Tsang-King-Sang (2000), 'The Bouchereau Woodland and the transmission of socio-ecological economic value', *Ecological Economics*, **34**, 247–66.

Norgaard, R.B. (1988), 'Sustainable development: A co-evolutionary view', *Futures*, 20, 606–20.

Norgaard, R.B. (1990), 'Economic indicators of resource scarcity: A critical essay', *Journal of Environmental Economics and Management*, **19**, 19–25.

Norgaard, R.B. (1994), *Development Betrayed: The End of Progress and a Coevolutionary Revisioning of the Future*, London: Routledge.

O'Connor, M. (1989), 'Codependency and indeterminacy: A critique of the theory of production', *Capitalism, Nature, Socialism*, **3**, 33–57.

O'Connor, M. (ed.) (1994), *Is Capitalism Sustainable? Political Economy and the Politics of Ecology*, New York: Guilford Publications.

O'Connor, M. (1996), 'Cherishing the future, cherishing the other: A Post-Classical theory of value', in S. Faucheux, D. Pearce and J. Proops (eds), *Models of Sustainable Development*, Cheltenham, UK and Brookfield, US: Edward Elgar, pp. 223–48.

O'Connor, M. (1997a), 'The internalization of environmental costs: implementing the polluter pays principle in the European Union', *International Journal of Environment and Pollution*, **7**, 450–82.

O'Connor, M. (1997b), 'Environmental valuation from the point of view of sustainability', in A. Dragun and K. Jacobbson (eds), *Sustainability and Global Environmental Policy: New Perspectives*, Cheltenham, UK and Lyme, NH, US: Edward Elgar, pp. 147–79.

O'Connor, M. (1998), 'Walking in the Garden(s) of Babylon: An overview of the VALSE Project', Rapport de Recherche, Guyancourt: C3ED, Université de Versailles St-Quentin-en-Yvelines, France.

O'Connor, M. (1999), 'Dialogue and debate in a post-normal practice of science: a reflection', *Futures*, **31**, 671–87.

O'Connor, M. (2000), 'Pathways for environmental valuation: A walk in the (Hanging) Gardens of Babylon', *Ecological Economics*, **34**, 175–94.

O'Connor, M. (2002), 'Social costs and sustainability', in D.W. Bromley and J. Paavola, *Economics, Ethics and Environmental Policy: Contested Choices*, Oxford, UK and Malden, MA, US: Blackwell Publishing.

O'Connor, M. and J. Martinez-Alier (1997), 'Ecological distribution and distributed sustainability', in S. Faucheux, M. O'Connor and J. van der Straaten (eds), *Sustainable Development: Concepts, Rationalities and Strategies*, Dordrecht: Kluwer, pp. 33–56.

O'Connor, M. and G. Ryan (1999), 'Macro-economic cost-effectiveness for the estimation and the use of multi-sectoral dynamic modelling as an environmental valuation tool', *International Journal of Sustainable Development*, **2**, 127–53.

O'Connor M. and C.L. Spash (eds) (1999), *Valuation and the Environment: Theory, Method and Practice*, Cheltenham, UK and Northampton, MA, USA: Edward Elgar.

O'Neill, J. (1993), *Ecology, Policy and Politics: Human Well-Being and the Natural World*, London: Routledge.

Peet, J. (1992), *Energy and the Ecological Economics of Sustainability*, Washington, DC: Island Press.

Pezzey, J. (1997), 'Sustainability constraints, present value maximisation and intergenerational welfare', *Land Economics*, **73**, 448–66.

Pezzey, J. and C. Withagen (1998), 'The rise, fall and sustainability of capital-resource economies', *Scandinavian Journal of Economics*, **100**, 513–27.

Sachs, I. (1980), *Stratégies de l'écodéveloppement*, Paris: Les Editions Ouvrières.

Sachs, I. (1984), *Développer les champs de planification*, Paris: Maison des Sciences de L'Homme; English translation (1987) by Peter Fawcett, *Development and Planning*, Cambridge: Cambridge University Press.

Samuels, W.J. (1992), *Essays on the Economic Role of Government Vol.I Fundamentals; Vol.II Applications*, London: Macmillan.

Schütz, J. (2000), 'Sustainability, systems and meaning', *Environmental Values*, **9**, 373–82.

Spash, C. (1994a), 'Trying to find the right approach to greenhouse economics: some reflections upon the role of CBA', *Analyse & Kritik: Zeitschrift für Socialwissenschafen*, **16**, 186–99.

Spash, C. (1994b), 'Double CO_2 and beyond: Benefits, costs and compensation', *Ecological Economics*, **10**, 27–36.

3. Multicriteria-based environmental policy

Silvio O. Funtowicz, Juan Martinez-Alier, Giuseppe Munda and Jerry Ravetz

POST-NORMAL SCIENCE AS A BRIDGE BETWEEN COMPLEX SYSTEMS AND ENVIRONMENTAL POLICY

The *multiplicity of perspectives* on a situation is one of the essential features of complexity, as it is now understood. Another is that the system in question consists of a *structure of subsystems*. Much of the motivation for applying complex systems theory to environmental problems has come from the failure of attempts to manage ecosystems as if they were simple or merely complicated systems.

In such contexts of complexity, there is a new role for science. The facts that are taught from textbooks are still necessary, but are no longer sufficient, for these relate to a standardized version of the natural world, frequently the artificially pure and stable conditions of a laboratory experiment. Such a style of work has proved highly successful in academic and industrial research, but for the problems of achieving sustainability it is no longer appropriate. An approach for managing complex policy-related research issues is 'Post-Normal Science' (Funtowicz and Ravetz, 1991; Kuhn, 1962). The insight leading to post-normal science is that, in the sort of issue-driven problems characteristic of policy-related research, *typically facts are uncertain, values in dispute, stakes high and decisions urgent.* It focuses on aspects of problem solving that tend to be neglected in traditional accounts of scientific practice: uncertainty and value loading. Post-normal science provides a coherent explanation of the need for greater participation in science policy processes, based on the new tasks of quality assurance in these problem areas. Some might say that such problems should not be called 'science'; but the answer could be that such problems are everywhere, and when science is (as it must be) applied to them, the conditions are anything but normal, since the previous distinction between 'hard', objective scientific facts and 'soft', subjective value judgments is now inverted. All too often, we must make hard policy decisions where our only scientific inputs are irremediably soft.

One innovation of post-normal science is the inclusion of 'decision stakes' for 'science', which had traditionally been assumed to be 'value-free'. But in any real problem of environmental management, the two dimensions are inseparable. When conclusions are not completely determined by the scientific facts, inferences will (naturally and legitimately) be conditioned by the values held by the agent. This is a necessary part of ordinary research practice: all statistical tests have values built in through the choice of numerical 'confidence limits', and the management of 'outlier' data calls for judgments that can sometimes approach the post-normal in their complexity. If the stakes are very high (as when an institution is seriously threatened by a policy), a defensive policy will involve challenging every step of a scientific argument, even if the system's uncertainties are actually small. Such tactics become wrong only when they are conducted covertly, as by scientists who present themselves as impartial judges when they are actually committed advocates.

There are now many initiatives, increasing in number and significance all the time, for involving wider circles of people in decision making and implementation on environmental issues. Examples of 'post-normal science' are to be found wherever local communities engage in scientific research and dialogue on the state of their personal and environmental health. One important case is the 'popular epidemiology' movement connected to the Environmental Justice movement in the United States (Novotny, 1994). A number of grassroots movements struggled for years against all official agencies, including the academics, to try and establish the case that their communities were being harmed. In the most famous case, the authorities were eventually forced to admit that a collection of symptoms was the manifestation of a real condition, ever after known, using the town's name, as Lyme Disease.

'TAKING NATURE INTO ACCOUNT': THE INCOMMENSURABILITY PRINCIPLE

Environmental policy deals with reflexive phenomena. An effective assessment, in order to be realistic, should consider not merely the measurable and contrastable dimensions of the simple parts of the system that, even if complicated, may be simulated technically; it should also deal with the higher dimensions of the system. These are the dimensions in which power relations, hidden interests, social participation, cultural constraints and other 'soft' values become relevant, and unavoidable variables heavily, but not deterministically, affect the possible outcomes of the strategies to be adopted.

A mathematical model of, for example, an ecosystem, although legitimate in its own terms, cannot be sufficient for a complete analysis of its reflexive properties, which include the human dimensions of ecological change and the transformations of human perceptions along the way. The learning process that takes place while analysing the issue and defining policies will itself influence perceptions and alter significantly the decisional space in which alternative strategies are chosen. At the other end, institutional and cultural representations of the same system, also legitimate, are on their own insufficient for specifying what should be done in practice in any particular case. The various dimensions are not totally disjointed; thus the institutional perspective can be a basis for the study of the social relations of the scientific processes. To take any particular dimension as the true, real or total picture amounts to *reductionism*, whether physical or sociological.

As a consequence, any attempt to fit the real world to a closed model leads to a simplification, to violence to the description of reality. In most cases the sacrificed dimensions are precisely the reflexive properties of the systems. These characterize the problem in a fundamental way but are hardly identifiable and measurable. For example, in conventional economics only the quantitative properties and a single perspective, economic efficiency, are considered (Munda, 1996). The environment is a site of conflict between competing values and interests and different groups and communities that represent them. How are such conflicts to be resolved? Conventional economics assumes the existence of value commensurability. Is that assumption justified? In the following, we argue that it is not.

From a philosophical perspective, it is possible to distinguish between the concepts of *strong commensurability* (a common measure of the different consequences of an action based on a cardinal scale of measurement), *weak commensurability* (a common measure based on an ordinal scale of measurement), *strong comparability* (there exists a single comparative term by which all different actions can be ranked) and *weak comparability* (irreducible value conflict is unavoidable but compatible with rational choice employing practical judgment) (Martinez-Alier *et al.*, 1998; O'Neill, 1993).

The arguments about economic commensurability and its place in decision making about the environment are not new to the economic debate. It was precisely the relation between rational decision making and economic commensurability which was the main point in the opening stage of the famous debate of the 1920s and 1930s on economic calculus in a socialist economy. The debate, started in central Europe (Hayek, 1935), focused on disagreement on how an economy could work when the means of production were socialized, and therefore were not in the market. The question seemed practically relevant in the aftermath of the war of 1914–18 because of the wave of revolutions in central and eastern Europe.

Neurath explained the essence of economic incommensurability by means of the following example (Neurath, 1919). Let us consider two capitalist factories, achieving the same production level of the same type of product, one with 200 workers and 100 tons of coal, the second one with 300 workers and only 40 tons of coal. Both would compete in the market, and the one using a more 'economic' process would achieve an advantage. However, in a socialist economy (where the means of production are socialized), in order to compare two economic plans, both of them achieving the same result, a present value should be given to future needs for coal (and, we would now add, a present value should be given also to the future impact of carbon dioxide emissions). We must not only decide, therefore, a rate of discount and a time horizon, but also guess the changes in technology: use of solar energy, use of waterpower and use of nuclear power. In Neurath's own words (Neurath, 1928, p. 263), the answer to the question whether coal-intensive or labour-intensive methods should be used 'depends for example on whether one thinks that hydraulic power may be sufficiently developed or that solar heat might come to be better used. If, however, one is afraid that, when one generation uses too much coal, thousands will freeze to death in the future, one might use more human power and save coal. These and many other non-technical matters determine the choice of a technically calculable plan … we can see no possibility of reducing the production plan to some kind of unit and then comparing the various plans in terms of such units'.

MULTICRITERIA EVALUATION AS A TOOL FOR ENVIRONMENTAL POLICY UNDER COMPLEXITY

A typical multicriteria problem (with a discrete number of alternatives) may be described in the following way: A is a finite set of n feasible actions (or alternatives); m is the number of different points of view or evaluation criteria g_i $i = 1, 2, \ldots, m$ considered relevant in a decision problem, where the action a is evaluated to be better than action b (both belonging to the set A) according to the ith point of view if $g_i(a) > g_i(b)$. In this way a decision problem may be represented in a tabular or matrix form. Given the sets A (of alternatives) and G (of evaluation criteria) and assuming the existence of n alternatives and m criteria, it is possible to build an $n \times m$ matrix **P** called the evaluation or impact matrix whose typical element p_{ij} $(i = 1, 2, \ldots, m; j = 1, 2, \ldots, n)$ represents the evaluation of the jth alternative by means of the ith criterion (see Table 3.1). The impact matrix may include quantitative, qualitative or both types of information (Munda *et al.*, 1994a; Munda, 1995).

In general, in a multicriteria problem, there is no solution optimizing all the criteria at the same time and therefore the decision maker has to find

Table 3.1 Example of an impact matrix

		Alternatives			
Criteria	Units	a_1	a_2	a_3	a_4
g_1		$g_1(a_1)$	$g_1(a_2)$	.	$g_1(a_4)$
g_2		.	.	.	.
g_3		.	.	.	.
g_4		.	.	.	.
g_5		.	.	.	.
g_6		$g_6(a_1)$	$g_6(a_2)$	.	$g_6(a_4)$

compromise solutions. It is clear that in policy-relevant economic–environmental evaluation models, socioeconomic and nature conservation objectives are to be considered simultaneously. Consequently, multicriteria methods are in principle an appropriate modelling tool for environmental decision-making issues: a compromise solution taking into account different conflicting values can in principle be identified.

As a tool for conflict management, multicriteria evaluation has demonstrated its usefulness in many environmental management problems. From an operational point of view, the major strength of multicriteria methods is their ability to address problems marked by various conflicting evaluations. Multicriteria evaluation techniques cannot solve all conflicts, but they can help to provide more insight into the nature of conflicts and into ways in which to arrive at political compromises in case of divergent preferences, thereby increasing the *transparency* of the choice process.

The main advantage of multicriteria models is that they make it possible to consider a large number of data, relations and objectives that are generally present in a specific real-world decision problem, so that the decision problem at hand can be studied in a multidimensional fashion. It may easily happen that an action A may be better than an action B according to one criterion and worse according to another. When different conflicting evaluation criteria are taken into consideration, two cases are possible (Munda, 1993): (1) leaving the decision maker total freedom to make the decision (decisionism) and (2) introducing restrictive hypotheses, consciously or not, so that the problem can be solved by a classical method (rationalism).

Decisionism in practice maintains that decisions are blind actions, inspired by the subconscious and by passion, so that the act of reasoning over a decision is meaningless. On the contrary, rationalism assumes that in any decision problem an optimal precise solution always exists and that it is possible to find it by reasoning over the problem. Thus, using Socrates' words, 'ignorance is the only cause of foolish or evil acts'. The methods used in multicriteria analysis lie between these two extremes. Thus the concept of 'decision process' has an essential importance.

As a consequence, the validity of a given multicriteria evaluation study depends on the inclusion of the several legitimate perspectives, as well as on the non-omission of the reflexive properties of the system, even though these are not easy to deal with. Once the premises of a particular multicriteria approach are known, the decision makers are aware of the consequences of the assumption. This requires transparency in relation to two main factors: (1) mathematical and descriptive properties which make the models used conform to given requirements, and (2) the way such models are used and integrated in a decision process. The importance of the decision process has recently been emphasized by different authors. According to Simon (Simon, 1972, 1978, 1983), a distinction must be made between the general notion of rationality as an adaptation of available means to ends, and the various theories and models based on a rationality which is either substantive or procedural. This terminology can be used to distinguish between the rationality of a decision considered independently of the manner in which it is made (in the case of substantive rationality, the rationality of evaluation refers exclusively to the results of the choice) and the rationality of a decision in terms of the manner in which it is made (in the case of procedural rationality, the rationality of evaluation refers to the decision-making process itself) (Froger and Munda, 1998).

Roy (1985) states that in general it is impossible to say that a decision is a good one or a bad one by referring only to a mathematical model: all aspects of the whole decision process which lead to a given decision also contribute to its quality and success. As a consequence, it becomes impossible to base the validity of a procedure either on a notion of approximation or on a mathematical property of convergence. The final solution is more like a *creation* than a discovery.

This new way of looking at rationality implies *a new concept of quality*. What we can now evaluate is the process leading to a given decision, not the final product, that is, the final decision. Is it possible to improve the quality of a decision process?

A NEW CONCEPT OF QUALITY AND 'EXTENDED PEER COMMUNITIES'

The approach of post-normal science starts with the acceptance that the goals of the achievement of the true and the advancement of the good are no longer realistic or appropriate for policy-related research. There are alternative bases for the proper evaluation and guidance of the scientific endeavour; they come through the idea of *quality*. In some ways this idea has become very familiar to anyone involved in institutional work. Quality has become the name of many games, with audits and evaluations applied to a vast range of human activities, including teaching and research itself. We even have explicit instructions for quality assurance, encoded in International Standards, and effectively possessing statutory force. For those with experience of such exercises, quality may seem to be a rather weak, or at best flexible, basis for security in science. For many have learned, sometimes through bitter experience, that quality is not a simple, absolute measure like length. The quality of the quality-assessment exercise is frequently compromised, sometimes with official and unofficial systems competing for credibility (Funtowicz and Ravetz, 1990).

It could seem that we are arriving at a paradoxical and indeed troubling conclusion: with the true and the good compromised as sources of security for science, we have just proposed quality; and yet this is hardly an unproblematic concept in itself. Worse, the problem of quality of science becomes really acute in the case of the environmental sciences. These lack the informal closed communities of the old 'little science', and their results are generally incapable of immediate direct testing through experiment or observation. Even when apparently straightforward research is done, the appropriate quality criteria may be different for policy application from those that apply in the former, restricted, world of the lab, since such work is assessed only secondarily as a contribution to knowledge and a stimulus to further research. Rather, what is crucial is its relevance and reliability for policy conclusions. Who is to assess quality by those criteria, and who is to assess the assessors?

We suggest the idea of an 'extended peer community' in cases of post-normal science, where neither traditional research nor market mechanisms are at all adequate for the tasks of quality assurance. In this case, the extended peer community consists not merely of persons with some form or other of institutional accreditation, but rather of all those with a desire to participate in the resolution of the issue. Seen out of context, such a proposal might seem to involve a dilution of the authority of science, and its dragging into the arena of politics. However, here we are not talking about the traditional areas of research and industrial development, but about those situations where issues of quality are crucial, and traditional mechanisms of quality assurance are patently inadequate. Since this context of science is one involving policy, we might see this extension of franchise to peer communities as analogous to earlier extensions of franchise in other fields, such as allowing workers to form trade unions and women to vote. In all such cases, there were prophecies of doom which did not materialize.

For the formation of environmental policy under conditions of complexity, it is hard to imagine any viable alternative to extended peer communities. They are already being created, in increasing numbers, either when the authorities cannot see a way forward, or when they know that, without a broad base of consensus, no policies can succeed. They are called 'citizens' juries', 'focus groups' or 'consensus conferences', or any one of a great variety of names, and their forms and powers are correspondingly varied. But they all have one important element in common: they assess the quality of policy proposals, including the scientific and technical component, and their verdicts all have some degree of moral force and hence political influence. Here the quality is not merely in the verification, but also in the *creation*, as local people can imagine solutions and reformulate problems in ways that, with the best will in the world, do not come naturally, even to the accredited experts.

None can claim that the restoration of quality through extended peer communities will occur easily, and without its own sorts of errors. We are beyond the search for absolute guarantees, and the very idea of quality, as we have articulated it, should warn against that. But in the processes of extension of peer communities through the approach of post-normal science, we can see a way forward for science as much as for the complex problems of the environment. The following examples illustrate the divergence among stakeholder interests and perceptions in environmental policy and show how very conflictual policy issues can be opened up for resolution by means of decision aids applied in a self-aware and transparent fashion.

MULTICRITERIA EVALUATION IN ENVIRONMENTAL POLICY: SOME REAL-WORLD EXAMPLES

Land Use Conflicts in The Netherlands

This illustrative application concerns a study on environmental management in The Netherlands in the southern part of Limburg. The problem at hand can be briefly illustrated as follows (for more information, see Munda *et al.*, 1994b).

A company having almost absolute dominance in the Dutch cement industry had a concession to extract marl on one of the hills in south Limburg, but this concession was to end in the near future; thus alternative areas had to be explored. Among the new possible areas, the most appropriate was the Plateau van Margraten; this is a rather flat area used for agriculture and for some recreation. It has a unique physical structure and is a rather characteristic area in the landscape of the region. Designation of this area for marl mining would have fundamentally affected its social and ecological value; on the other hand, if the authorities had refused to grant permission for marl mining to the company, this would have led to an almost total destruction of the national cement industry and to serious unemployment effects for this already weak economic region. This situation clearly demonstrates the sharp conflicts between environmental and economic interests.

A first meaningful step towards an evaluation analysis for this land use problem was to identify a set of feasible and relevant alternatives. These alternatives were as follows.

1. Implementation of the original plans of the company (that is, a concession for the Plateau van Margraten area). This would have guaranteed the future position of the national cement industry and also favoured employment and welfare in the region. Agriculture would have suffered from some negative impacts, while the negative social impacts (for recreation and so on) would have been rather high. Finally, the environmental damage would have been very high.

   Clearly, this is the best alternative for the interest groups supporting the company.
2. The use of an alternative area (the Rasberg area, in the same region) for marl mining. However, this area is much smaller and the physical condition of the soil would have hampered profitable cement production at the going prices. On the other hand, the ecological damage would have been less serious.

   This alternative could be interpreted as a compromise between the authorities and the company (here a concession would have been granted, but the location would have been decided by the political authorities and not by the company).
3. The provision of a concession for one half of the area (Plateau van Margraten). This would have led to fewer agricultural losses, while the environmental damage would also have been lower. The economic impacts would have been less favourable than those of the first alternative.

   This was a possible base for compromise. However, it could have been very dangerous for the political authorities, since it could maximize the opposition (by making nobody happy).
4. A concession given by the political authorities for marl mining on the existing area. This was only a short-term solution (since it was not possible from a technical point of view to prolong the extraction of marl at that site as it was becoming less attractive from an economic point of view).

   Clearly, this alternative was not homogeneous with the others with respect to the time horizon. It reflected a typical attitude of politicians all over the world: 'Let's try to shift the problem on to somebody else' (the winners of the next elections).

5. Import of marl from the Plateau van Vroenhoven, an area in Belgium.

   This solution might have been attractive from a national standpoint, but if we take into account the global environmental consequences (the environmental impact of extraction in Belgium and the transport of marl) it was clearly the worst option from an environmental point of view. This alternative also showed the importance of the hierarchical level used to describe a problem (region, country, European Union).
6. A restructuring of the company so that it became a trade and research organization for cement instead of a production unit for cement. This would have led to a certain loss of employment, while the future need for such an organization was unclear.

   This alternative could have been attractive for anyone not having an economic interest in the company.
7. A closing-down of all productive activities of the company.

   This might have been favourable from the viewpoint of environmentalists and people who used the Plateau for recreation, but it would have led to serious economic problems for the region.

These alternatives were to be judged on the basis of various evaluation criteria. Three main groups of criteria could be distinguished: economic, social and environmental. These three classes could be subdivided into various components.

A Economic criteria

- employment in agriculture,
- employment in the cement industry (including marl mining),
- agricultural production,
- national production of marl,
- value added in the cement industry.

B Social criteria

- residential attractiveness,
- recreational attractiveness (daily),
- tourist attractiveness,
- congestion created in transport infrastructure.

C Environmental criteria

- quality of geophysical structure,
- diversity and scarcity of eco- and bio-components,

- consistency with existing landscape components,
- consistency with existing cultural–historical components.

Of course, the alternatives and criteria illustrated are only some of the possible ways to tackle the problem at hand. They are the result of the decision-making process developed on that occasion. However, it should be noted that the transparency is really very high. It is easy to understand the interests that were behind each alternative.

It had to be decided whether to measure the environmental impacts of the various alternatives only in The Netherlands, or both in The Netherlands and in Belgium. Of course, the 'solutions constructed' were different, according to the choice made. In any case, it was clear that such a choice implied a value judgment, that is the implementation of a weak or strong sustainability philosophy.

At this point in the discussion, one question arose: who was to take the decisions? Some critics of multicriteria evaluation say that, *in principle*, in cost–benefit analysis, votes expressed on the market by the whole population can be taken into account (of course with the condition that the distribution of income is accepted as a means to allocate votes). On the contrary, multicriteria evaluation can be based on the priorities and preferences of some decision makers only (we could say that the way these decision makers have reached their position is accepted as a way to allocate the right to express these priorities). This criticism may be correct if a 'technocratic approach' is taken, where the analyst constructs the problem relying only upon experts' inputs. By 'experts' we mean those who know the 'technicalities' of a given problem.

To clarify this point we will briefly consider a case study of water management in Sicily. For more details on this project, see (De Marchi *et al.* (2000), Funtowicz *et al.* (1998).

Water Management Issues in Troina, Sicily: a Multicriteria Process

Troina is a small town (10 000 inhabitants) in north-eastern Sicily, Italy. On the one hand, it was commonly assumed that there was an actual water shortage in Troina, which could be remedied by more effective use of existing resources. (Paradoxically, although real water shortage is common in Sicily, Troina is an exception.) On the other hand, there was a complex and heterogeneous collection of interests in the Troina water issue, who had hitherto had no effective dialogue. Hence an effective structuring of the water problem at this early stage was an important task, so that eventual negotiations among stakeholders could have a better chance of a positive outcome. The steps of the overall evaluation process followed are schematized in Figure 3.1.

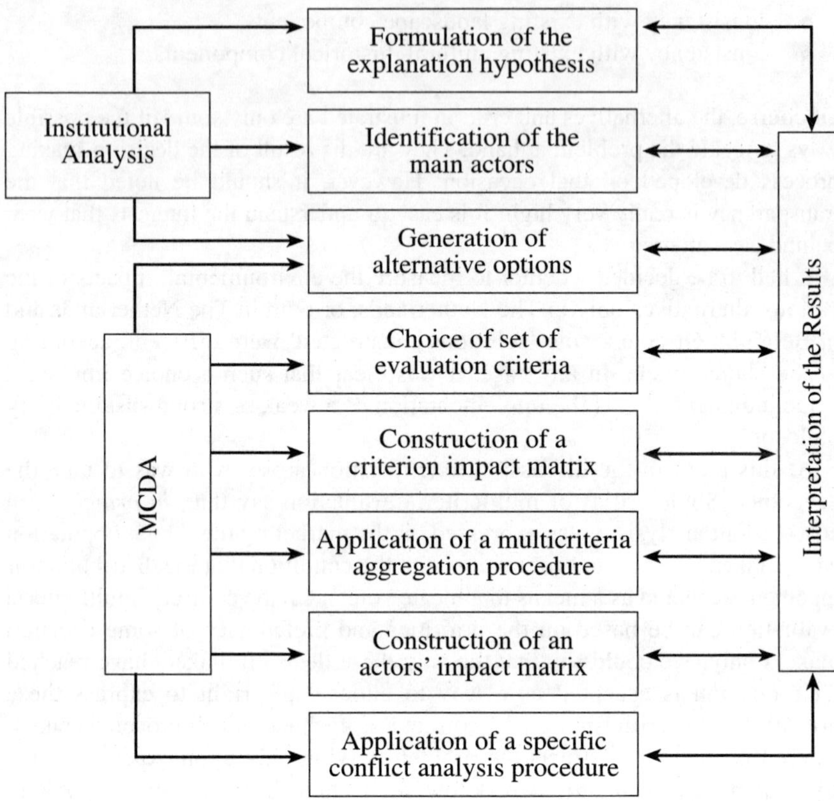

Figure 3.1 Scheme of the evaluation process

It needs to be noted that evaluation is not a 'one-shot' activity; on the contrary, it takes place as a *learning process*. It has to be realized that the evaluation process is usually highly dynamic, so much so that judgments regarding the political relevance of items, alternatives or impacts may present sudden changes, requiring a policy analysis to be flexible and adaptive in nature. This is the reason why evaluation processes have a *cyclic nature*. By this is meant the possible adaptation of elements of the evaluation process by means of continuous feedback loops among the various steps and consultations among the actors involved (Nijkamp *et al.*, 1990).

The first question to be asked was the following: Is 'business as usual' a possible option in the long run? Business as usual was a situation where power and water management was fragmented among the main actors and where infrastructure actions were the only ones not requiring agreements. This can be considered the classic case of non-cooperative resource exploitation.

For instance, the municipality of Troina was trying to become self-sufficient with respect to its drinking water needs by using its own spring water sources, even if this could be perceived as inefficient. To evaluate the 'business as usual' option properly, it had to be compared to a set of different possible options on the basis of some evaluation criteria. At this point, an issue immediately arose: alternatives and criteria for whom? This led to a need to take into account the preferences of some of the actors playing an important role in the problem at hand.

Initially (as a result of the institutional analysis), only the actors playing an important role in the community of Troina were taken into account. Later on, as a surprising feedback of the process of generation of alternative options, it was clear to everybody that additional interest groups outside Troina also had to be taken into account. This learning process was very interesting, particularly for the local administrators of Troina, who fully realized the importance of Troina water resources outside their own territory. As the mayor acknowledged, such a process of structuring the problem at hand was extremely useful for understanding the hierarchy of interests that is behind the exploitation of local natural resources.

A set of options with a short/medium temporal scale, a low cost and a high probability of being absorbed by the community without any strong impact was generated. These alternatives could be considered small additions/changes to business as usual. The first was to use some spring water sources located in the forest to produce bottled mineral water. This policy option was strongly supported by the then town administration. At the time, this water flowed freely in the forest; thus, if it were bottled, no water use conflict would exist. It was thought that the symbolic value of this option for the community could have been very big (to have bottled Troina water might have created a feeling of reappropriation of local natural resources). Some uncertainty still exists on the financial impacts of such an option.

The second option was to combine mineral water with some recreational activities in the forest. These recreational activities were to be connected with the restoration of existing country houses, the property of the municipality. This would allow the opening (for example), of a small hotel or a restaurant in the woods, but would also finance the rediscovery by the population of Troina of the habit of spending some time in the forest.

The third option was to develop a massive information campaign about local water resources (water cycle, water process, technological uses of water, water management, water distribution). The objective of this action would have been to increase public knowledge. This would probably have led to the least protest by citizens. On the other hand, various powerful actors might not have liked such transparency.

Implementation of the 'Galli framework law' was the fourth option. This concerned the creation of a water basin authority, and normally was to be implemented by a decree of the central government. In Sicily the situation is more complex because the subject of water is 'a reserved topic' of the regional government. This promised great difficulties in the implementation of a law creating a new power.

Self-sufficiency of Troina in its drinking water needs was a fifth possibility. This was the main short-term goal of the town administration.

The sixth option was compensation to the Troina community (for the fact that someone else outside the community was appropriating its water). Apparently, this seemed the main objective of the population at large. It was not clear what form such compensation should take in practice.

The final option, changes to the water irrigation infrastructure in Catania (pipelines and so on), would have improved the efficiency of the water use by Catania farmers, thus saving more water for Troina. This process of renovating the pipelines is already in progress.

Consensus was reached on the use of the following set of criteria:

1. use of water (in the sense of efficiency),
2. financial analysis (in the subsequent applications, this was done by taking into account returns and financial constraints),
3. employment,
4. flexibility of the social power structure (connected to community vulnerability),
5. community identity (symbolic value of water),
6. accountability and transparency of the water management,
7. social awareness or participation,
8. environmental impact (in the subsequent applications, this was taken into consideration by means of the precautionary principle).

Given the time and resource constraints, it was decided to construct a qualitative multicriteria impact matrix. The criterion scores, modelled as linguistic variables, were determined on the base of intuition and knowledge of the problem at hand. The NAIADE method (Munda, 1995) was chosen because of its capability to deal with qualitative information and conflict analysis issues.

By looking at the conflict analysis for all actors as well as at the results of multicriteria analysis, some interesting conclusions could be drawn. According to these settings, the *mineral water plus recreation* option seemed a good compromise from the point of view of the conflict analysis (it was the only change in the status quo that did not meet any strong opposition). It could be considered more or less 'defensible' from the multicriteria analysis point of view, and, though not top priority (it was fourth in the final ranking), it was widely preferred to 'business as usual'.

Compensation seemed to present a medium/low degree of attractiveness for all actors. A possible explanation could be that it did not directly affect the powerful actors. Only the population at large could receive some benefits from it (and its interests, we suppose, were represented by the municipality, which did not, however, consider that as the highest priority). One should note that the multicriteria analysis put compensation in third place, thus it could also be considered defensible but not highly attractive.

The multicriteria analysis put the *information campaign* at the top of the list of priorities, but we also know that strong opposition to such a policy option probably existed. What was to be done in this case? This is a clear example of a situation where the decision maker (in our case the municipality) had to decide whose interests had priority; no escape from value judgments is possible.

During the study, the top position of the information campaign was unexpected. The response to this surprise was the idea of implementing, within a very short time horizon, an exposition on water management issues in the town of Troina. The mayor and the municipal administration thought that the implementation cost of such a policy measure was quite low and the positive impacts on the community could be very high. Of course, the political risks for the administration could also be very high. This point led us back to the initial and principal question, was 'business as usual' a defensible option?

It should be noted that 'business as usual' ranks almost bottom in the multicriteria analysis. In the conflict analysis, however, it is in a low position for some actors (municipality, neighbouring and Agrigento municipalities, non-resident Troina farmers and the construction/building industry) and in a high/medium position for all the others. To this second group belong almost all the powerful social actors of the Troina community. We could say that the status quo is a compromise solution among the opposing internal interests. This can explain why nobody was willing to change the existing situation (though it was very risky for the community at large). This situation, however, looked much more like an *impasse* than like a real equilibrium (except where the Catania farmers, who had an evident self-interest in maintaining the status quo, were concerned).

This study attempted to avoid the pitfalls of the technocratic approach by applying different methods of sociological research. The institutional analysis, performed mainly on historical, legislative and administrative documents, provided a map of the formal decision makers. Much insight was offered by 'participant observation' as some contributors to the study were also members of the community and knowledgeable about its internal dynamics. The possible biases of this 'insider perspective' were checked against the information obtained from in-depth interviews with key local actors. Finally, a survey was performed on a random sample of the resident population, so as to explore its perception of the water issue in Troina.

Thanks to the knowledge and insight derived from the previous phases of our research, it was possible to prepare a questionnaire using mainly prestructured (or closed-ended) questions. These consisted of a query followed by a limited number of answers, among which the respondents selected the one which matched their opinion/knowledge/belief most closely. Some open-ended questions were also included, allowing the interviewees to express their opinions in their own words. The latter option was preferred, for example, when aiming at clarification of the answer provided to a previous, closed-ended question.

This triangulation of methods, which proves powerful in sociological research, becomes even more so when integrated into a study like the present one, applying multicriteria methods to a problem of environmental valuation. Ideally, in this case the results obtained by the researcher (that is, his or her data, findings, interpretations and insights) are returned to the community, which uses them, not as a given, but rather as an input into the decision-making process.

In synthesis, it should not be forgotten that the classical schematized decision maker–analyst relationship is indeed embedded in a social framework that is of a crucial importance in the case of public policy decisions. We believe that this type of extended evaluation process can be very effective since it accomplishes the goals of being transdisciplinary (with respect to the research team) and also participatory (with respect to the local community).

MULTICRITERIA EVALUATION IN MACROECONOMICS: GREEN NATIONAL ACCOUNTING AND PHYSICAL INDICES OF (UN)SUSTAINABILITY

Traditionally, gross national product (GNP) has been considered as the best performance indicator for measuring national economy and welfare. But if resource depletion and degradation are factored into economic trends, what emerges is a radically different picture from that depicted by conventional methods. In environmental terms, the GNP measure is plainly defective because (a) no account is taken of environmental destruction or degradation, (b) natural resources as such are valued at zero, and (c) repair and remedial expenditure such as on pollution abatement measures and health care is counted as a positive contribution to GNP inasmuch as it involves expenditures on economic goods and services (Faucheux and O'Connor, 1998).

The purpose of 'green accounting' is to provide information on the ecological (un)sustainability of the economy, but there is no settled doctrine on how to combine different and sometimes contradictory indices in a way that is immediately useful for policy (in the way that GNP or other macroeconomic statistics have been useful for policy). How to account for depletion of resources when they are not inventoried, or when no property rights exist? How to put money value on non-market impacts (because of trade or because of international externalities such as carbon dioxide 'exports') outside the European borders? Leaving money values aside, how to integrate the physical indicators themselves? Different physical indicators will sometimes show contradictory trends, and then 'aggregation' of indicators (in order to be able to rank situations) becomes difficult. For instance, statistics are available which show that The Netherlands is sustainable (in the 'weak' sense of the word), while other statistics (on environmental space) show the inhabitants of The Netherlands occupying fifteen times their own territory: that is, appropriating the 'carrying capacity' of a much larger territory than their own. Such incongruencies (if such they are) also apply to Europe as a whole. For this reason, for some authors, the main requirement would be that the total value of the natural resource stocks should remain constant in money terms (Pearce and Turner, 1990).

By valuing each resource stock in money terms, the total value of natural capital can be measured. One obvious problem here is that many natural resources (such as air, water or wilderness) do not have observable prices. Thus one would need to find implicit or shadow prices in some way. Even those prices that do exist may not be useful; they may be affected by market imperfections and taxes, and they may exclude externalities involved with the production and use of the resource. Moreover, the economic values of non-traded and traded environmental services or of negative externalities depend on the endowment of property rights and on the distribution of income (Martinez-Alier, 1991).

There are additional problems in using market prices to value the aggregate stock of natural capital. Resource prices or net prices reflect conditions at the margin and to use these to value entire stocks can give perverse results. Although the idea of a constant capital stock is quite important and desirable (maintaining the natural capital seems to be an important prerequisite for sustainability), we should admit that the above considerations demonstrate that the development of relevant monetary indicators of sustainable development connected to this idea is quite difficult (Cabeza-Gutes, 1996).

The assumption that the scale of the economy has a maximum limit defined by either the regenerative or the absorptive capacity of the ecosystem leads to the concept of *strong sustainability*. Such a definition is based on the assumption that certain sorts of natural capital are deemed critical, and not readily substitutable by human-made capital. In particular, the characterization of sustainability in terms of the 'strong' criterion of non-negative change over time in stocks of specified natural capital provides a strong justification for development of non-monetary indicators of ecological sustainability based on *direct physical measurement* of important stocks and flows (Faucheux and O'Connor, 1998; Munda, 1997). One has to keep in mind that the very definition of sustainability depends on what we define as identity for the system, and the time-scale adopted to define the system under investigation. For example, the recent literature on physical indices includes the following.

HANPP

HANPP (human appropriation of net primary production) was proposed by Vitousek *et al.* (1986). The NPP is the amount of energy that primary producers, the plants, make available for the rest of living species, the heterotrophs. Of this NPP, humankind occupies about 40 per cent in terrestrial ecosystems according to the calculations of Vitousek *et al.* The higher the HANPP, the less biomass is available for 'wild' biodiversity.

The proportion of NPP appropriated by humans is increasing because of population growth, and also because of increasing demands on land per person, for urbanization, foodstuffs and timber ('Plantations are not forests', is a slogan of environmental activists in the Tropics).

This indicator should be regionalized. In Latin America as a whole, the part of NPP 'coopted' by the local population is still much lower than in Europe or in Southeast Asia. However, pressure on NPP comes not only from population density in the region itself, but also from pressure from exports. Therefore HANPP and 'environmental space' (or 'ecological footprint') are related measures.

MIPS

MIPS, which has been developed at the Wuppertal Institute (Schmidt-Bleek, 1994), adds up all the materials used for production both directly and indirectly (the 'ecological rucksack'), including mineral ores, the energy carriers such as coal or oil, and including all biomass, measured over the whole product 'life cycle', that is, the disposal or recycling phases. This is the material input that is *measured in tons.* It then compares the material input, also measured in tons, with the services provided, sector by sector (and, in principle, for the whole economy). For instance, in order to provide the service of travel of one passenger for one kilometre, or in order to provide the service of living space of so many square metres, what is the amount of materials involved, comparing different regions in the world, or historically?

Comparisons of MIPS will show whether there is really a trend towards *dematerialization* of the economy. It may of course be objected that tons of materials say nothing about the toxicity of the materials used or of their residues. MIPS is a synthetic indicator, *but again, not the only one*.

EROI

This acronym stands for energy return on (energy) input, and it was the first physical indicator widely employed in ecological economics in the 1970s, mainly by direct or indirect disciples of Howard Odum. Clearly, for an economy to be sustainable, the energy productivity of human labour (that is, how much energy is made available per day by one day of human work) must be higher than (or equal to, if everybody is working) the efficiency of the transformation of energy intake into human work. This is a minimum condition for sustainability. However, as Podolinsky wrote, the economies of hunter-gatherers and of agriculturalists were different from industrial economies (Martinez-Alier, 1987). The energy productivity of a coal miner was much greater than that which a primitive agriculturalist could obtain, but this energy surplus from fossil fuels was transitory, it was not sustainable because coal reserves were limited. We may ask: is there a trend towards an increasing energy cost of obtaining energy (Cleveland, 1991)?

In the 1970s there were a number of studies on energy flow in agriculture, of which the best known was that of Pimentel *et al.* (1973), showing the decreasing energy efficiency in maize cultivation in the United States. The human labour input had become very small, but energy inputs, in the form of fuel for machinery, pesticides and fertilizers, increased in proportion more than the energy in the crop. Perhaps in Europe the trend towards decreasing energy efficiency in agriculture was halted in the 1970s because of the increase in oil prices (Bonny and Dauce, 1989; Passet, 1996). In any case, a fruitful new field of research was opened by such studies (historic and cross-section) on the efficiency of the use of energy in different sectors of the economy, including the energy sector itself.

Naturally, although all kinds of energy can be counted in the same units, not all sources of energy have the same meaning from other points of view. In their use, some forms of energy are more versatile than others. In their origin, some arise from non-renewable resources, and/or in their use they have more negative impacts than other sources. There have been attempts at giving equivalencies between types of energy (aside from their energy contents) but the ratios for transforming the values of different types of energy seem to be based (in our view) on ad hoc decisions.

Ecospace and Ecological Footprint

Both these concepts, with similar contents, address the following issue: what is the demand for natural resources that an economy makes, expressing this demand in terms of space? The authors who have developed the ideas on environmental space, ecospace or the ecological footprint (Opschoor, 1995; Rees, 1996) would concur on the crucial importance of time in ecological economics. However, for practical purposes, they chose to give a spatial representation of the environmental load of the economy. Rather than asking what population a particular region or country can support sustainably – which would depend not only on its geography and resources but also on its average level of exosomatic consumption of energy and materials, on the material and energy intensity of the technologies employed, and on the ecological terms of trade (that is, whether the region is a victim of, or profits from, ecologically unequal exchange) – the question of carrying capacity asks: how large an area of productive land is needed in order to sustain a given population indefinitely, at its current standard of living, and with current technologies?

The main categories of land use for the calculation of the ecological footprint would be as follows:

- crop and grazing land required to produce the current diet (the sea area could also be included);
- land for wood plantations for timber and paper;
- land occupied or degraded or built over, as urban land;
- land needed to absorb CO_2 emissions through photosynthesis, or alternatively
- land required to produce the ethanol equivalent to current fossil energy consumption.

Similar computations, not for cities or metropolitan regions (whose 'ecological footprint' is hundreds of times larger than their own territories) but for whole countries, show that some densely populated European countries (assuming per capita eco footprints of only 3 hectares) or Japan or Korea (with per capita eco footprints of only 2 hectares) occupy eco-spaces ten times larger (for The Netherlands, fifteen times larger) than their own territories.

It is interesting to reflect on how a development should be judged in which a synthetic indicator such as MIPS improves, while HANPP deteriorates; this is a sort of macroeconomic multicriteria evaluation. This discussion may be phrased also in the framework of recent work on the so-called 'inverted U curve' (or so-called 'Kuznets environmental curve': for a critical viewpoint, see Arrow *et al.* (1995), Selden and Song (1994). For instance, as incomes grow, in urban situations sulphur dioxide emissions first increase and then decrease. But carbon dioxide emissions increase with incomes. If something improves and something deteriorates, the first reaction from the conventional economist will be to give weights or to put prices on such effects, in the pursuit of strong comparability of values. However, there is so much uncertainty and complexity involved in such situations, and there are also so many distribution conflicts involved (the prices of externalities would depend on the distribution of property rights, of power and of income), that the economists' accounts would be convincing only for the faithful.

We must learn to live with weak comparability of values. The interplay between physical uncertainties, distributional issues and temporal scales appears very clearly in the well-known case of integrated economic–environmental assessment of climate change. Attempts at cost–benefit analysis of the increased greenhouse effect are not convincing because of the arbitrariness of the discount rate (Azar and Sterner, 1996), because of the inseparable links between (in)equity and efficiency, and also because many items are not easily measured in physical terms, much less easily valued in money terms (Funtowicz and Ravetz, 1994b).

CONCLUSIONS

A mathematical model of, for example, an ecosystem, although legitimate in its own terms, cannot be sufficient for a complete analysis of its complex properties, which include the human dimensions of ecological change and the transformations of human perceptions along the way. The various dimensions are not totally disjoint; thus the institutional perspective can be a basis for the study of the social relations of the scientific processes. To take any particular perspective as the true, real or total picture results in a totally inadequate description of the problem. In most cases the sacrificed perspectives are those defining the problem in a fundamental way, but which are hardly identifiable and measurable.

A possible reduction of complexity, a precondition for management actions, consists in the aggregation of non-equivalent representations which arise in the interaction between the various observer subjects and the different systemic levels. The reduction of the number of non-equivalent representations introduces the problem of the descriptors: indicators and indices. The expression 'taking nature into account' (much used both in the United Nations system and in the European Union) hides the tension between money valuation and appraisal through physical indices (which themselves might show contradictory trends). So far, the elementary question of whether the European economy is moving towards sustainability or away from sustainability cannot be answered with consensus on the 'measuring rod(s)' to be employed.

The question then arises as to how such indicators could be aggregated. Often, some indicators improve while others deteriorate. For instance, when incomes grow, SO_2 might go down while CO_2 increases; or, at a different level of aggregation, MIPS might improve while HANPP deteriorates. It has to be noted that this is the classical conflictual situation studied in multicriteria evaluation theory. Since multicriteria evaluation techniques are based on a 'constructive' rationality and allow one to take into account conflictual, multidimensional, incommensurable and uncertain effects of decisions, they appear to be a promising assessment framework for (micro and macro) environment policy under conditions of complexity. Multicriteria evaluation techniques cannot solve all conflicts, but they can help to provide more insight into the nature of conflicts and into ways in which to arrive at political compromises in the case of divergent preferences, and so to increase the transparency of the choice process.

However, one should remember that we are in a 'second-best' world. A useful analogy here is with *Flatland*, the classic Victorian science fiction and social parody (Abbott, 1935). There, the inhabitants of spaces with more dimensions had a richer awareness of themselves, and also could see beyond and through the consciousness of the simpler creatures inhabiting fewer dimensions. At this stage it is not unfair to reveal the dénouement of the story, namely that the Sphere of three-dimensional space showed himself to be just another Flatlander at heart, when he angrily refused to accept the reality of higher dimensions of being.

There is a complex 'feedback' relationship between scientific theories and scientific understanding of ecosystem change, on the one hand, and the evolution of social institutions and the cultural imaginary (habits of thought and norms) concerning the environment, on the other. One implication of this complexity is that the role of scientific inputs in policy design becomes less simple to define than in the industrial age. Dealing with environmental problems therefore requires opening the analytical and decision-making processes to broader categories of facts and actors than those traditionally legitimated. On the one hand, the old distinction between hard facts and soft values is being replaced by a 'soft facts/hard values' framework. On the other hand, the distinction between experts and non-experts is losing significance. In a sense, when facing an environmental problem, all stakeholders are experts in different ways, from different points of view, and with regard to different aspects of the problem. We have seen that indicators of environmental loading cannot be plausibly or usefully reduced to a single 'true' numeraire. Where multicriteria evaluation has been effective, it has been applied in a self-aware and transparent fashion. Its goal has not been to provide a demonstration by experts, but to enhance dialogue among stakeholders. In that way it is an exemplification of post-normal science, and contributes to its growth.

REFERENCES

Abbott E.A. (1935), *Flatland: A Romance of Many Dimensions,* Boston: Little, Brown & Co.

Arrow, K.J. *et al.* (1995), 'Economic growth, carrying capacity and the environment', *Ecological Economics*, **15**, 91–6.

Azar C. and T. Sterner (1996), 'Discounting and distributional considerations in the context of global warming', *Ecological Economics*, **19**, 169–84.

Bonny, S. and P. Dauce (1989), 'Les nouvelles technologies en agriculture, une approche technique et économique', *Cahiers d'Economie et de Sociologie Rurale*, INRA-ESR, **13**.

Cabeza Gutes, M.(1996), 'The concept of weak sustainability', *Ecological Economics*, **17**, 147–56.

Cleveland, C. (1991), 'Natural resource scarcity and economic growth revised: economic and biophysical perspectives', in R. Costanza (ed.), *Ecological Economics: the Science and Management of Sustainability*, New York: Columbia University Press.

Cohen, R.S. and M. Neurath (eds) (1983), *Philosophical Papers 1913–1946*, Dordrecht: Reidel.

De Marchi, B., S.O. Funtowicz, S. Lo Cascio and G. Munda (2000), 'Combining participative and institutional approaches with multicriteria evaluation. An empirical study for water issue in Troina, Sicily', *Ecological Economics*, **34**, 267–82.

Faucheux, S. and M. O'Connor (1998), 'Weak and strong sustainability', in S. Faucheux and M. O'Connor (eds), *Valuation for Sustainable Development: Methods and Policy Indicators*, Cheltenham, UK and Lyme, NH, US: Edward Elgar.

Froger, G. and G. Munda (1998), 'Methodology for environmental decision support', in S. Faucheux and M. O'Connor (eds), *Valuation for Sustainable Development: Methods and Policy Indicators*, Cheltenham, UK and Lyme, NH, US: Edward Elgar.

Funtowicz S.O. and J.R. Ravetz (1990), *Uncertainty and Quality in Science for Policy*, Dordrecht: Kluwer Academic Publishers.

Funtowicz, S.O. and J.R. Ravetz (1991), 'A new scientific methodology for global environmental issues', in R. Costanza (ed.), *Ecological Economics*, New York: Columbia University Press, pp. 137–52.

Funtowicz, S.O. and J.R. Ravetz (1994a), 'Emergent complex systems', *Futures*, **26** (6), 568–82.

Funtowicz, S.O. and J.R. Ravetz (1994b), 'The worth of a songbird: ecological economics as a post-normal science', *Ecological Economics*, **10**, 197–207.

Funtowicz, S.O., B. De Marchi, S. Lo Cascio and G. Munda (1998), 'The Troina water valuation case study', unpublished research report, European Commission, Joint Research Centre, ISIS, Ispra.

Funtowicz, S.O., J. Martinez-Alier, G. Munda and J. Ravetz (1999), 'Information tools for environmental policy under conditions of complexity', *European Environmental Agency, Experts' Corner, Environmental Issues Series*, no. 9.

Hayek, F.A. (ed.) (1935), *Collectivist Economic Planning*; reprinted New York: Augustus M. Kelley, 1970.

Kuhn, T.S. (1962), *The Structure of Scientific Revolutions*, Chicago: University of Chicago Press.
Martinez-Alier, J. (1987), *Ecological Economics*, Oxford: Basil Blackwell.
Martinez-Alier, J. (1991), 'Environmental policy and distributional conflicts', in, R. Costanza (ed.), *Ecological Economics: The Science and Management of Sustainability*, New York: Columbia University Press, pp. 118–36.
Martinez-Alier, J., G. Munda and J. O'Neill (1998), 'Weak comparability of values as a foundation for ecological economics', *Ecological Economics*, **26**, 277–86.
Munda, G. (1993), 'Multiple criteria decision aid: some epistemological considerations', *Journal of Multi-Criteria Decision Analysis*, **2**, 41–55.
Munda, G. (1995), *Multicriteria Evaluation in a Fuzzy Environment: Theory and Applications in Ecological Economics*, Heidelberg: Physica-Verlag.
Munda, G. (1996), 'Cost–benefit analysis in integrated environmental assessment: some methodological issues', *Ecological Economics*, **19**, pp. 157–68.
Munda, G. (1997), 'Environmental economics, ecological economics and the concept of sustainable development', *Environmental Values*, **6**(2), 213–33.
Munda, G., P. Nijkamp and P. Rietveld (1994a), 'Qualitative multicriteria evaluation for environmental management', *Ecological Economics*, **10**, 97–112.
Munda, G., P. Nijkamp and P. Rietveld (1994b), 'Fuzzy multigroup conflict resolution for environmental management', in J. Weiss (ed.), *The Economics of Project Appraisal and the Environment*, Aldershot, UK and Brookfield, VT, US: Edward Elgar, pp. 161–83.
Neurath, Otto (1919), 'Through war economy to economy in kind', reprinted in R.S. Cohen and M. Neurath (eds) (1983), *Philosophical Papers 1913–1946*, Dordrecht: Reidel.
Neurath, Otto (1928), 'Personal life and class struggle', in R.S. Cohen and M. Neurath (eds) (1983), *Philosophical Papers 1913–1946*, Doredrecht: Reidel.
Nijkamp, P., P. Rietveld and H. Voogd (1990), *Multicriteria Evaluation in Physical Planning*, Amsterdam: North-Holland.
Novotny, P. (1994), 'Popular epidemiology and the struggle for community health: alternative perspectives from the environmental justice movement', *Capitalism, Nature, Socialism*, **5**(2), 29–42.
O'Connor, M., S. Faucheux, G. Froger, S.O. Funtowicz and G. Munda (1996), 'Emergent complexity and procedural rationality: post-normal science for sustainability', in R. Costanza, J. Martinez-Alier and O. Segura (eds), *Getting Down to Earth: Practical Applications of Ecological Economics*, Washington, DC: Island Press/ISEE, pp. 223–48.
Odum, H.T.(1971), *Environment, Power and Society*, New York: Wiley.
O'Neill, J. (1993), *Ecology, Policy and Politics*, London: Routledge.
Opschoor, J.B.(1995), 'Ecospace and the fall and rise of throughput intensity', *Ecological Economics*, **15**(2), 137–40.
Passet, R. (1996), *L'économique et le vivant*, 2nd edn, Paris: Payot.
Pearce, D.W. and R.K. Turner (1990), *Economics of Natural Resources and the Environment*, Baltimore: The Johns Hopkins University Press.
Pimentel, D. *et al.* (1973), 'Food production and the energy crisis', *Science*, **182**, 443–9.
Rees, W.E. (1996), 'Revisiting carrying capacity: Area-based indicators of sustainability', *Population and Environment: A Journal of Interdisciplinary Studies*, **17**(39), January.
Roy, B. (1985), *Méthodologie multicritère d'aide à la decision*, Paris: Economica.

Schmidt-Bleek, F. (1994), *Wieviel umweltbraucht der mensch? MIPS Das Mass für ökologisches wirtschaften*, Berlin: Birkh user.

Selden, T. and D. Song (1994), 'Environmental quality and development: is there a Kuznets curve for air pollution emissions?', *Journal of Environmental Economics and Management*, **27**, 147–62.

Simon, H.A. (1972), *Theories of Bounded Rationality: Decision and Organization*, ed. C.B. Radner and R. Radner, Amsterdam: North-Holland.

Simon, H.A. (1978), 'On how to decide what to do', *The Bell Journal of Economics*, **9**, 494–507.

Simon, H.A. (1983), *Reason in Human Affairs*, Stanford: Stanford University Press.

Vitousek, P., P. Ehrlich, A. Ehrlich and P. Matson (1986), 'Human appropriation of the products of photosynthesis', *Bioscience*, **34**(6), 368–73.

4. Integrated assessment: current practices and challenges for the future

Jan Rotmans and Marjolein B.A. van Asselt

INTRODUCTION

Over the last decade integrated assessment (IA) has become a rapidly evolving field. However, IA is often loosely defined, which makes the field rather cluttered. So the question arises: what is IA? In our opinion, IA can probably best be described as an interdisciplinary and participatory process of combining, interpreting and communicating knowledge to allow a better understanding of complex phenomena. The aim is thus to analyse, explore and evaluate past, current and future developments in terms of plausibility, desirability and feasibility. Integrated assessments should result in added value compared to insights derived from disciplinary research. IA has the explicit purpose to inform policy and to support decision making. It is important to realize that IA is not a pure scientific activity. It requires involvement of scientific experts, stakeholders and decision makers. Communication between those different actors is at the very heart of IA (Cohen, 1997; Parson, 1997; Toth and Hizsnyik, 1998; Rotmans and van Asselt, 1996; Rotmans, 1998c; Kasemir *et al.*, 1999).

This chapter rests on a framework proposed by Rotmans and van Asselt (1996) (see Figure 4.1). This framework describes IA as a cyclic and participatory process comprising various parallel actions and a wide diversity of actors. The two pillars are (a) the participation of scientists in the form of interdisciplinary research, and (b) the participation of representatives of societal actors, such as the policy community, the business community, non-governmental organizations (NGOs) and the general public. This framework defines IA as an active dialogue in which interdisciplinary science outlines the state-of-the-art knowledge pertaining to the issue under concern, including the inherent uncertainties, value judgements and preferences. The societal actors then indicate what is desirable, and come out with options that satisfy societal constraints. The visions resulting from this participatory process may then facilitate the decision-making processes.

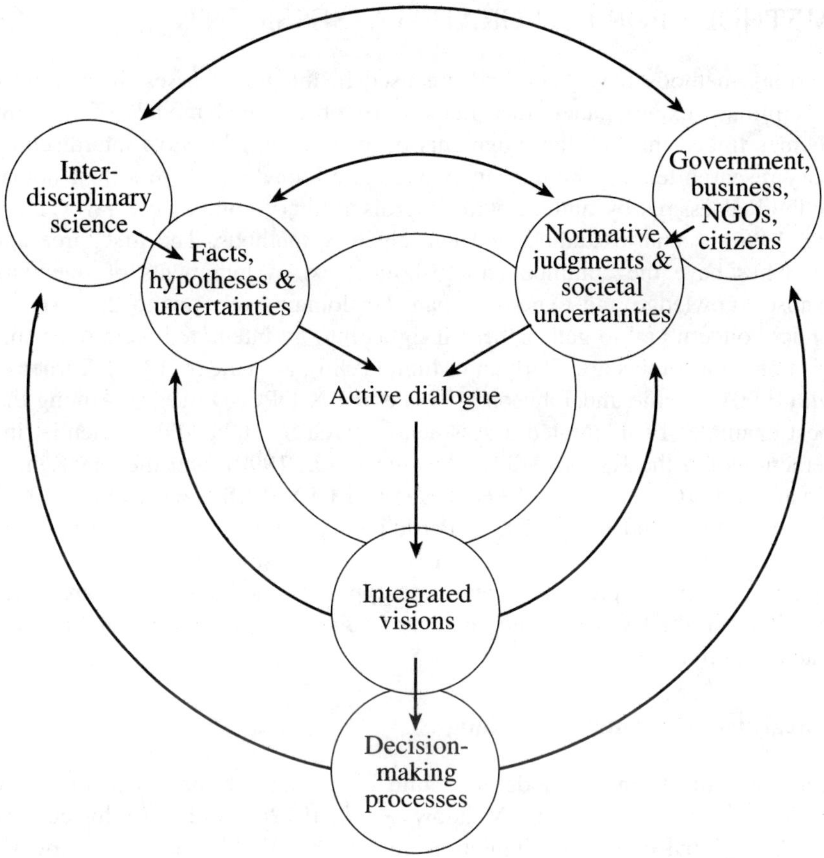

Source: Rotmans and van Asselt (1996).

Figure 4.1 Framework for IA

The framework sketched above is considered attainable, but does not reflect the current state of IA. So far IA has been merely an intuitive process, where the integrative stakeholder approach has often been troubled by the limited scope of the disciplinary sciences. But even an immature stakeholder approach does make sense, because it makes the heterogeneity of values, beliefs and perceptions explicit.

The aim of this chapter is to provide an overview of current practices in integrated assessment. It describes where the IA community stands now and, on the strength of this overview, we will provide some more food for thought on the issue of quality in IA.

METHODS FOR INTEGRATED ASSESSMENT

Various methods have been and are used in integrated assessment: multidisciplinary expert panels (see Parson, 1996b); formal models of relevant themes linked through the judgments of experts, collaborative interdisciplinary research teams who exchange and share knowledge across their fields; individual essays by authors with interdisciplinary competence (Weyant *et al.*, 1996); scenario-studies; and participatory methods. The first three approaches have the common aim to collect expert judgments of scientists whose knowledge and expertise span the domains relevant to the issue(s) under concern and to gather these insights into an integrated picture. Examples of such studies are Clark and Munn (1986), Schneider (1989), Turner *et al.* (1990), Chenje and Johnson (1994) and UN-DPCSD (1997). Among the best examples of integrated assessments driven by stakeholder–scientist interactions are the RAINS study (Alcamo *et al.*, 1990), and the MacKenzie Basin study (Cohen, 1993, 1994, 1997) and ULYSSES (Jaeger *et al.*, 1997; Kasemir, Jäger and Jaeger, 2001). Participatory methods are explicitly developed and used to involve non-scientists in the assessment effort.

The present chapter discusses three types of methods which are quite dominant in the IA community, namely IA modelling, scenarios and participatory approaches.

Integrated Assessment Modelling

Current projects in IA modelling build on a tradition started in the early 1970s by the Club of Rome (Meadows *et al.*, 1972a, 1972b). In this context the first global computer simulation model, the World3 model, was developed. This model inspired the development of numerous global models, focusing on resource depletion, population and pollution. A review of the first decade of IA modelling *avant la lettre* can be found in Meadows *et al.* (1982).

The next generation of IA models explicitly addressed environmental issues. The first among these models emerged in the late 1970s from earlier energy modelling (Nordhaus, 1979; Edmonds and Reilly, 1985). The RAINS model of acidification in Europe was developed in the 1980s (Alcamo *et al.*, 1990).

The phenomenon of global climate change has prompted the development of a new class of IA models. The first steps to an integrated model of climate change were taken by Rotmans (1986), Mintzer (1987), and Lashof and Tirpak (1989). The first model that comprised a fully integrated representation of climate change from sources to impacts was the IMAGE 1.0 model (Rotmans, 1990). Since then approximately 40 IA models of climate change have been developed (van der Sluijs, 1997). Overviews of IA modelling activities in the field of climate change can be found in Rotmans and Dowlatabadi (1998), Schneider (1997) and Parson and van den Fisher (1997).

Modelling methods

There is general agreement that two types of IA models can be distinguished. Weyant *et al.* (1996) classify them as (a) policy optimization models, which try to optimize key policy variables such as carbon emission control rates and carbon taxes, given certain policy goals (such as maximizing welfare or minimizing costs of climate policy), and (b) policy evaluation models which try to evaluate the environmental, social and economic consequences of specific policy strategies. However, a number of IA models that are characterized as policy evaluation models can also be used for optimization experiments (such as RAINS). We consider it more appropriate to refer to the two schools of modelling by classifying them according to their origins: the *macroeconomic-oriented school*, that represents simple, fully parameterized decision-analytic formulations of a policy-relevant complex problem, and the *biosphere-oriented school*, that represents a more comprehensive, process-oriented description of a complex problem.

The most widely known exponent of the macroeconomic-oriented school is the DICE model (Nordhaus, 1992, 1994). Other variants have been developed later on, such as a regionalized version RICE (Nordhaus and Yang, 1995), and another with uncertainty ranges in key parameter values, that is PRICE (Nordhaus and Popp, 1997). Other well-known examples of this school are the CETA model developed by Peck and Teisberg (1992) and the MERGE model (Manne *et al.*, 1994). Representative of the biosphere-oriented school of IA modelling are the IMAGE models (IMAGE 1.0 (Rotmans, 1990) and IMAGE 2.0 (Alcamo, 1994)). Other important models in this school are AIM (Morita *et al.*, 1995), the MIT model (Yang *et al.*, 1996), and TARGETS (Rotmans and Vries, 1997d; Rotmans and van Asselt, 1999; van Asselt and Rotmans, 2002). Some attempts are under way to combine the best of both worlds, yielding a hybrid of the two categories above. Therefore the above two classes should be considered as the polar ends of a continuum populated by many IA modelling efforts. Examples of such hybrid IA models are ICAM (Dowlatabadi and Morgan, 1993a, 1993b) and GCAM (Edmonds *et al.*, 1994).

Current trends and challenges for the future

In current IA modelling activities, four important trends can be distinguished:

- growing interest in regional assessments to complement the global studies;
- broadening the scope from climate change to global change and sustainable development;

- emphasis on uncertainty and subjectivity in modelling efforts;
- rising interest in linking models with qualitative approaches.

Most current IA models are global models. Geographical differences and heterogeneities are dealt with in the form of a subdivision into world regions, or by introducing classes, such as land use and vegetation classes. The number of regions included varies from two (usually industrialized countries versus industrializing countries) to sixteen in the GCAM model (Edmonds *et al.*, 1994). Notwithstanding the dominant orientation towards global modelling, the interest in regional integrated assessments is gradually increasing. Examples of regional models are the ESCAPE model for Europe (Rotmans *et al.*, 1994b), the IMAGE 2.0 model (Alcamo, 1994), and the Asian–Pacific Integrated model (AIM)(Morita *et al.*, 1994; Matsuoka *et al.*, 1995). The Mackenzie Basin Impact study (Cohen, 1993, 1994; Cohen *et al.*, 1997) and CLEAR (Cebon *et al.*, 1997) are examples of an IA activity with a subnational focus.

Another current trend in IA modelling is the gradual shift in focus from climate change to global change and sustainable development. Such a broadening does not belittle the importance of climate change, but does place it within a broader context of the multitude of environmental problems being faced around the world. An IA model for global change involves addressing issues such as economic developments, demography, human health, urbanization, political processes, industrial transformation, energy, agriculture, food security, technology, fresh water, resources, pollution and waste, forests, land cover and land use, and biodiversity (Rotmans, 1998a). A first attempt to build an IA model on global change is the TARGETS model (discussed later in the chapter). Other modelling projects have recently been broadening their scope from pure climate assessment to global change research, for example at Carnegie Mellon University (CMU) and at Battelle's PNNL (Pacific Northwest National Laboratory).

The emphasis on uncertainty treatment is also increasing. New approaches for dealing with uncertainty in IA modelling have been introduced. First, there is the probabilistic modelling approach as advocated by Morgan and Henrion (1990) and applied to the ICAM model (Dowlatabadi and Morgan, 1993a, 1993b). Second, a multiple perspective approach is advocated (Lave and Dowlatabadi, 1993; van Asselt and Rotmans, 1995, 1996, 2002; van Asselt, 2000), discussed later. In this approach the IA model does not merely include one perspective, but comprises plural perspectives by providing multiple 'model routes' (van Asselt and Rotmans, 1995, 1996, 2002; van Asselt, 2000), or by adopting the 'QUESTionnary' approach (see Chapter 8, this volume). The 'QUESTionnary' approach implies a design in which the users are explicitly involved to enter their own subjective values in an interactive dialogue using questionnaire-like screens.

In line with the attempt to make uncertainties explicit in modelling, modellers as well as non-modellers argue more and more that we need to find ways of including semi-quantitative and qualitative knowledge in models and dealing with ignorance and indeterminacy in an adequate way. Seeds for this trend can be abundantly found elsewhere in the present book.

The major challenge concerning modelling methods for IA is to broaden and deepen the current tools and methods. The following challenges for the future can be derived from the above trends:

- the need for a *framework* that enables use of regional and global assessments in a *complementary* way so that they enrich each other;
- the need for a broader *conceptual model* that allows us to address the issue of *sustainable development*, whatever its subjective interpretation may be;
- the challenge to make the *management of uncertainty* the heart of modelling activities;
- the need for *alternative uncertainty analysis methods* (such as the perspective-based approach) to mature;
- the link with *qualitative methods*.

Scenarios

Thinking about the future is often done by the development of scenarios. What the diverse IA projects have in common is that the development of scenarios is generally either an explicit aim or part of the process. Scenarios are hypothetical sequences of events, constructed for the purpose of focusing attention on causal processes and decision points (Kahn and Wiener, 1967). In practice, scenarios are archetypal descriptions of alternative images of the future, created from mental maps or models that reflect different perspectives on past, present and future developments (van Asselt *et al.*, 1998; Rotmans, 1998c).

Scenarios can be useful tools to help us frame our key considerations and assumptions, and to identify gaps, inconsistencies and ignorance in a systematic way. They can help us to explore different and new perspectives and thereby challenge conventional thinking. Finally, a variety of policy strategies can be analysed by using scenarios. This can help us to expand our capacity to cope with complexity and uncertainty. In this way, scenario analysis may facilitate decision-making processes (Rotmans, 1998c; van Notten and Rotmans, 2001).

Methods for scenario analysis

Different methods for scenario development (see table 4.1) have been applied during the last 25 years. The first method is model-based scenario analyses.

Table 4.1 Scenario methods

Scenario method	Examples
Modelling approach	Alcamo et al. (1990) Rotmans et al. (1997b)
Global scenarios with a strong narrative component	Kassler (1994), UN-DPCSD (1997), UNEP (1997), Gallopin *et al.* (1997)
Single-issue scenarios	WRR (1994), IPCC (1996)
Regional scenarios	EC-DGXI (1996)

Another class of scenarios involves scenarios with a strong narrative component. Apart from these two approaches, we can discriminate between scenarios that are developed around a specific issue or sector (such as food or energy) and scenarios that focus on a specific region, such as Europe or Latin America (Anastasi, 1997).

Current scenarios are characterized by a number of weaknesses. First, they are often developed from narrow, disciplinary based perspectives, displaying *a lack of diversity*. They are commonly *extrapolations of existing trends*, excluding surprises. Many scenarios do have a 'business-as-usual' or 'conventional development' type of character, assuming that current conditions will continue to exist for decades, which is, however, highly implausible. Further, current scenarios are often based on a *very limited* set of standard economic assumptions and, to a lesser extent, environmental indicators. In particular, social and institutional indicators need to be included in integrated scenarios, even if they cannot yet be quantified. Finally, scenarios are often *not transparent* in the sense that key assumptions and underlying implicit judgments and preferences are not made explicit.

Current trends and challenges for the future

The challenge for IA is to develop integrated scenarios, which can help prudent decision makers to understand past and current developments, to anticipate the future and to evaluate policy strategies. The following lessons relevant to IA can be learned from two decades of scenario analysis (compare Anastasi, 1997).

- Scenarios that have a strong narrative, as well as a quantitative component, are able to engage key stakeholders;
- Models can play an important underpinning role, providing a valuable consistency check;
- Social dimensions need to be addressed in scenarios;
- A group of individuals with different, yet complementary, knowl-

edge, experiences and perspectives is needed to provide scenario 'richness';
- Active dissemination is needed to ensure that stakeholders make best use of scenarios.

Integrated scenarios should include economic, environmental, social and institutional indicators, which is currently not the case. IA scenarios should aim to cover a broad range of possible futures, including bifurcations and surprises.

In order to fulfil its decision-support role, it is important that the consistency of the scenarios is checked among different sectors, problems and scales. Future energy use, for instance, has to be interrelated with future demands for land and water. For example, the Dutch WRR study (WRR, 1994) in which scenarios are developed for different sectors (food, energy, environment, resources and water) explicitly lacks such a consistency check. This lack of integration prevents those scenarios from being useful tools in the sustainable development debate. There is a need for IAs that condense critical developments on different temporal, spatial and aggregational scales into coherent narratives useful for decision making.

Taking into account the lessons learned over the last 20 years, future challenges for scenario analysis in the context of integrated assessment can be identified. In order to fulfil a valuable role in the decision support processes, we have to explore approaches so that IA scenarios

- describe dynamic patterns of changes;
- are transparent with regard to assumptions and choices;
- include a variety of perspectives;
- include a balanced set of social, economic, environmental and institutional indicators;
- are consistent among different sectors, problems and scales;
- are coherent, plausible and challenging, with a strong narrative as well as quantitative component;
- are developed in an iterative way involving a heterogeneous group of people;
- are actively disseminated among the target group(s).

Participatory Methods for IA

'Participatory methods' is an umbrella term describing approaches for assessment in which non-scientists, such as policy people, stakeholders or even lay people, play an active role. Brewer (1986) first referred to the idea of using participatory approaches in assessment efforts; however, only recently have IA projects sought to apply such methods for IA purposes.

Participatory methods are able to integrate quantitative with qualitative knowledge (Parson, 1997). Qualitative knowledge cannot (yet) be grasped by IA models. In this way, participatory methods can complement IA models and scenarios. It is furthermore argued that involvement of non-scientists is needed to ensure the relevance and later acceptance of the analytical (modelling) approach (Hordijk, 1991; van Asselt, 1994; Costanza and Ruth, 1996; Alcamo *et al.*, 1996). Participatory methods are needed to set up such a dialogue between analysts and societal actors; they are also justified on arguments inspired by the nature of democracy. Policies for managing sustainability will be effective only if they have the moral support of a great mass of people (Ravetz, 1997). It is therefore argued that assessments should comprise the opinions and attitudes of stakeholders and citizens.

Participatory methods

Participatory methods are not new. Focus groups, for example, have been applied in market research since the 1970s (Cox and Higginbotham, 1976), while consensus conferences have been applied in technology assessment (for example, on the issue of predictive genetic research, Platform on Science and Ethics, 1995)). Gaming approaches have been prominently in use for training purposes (such as military and business games) (Hausrath, 1971). There is not a great difference in employing such methods in IA. However, IA's complexity, multidisciplinary character and wide variety of societal actors present special challenges. The use of participatory methods in IA, therefore, requires substantial adjustment of existing procedures and the development of new tools and methods. Projects like the ULYSSES project (Dürrenberger *et al.*, 1997; Jäger, 1998; Kasemir *et al.*, 1999; Toth and Hizsnyik, 1998), the IIASA policy exercise effort (Parson, 1996a) and the VISIONS project (Rotmans *et al.*, 1999a, 2001) explore the necessary features of participatory methods for IA.

Participatory methods for IA differ with regard to the profile of the participants, the goal of participation and the degree of participation (compare van Asselt and Rijkens-Klomp, 2002). We distinguish three classes of methods: dialogue methods, policy exercises, and mutual learning methods (van Asselt, 2000). The dialogue method is applied in cases where the intended users are considered as a source of information necessary for the analysts to perform the assessment. The goal of participation is to extract this essential information from the intended users. Within this class, we can discriminate between continuous dialogues and cases in which the dialogue takes place in a specific phase of the assessment. In the first case, the role of the intended users can be described as that of *co-designer*. In the cases where the dialogue takes place in the design phase, the role of the intended users is to contribute to the design principles by sketching their wants and needs. This type of dialogue can be described as a *user-platform*. If the dialogue is part of the final stage, the participants can be described as a *test-group* that helps to determine how the results of the assessment will be brought to the fore. Van Asselt (1994) sketches an example in which a dialogue[1] was intended to serve as a user-platform. In adaptive ecological modelling (Holling, 1978; Costanza and Ruth, 1998), the explicit aim is that the crucial design choices are made by the user community. The Delft process around the IMAGE model (van Daalen *et al.*, 1997) can be considered an example of a test group. In the RAINS project the role of the policy makers was close to that of co-designer (Hordijk, 1991).

Policy exercises build upon the tradition of simulation games. A policy exercise can be described as a flexibly structured process designed as an interface between scientists and policy makers (Toth, 1988), in which a complex system is represented by a simpler one with relevant behavioural similarity, and in which decision making is partly through human participants (Parson, 1997). In general, a game is set up that represents a negotiation process in which the different teams are responsible for a certain country or region. Policy exercises quite often make use of computer support. A computer model can be used as a consulting device or as a tool to convert the negotiated agreements into a new state of the world. Characteristic of policy exercises is that (a) the participants play roles, and (b) the participants do not explicitly take part in the assessment process. A policy exercise is a way to obtain information on human behaviour and policy preferences necessary for the assessment the analysts produce. Examples of policy exercises in IA are the climate policy exercises (Parson, 1996a) and RIVM's SusClime-exercises (de Vries, 1995). Both efforts made use of IA models, respectively a 'tailor-made' version of the GCAM model (Edmonds *et al.*, 1994) and a preliminary version of the TARGETS model (Rotmans *et al.*, 1997b; Hilderink *et al.*, 1998).

The principle behind mutual learning is that participation of stakeholders and citizens enriches the assessment by a multiplicity of perspectives, skills and competences. The participants are considered as co-producers of knowledge. They are not selected according to whether the assessment is of use to them, but whether their perspectives, skills or competences complement the scientists' expertise and knowledge. We distinguish two forms of mutual learning: the *focus group approach*, in which scientists play the role of facilitator and observer, and the *interactive approach*, in which scientists are actively involved as participants. In the first case, special groups are composed, typically consisting of citizens, policy makers or other stakeholders who are provided with scientific input. The assessments of these groups are then used in a broader IA process. In interactive analysis (Grin *et al.*, 1997), problem definitions and proposed solutions are integrated into a joint assessment that makes sense to both stakeholders and scientists. The ULYSSES project involves IA focus groups with lay people (Dürrenberger *et al.*, 1997). The VISIONS project (Rotmans et al., 1999b, 2001) can be considered as a first example of the interactive approach.

Challenges for the future

The major challenge is to gain more experience with participatory methods in IA (see also van Asselt and Rijkens-Klomp, 2002). The evaluation of these exploratory experiences should lead to an overview of strengths and weaknesses of the various approaches. Such an overview indicates the requirements associated with participatory methods for integrated assessment. Such insights should then lead to the development of appropriate tools, procedures and, ideally, manuals that make it possible to test and improve participatory methods for IA.

Towards an Integrated Assessment Toolkit

Models, scenarios and participatory methods are not mutually exclusive alternative methods for integrated assessment. Models can be used as a tool to develop scenarios. On the other hand, models and scenarios could be the result of participatory processes. Dialogue approaches can be oriented towards the development and/or use of IA models. Within policy exercises, models can be used as reference frameworks. In the ULYSSES focus groups, IA models are used as expert input into the group discussions. In mutual learning approaches, models might be helpful for comparing scenarios developed by participants with scientific insights.

The major methodological challenge for IA is to take advantage of the existence of multiple methods. Figure 4.2 suggests how the various methods can be used in a complementary manner. This cyclic scheme can thus serve as an heuristic to design a variety of sensible procedures using both models, scenarios and participatory approaches. Starting with participatory methods and then turning clockwise, the figure sketches a project in which participatory methods provide the basis for the development of an IA model that, in its turn, is used to develop scenarios. These scenarios are then input to the next round of participatory meetings, after which the developed models are adjusted, and so on. Starting with IA models and turning anti-clockwise results in the following iterative process: an IA model is developed as an interdisciplinary scientific effort and is then used as scientific input to participatory processes in which a variety of scenarios is developed. The consistency of these scenarios is then checked using IA models, or scenario narratives can be illustrated by means of trends derived from model analysis. These improved scenarios serve as input for participatory processes, and so on.

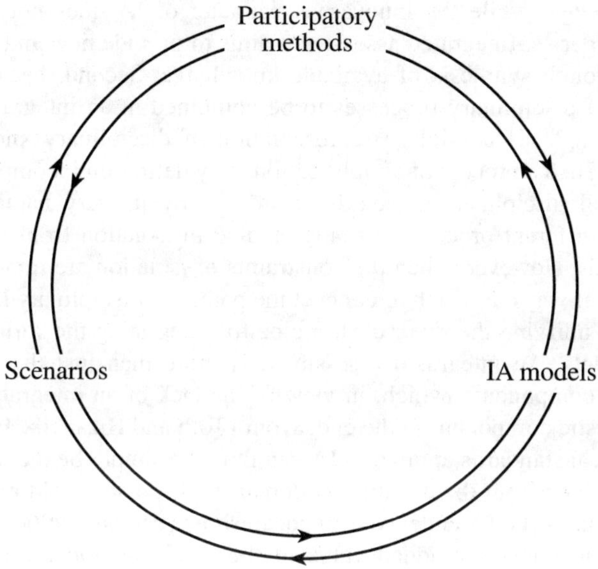

Figure 4.2 IA methods cycle

GOOD PRACTICE AND HIGH QUALITY

Another important challenge for IA, and the most crucial one if IA wants to grow into a mature approach, is the development of codes for good practice and quality criteria. Critical reflection on the practice and results of IA activities is not a luxury, but urgently needed (Ravetz, 1997; Rotmans, 1998c; van Asselt, 2000). Codes of good practice and quality criteria are necessary to be able to evaluate and compare IA studies. Where codes of good practice mainly address the assessment process itself, quality criteria are needed to judge the products associated with IA. An accepted set of codes for good practice and quality criteria that enable us to evaluate and compare IA studies will in the end improve the credibility of integrated assessment as an approach to decision support on complex issues.

Dilemmas

Why not simply apply standard scientific criteria to evaluate integrated assessments? The reason is that the interdisciplinary nature of IA hampers the application of disciplinary standards to IA, which can be shown at three different levels. First, the ambitions of disciplinary research and integrated assessment differ fundamentally. The disciplinary enterprise is focused on new knowledge, while the innovative character of IA does not lie in new knowledge per se. Integrated assessment aims to provide new and innovative insights through synthesis of available knowledge. Second, because of the multitude of disciplinary processes to be combined in an integrated assessment, as simple as possible a representation of disciplinary knowledge is preferable. Such a process of simplification is by definition incompatible with satisfying all disciplinary standards. Third, IA by its very nature involves combining different processes usually studied in isolation from other disciplinary fields. However, when the constraints of isolation are removed, there is a variety of ways in which to connect the pieces of disciplinary knowledge. There is no unifying theory or clear recipe for integrating the various knowledge elements. An integrated assessment is more than just the sum of its knowledge components, which, in view of the lack of an integration theory, adds an artistic component to the endeavour (Toth and Hizsnyik, 1998).

The critical standards applied to IA can thus not simply be the intersection of the standards from the constituent domains. To do so would be to reduce all evaluation of the IA endeavour to cheap shots (Parson, 1996c) and would by definition ignore the added value of the synthesis. On the other hand, however, disciplinary-based standards are necessary to evaluate the quality of the inputs from the various disciplines on which the integrated assessment builds. The theories, data and expert models used, and the assumptions made, should be recognized as valid by the disciplinary community.

Integrated assessment also differs from interdisciplinary research on account of its decision-support purpose. If IA is considered as a kind of decision aid, it should be tested through use. However, what does use mean in the context of IA? And how to judge that the use of IA improves decision making? It takes decades or more before the effects of present decisions can be discerned, and that those changes are only partly policy-driven (Ravetz, 1997). So if it is difficult to judge the quality of a decision, how can we then recognize whether the assessment supports decision making? IA practitioners, such as Robinson (1992) and Rotmans (as cited in van Asselt, 1994) argue that studies that correspond to their own perceptions and political agenda have a greater likelihood to be considered by decision makers. Are such assessments better? If so, factors such as political utility and timeliness would overrule scientific criteria. Such criteria prevent integrated assessment from being beyond current political interests. Taking the decision support aim seriously, implies that, notwithstanding the above difficulties, we need to find ways to evaluate the political quality (Robinson, 1992) of integrated assessments.

Another feature of IA complicates the quality issue even further. Integrated assessment aims to clarify complex issues. Owing to the character of complex issues, every IA study is by definition incomplete and at its best only partially integrated. The level of integration (Schneider, 1997) may serve as a quality criterion, but full integration as a yardstick makes any integrated assessment a 'mission impossible'. There seems to be no way to prove that the assessment is correct. The future is likely to be influenced by assessment activities. Assessments may foster decisions that prevent forecasts taking place. Malthus' fears and the 'Limits to Growth' dooms have clearly influenced political thinking and decision making. The current state of the world (no mass starvation or depleted resources) does not make those past assessments of a poor quality.

These dilemmas indicate that designing codes of good practise and quality criteria for IA is not an easy job. It is nevertheless urgently needed in order to be credible in the long term. At the moment, it is too difficult, and it would probably even be counterproductive, to formulate strict rules and hard criteria. In view of this, we attempt to formulate rough guidelines and a kind of checklist as a next step in this challenging endeavour. It is important to realize that these guidelines and the checklist do not represent the current state of the art. These quality aspects first and above all picture an image of desired IA.

Rough Guidelines for Good Practice

Different authors in IA have addressed the issue of developing guidelines for good practice. Ravetz (1997) states that the quality of integrated assessment is assured only by the quality of its production. Risbey *et al.* (1996) emphasize that process-based criteria should be developed. Bailey *et al.* (1996) seek to identify key aspects of good practice in IA. Morgan and Dowlatabadi (1996) propose hallmarks of a good integrated assessment. Clark and Majone (1985) derived four 'meta-criteria' that capture what practitioners and users have in mind when they cite a particular assessment as being noteworthy or important. Others, such as Parson (1996c), Schneider (1997), Jäger (1998) and van Asselt (2000) in turn have interpreted and extended these contributions.

It is a commonly shared view that good practice primarily depends on craftsmanship. An IA study is designed with a particular function or policy question in mind. To know what to do when, and what to leave aside, is a crucial part of the craft. In the case of integrated assessment, 'best' is conditioned by the context, time-frame, costs and conditions of use.

The above authors agree that the general functions assigned to IA imply that the IA process should involve a dialogue between users and analysts. Good practice thus means that IA, at least in its crucial stages, embraces communication between IA practitioners, stakeholders and the broad audience. This implies that participatory methods are needed in the IA process. Ideally, the various societal actors should participate in all stages of the IA process, but we should keep in mind that this may be too demanding for both the IA practitioners and the stakeholders. Within the VISIONS project, we observed that it is difficult to get stakeholders 'on board', irrespective of the participatory methods used and the scale of the assessment (Rotmans *et al.*, 1999a). Fair management is needed to ensure that the different participants are good discussion partners and that solutions are worked out that do not entirely ignore the interests of anyone across the spectrum of societal actors. Furthermore, stakeholders are not used to this kind of science–society interaction, so the structure of the participatory process and the process facilitators have to provide help (ibid.). In this context, it is again extremely relevant that more experience is gained with participatory methods in IA in order to find out which methods seem to be suitable for what kind of contexts and to develop procedures and formats for applying participatory methods.

On the other hand, it is commonly shared that IA is more than a participatory process. The analytical dimension, that is, gathering and synthesizing knowledge elements from different disciplines and knowledge domains, is as crucial as the participatory process. Building upon the state of the art in IA, we conclude that the following analytical steps are essential in any IA process (Rotmans, 1998c; ICIS, 1998, 1999; van Asselt, 2000).

- A scan of the relevant economic, sociocultural, environmental and institutional dimensions of the case under consideration to get a first rough picture of the issues and processes that should be considered.
- Design and selection of indicators that are crucial for the analysis. Ideally, this step should be taken as a participatory effort. In this context the distinction between stock and flow indicators is relevant. Flow indicators indicate the short-term changes, while stock indicators describe long-term developments.
- An historical analysis of the development of the selected indicators, in order to be able to understand the crucial dynamics and to clarify cause–effect chains. Part of this step involves an inventory of data pertaining to the key issues and processes so as to be able to sketch the state of the art.
- Identification of salient uncertainties and risks.
- Trend analysis to get a feeling for future prospects and the articulation of desired futures.
- Assessment of options for decision making in the view of historical developments, the current state of the art, the salient uncertainties and future risks.

There is agreement within the IA community that the step of identifying major uncertainties and risks is crucial, but problematic. It is commonly felt that IA lacks the methods or procedures that make it possible to incorporate uncertainty in an adequate way into trend analysis and to use the concept of risk in the final assessment. Notwithstanding the different steps identified above, it is agreed that integrated assessment can never be a linear endeavour. This implies that the followed approach should be iterative and cyclical.

Quality Criteria[2]

What holds for the process also holds for the product: the quality of the product is dependent on the purpose and context of the study in question. It is thus by definition impossible to come up with general quality standards that measure all IAs with the same yardsticks. Nevertheless, it is useful to think about rough rules for assessing the quality of IA studies within the scope of their own purpose.

Building upon Robinson (1992), we distinguish three types of quality criteria: (a) analytical quality,[3] (b) methodological quality and (c) usability[4] that can be defined respectively as criteria concerning the credibility of the underlying data sources and theories, the validity of techniques/models used, the level of integration, and the logic of the conclusions; criteria addressing the quality of the methods and approaches adopted; and criteria involving the degree of relevancy of the assessment for decision making (compare Rotmans, 1998b, 1998c; van Asselt, 2000).

The latter category is unique and reveals the explicit decision-support aim of IA. For that reason, IA studies have to be subjected to additional criteria that go beyond interdisciplinarity. Analytical and methodological quality are a necessary, but insufficient condition for every IA study. We can thus distinguish between two hierarchical levels, internal quality of the assessment[5] ('have we done a good job?') and external quality ('is the assessment useful?') (see Figure 4.3). The aim is a balanced quality judgment, involving both internal and external quality, which would enable us to distinguish between 'better' and 'worse' IA studies, to separate the sheep from the goats.

In order to arrive at a checklist, it is necessary to investigate what kind of specific items the different types of quality comprise. On the other hand, we should not aim at an exhaustive checklist. For each type of criteria, we have tried to identify seven key questions.[6]

Analytical quality criteria involve what Risbey *et al.* (1996) call 'discipline-based criteria to evaluate IA components'. An assessment of the analytical quality thus involves addressing the following questions:[7]

1. What are the data sources (field data, survey data, laboratory experiments, statistical data, computer simulations, educated guesses and so on), how credible are they and are the data confirmed by different studies?

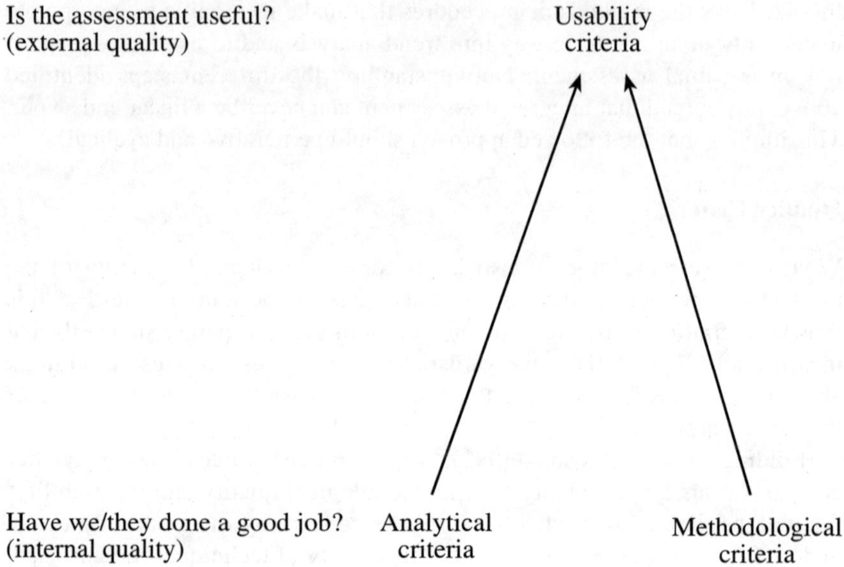

Figure 4.3 Two levels of quality

2. Are the theoretical assumptions derived from state-of-the-art theory, are the concepts and laws used interpreted and formulated in accordance with disciplinary standards, and are the models used in the assessment calibrated[8] and validated?[9]
3. Is there a balance between aggregation and disaggregation, and is it based on a sound protocol?
4. Is the adopted time-horizon long enough to capture the relevant time-scales, and how is this long-term perspective related to short-term decision making?
5. Are autonomous processes and processes that are or may be affected by human activities and/or policy strategies distinguished in the assessment?
6. To what extent is the study integrated: are the key social, economic and environmental dimensions addressed in a balanced way and does the assessment adequately address mutual interactions as well as positive and negative feedbacks?
7. Is the study consistent, are the conclusions supported by evidence and/or logical and plausible argumentation,[10] can the results be generalized (either analytically or statistically) and do the conclusions transcend disciplinary insights and provide innovative findings?

Methodological quality addresses the quality of the integrated assessment process and the methods and approaches adopted. Therefore, the guidelines for good practice reappear to a greater or lesser extent as methodological criteria. Issues relevant in this context are the following:

1. Are the research questions and the research priorities appropriate in view of the aims, time-frame, costs and conditions of use?
2. Is the research guided by a framework that is integrated and comprises the essential analytical steps as indicated under codes of good practice?
3. Are the chosen analytical and participatory methods and approaches state-of-the-art, appropriate and legitimate in the context of the aim of the study?
4. Is the study of an interdisciplinary or multidisciplinary nature?
5. Is the use of disciplinary knowledge elements and the simplification of this knowledge into building blocks for the IA study done in close collaboration with disciplinary experts (disciplinary peer review)?
6. What is the level of participation by what kind of stakeholders, and how were they selected?
7. How is uncertainty dealt with and are values, preferences and bias made explicit so that it is clear to what extent value judgments influence the scientific conclusions?

Usability addresses the relevance of the IA study for society in general, and decision making in particular. As discussed before, it is difficult, if not impossible, to come to a definite judgment taking into account the nature of decision-making processes and the delayed response to actual decisions. However, the following key questions may help us to get an impression of the usability of IA-studies:

1. Does the problem formulation make sense to the stakeholders and the decision makers, and does the study address important decision-making issues?
2. Are the stakeholders, views and dimensions relevant for the decision-making process taken into account (Clark *et al.*, 1985; Jäger, 1998)?
3. Is the assessment comprehensible to the audience and users, and are the recommendations concrete?
4. Is the study useful for disciplinary sciences, in the sense that it helps to set disciplinary research agendas?
5. To what extent has the IA study been able to address societal concerns and needs, and, if it has, in what way do stakeholders and the general public benefit from the integrated assessment?
6. Does the study facilitate in any way one or more of the following deci-

sion-making processes: framing the issue(s), agenda setting, scenario development, analysis of policy options, evaluation of consequences, identification and exploration of scientific uncertainties or evaluation in terms of equity (compare Parson, 1996b)? To what extent did the study change, stabilize or advance the relevant debate?
7. Is the assessment timely?

The above checklist is summarized in Table 4.2, where the major items associated with the various quality criteria are listed. Three kinds of items can be distinguished: criteria that hold for any scientific study (normal type), criteria pertaining to interdisciplinary research in general (*italic*) and criteria that hold for IA in particular (**bold**).

Table 4.2 Quality checklist

ANALYTICAL QUALITY	METHODOLOGICAL QUALITY	USABILITY
Credibility of data sources	Suitability of research agenda	**Value of problem definition**
Disciplinary quality of used knowledge elements	*Integrated character of research methodology*	**Legitimacy**
Balance aggregation – disaggregation	Choice of methods	Transparency
Integration of time-horizons	*Interdisciplinarity*	*Disciplinary benefit*
Distinction between autonomous and policy-driven	*Level of collaboration with disciplines*	**Societal benefit**
Level of integration	**Level of participation**	**Effectiveness**
Consistency and 'transdisciplinary' character of conclusions	**Uncertainty treatment**	**Timeliness**

REFLECTIONS ON THE TARGETS PROJECT

The present authors led the TARGETS project, which was officially labelled 'Global Dynamics and Sustainable Development'. In 1992, the project was launched at the Dutch National Institute for Public Health and Environment (RIVM). The development of the integrated assessment model, TARGETS (Rotmans and Vries, 1997; Hilderink et al., 1998; Rotmans and van Asselt, 1999), which stands for 'Tool to Assess Regional and Global Environmental and Health Targets for Sustainability', was central to the project. About 30 people, comprising researchers, PhD students, trainees and support staff participated in the research. The philosophy underlying the project, the details of the TARGETS model and an assessment of global change are comprehensively described in Rotmans and Vries (1997). In the following sections, we will reflect on the TARGETS project from a quality assessment point of view in order to further assess current practices by means of an example.

Introduction to the TARGETS Project

The TARGETS project can be considered as a scientific assessment of global change taking into account plural social and cultural perspectives (Figure 4.4). The TARGETS model enables evaluation of a number of environmental, social and economic consequences of several types of human activities simultaneously. System theory provided the main building blocks for the conceptual framework. At the highest level of aggregation, the TARGETS model comprises a human and environmental system. Following a modular approach, the model consists of a population and health submodel, an energy submodel, an economic module, a biophysics submodel, a land/soil submodel and a water submodel. Interactions and feedback loops between the submodels are taken into account in each time step of the simulation period. The time horizon for the TARGETS 1.0 model spans two centuries (1900–2100). The general time step used within the TARGETS 1.0 framework is one year, with the exception of the calculation of some physically related processes which require a time step of a month (hydrological processes) or a season (biogeochemical processes).

A crucial feature of the TARGETS model is that it incorporates multiple model routes. These are coloured interpretations of the uncertainties prevalent in the model. The model routes are fleshed out according to three cultural perspectives, namely the hierarchist, the egalitarian and the individualist. This typology of perspectives builds upon insights derived from anthropology and cultural theory (Douglas, 1982; Douglas and Wildavsky, 1982; Rayner, 1984, 1991; Thompson *et al.*, 1990; Thompson, 1997). The freedom of inter-

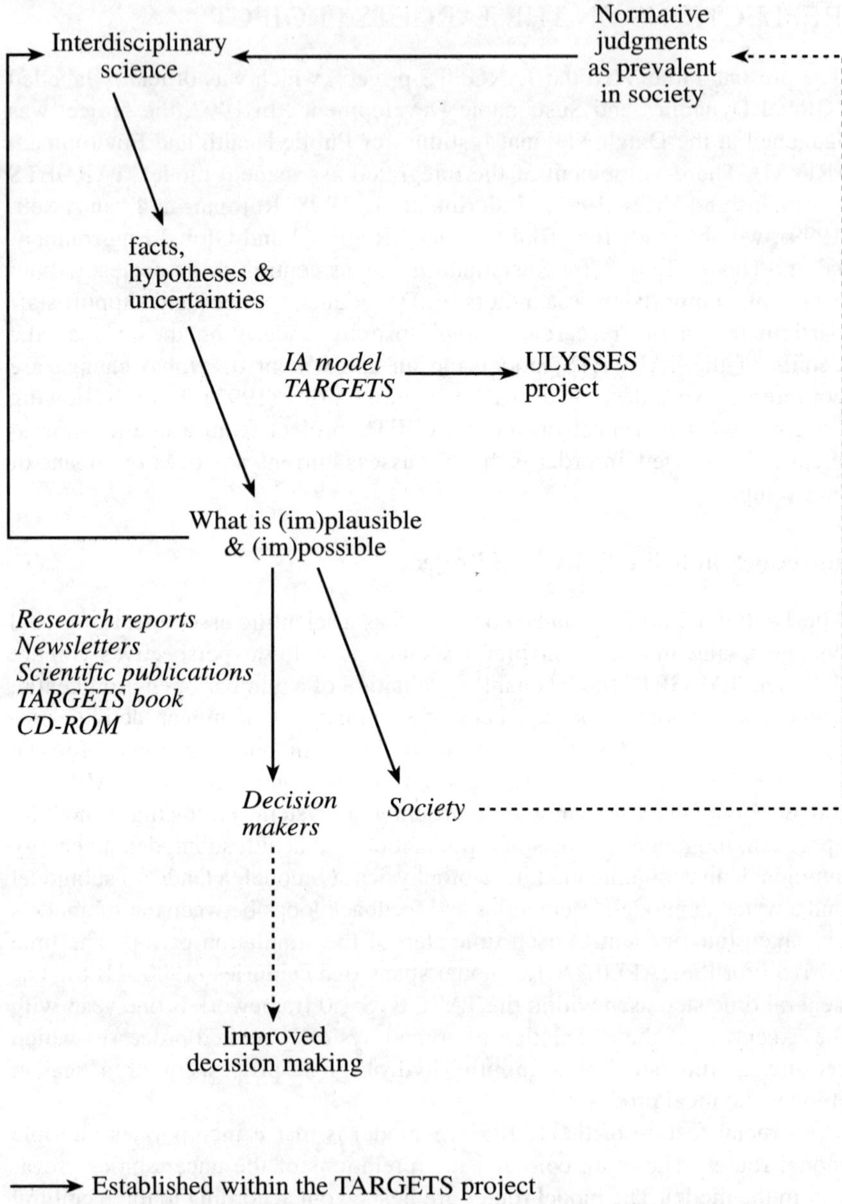

Figure 4.4 Representation of the TARGETS project compared to the cyclical IA framework

pretation is bounded by two criteria: the range of freedom is determined by the variety of quantitative and qualitative estimates found in scientific literature, and the historical trajectories (generally from 1900 until the present) generated by each model route have to represent the observed time-series. The model routes were used as building blocks for performing scenario experiments in a systematic way. If policy preferences (management style) and the social, economic and environmental processes (world view) are in accordance with one perspective, this is called a utopia. Mismatches are called dystopias. A comprehensive discussion of this methodology for uncertainty management can be found in van Asselt and Rotmans (1996, 1997) and van Asselt (2000).

How are these model routes constructed? Model routes consist of chains of alternative formulations of model relations and quantities. In the first step those relations and quantities that express a subjective interpretation are identified, which involves a continuous dialogue between modellers and disciplinary experts. The next step involves translation of the qualitative descriptions of the perspectives into model terms. This means that alternative relations have to be formulated, and/or alternative values have to be determined. In its simplest form, only parameter values are changed. Finally, the different parameter values and model relations are implemented in the model, and the model is run for the different perspective-based model routes. Each model route projection can then be surrounded by an uncertainty range, using classical uncertainty methods (sampling techniques). For an elaborate description of the construction of the model routes in the TARGETS model, the reader is referred to Rotmans and Vries (1997).

Insights

The TARGETS project brought some counterintuitive insights to the fore which are beyond the reach of disciplinary science and common sense. What kind of insights did the study produce that enhance a better understanding of complex global change issues? In answer, we will summarize the major and counterintuitive model-based results that our integrated assessment (Rotmans *et al.*, 1997c; Rotmans and van Asselt, 1999) produced in response to the question; 'Can we provide a future world population with enough food, clean water and energy to guarantee a healthy life, while safeguarding our natural resources base?'

The differences between the utopias are salient. Whereas the individualistic utopia has the highest pressures and the highest social and economic impacts, the state of the environment is the least deteriorated, and water and energy prices are lowest. The reason is that this is a world of abundance and resilience: energy, land and water resources are huge and the environmental system is supposed to be quite insensitive to human disturbances. The egalitarian utopia shows the opposite picture: at much lower pressure and impact levels, and despite rather radical response measures, parts of the environment, notably land and climate, are in worse shape. The hierarchist utopia has high energy-related indicators, which means that this scenario symbolizes an energy-intensive future. The environmental impacts are considerable: the environment is more deteriorated than in the individualist utopia, but less than in the egalitarian one.

The intriguing aspect that arose from the simulated utopias briefly described above is that they are not strictly utopian in the sense of self-fulfilling prophecies: not all is rosy, as we expected beforehand. This is due to the variety of choices over widely differing issues that have to be internally consistent. While the rosy future picture is most clear-cut in the individualist utopia, both the egalitarian and hierarchist utopia are characterized by a gloomy future environmental state.

Although the utopias are quite interesting as experiments, the dystopias are more interesting. Dystopias are scenarios in which the world-view and management style do not match. That means that they represent the potential risk of switching from one style of management to another, or of a drastic switch in world-view.

Our assessment indicated that the most catastrophic future is the one in which an egalitarian world-view is combined with an individualist management style. In this case, the world would be confronted by significant changes in the global climate and, partly as a consequence, by serious food and water shortages. Life expectancy only increases slightly compared to the present world average, and the resource base is squandered. The main conclusion here is that, if policy makers want to reduce the risks of such a catastrophic future, they should pursue an egalitarian government policy that aims at a high quality of human life (in particular health care and education for women), carbon tax, R&D programmes on renewable resources and small-scale technology, water taxing, public water supply policy, and eco-forestry and eco-agriculture policies. However, analysing the egalitarian management style in general, it is obvious that it contains the potential risk of reducing socioeconomic benefits in terms of a lesser improvement of quality of life and human health. A further interesting observation is that detrimental climate impacts are absent in a future where the world functions according to the individualistic world-view and egalitarian policy measures are carried out. The counterintuitive result means that an egalitarian government in combination with an adverse world-view (that of the individualist) turns out to be more effective in terms of socioeconomic and environmental prosperity than in the case of the egalitarian utopia. Our assessment reveals the following:

- the individualistic management style (market-oriented health policy, market pricing of water, high-tech R&D programmes, protection of industrial sectors, and intensive agriculture, including genetic engineering) is the most risky in terms of climate risks as global mean temperature and sea level rise;
- the hierarchist management style (family planning, selective health care policy (cure), moderate R&D programmes for energy efficiency and new energy supply options, reforestation policy and agricultural planning) is least effective when evaluated in terms of improvements in resource efficiency;
- the observation that a transition to a less energy-intensive society is foreseen in both the egalitarian and individualist utopia reveals that both a market-driven energy policy and a strict carbon-tax policy are potentially promising strategies to support such a shift. This result again underlines the importance of developing less energy-intensive technologies;
- the egalitarian management style (investments in human quality, taxing systems, R&D programmes on new technologies, and eco-friendly policies) is the most effective in curbing population growth, although it should be noted that this is at the expense of a significant improvement in life expectancy.

Our major conclusion is that a global catastrophe does not appear to be imminent. But the projections generated with the TARGETS model clearly indicate that pursuit of current trends is most unlikely to result in a sustainable future, whatever the perspective. Our major insight referring to the fundamental controversy on global change is that it seems possible to provide a future world population with more food per capita than the current level, and that there are several potentials for a transition to a less energy-intensive, but healthy, economy. It is most likely that the global population on average will live longer and be healthier than today, which, however, does not imply an equitable distribution of health. The resource base is at risk, but there are many promising ways to safeguard the environment for future generations. However, there is a serious risk that water may become scarce, even at the global level.

Analytical Quality of the TARGETS Project

How does the TARGETS project 'score' in terms of analytical quality? The model covers social, economic and environmental dimensions of the issue of sustainable development. The treatment of the various dimensions is more balanced than in existing IA models, which either overemphasize the

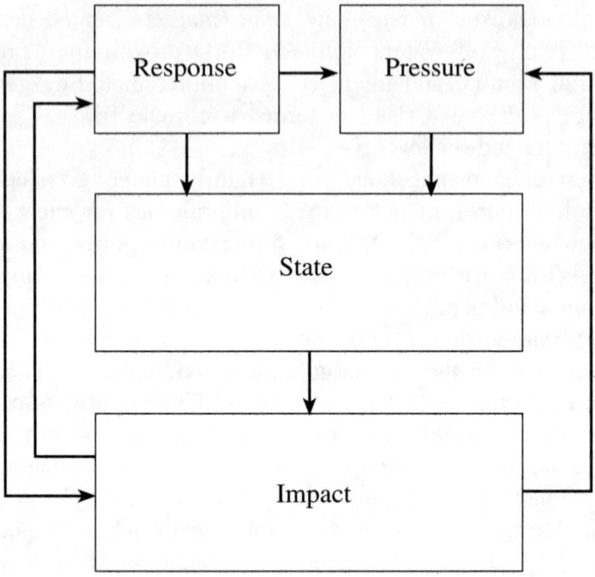

Source: Rotmans *et al*. (1994).

Figure 4.5 PSIR scheme

economic dimension (the macroeconomic school) or favour environmental processes and neglect important social and economic dimensions (most biosphere-oriented models). Horizontal integration was a central point of departure in the TARGETS project. The Pressure–State–Impact–Response (PSIR) concept was used as a frame to structure the integrative effort (see Figure 4.5). Interrelations between social, economic and environmental issues were investigated in terms of common pressures, common impacts and common responses:

- The *pressure* system describes the developments in human population and health, resources, economy, land, soil and water use and the mutual interrelations between these developments.
- The *state* dynamics system describes the state of the environmental system and the social and economic state of the human system, which are of course interrelated. The state modules can be conceived as describing the state of the various environmental, economic and social reservoirs, namely terrestrial, biospheric, aquatic and atmospheric reservoirs, on the one hand, and demographic and resources reservoirs, on the other.

- The *impacts* are divided into three types, namely impacts indicating (a) the effect of multiple stress on the environment; (b) the impact of global change on human health; and (c) the socioeconomic effects of large-scale environmental problems.
- The *response* system contains those variables which can be used to influence human activities and/or the environment. The response variables are all information variables, while the majority of the variables within the PSIR system are of a physical character. We distinguish the following policy variables: financial incentives, regulation, information programmes and research, development and demonstration programmes (RD&D).

In this way the issues of population and human health, energy, water, food and environmental quality are put in the broader context of global change and sustainable development. The TARGETS model is, furthermore, vertically integrated, because for each global change issue the causal chains are assessed.

The TARGETS model is a quantitative and deterministic framework. Semi-quantitative information, qualitative and vague information are just used in an informal way to arrive at parameter estimates. The TARGETS model has been set up as a generic framework so that, in principle, it can be applied at different levels of aggregation. TARGETS 1.0 is a global model, in which classes (such as vegetation and land-use classes) are used to account for geographical differences. For example, the following land-use classes are distinguished: irrigated arable land, rain-fed arable land, grassland, forest, and other, which division is further subdivided into a developing and a developed region.

In order to test whether the disciplinary knowledge has been represented in an adequate way, the submodel documentation was reviewed in 1996 by RIVM and external disciplinary experts. Their comments were used to improve the various submodels. The TARGETS model is extensively calibrated and validated against available data, other IA models and experts models, if available. In the context of model validation, submodels, such as population and health, energy and water, have been implemented for specific regions, such as India, the United States and the Zambezi river basin. The explicit policy was to seek publication in disciplinary journals such as a publication on the biogeochemical submodel in *Biogeochemical Cycles* (den Elzen *et al.*, 1997a).

The following procedure was designed for submodel and integrated experiments in order to provide consistency among the scenario results (see Rotmans *et al.*, 1997a):

- Three economic scenarios (in terms of gross world product) have been generated, building upon previous scenario studies by others.
- The integrated model was run with the hierarchist settings, which resulted in projections for population, health, energy, water, food and environmental quality. These generated projections are referred to as 'reference projections'.
- Then, in sequence, the submodels were run using the output from the previous model runs, in the following order: population, energy, water, land and food and the biogeochemical cycles submodel.
- After the submodel experiments, integrated experiments have been carried out with the whole TARGETS model and have been compared with the submodel experiments.

The generated scenarios have been compared with existing scenarios, and differences and comparisons have been discussed.

This leads to interesting cross-fertilizations. For example, comparison of the population scenarios generated with TARGETS and the established UN population scenarios (UN, 1993, 1995) indicates that the low UN projection is rather implausible. The population number in 2100 associated with the low UN projection (about 5 billion world citizens) can be reproduced with the egalitarian model route and assumed food and water crises. However, the extraordinary fast rate of decline in this UN projection cannot be explained by our systematic experiments.

Methodological Quality of the TARGETS Project

The TARGETS project has followed the iterative and cyclic approach shown in Figure 4.6. As a starting-point we have selected a limited number of global change issues: population and health, energy, land and food, water and element cycles. The key issues have been selected through a literature review, and have been studied in close collaboration with disciplinary experts. The conceptual framework that served as a starting point for the assessment was the result of brainstorm discussions among members of the core research team in the very first year. The aim was first to implement this conceptual model and then, on the basis of the first series of experiments, to decide whether or not to extend the conceptual model. In spite of its limitations, the conceptual model turned out to be adequate and complicated enough to implement, so that no further extension and disaggregation took place. In view of the complexity of these issues and the fundamental uncertainties surrounding them, we addressed those global change issues in terms of controversies. Each controversy was then analysed as a knowledge pattern that consists of a sequence of uncertainties. On the basis of expert knowledge and literature search, those uncertainties

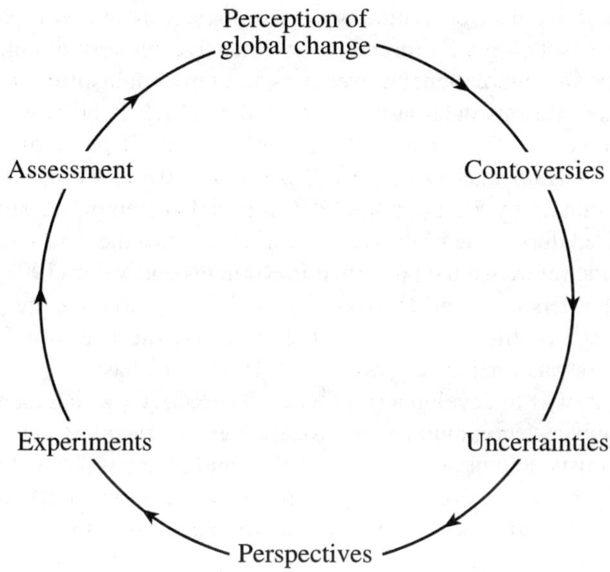

Figure 4.6 TARGETS research cycle

found to be crucial were selected, up to a maximum of ten per controversy. Then the knowledge pattern of chained uncertainties was coloured according to the different perspectives, so that consistent clusters of interpretations of those uncertainties were created. The next step involved the translation of the perspective-based, qualitative description of the controversies into model terms in the form of perspective-based model routes.

In the next step, a series of experiments was done with the model in a systematic manner. Projections were structured according to the lines of utopias and dystopias. Then we aimed to indicate the risks associated with a specific global change issue by evaluating the whole range of utopian and dystopian futures, as well as those futures that result from the case studies. This came down to assessing whether the majority of the resulting images of the future show (un)desirable trends. This combined risk and uncertainty assessment enabled us to address the controversy under concern in an evaluative, integrated way. The insights derived from such an integrated assessment may reveal a description of the global change issue in question that differs from the initial perception. Such lessons can provide the starting point for another iteration of the research cycle.

The TARGETS project was definitively an interdisciplinary research effort. Exponents of the following disciplines were actively involved: agricultural science, arts, computer science, demography, econometrics, energy studies, environmental science, epidemiology, hydrology, mathematics, philosophy, physics and psychology. Furthermore, an extensive network of collaboration with national and international universities and research institutes contributed to the project. Various data-bases (such as the HYDE data base), statistical yearbooks (such as the annual *World Development Reports* of the World Bank, the UN *Human Development Reports*, the *World Resources Reports* presented annually by WRI and the IPCC reports) and empirical studies have been consulted during the project. For a full account of the data sources used, we refer to the reference list published in Rotmans and Vries (1997).

No stakeholders or potential users were actively involved in the project. In the early stage of the project a limited study on the needs and wants of potential users was carried out (van Asselt, 1994). The basic idea, at the onset of the project, was to develop a prototype of TARGETS which then could be used in the intricate communication process between the modellers and disciplinary scientists, and between the modellers and policy makers. To this end, it was attempted to develop a policy exercise setting in which the TARGETS model could be used. Notwithstanding the first attempts in that direction, this ambition failed. However, in the ULYSSES project, the usefulness of the TARGETS model as a tool to initiate and facilitate discussions among the general public has been explored (van Asselt and Rotmans, 2001).

Although the development of the TARGETS model was central to the project, the development of long-term, coherent and consistent scenarios was

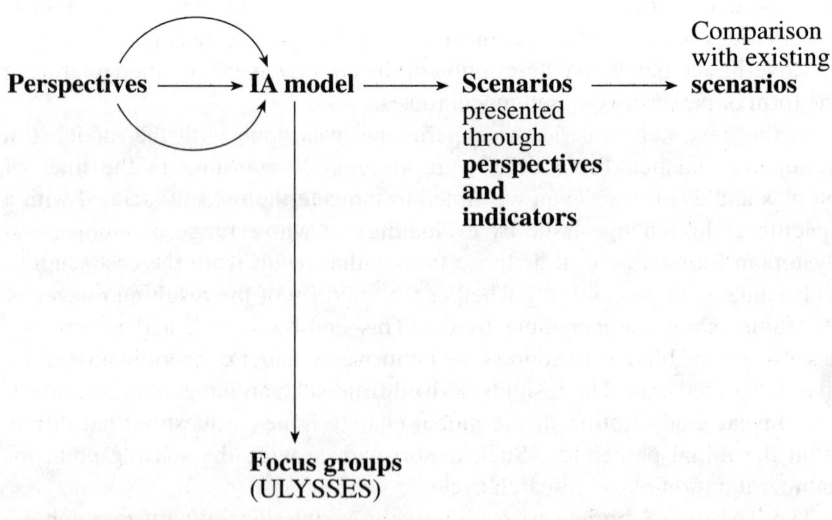

Figure 4.7 Complementary use of multiple methods in the TARGETS project

clearly an important aim. Furthermore, existing scenarios were used as a way to better understand complex processes. The way in which the multiple methods (IA model, perspectives, scenarios and, indirectly, focus groups) are used in combination is shown in Figure 4.7. Innovative methodological features of the TARGETS model were the following:

- the perspective-based model routes;
- the high level of integration (both horizontally and vertically) of a range of global change issues into one framework;
- the development of a hierarchical framework of indicators that is interlinked with the modelling framework;
- the development of a new modelling and visualization language (M), that facilitates communication within the interdisciplinary research team;
- the use of the concept of transitions as a frame to describe and understand the complex dynamics of global change.

Quality of TARGETS in Terms of Usability

The TARGETS project was clearly inspired by the international societal and policy interest in the issue of sustainable development following the Rio conference in 1991. The main objective of the project was to operationalize, and to render applicable, the concepts of global change and sustainable development, in such a way that these notions can be used in the decision-making process (Rotmans et al., 1994a).

In the course of the project various scientific reports and journal articles were written that allowed colleague researchers to gain knowledge of our efforts. The TARGETS book (Rotmans *et al.*, 1997c) is explicitly aimed at being understandable for and appealing to a broad audience, from scientists and modellers to policy analysts, decision makers and students of all aspects of global change. Furthermore, a CD-ROM (Hilderink *et al.*, 1998) has been made that allows the broad audience to experiment with the TARGETS model themselves.

What can disciplinary science learn from our investigations? First of all, the TARGETS study puts disciplinary facts, theories and hypotheses in a broader context. This may shed some light on the societal and environmental consequences of processes which have thus far been studied in isolation. For example, with regard to energy, our integrated assessment shows that the time needed for a transition from fossil fuels to renewables is generally underestimated. Whatever the policy measures, such a transition takes about two generations, owing to the interlinkages with the social and economic transition. Our work suggests that an integrated systems approach can also be valuable in areas where it is not, or not very often, used. Examples are demography, water, epidemiology, land use and food production and economic demand-and-supply mechanisms. It showed, furthermore, that questions which have bothered disciplinary scientists for a long time can be examined using an integrated approach. A striking example is the issue of the missing sink of carbon, which imbalance is unsolved as yet in biogeochemistry and climatology. Experiments with the biogeochemical submodel CYCLES suggest that only a complex interplay between processes in the global carbon cycle and nitrogen cycle can explain a balanced carbon budget (den Elzen *et al.*, 1997a, 1997b). In many cases the state of the art in the underlying disciplines did not allow an adequate representation of certain relevant issues in our integrated framework. Examples are erosion, the social dynamics behind agricultural shifts and the issue of labour in economic and social processes. Such an identification of gaps in knowledge could be useful for disciplinary agenda setting.

A Quality Assessment of the TARGETS Project

Building upon the above we arrive at the following reflexive assessment of the quality of TARGETS (Table 4.3), in which '?' indicates that the issue cannot be addressed by the authors at this moment, '0' means no clear opinion, '–' means a negative quality judgment and '+' indicates a positive judgment. Taking into account the positive evaluations on IA specific items, the conclusion of this reflexive quality assessment should be that the TARGETS project can be appropriately qualified as an IA study.

CHALLENGES FOR THE FUTURE

This chapter provides a picture of IA by describing current practices, challenges for the future, a framework for quality assessment and a critical reflection on our own IA efforts. We have tried to sketch what integrated assessment can be if IA practitioners attempt to address the described challenges in a creative and responsible way. The following items are perhaps critical to the future utility of IA:

- development of scientific methods for participatory processes;
- protocols for integrated uncertainty management;
- further development of quality assessment procedures;
- development of protocols for aggregation and disaggregation;
- linking different spatial and temporal scales to identify the role of individuals and institutions, and their systems of governance (scaling issues);

Table 4.3 Quality assessment of the TARGETS project

Analytical quality		Methodological quality		Usability	
integration of scales	+	**integrated framework for performing study**	+	**societal relevance**	+
exogenous & endogenous	?	**sound aggregation protocol**	+	innovative	+
consistency	0	**iterative & cyclic**	+	achievement of goals	0
coherency	+	interdisciplinary	+	**policy relevance**	?
horizontal integration	+	transparency	+	concrete recommendations	–
vertical integration	+	competency & craftsmanship	0	disciplinary relevance	+
quantitative & qualitative	–	**participation & pluralism**	–/+	dissemination	?
balance	+	multiple methods	0	**insights**	?
reliability, generic character & robustness	+	**uncertainty management**	+		

- procedures for active dissemination of insights to societal stakeholders and the general public;
- an IA toolkit that comprises a wide variety of well-documented tools and methods, and suggestions for the way the various methods can be used in a complementary manner.

We have tried to provide some food for thought. As a special dish we have analysed our own IA efforts in terms of quality. The main aim of this chapter is to provide a state-of-the-art overview of an evolving approach and to inspire those who already perform integrated assessments. But, more than that, we hope that this contribution encourages researchers from a variety of disciplines to embark on the adventurous journey towards an integrated understanding of our complex human–environment system.

ACKNOWLEDGEMENTS

We are grateful to Hadi Dowlatabadi and Sylvia Tognetti and two anonymous reviewers for their very constructive comments which have considerably improved this chapter. We would like to thank Susan van 't Klooster, Nienke van Kuijeren and Hans Maessen for their help with the editing.

NOTES

1. Analysts and intended users in the policy community did not meet directly, but were informed about each others' perspectives and attitudes via interviews.
2. In this effort to propose quality criteria, the Bellagio principles as formulated by the International Institute for Sustainable Development (IISD) (*http://iisd1.iisd.ca/*) served as another source of inspiration.
3. Also referred to as 'scientific quality' (Toth and Hizsnyik, 1998) or technical adequacy (Clark and Majone, 1985).
4. Also referred to as practical achievement (Toth and Hizsnyik, 1998).
5. Clark and Majone (1985).
6. Of course this number is somewhat arbitrary, as any number would be. The general message should be that there has to be a balance between the three types, and for that reason we wanted to have the same number of issues for each type of criteria. The only 'justificant' for seven may be that this number has the cultural (religious) meaning of representating completeness.
7. Compare Funtowicz and Ravetz (1990).
8. Calibration is defined as the procedure to gauge the most important parameters in such a way that the model simulations come close to the observations.
9. Validation is defined here as testing model performance.
10. That is, to what extent are the conclusions compatible with data, model results and qualitative insights?

REFERENCES

Alcamo, J. (1994), *IMAGE 2.0: Integrated Modeling of Global Climate Change*, Dordrecht: Kluwer Academic Publishers.

Alcamo, J., E. Kreileman and R. Leemans (1996), 'Global Models meet Global Policy', *Global Environmental Change*, **6** (4), 1–5.

Alcamo, J., R. Shaw and L. Hordijk (1990), *The RAINS Model of Acidification: Science and Strategies in Europe*, Dordrecht: Kluwer Academic Publishers.

Anastasi, C. (1997), 'Lessons Learned from Two Decades' Scenario Development', Open meeting of the Human Dimensions of Global Environmental Change Research Community, Laxenburg, Austria.

Bailey, P., C. Gough, M. Chadwick and G. McGranahan (1996), 'Methods for Integrated Environmental Assessment: Research directions for the European Union', Stockholm Environment Institute (SEI), Stockholm, Sweden.

Brewer, G.D. (1986), 'Methods for Synthesis: Policy Exercises', in W.C. Clark and R.E. Munn (eds), *Sustainable Development of the Biosphere*, Cambridge: Cambridge University Press, pp. 455–73.

Cebon, P., H. Davies, D. Imboden and C. Jaeger (eds) (1997), *Climate and Environment in the Alpine Region: An Interdisciplinary View*, Cambridge, MA: MIT Press.

Chenje, M. and P. Johnson (eds) (1994), *State of the Environment in Southern Africa*, Johannesburg: The Penrose Press.

Clark, W.C. and G. Majone (1985), 'The Critical Appraisal of Scientific Enquiries with Policy Implications', *Science, Technology and Human Values*, **10** (3), 6–19.

Clark, W.C. and R.E. Munn (1986), *Sustainable Development of the Biosphere*, Cambridge: Cambridge University Press.

Cohen, S.J. (1993), *MacKenzie Basin Impact Study: Interim Report 1*, Downsview, Canada: Environment Canada.

Cohen, S.J. (1994), *MacKenzie Basin Impact Study: Interim Report 2*, Downsview, Canada: Environment Canada.

Cohen, S.J. (1997), 'Scientist–Stakeholder Collaboration in Integrated Assessment of Climate Change: Lessons from a Case Study of Northwest Canada', *Environmental Modelling and Assessment*, **2** (4), 281–93.

Cohen, S.J., R. Barrett, S. Irlbacher, P. Kertland, L. Mottsch, L. Pinter and T. Zdan (1997), *MacKenzie Basin Impact Study. Final Report*, Vancouver: Environment Canada and University of British Colombia.

Costanza, R. and M. Ruth (1996), 'Dynamic Systems Modelling for Scoping and Consensus Building', European Chapter of the International Society for Ecological Economics, University of Versailles, Paris.

Costanza, R. and M. Ruth (1998), 'Using Dynamic Modeling to Scope Environmental Problems and Build Consensus', *Environmental Management*, **22** (2), 183–5.

Cox, K.K. and J.B. Higginbotham (1976), 'Application of Focus Group Interview in Marketing', *Journal of Marketing*, **40**, 77–80.

de Vries, B. (1995), *SusClime: A Simulation Game on Population and Development in a Resource- and Climate-constrained Two-country World*, Global Dynamics and Sustainable Development Programme, GLOBO Report series no. 11, Bilthoven: RIVM.

den Elzen, M.G.J., A.H.W. Beusen and J. Rotmans (1997a), 'An Integrated Modelling Approach to Global Carbon and Nitrogen Cycles: Balancing their Budgets', *Global Biogeochemical Cycles*, **11** (2), 191–215.

den Elzen, M.G.J., A.H.W. Beusen, J. Rotmans and H.W. Koster (1997b), 'The Biogeochemical Submodel: CYCLES', in J. Rotmans and H.J.M. de Vries (eds), *Perspectives on Global Change: The TARGETS Approach*, Cambridge: Cambridge University Press.

Douglas, M. (1982), *Essays in the Sociology of Perception,* London: Routledge & Kegan Paul.

Douglas, M. and A. Wildavsky (1982), *Risk and Culture: Essays on the Selection of Technical and Environmental Dangers*, Berekley: University of California Press.

Dowlatabadi, H. and M.G. Morgan (1993a), 'Integrated Assessment of Climate Change', *Science*, **259**, 1813–14.

Dowlatabadi, H. and M.G. Morgan (1993b), 'A Model Framework for Integrated Studies of the Climate Problem', *Energy Policy*, **21** (3), 209–21.

Dürrenberger, D., J. Behringer, U. Dahinden, A. Gerger, B. Kasemir, C. Querol, R. Schüle, D. Tabara, F. Toth, M. van Asselt, D. Vassilarou, N. Willi and C. Jaeger (1997), 'Focus Groups in Integrated Assessment: A Manual for a Participatory Tool', ULYSSES working paper WP-97-2, Darmstadt University of Technology, Darmstadt, Germany.

EC-DGXI (1996), 'Vision 2020: Scenarios for a Sustainable Europe', European

Commission, Directorate General XI, Environment, Nuclear Safety and Civil Protection, General Consultative Forum, Brussels.
Edmonds, J. and J.M. Reilly (1985), *Global Energy: Assessing the Future*, Oxford: Oxford University Press.
Edmonds, J., H. Pitcher, N. Rosenberg and T. Wigley (1994), 'Design for the Global Change Assessment Model', in *Integrative Assessment of Mitigation, Impacts and Adaptation to Climate Change*, Laxenburg, Austria: IIASA.
Funtowicz, S.O. and J.R. Ravetz (1990), *Uncertainty and Quality in Science for Policy*, Dordrecht: Kluwer.
Gallopin, G., A. Hammond, P. Raskin and R. Swart (1997), 'Branch Points: Global Scenarios and Human Choice: A Resource Paper of the Global Scenario Group', Polestar Series Reports no. 7, Stockholm Environment Institute, Sweden.
Grin, J., H. van de Graaf and R. Hoppe (1997), *Technology Assessment through Interaction: A guide*, The Hague: SDU.
Hausrath, A. (1971), *Venture Simulation in War, Business and Politics*, New York: McGraw-Hill.
Hilderink, H.B.M., E. Mosselman, A.H.W. Beusen, M.B.A. van Asselt, M.G.J. den Elzen, P.J.F. de Vink and J. Rotmans (1998), *Targets 1.0 (CD-ROM)*, Bussum, The Netherlands: Baltzer Science Publishers.
Holling, C.S. (1978), *Adaptive Environmental Assessment and Management*, London and New York: Wiley; revised 1990.
Hordijk, L. (1991), 'Use of the RAINS Model in Acid Rain Negotiations in Europe', *Environmental Science and Technology*, **25** (4), 596–603.
ICIS (1998), *Limburg in Perspective: A first inventory* (in Dutch), Maastricht: International Centre for Integrative Studies (ICIS).
ICIS (1999), *Het Denkmodel voor POL*, Maastricht: International Centre for Integrative Studies (ICIS).
IPCC (1996), *Climate Change 1995: Impacts, Adaptations and Mitigation of Climate Change: Scientific – Technical Analyses*, Cambridge: Cambridge University Press.
Jäger, J. (1998), 'Current Thinking on Using Scientific Findings in Environmental Policy Making', *Environmental Modelling and Assessment*, special issue: 'Challenges and Opportunities for Integrated Environmental Assessment', ed. J. Rotmans and P. Vellinga (eds), **3** (3), 143–53.
Jaeger, C. *et al.* (1997), *ULYSSES – Urban Lifestyles, Sustainability and Integrated Environmental Assessment – Towards a Polylogue on Climate Change and Global Modelling*, Darmstadt, Germany: Darmstadt Technical University.
Kahn, H. and A. Wiener (1967), *The Year 2000*, New York: Macmillan.
Kasemir, B., J. Jäger and C. Jaeger (2001), *Public Participation in Sustainability Science*, Cambridge: Cambridge University Press.
Kasemir, B., M.B.A. van Asselt, G. Dürrenberger and C.C. Jaeger (1999), 'Integrated Assessment: Multiple Perspectives in Interaction', *International Journal of Environment and Pollution*, **11** (4), 407–25.
Kassler, P. (1994), 'Energy for Development', *Shell Selected Papers*, London: Shell.
Lashof, D.A. and D.A. Tirpak (1989), *Policy Options for Stabilizing Global Climate*, Washington: US Environmental Protection Agency.
Lave, L.B. and H. Dowlatabadi (1993), 'Climate Change: The Effects of Personal Beliefs and Scientific Uncertainty', *Environmental Science and Technology*, **27** (10), 1962–72.
Manne, A.S., R. Mendelsohn and R.G. Richels (1994), 'MERGE: A Model for Evaluating Regional and Global Effects of GHG Reduction Policies', in *Integra-*

tive Assessment of Mitigation, Impacts and Adaptation to Climate Change, Laxenburg, Austria, pp. 143–2.

Matsuoka, Y., M. Kainuma and T. Morita (1995), 'Scenario Analysis of Global Warming using the Asian–Pacific Integrated Model', *Energy Policy*, **23** (4/5), 357–72.

Meadows, D., J. Richardson and G. Bruckmann (1982), *Groping in the Dark: The first decade of global modeling*, New York: John Wiley & Sons.

Meadows, D.H., D.L. Meadows, J. Randers and W.W. Behrens (1972a), *The Limits to Growth*, New York: Universe Books.

Meadows, D.L., D.H. Meadows and J. Randers (1972b), *Dynamics of Growth in a Finite World*, Cambridge: Wright-Allen Press.

Mintzer, I. (1987), 'A Matter of Degrees: The potential for controlling the greenhouse effect', Research Report no. 5, World Resource Institute: Washington.

Morgan, G.M. and M. Henrion (1990), *Uncertainty: A Guide to Dealing with Uncertainty in Quantitative Risk and Policy Analysis*, New York: Cambridge University Press.

Morgan, M.G. and H. Dowlatabadi (1996), 'Learning from Integrated Assessment of Climate Change', *Climatic Change*, **34**, 337–68.

Morita, T., Y. Kaihuma, H. Harasawa, K. Kai, L. Dong-Kun and Y. Matsuoka (1994), 'Asian–Pacific Integrated Model for Evaluating Policy Options to Reduce GHG Emissions and Global Warming Impacts', National Institute for Environmental Studies, Tsukuba, Japan.

Morita, T., M. Kainuma, H. Harasawa, K. Kai, L. Dong-Kun and Y. Matsuoka (1995), 'The Asian Pacific Integrated Model: What can it Predict? A collection of AIM simulation results, National Institute for Environmental Studies, Tsukuba, Japan.

Nordhaus, W.D. (1979), *The Efficient Use of Energy Resources*, New Haven: Yale University Press.

Nordhaus, W.D. (1992), 'The DICE Model: Background and Structure of a Dynamic Integrated Climate Economy', Yale University.

Nordhaus, W.D. (1994), *Managing the Global Commons: The Economics of Climate Change*, Cambridge, MA: MIT Press.

Nordhaus, W.D. and D. Popp (1997), 'What is the Value of Scientific Knowledge? An Application to Global Warming using the PRICE Model', *Energy Journal*, **18** (1), 1–45.

Nordhaus, W.D. and Z. Yang (1995), 'RICE; a regional dynamic general equilibrium model of optimal climate-change policy', *American Economic Review*, **86**, 741–65.

Parson, E.A. (1996a), 'A Global Climate Change Policy Exercise: Results of a test run, July 27–29, 1995', International Institute for Applied Systems Analysis (IIASA), Laxenburg, Austria.

Parson, E.A. (1996b), 'How Should We Study Global Environmental Problems? A plea for unconventional methods of assessment and synthesis', International Institute for Applied Systems Analysis (IIASA), Laxenburg, Austria.

Parson, E.A. (1996c), 'Three Dilemmas in the Integrated Assessment of Climate Change', *Climatic Change*, **34**, 315–26.

Parson, E.A. (1997), 'Informing Global Environmental Policy-making: A Plea for New Methods of Assessment and Synthesis', *Environmental Modelling and Assessment*, **2** (4), 267–80.

Parson, E.A. and K. van den Fisher (1997), 'Integrated Assessment Models of Global Climate Change', *Annual Review of Energy and the Environment*, **22**, 589–628.

Peck, S.C. and T.J. Teisberg (1992), 'CETA: A Model for Carbon Emissions Trajectory Assessment', *The Energy Journal*, **13** (1), 55–77.
Platform on Science and Ethics (1995), 'Workshop reports on the societal debate on genetic research', Rathenau Institute, The Hague.
Ravetz, J.R. (1997), 'Integrated Environmental Assessment Forum: Developing Guidelines for Good Practice', ULYSSES WP-97-1, Darmstadt University of Technology, Darmstadt: Germany.
Rayner, S. (1984), 'Disagreeing about Risk: The Institutional Cultures of Risk Management and Planning for Future Generations', in S.G. Hadden (ed.), *Risk Analysis, Institution and Public Policy*, Port Washington: Associated Faculty Press.
Rayner, S. (1991), 'A Cultural Perspective on the Structure and Implementation of Global Environmental Agreements', *Evaluation Review*, **15** (1), 75–102.
Risbey, J., M. Kandlikar and A. Patwardhan (1996), 'Assessing Integrated Assessments', *Climatic Change*, **34**, 369–95.
Robinson, J.B. (1992), 'Of Maps and Territories: The Use and Abuse of Socioeconomic Modelling in Support of Decision-making', *Technological Forecasting and Social Change*, **42**, 147–64.
Rotmans, J. (1986), 'The Development of a Simulation Model for the Global CO_2 Problem', RIVM 840751001, Bilthoven, The Netherlands (in Dutch).
Rotmans, J. (1990), *IMAGE: An Integrated Model to Assess the Greenhouse Effect*, Dordrecht: Kluwer Academic.
Rotmans, J. (1998a), 'Global Change and Sustainable Development: Towards an Integrated Conceptual Model', in H.-J. Schellnhuber and V. Wenzel, *Earth System Analysis : Integrating Science for Sustainability*, Berlin: Springer, pp. 421–53.
Rotmans, J. (1998b), 'Integrated thinking and acting: a necessary good', ICIS, Maastricht, the Netherlands (in Dutch).
Rotmans, J. (1998c), 'Methods for IA: The Challenges and Opportunities Ahead', *Environmental Modelling and Assessment*, **3**(3), 155–79.
Rotmans, J. and H. Dowlatabadi (1998), 'Integrated Assessment of Climate Change: Evaluation of Methods and Strategies', in S. Rayner and E. Malone (eds), *Human Choice and Climate Change: An International Social Science Assessment*, Washington: Battelle Press, pp. 292–377.
Rotmans, J. and M.B.A. van Asselt (1996), 'Integrated Assessment: A growing child on its way to maturity', *Climatic Change*, **34** (3/4): 327–36.
Rotmans, J. and M.B.A. van Asselt (1999), 'Perspectives on a Sustainable Future', *International Journal for Sustainable Development*, **2** (2): 201–30.
Rotmans, J. and B.d. Vries (1997), *Perspectives on Global Change: The TARGETS Approach*, Cambridge: Cambridge University Press.
Rotmans, J., M.B.A.v. Asselt, A.J.d. Bruin, M.G.J.d. Elzen, J.d. Greef, H. Hilderink, A.Y. Hoekstra, M.A. Janssen, H.W. Koester, W.J.M. Martens, L.W. Niessen and H.J.M.d. Vries (1994a), 'Global Change and Sustainable Development', RIVM (National Institute of Public Health and the Environment), Bilthoven, The Netherlands.
Rotmans, J., M. Hulme and T. Downing (1994b), 'Climate Change Implications for Europe: An Application of the ESCAPE Model', *Global Environmental Change*, **4** (2), 97–124.
Rotmans, J., M.B.A. van Asselt, A.J. de Bruin, M.G.J. den Elzen, J. de Greef, H. Hilderink, A.Y. Hoekstra, M.A. Janssen, H.W. Koster, W.J.M. Martens, L.W. Niessen and H.J.M. de Vries (1994c), 'Global Change and Sustainable Development: A

Modelling Perspective for the Next Decade', National Institute of Public Health and the Environment (RIVM), Bilthoven, The Netherlands.
Rotmans, J., H.J.M. de Vries, M.B.A. van Asselt, A.H.W. Beusen, M.G.J. den Elzen, H.B.M. Hilderink, A.Y. Hoekstra and B.J. Strengers (1997a), 'Towards Integrated Assessment of Global Change', in J. Rotmans and H. J. M. de Vries (eds), *Perspectives on Global Change: The TARGETS approach*, Cambridge: Cambridge University Press, pp. 223–38.
Rotmans, J., M.B.A. van Asselt and H.J.M. de Vries (1997b), 'Global Change and Sustainable Development', in J. Rotmans and H. J. M. de Vries (eds), *Perspectives on Global Change: The TARGETS approach*, Cambridge: Cambridge University Press, pp. 1–14.
Rotmans, J., M.B.A. van Asselt, H.J.M. de Vries, A.H.W. Beusen, M.G.J. den Elzen, H.B.M. Hilderink, A.Y. Hoekstra, M.A. Janssen, H.W. Koster, L.W. Niessen and B.J. Strengers (1997c), 'The TARGETS model', in J. Rotmans and H.J.M. de Vries (eds), *Perspectives on Global Change: The TARGETS approach*, Cambridge: Cambridge University Press, pp. 33–54.
Rotmans, J., M.B.A. van Asselt, S. Peters and J. Mellors (1999a), 'VISIONS Progress Report 1998–99', ICIS, Maastricht.
Rotmans, J., C. Anastasi, M.B.A. van Asselt, S. Peters, J. Mellors, S. Greeuw and D. Rothman (1999b), 'VISIONS for Europe', ICIS, Maastricht, The Netherlands.
Rotmans, J., M. van Asselt, C. Anastasi, D. Rothman, S. Greeuw and C. van Bers (2001), 'Integrated Visions for a Sustainable Europe: Summary of Project Results and Visions', ICIS, VISIONS, Maastricht, the Netherlands.
Schneider, S. (1997), 'Integrated Assessment Modelling of Climate Change: Transparent rational tool for policy making or opaque screen hiding value-laden assumptions?', *Environmental Modelling and Assessment*, **2** (4), 229–50.
Schneider, S.H. (1989), 'The Changing Global Climate', *Scientific American*, **261** (3), 38–47.
Thompson, M. (1997), 'Cultural Theory and Integrated Assessment', *Environmental Modelling and Assessment*, **2** (3), 139–50.
Thompson, M., R. Ellis and A. Wildavsky (1990), *Cultural Theory*, Boulder, CO: Westview Press.
Toth, F.L. (1988), 'Policy Exercises', *Simulation and Games*, **19** (September), 235–76.
Toth, F.L. and E. Hizsnyik (1998), 'Integrated Environmental Assessment Methods: Evolution and applications', *Environmental Modelling and Assessment*, special issue: 'Challenges and Opportunities for Integrated Environmental Assessment', J. Rotmans and P. Vellinga (eds), **3** (3), 193–207.
Turner, B.L., W.C. Clark, R.W. Kates, J.F. Richards, J.T. Mathews and W.B. Meyer (eds) (1990), *The Earth as Transformed by Human Action*, New York: Cambridge University Press.
UN (1993), 'World Population Prospects: The 1992 revision', United Nations, Department for Economic and Social Information and Policy Analysis, New York.
UN (1995), 'World Population Prospects: The 1994 revision', New York: United Nations.
UN-DPCSD (1997), 'Critical Trends: Global change and sustainable development', Department for Policy Coordination and Sustainable Development, New York: United Nations.
UNEP (1997), *Global Environmental Outlook*, Oxford: Oxford University Press.

van Asselt, M.B.A. (1994), 'Global Integrated Assessment Models as Policy Support Tools: A Triangular Approach', University of Twente, Enschede.

van Asselt, M.B.A. (2000), *Perspectives on Uncertainty and Risk: The PRIMA approach to decision support*, Dordrecht: Kluwer Academic Publishers.

van Asselt, M.B.A. and N. Rijkens-Klomp (2002), 'A Look in the Mirror: Reflection on Participation in Integrated Assessment from a Methodological Perspective', *Global Environmental Change*.

van Asselt, M.B.A. and J. Rotmans (1995), 'Uncertainty in Integrated Assessment Modelling: A Cultural Perspective-based Approach', National Institute of Public Health and the Environment (RIVM), Bilthoven.

van Asselt, M.B.A. and J. Rotmans (1996), 'Uncertainty in Perspective', *Global Environmental Change*, **6** (2), 121–57.

van Asselt, M.B.A. and J. Rotmans (1997), 'Uncertainties in perspective', in J. Rotmans and B. de Vries (eds), *Perspectives on Global Change: the TARGETS approach*, Cambridge: Cambridge University Press, pp. 205–22.

van Asselt, M.B.A. and J. Rotmans (2001), 'From project to programme: Ulysses' journey from targets to visions', in B. Kasemir, J. Jäger and C. Jaeger (eds), *Public Participation in Sustainability Science*, Cambridge: Cambridge University Press.

van Asselt, M.B.A. and J. Rotmans (2002), 'Uncertainty in Integrated Assessment modelling: From positivism to pluralism', *Climatic Change*, **54**, 75–105.

van Asselt, M.B.A., C.A.H.M. Storms, N. Rijkens-Klomp and J. Rotmans (1998), 'Towards Visions for a Sustainable Europe: An overview and assessment of the last decade of European scenario-studies', ICIS, Maastricht, The Netherlands.

van Daalen, C.E., W.A.H. Thissen and M.M. Berk (1997), 'The Delft Process: Experiences with a dialogue between policy makers and global modellers', Delft University of Technology Faculty of Technology Policy and Management.

van der Sluijs, J.P. (1997), 'Anchoring amid Uncertainty: On the management of uncertainties in risk assessment of anthropogenic climate change', Utrecht University, Utrecht.

van Notten, P. and J. Rotmans (2001), 'The future of scenarios', *Scenario and Strategy Planning*, **3** (1), 4–8.

Weyant, J., O. Davidson, H. Dowlatabadi, J. Edmonds, M. Grubb, E.A. Parson, R. Richels, J. Rotmans, P. Shukla, R.S.J. Tol, W. Cline and S. Frankhauser (1996), 'Integrated Assessment of Climate Change: An overview and comparison of approaches and results', in J.P. Bruce, H. Lee and E. F. Haites (eds), *Economic and Social Dimensions of Climate Change*, Cambridge: IPCC, Cambridge University Press, pp. 371–96.

WRR (1994), *Sustained Risks: A Lasting Phenomenon*, The Hague: SDU Uitgeverij.

Yang, Z., R.S. Eckaus, A.D. Ellerman, J. Fitzmaurice and H.D. Jacoby (1996), *The MIT Emissions Prediction and Policy Analysis (EPPA) Model*, Cambridge, MA: MIT.

PART II

Participatory Frameworks

5. Ecological and economic context of the proposed Paraguay–Paraná Hidrovia and implications for decision making

Emiko Kawakami de Resende and Sylvia S. Tognetti

INTRODUCTION

In complex and controversial environmental decisions, a question that is often the subject of controversy is whether all of the costs and benefits of the proposed action have been considered, how these have been determined, and how they are distributed among various stakeholders. In a watershed context, it is difficult or impossible ever to have the complete information necessary to determine this, because of inherent uncertainty regarding the links between causes and effects: there are multiple causes of environmental degradation, while effects depend on vulnerability and response capacity, as well as on what is measured and counted; this in turn depends on what is valued. In addition, benefits and costs are geographically separated between those upstream and those downstream. This chapter considers the implications for decision making of using information derived from the different methodological approaches used to analyse the potential consequences of developing the proposed Paraguay–Paraná 'Hidrovia' or waterway. Special attention is given to the conservation of biodiversity in the Pantanal. The decision to develop the Hidrovia is generally illustrative of problems associated with development in large river basins, and of conserving biodiversity.

We begin with an overview of the complex ecological and socioeconomic context in which this development scenario occurs, the potential impacts and the assessments that were made. We then contrast these assessments with a participatory approach to integrated assessment. The aim of this is to establish a process for stakeholders to reconsider their values in light of new information, by engaging them in a process of mutual learning; and in negotiation and conflict resolution regarding their rights and responsibilities and the distribution of costs and benefits of potential unintended consequences. It is a process in which stakeholders also provide information about how they might be affected, based on local knowledge, which may contribute towards the generation of new options made possible by this learning process. We show that the main obstacle to implementing such an approach is an institutional one.

DESCRIPTION OF THE AREA

The Pantanal is the largest freshwater wetland in the world and is located in the Upper Paraguay River Basin, which is at the interface of three national political boundaries: of the 496 000 km^2 that it covers, 396 000 km^2 lie in central western Brazil in the states of Mato Grosso and Mato Grosso do Sul. The remainder is found in eastern Bolivia and north-eastern Paraguay. It is also at the interface of four major South American ecosystems that contribute to its vegetation composition – the Amazon tropical rainforest, the cerrado scrub forests of central Brazil, the Chaco semi-arid scrub forest, and subtropical Atlantic humid forest. Within it, ten different ecological subregions have been identified, controlled primarily by the annual flood/drought cycle whose degree of fluctuation also varies in a multi-year pattern, and which regulates water flow downstream by releasing it very slowly. The annual floods are also a source of nutrients responsible for high primary production in otherwise poor and sandy soils. Biodiversity in the Pantanal includes over 650 species of birds (Thomás, personal communication), over 250 species of fish (Britski *et al.*, 1999), of which about ten are caught for commercial purposes, approximately 90 species of mammals, 50 species of reptiles, 1050 butterflies (Brown, 1986), over 1000 plants, and many unidentified insects.

Home to all of this is an immense alluvial plain with a very small elevational gradient. Within the Pantanal, the slope is only 1–3 cm/km from north to south, and 6–12 cm/km from east to west. Thus the rivers are very meandrous, with many oxbow lakes and four large lakes in the western part. In contrast, altitudes in the upper basin range from 80 to 150 metres on the plains, to over 250 metres in the highlands, with some isolated peaks of over 1000 metres (Wade *et al.*, 1993). The rivers, which originate in the highlands, generally drain sandy soils, and deposit large amounts of sediment when they reach the plain. Most of these rivers have elevated sand banks along their margins and, in extreme cases such as the Taquari River, have beds higher than the plain. During the rainy season, the water exceeds these margins, invades the grasslands, and spreads and forms a very extensive inundated area. Because of low declivity, the rain water on the plain produces temporary rivers, regionally called 'corixo' and 'vazante', and replenish the lagoons or 'baias'.

The Pantanal ecosystem is regulated by an annual cycle of flooding and drought, including a multi-year pattern of variability in the magnitude of the fluctuations, or pulses, in the cycle. Hydrologically, it functions as a large sponge that slowly releases the flow of water coming from the upper lands. In 1988, the highest flood of the century occurred, in which all of the Pantanal appeared to be a big freshwater sea, justifying its ancient name, Xaraes Sea. On the other hand, from 1960 to 1974, the floods were so low that people were saying that the Pantanal was drying up and becoming a large desert. When a big flood came in 1974, local people were surprised – most ranchers had no time to save the cattle and many animals died, including native ones.

Total yearly rainfall in the basin is approximately 1100–1500mm, 80 per cent of which falls between November and March (Alfonsi and de Camargo, 1986). Beginning in November, the Pantanal is inundated from north to south along the Paraguay river and from east to west along the main tributaries, the São Lourenço and Taquari rivers, turning it into a vast, shallow inland sea, interspersed with higher unflooded areas. Flooding may last from three to nine months, depending on local elevation, with maximum water levels normally occurring in January and February in the northern and eastern reaches of the Paraguay and its tributaries, and during May and June in the southern areas. After peak floods, the system dries slowly through evaporation, evapotranspiration, absorption and outflow. The area changes to a huge savanna, with open grasslands, isolated pockets of cerrado vegetation, and many shallow water bodies in which a large number of trapped fish attract wading birds and other wildlife.

The Pantanal is one of the world's largest breeding grounds for wading birds, an important migratory bird stopover point, and probably the most important area in South America for wetland birds. Its other wildlife includes a number of unique animals in the world, some of which are nearly extinct elsewhere in Brazil. Among these are the giant anteater, giant river otter, maned wolf, tapir, jaguar, puma, neotropical river otter (*Lutra longicaudis*) and bush dog (*Speothos venaticus*). Most of these are included in the international red book list of endangered species (da Fonseca *et al.*, 1994).

Fish migration, plant flowering, bird breeding and caiman nesting are strongly regulated by, and dependent on, water level. For example, when water levels begin to decrease, migratory fishes (such as curimbata, *Prochilodus lineatus*, a very abundant detritivorous fish), many of which have market value, start to shoal and, by the end of the dry season (generally by September/October), are migrating upstream, forming spectacular shoals. After breeding on the upper reaches of the rivers, they move again downstream (by January/February) and enter the flooded areas to feed. A similar process occurs to alewives carried passively by the river currents into the flooded areas, in which they find food and shelter. They stay there until the water level begins to fall, when the adults return to the main channel (by June/July), and begin another upstream migration.

Success of caiman nesting is also related to flooding intensity and duration. Low and short floods mean few nests and reduced breeding success. The same happens to fish-eating birds like the jabiru stork, woodstork and spoonbill, and to animals like the giant otter and neotropical river otter. They are largely dependent on the flooding and subsequent drought that enable them to get enough food (fish) for their young and themselves.

Population density in the Pantanal region is very low, concentrated on widely scattered ranches, each typically occupied by three or four families. Cattle ranches, which constitute the main economic activity in the Pantanal, are owned by approximately 3500 'fazendeiros' or ranchers. The tradition of cattle ranching in the Pantanal goes back some 200 years. The cattle are raised in a very extensive system (one animal per three hectares) that is based on native pastures. By some estimates, each ranch needs at least 10 000 hectares to be economically viable (Cadavid-Garcia, 1986).

Another traditional activity is fishing, now performed by about 3000 fishermen. It is also attracting increasing numbers of tourists: 46 000 in 1994 (just to fish in the Southern Pantanal) (Catella *et al.*, 1996), and an estimated 60 000 in the entire Pantanal. This has led to increased employment for the local population, in tourism agencies, hotels, airline companies, local commerce and on ships and boats. There is also an increase in ecotourism, for photographing and sightseeing, as well as a special kind of 'jungle tourism' done by young foreign tourists.

Other potential uses of Pantanal resources are natural population management of caiman for skin, meat and other products, capybara for meat and leather, and a feral pig for meat production, now under research by the Pantanal Agricultural Research Center, EMBRAPA, at Corumbá, in the state of Mato Grosso do Sul.

Most of the region's population of about two million live in the highlands surrounding the Pantanal where, in the last 20 years, land use has shifted dramatically towards intensive agriculture and cattle production. Use of great amounts of agrochemicals and poorly planned water management systems have chronic long-term negative effects on the biology and hydrology of the area. Though public attention has recently begun to focus on the impacts of large-scale agricultural operations, given the continuing economic crisis in Brazil and traditionally low concern for environmental values, it may be difficult to achieve meaningful change in agricultural practices in the near future. An exception was the county of Sao Gabriel D'Oeste, which developed an extensive programme of soil conservation in the Coxim River basin, a tributary of the Taquari River.

THE HIDROVIA PROJECT

Historically, the Paraguay River has been used as a waterway for the transport of commercial goods. It has also been an important trade route, both in colonial and modern times. In recent years, because of improved road transport, at least in Brazil, navigation has decreased and a number of operational port facilities have fallen into disuse. The revitalization of this waterway through a development project known as 'Hidrovia' was agreed upon in the late 1980s by the La Plata Basin countries – Argentina, Bolivia, Brazil, Paraguay and Uruguay – as a way to ensure permanent navigation of the Parana–Paraguay waterway, from the interior regions of Brazil and Bolivia to the Atlantic Ocean near Buenos Aires in Argentina (Bucher *et al.*, 1993). It was also seen as a way to integrate the economies of these countries by providing a low-cost transport system for commercial goods. The main objectives of the countries are to transport, along the Paraguay and Parana Rivers, grain, timber, paper and pulp, iron and manganese ores, energetic and vegetal coal, clinker, steel, plaster, calcareous stone, limestone for agriculture, cotton, liquid fuel and fertilizers.

In September 1989, an Intergovernmental Committee on the Paraná–Paraguay Hidrovia (CIH) was created (a) to identify specific projects; (b) to determine the priority of works and projects to be undertaken; and (c) to study the compatibility of applicable laws of the La Plata Basin countries. In 1991, the InterAmerican Development Bank provided the CIH with US$7.5 million to develop technical, financial, social, economical, legal, institutional and environmental studies (Lammers *et al.*, 1994). Support was also provided by UNDP (US$485 000), Fonplata (US$ 1.66 million) and national governments (US$1.35 million), for a total budget of US$11 million.

The main concerns of opponents were that the Hidrovia would involve dredging and straightening of river channels as well as removal of the rock outcrops that regulate the flow of water from the Pantanal. This could have profound effects on flooding and sedimentation problems throughout the river basin (Ponce, 1995), on the biodiversity of the Pantanal itself, as well as on the regional economies. It would also be a catalyst for other related development activities that would lead to industrialization of the region, with cumulative impacts.

The feasibility studies, required to obtain a loan from the InterAmerican Development Bank, included two potential levels of development of 'Hidrovia', modules A and B. Module A represented a short-term, more restricted project, consisting mainly of dredging from Santa Fe (Argentina) to Corumba/Puerto Quijarro (Brazil–Bolivia), including the Tamengo Channel, and signposting from Corumba to Nueva Palmira (Uruguay). This module included the Pantanal region marginally, if removal of the rock bed at Passo do Remanso Castilho in Paraguay were not considered.

Module B was a more ambitious, long-term project intended to make the 1670 kilometres of the Paraguay River navigable through the Pantanal region all year round. Module B entailed the following:

- dredging of the main channel to achieve a permanent width of 50 metres and depth of 3 metres;
- cutting off existing meanders, to reduce travel from Caceres to Corumba by 62 km;
- extraction of rock beds in some places;
- construction of 32 dikes to close river arms between Caceres and Corumba;
- construction of a slope protection system;
- improvement of existing harbours by dredging and constructing new terminals as well as modernization and re-equipment of the existing terminals.

It was estimated that 86.6 million cubic metres would be dredged in ten years. The estimated budget was US$1.1–1.3 billion for construction and US$2.6–3 billion for maintenance and operation, during the period from 1990 to 2015.

ASSESSMENT OF EFFECTS

Under the Brazilian National Environmental Policy, an environmental impact assessment is mandatory. The Pantanal must be given special consideration because it has been designated as a National Heritage site in the Brazilian Constitution, and includes two national protected areas along the Paraguay River: the National Park of Cará-Cará and the Ecological Station of Taiamã. Within Brazil, legal and jurisdictional complexities arise from the fact that the Pantanal region is in the territory of two states – two-thirds is in the state of Mato Grosso do Sul and one third in the state of Mato Grosso. Regionally, there is concern because Argentina, Paraguay and Uruguay have no environmental impact assessment legislation.

Key issues identified in the assessment were hydrological and ecological effects which have consequences for land use and socioeconomic factors.

Hydrological Effects

A principal concern is that channel dredging, cutting off meanders and constructing of dikes and slope protection systems will alter the hydrological regime of the Paraguay River by accelerating water flow, reducing the floodable area and the flooding period. If, as is suggested, the rock beds were removed, the Pantanal would likely lose its sponge-like character which serves as a natural buffer and is responsible for the exceptional stability of water flow through the Paraguay River. In turn, this would result in an overlap of the peak flooding period in both the Parana and Paraguay rivers which would increase the risk of catastrophic rises in the lower Parana River, affecting all the existing human activities, which include petrochemical, chemical and frozen meat processing plants; power plants (including one atomic power plant) and also the city of Buenos Aires. During the dry season, extreme low water levels would be expected along the middle and lower Parana River.

The Pantanal is a region still being formed by the sediments brought down from the highlands. The cutting off of existing meanders and the removal of rock beds would increase the water velocity. As a consequence, sediments currently in the process of stabilization could be carried away by the fast waters, which would initiate a process of erosion from the region and deposition downstream, thereby strongly increasing existing navigation problems on the lower Parana River. More and continuous dredging would then be needed, which would increase the previously estimated costs of the Hidrovia.

Another expected consequence is the lowering of the water table, which would progressively lead to a drier condition and, most likely, to a 'desert', because of the existing sandy soils in most areas of the Pantanal, and to loss of nutrients. As is typical in floodable areas, the nutrient cycle is highly dependent on the nutrients brought from the highlands and deposited in the lowlands by the flood. Life is also directly dependent on the flood level and flooding duration. Hazardous loads transported by the Hidrovia could have strong effects on the Pantanal if spillage occurred, particularly during the flood season.

Ecological Effects

Alteration of the hydrological regime would drastically modify the relationship between land, water and the floodable area. Terrestrial habitats would increase and aquatic habitats would be reduced both temporally and spatially, affecting wetlands, particularly lentic habitats. This would in turn have complex ramifications for the existing food web in the Pantanal region, as is illustrated in the following characterization of ecological relationships.

During the flooding period, detritovorous fishes like *Prochilodus scrofa*, an important commercial fish, enter very shallow water, in order to feed on the periphyton and organic load brought by inundation. Thousands of them can be seen feeding during the flooding season in shallow waters no more than 20 to 50 centimetres deep, where periphyton and organic particulate matter are very abundant. Periphyton grows fast in these shallow areas on submerged vegetation. Young and small fishes feed on zooplankton in open areas and on aquatic insects from the macrophytes. These fishes are eaten in particular by biguá (*Phalacrocorax olivaceus*), a very abundant fish-eating bird, and by most commercial fish. Gastropods and crabs that feed on periphyton beneath the macrophytes are eaten by several economically important fishes, such as pacu (*P. mesopotamicus*) and piavucu (*Leporinus macrocephalus*). The snail-hawk, named gavião-caramujeiro, feeds only on aquatic gastropods.

A particularly vulnerable fish species is *Gymnotus carapo,* widely used as fish bait to catch large catfishes like pintado *(Pseudoplatystoma corruscans)*, cachara (*Pseudoplatystoma fasciatum)* and jaú (*Paulicea luetkeni)*. Both young and adults are only found beneath the macrophytes, where they are protected from predators and feed on abundant aquatic insects. Other related gymnotoid fishes like the *Eigenmannia* species also live only beneath macrophytes, and are also particularly vulnerable, as the growth of macrophytes is directly dependent on flooding.

Small and young fishes are primarily eaten by jabiru stork, woodstork, spoonbill and herons, whose reproductive behaviour is strongly related to the flooding season when food (that is, fish) is very abundant. Very large communal nesting of woodstork, herons and spoonbill can be seen between July and October, when the water level is falling and a great quantity of fish in drying oxbow lakes and temporary rivers is available. A long period of low and short floods, from 1960 to 1974, drastically reduced the population of these birds. Also, nesting and successful nesting of jabirus, a bird that is symbolic of the Pantanal, depends on available fish, which grow during the flood season. Giant otter, a threatened species outside the Pantanal, lives there in good condition, in rivers and oxbow lakes, feeding mainly on fishes.

The success of fish reproduction also depends largely on the flood season for food, growth and shelter. According to local inhabitants, during the long, low-flooding period, fish populations were so reduced in the Paraguay River that they could not see even one fish jumping in the water. Caiman populations at that time were so reduced that a law prohibited their hunting. In short, all these animals, most of them threatened in other parts of South America, would also be threatened in the Pantanal by the Hidrovia project.

The distribution of vegetation in the Pantanal, which comes from the cerrado, the amazonian forest, the Chaco and the subtropical forest, is also largely dependent on the water table. In the Pantanal, maximum differences in the mesorelief are no more than two metres. Small elevations named *cordilheiras* and *capoes* are covered by forests, mainly with cerrado trees, while the surrounding areas, less than two metres below, have grass coverage. Ponds, locally named *baias*, are shallow waters covered by floating and submerged vegetation. Along the rivers, amazonian vegetation influence can be seen through the occurrence of amazonian trees and amazonian victoria-régia, the largest aquatic leafed plant species.

A number of animals depend on grasses and aquatic vegetation. Capybaras live along the rivers and baias, feeding mainly on grasses and aquatic vegetation. Mating occurs in the water, each male having five or more females. When in danger, they dive and stay under water for long periods. The only vigorous and abundant population of marsh deer occurs in the Pantanal (Mauro, 1993), along the marshy areas of the rivers. Its diet consists of soft grasses that grow in these areas. Peccaries and feral pigs feed on roots, insects and small animals found around the ponds, and use the *cordilheiras* and *capão* forest for shelter. Pampas deer is abundant in open grasslands. Jaguars and pumas have abundant food, feeding on herbivorous species like capybara, pampas deer, wild and feral pigs and marsh deer.

Any alteration of the water table would lead towards predominance of forest-type vegetation. This would reduce available food for herbivores, reduce their population and probably reduce the marsh deer population below their minimum viable population size. Reduction of available food could also either reduce the population of jaguars and pumas directly, or induce them to kill more and more calves, in which case they would be increasingly threatened by hunting by the ranchers.

The vegetation distribution is very peculiar in the Pantanal. In some places there is dominance of some species with very large areas covered almost by a single species. Among these are Paratudais (*Tabebuia sp)*, carandazais (*Copernicia sp*) and cambarazais (*Vochysia divergens*), whose occurrence is dependent on the water table, flooding and soil type. So small differences in the water table can kill large areas of forest vegetation, drastically altering the vegetation cover of the region, and consequently, the abundance and distribution of large native animals.

Loss of soil fertility and lowering of the water table may also be expected to lead to depletion of nutrients and groundwater, which would then lead to the conversion of wetlands into dry lands in the areas of the Pantanal more distant from the rivers. Lands now used for cattle ranching could be invaded by woody weeds and rendered unusable (for that purpose).

Effects on Land Use and Livelihoods

In addition to direct impacts on the livelihood of fishermen, ranchers, those employed in tourism and their families, development of the Hidrovia is also expected to stimulate increased agricultural activities in the surrounding highlands, which would increase soil erosion. These were previously considered non-productive areas, which were converted to agricultural uses during the 'green revolution' of the 1960s.

For lack of experience and poor professional assistance, most farmers did not apply soil conservation management or use proper levels of fertilizers and agrochemicals. In the first years, many of them became sick from self-contamination by agrochemicals, and much soil was lost before conservation management practices were initiated. Even now, many farmers, particularly ranchers, are not conscious of the problem. Thus soils continue to be lost through erosion and continue to enter the Pantanal. If the Hidrovia project stimulates grain production, it is expected that even more land would be deforested and cultivated, and more soil eroded and deposited as silt in the Pantanal. Economic development, under these conditions, even if it generates more employment in the highlands, would not be sustainable.

The Hidrovia is also expected to reduce employment currently generated by road transportation of agricultural products. According to studies conducted by the Fundação Centro Brasiliero de Referencia e Apoio Cultural (CEBRAC) (Galinken et al., 1994), employment in road transport pays an average of US$300 a month, while employment generated by the Hidrovia would only pay US$108 a month. This would impoverish rather than improve the lives of workers.

Mineral products that would be transported by Hidrovia, mainly iron and manganese ores, from Bolivia and Brazil to Paraguay and Argentina, depend largely on international markets and also the ability of Paraguay and Argentina to process them for local use or for export. The future of these activities is not clear and international markets are highly uncertain.

Timber, from native forests in Brazil and Bolivia, may be exported, but would produce only temporary employment, because the activity is not sustainable, and would lead to a permanent loss of biodiversity. Native forests in these countries are not normally managed to sustain production, in part because there is not enough knowledge for this, and in part because of short-term economic considerations.

Also directly affected would be the lifestyle of the remaining indigenous populations, many of whom are negotiating return of land and recognition of property rights. The Guató indians who are negotiating the return to their island in the Paraguay River, in the Pantanal, would be directly affected by the Hidrovia, and their chances of survival reduced. Unemployment, as a consequence of the Hidrovia, of local fishermen, of local people involved in fishing tourism and of ranch-employed people would be permanent. The social consequences of unemployment of people who lack the skills required in a modern and rapidly changing society, such as social alienation, abandoned children and increase of teenage prostitution, have unfortunately become all too familiar, particularly in the developing countries.

ECONOMIC ANALYSIS OF THE HIDROVIA PROJECT

The first economic analysis of the Hidrovia project, conducted by Internave (1992), showed a positive net return for the project of 17.88 per cent for the spontaneous integration scenario and 26.22 per cent for the intentional integration scenario. The spontaneous integration scenario is the most conservative and assumes that growth in shipping will occur naturally, while the intentional integration scenario assumes that growth will be stimulated by the formation of a common market from countries of the La Plata Basin. The economic analysis is limited to a simple analysis of benefits resulting from savings in transport costs considering the costs of construction, maintenance and equipment. However, in a review of the Internave analysis, Bucher and Huszar (1995) found that, because of calculation errors, the internal rate of return of the project under such assumptions would actually be 6.2 per cent for the spontaneous integration scenario and 14.4 per cent for the intentional integration scenario.

Two additional shortcomings of the existing economic feasibility study were identified, suggesting that the savings in transport costs attributable to the project are overestimated: it was assumed that, without the project, shipping costs would increase as production in the region increased, but that with the project, these costs would be lower. Three other key assumptions were that transportation costs are US$0.007/ton/km by water, US$0.05/ton/km by road and US$0.017/ton/km by rail; that shippers would always select the least costly shipping method available; and that the only variable costs of water transport were the operating costs of the ships and barges, neglecting the constant dredging operations necessary to maintain the channel.

Another source of uncertainty identified by Bucher and Huszar (1995) that would directly affect shipping costs was that structural and institutional barriers could prevent producers from transferring their current shipping modes to water transport. For example, shippers would have invested in trucks and shipping terminals, have contracted with railroad and warehouses facilities, and would maintain formal and informal relationships with labour suppliers along existing routes. Changes would not be cost-free, or without risk. Moreover, even if there were a desire to change transportation modes, the need to depreciate existing capital before reinvesting in alternative transport equipment, facilities and long-term contracts could preclude shippers shifting from overland to water transport for a considerable time.

An analysis of the same data, by a group of non-governmental organizations (NGOs) –CEBRAC, ICV and WWF (Galinken et al., 1994) – found that, even if the Hidrovia were implemented as planned, and transported the maximum amount of Brazilian grain, the internal rate of return, in this most favourable situation, would be about 12 per cent, which is considered the minimum acceptable rate of return for this kind of project. In what they considered more realistic scenarios, the internal rate of return was lower than 12 per cent. If just some of the environmental costs were considered, even with the assumed maximum level of transport, they estimated that the internal rate of return would be two-thirds of the minimum value that would be accepted by the Intergovernmental Committee of the La Plata Basin.

Subsequent to the preliminary economic feasibility study discussed above, more extensive economic and engineering feasibility studies and an environmental assessment were conducted by the Intergovernmental Committee on the Paraná–Paraguay Hidrovia (CIH), with sponsorship from IDB and UNDP, which were intended to include environmental costs. However, an expert panel convened by two NGOs to review these assessments (Dunne *et al.*, 1997) found that the included costs were arbitrary and represented only a small fraction of potential costs; that impacts that appeared difficult to value were simply assumed to be negligible; and that cumulative impacts and uncertainty were ignored. Methods used to estimate those impacts that were valued were found questionable: for example, impacts were classified as high, medium or low, based on the percentage of resources in an area that were expected to be affected. Following this logic, estimates of decreased yields from fisheries were simply assumed to be a percentage equal to the percentage of water area affected by turbidity, ignoring the complexity of increased hydrological variability and of ecological interactions such as are described in this chapter. Although these studies included biological surveys and surveys of indigenous populations, this information is not reflected in the cost estimates and is presented descriptively, without analysis.

The final estimate of environmental costs, however, is simply based on estimated costs of proposed monitoring and mitigation measures ($1.7 million a year, compared with the $7 million spent on these assessments alone), which the expert panel judged to be a gross underestimate. According to Panayotou (1997) (a member of the expert panel), reasonable estimates of costs of potential impacts could have been obtained with standard contingent valuation surveys that assess willingness to pay to avoid harm and willingness to accept compensation for damages.

VALUATION IN A PARTICIPATORY, CONFLICT RESOLUTION FRAMEWORK

In calling for a 'broader analysis including all of the relevant benefits and costs' (Bucher and Huszar, 1995), an implicit unanswered question is how to decide and agree on what are to be included as costs. To a large extent, this is arbitrary and depends on how the problem is framed, which in turn depends on the interests and perspectives given a voice in the decision process; what are considered to be relevant factors in decision making; and the kinds of solutions proposed. Bucher and Huzsar avoid this issue by simply suggesting that the benefit–cost method is appropriate as a way to rule out areas where development is clearly not cost-effective – which they conclude it would not be if any additional environmental costs were included. However, this does not change the arbitrary nature of the task.

Standard valuation methods used to determine costs and benefits are also problematic when applied to complex problems, particularly in developing country settings. For example, Moran and Moraes (1999), who conducted a contingent valuation (CV) study in the Pantanal to assess the value of the sport fishery, call attention to the difficulty of surveying the affected populations with a single survey instrument, as they come from a wide range of socioeconomic classes. It is also difficult because the resource in question has significant subsistence and non-use values. Use of multiple survey instruments, on the other hand, contribute to a perceptual problem, that of determining what is being valued, and of reconciling the information obtained. Because of perceptual differences, there is also no objective verification of what is being valued and it is difficult to project the results of the survey beyond the socioeconomic group dominant among the survey respondents.

When faced with new kinds of complex problems that are beyond the response capacity of existing institutions, and in which uncertainty and value conflicts are inherent, an adaptive approach to valuation is called for, one that provides stakeholders with the opportunity to reconsider their values in light of new information, and to engage in a process of negotiation and conflict resolution between those with different perspectives. Valuation itself then becomes an institutional problem, of access to participation in the decision-making process (Wynne, 1997). This implies the need for qualitatively different kinds of information than when problems can be defined in narrow technical terms. Given that complete information is unobtainable, there is no 'right price' that can be determined using the 'right methods'. Prices are not simply a matter of supply and demand but, rather, are negotiated and reflect prevailing institutional structures such as property rights, power relationships and the ability to pay to avoid harm (O'Connor and Martinez-Alier, 1998). Standard valuation methods are also not appropriate when public goods are involved, because decisions affect others and cannot be justified on the basis of individual private preferences: to be seen as legitimate, they need to be justified on the basis of how they affect the public rather than individual interests (Jacobs, 1997). A key consideration is what is to be sustained, and this involves social objectives.

From this perspective, environmental problems are viewed as social and political conflicts regarding the distribution of risk among different social groups both in the present as well as between the present and the future (O'Connor, 1997). They may also give rise to conflicting values within individuals, derived from their multiple social roles and interests, as citizens and as consumers (Sagoff, 1988). Identification of existing and potential conflicts can serve to anticipate difficult decisions that will need to be made, and provides an opportunity to reframe problems in a broader context and reconsider what factors are considered relevant to the decision. Often 'explicit value statements about the environment emerge only when these principles are compromised or ways of life are threatened'. The objective of valuation then becomes one of finding an accommodation among multiple and often conflicting goals and aspirations for the future, identifying the resources needed to achieve them, and the difficult choices to be made or opportunities to be forgone (O'Connor, 1997). This implies 'satisficing' of needs and an ideal of achieving symbiosis between different interests, rather than optimization, which presumes a single correct choice in accordance with values revealed by the market.

Narrow and technical definitions of the problem and the use of deterministic valuation methods that do not take uncertainty into consideration merely reinforce such conflict by imposing a particular perspective. Also, by implying that there is a single correct answer, participation is reduced to an exercise in public relations intended to sell an expert point of view that pretends to be value-free. However, value judgments remain implicit in the problem definition. By viewing the problem in a larger context or frame of reference, we can also recognize that decision makers themselves are intrinsic to the system and are influenced by feedbacks, such as pressure from interest groups, rather than neutral external forces who may influence the system through policy and technological instruments for the sake of efficiency.

In the case of the environmental assessment for the Hidrovia project, narrow definition of the project and its impacts, limited to consideration of dredging the channel, in effect excludes not only the construction of ports, barges and service roads that would be associated with it (Dunne *et al.*, 1997), but also most of the issues considered important by many of the stakeholders. In addition to the direct impacts of dredging and consequences of altering the hydrology, a primary concern is with the cumulative impacts that would result from the broader vision of regional development that would be supported by the Hidrovia. This includes expansion of commercial agriculture, mining and processing of iron and manganese ore, and timber export.

For example, not considered are the impacts of expansion of trade and commercial agriculture that are implied by the development of the Hidrovia. These have the tendency to displace small and subsistence farmers, and to favour the larger-scale enterprises, which results in increased economic disparity and land use conflicts that, in a number of other cases, have also been violent. As illustrated by May and Bonilla (1997), previous expansion of trade in the southern cone region, which led to dislocation of Brazilian wheat production to Argentina, has already raised doubts as to whether there is in fact any overall net benefit – after considering the environmental and social costs of labour and land use dislocation in the push country, the environmental costs of intensification in the pull country, and increased transaction costs. If there was, it was not evident in the price of wheat flour in Brazil, which remained the same after opening of trade to Argentine wheat. According to May and Bonilla, the distribution of returns from trade accords and infrastructure investments has more to do with geopolitical imperatives and policy choices that are not revealed in econometric modelling of price response behaviour or cost–benefit analysis, which suggests that resolution of these conflicts requires a political rather than technical arena.

After the Pantanal workshop sponsored by the SCOPE/UNEP project on Ecological Economics and Integrated Assessment, a public forum was held. Participants, in addition to pointing to the need to consider cumulative impacts, specifically called attention to the lack of a relationship between the different assessments conducted for the region – specifically the Hidrovia assessment sponsored by IDB and UNDP, and the conservation assessment for the Upper Paraguay River Basin sponsored by the World Bank in conjunction with regional governments and research institutions. In the expert panel report (Dunne *et al.*, 1997), Panayotou points out that, even within the environmental assessment, there is little or no relationship between estimates of economic value and surveys that were conducted. Salati and Klabin also call attention to the need to evaluate the project in the context of cumulative impacts associated with global climate change.

Although multilateral development agencies in general, and UNDP in particular, are in principle committed to public participation in decision making, the expert panel found participation to be virtually non-existent in the assessment process. As implemented, 'participation' has consisted of unspecified interviews and public meetings for purposes of information exchange, following which public and NGO concerns were formulated as key questions that were then answered with information from the assessment. Information was not properly disseminated to those who would be most affected, who thus did not actually have an opportunity to influence the decision, and appear to have been invited to participate in a decision already made, rather than to negotiate a shared vision of regional sustainable development objectives.

Lack of transparency makes it difficult to determine whether the decision was based on anything other than geopolitical considerations and the interests of those who stand to benefit directly. According to the expert panel (Dunne *et al.*, 1997), no benchmark study of poverty was conducted that could provide a basis for determining whether the project would contribute to poverty alleviation. They also concluded that the project would most likely increase economic disparity. Failure to address such issues in the context of the Hidrovia and similar projects could lead to a crisis of legitimacy for those governmental and multilateral organizations who support these kinds of projects and who have at the same time committed themselves to public participation and to an interpretation of sustainable development as development that meets human needs in the present without sacrificing those of future generations.

Ultimately, the framing of issues and analytical methods used depends on the explicit or implicit policy objective. The cost–benefit analysis decision framework is associated with the objective of weak sustainability, because an underlying assumption is that manufactured capital can substitute for natural capital, that uncertainty can be at least probabilistically quantified, and that values are made commensurable by reducing them to a common denominator of monetary values. At a very minimum, this would need to include environmental costs through some of the standard environmental valuation techniques (for example, defensive expenditure, replacement cost, substitute goods, travel cost and contingent valuation). However, if the objective is strong sustainability, which implies the protection of natural capital, the magnitude of uncertainty and the high stakes associated with proposed and imminent large-scale irreversible development activities suggest the need for a broader approach. At a minimum, such an approach should allow consideration of the proposed development and its impacts in the same context as conservation planning, and provide all stakeholders with an opportunity to express their future aspirations for the region before such decisions are made. This could in turn provide a yardstick or criterion with which to evaluate the cost-effectiveness of the proposed development activities for achieving those aspirations, and to identify the trade-offs and the choices involved.

VALUATION AS AN INSTITUTIONAL CHALLENGE

Participatory processes present an institutional rather than a methodological challenge, and require a process of social learning and capacity building in developed and undeveloped countries alike. Social learning refers to attitude changes among participants in the process, as a result of involvement in working out a mutually acceptable solution to a problem (Webler *et al.*, 1995). By considering 'what is at stake' and 'what kind of a future they want to sustain', mutual interests can be identified that provide the legitimate basis for policy. Coexistence then becomes a problem of design and scenario negotiation. According to Davis (1997), many of the constraints have to do with styles of governance and administration which run counter to democratic or participatory modes of decision making, and cannot be changed by legislation alone or by holding public hearings that are in effect inaccessible to those most affected, and that do not actually provide an opportunity to influence the decision.

Although participation can be expensive and time-consuming, there are also arguments and historical cases showing that the costs of not using a participatory approach in the initial phase can similarly be quite high. According to Hanna (1995), participation can also contribute to economic efficiency because it allows for a better understanding of the resource context, that is, 'a description of resource users, processors, markets, and the analysis of social and economic characteristics of all resource interests'. This in turn provides the basis for designing more effective resource management programmes that reflect their social and environmental context, and allow for anticipation of regulatory implications and conflicts.

Even if the Hidrovia project were to go forward, processes for public participation in decision making would still be important because they would facilitate the development of social and institutional infrastructure that would be crucial to its success beyond the construction stage. According to Ostrom *et al.* (1993), social and institutional infrastructures may be equally important factors because they provide the structure of incentives that determine whether a project will be maintained. In an evaluation of 25 World Bank projects, efforts to enhance institutional capacity at the design stage were found to be a key factor that distinguished twelve of them that remained economically sustainable following the termination of financial and technical support. Such processes also provide a foundation for democracy and would give those affected a means of understanding and adapting to the magnitude of changes that are expected under such circumstances.

An illustration of the costs of not including stakeholders in the early planning stages is seen in the Mississippi river basin, where flood control structures have paradoxically led to an increase in flood damages. The marshlands of the Mississippi delta are also disappearing because these structures prevent silt transport and deposition in these areas. Not included in the extensive costs of flood damages are the costs of extensive basin-wide litigation, loss of trust and destruction of long-term relationships between state governments, as well as the destruction of ecosystems found in the basin of the Missouri river (the major tributary of the Mississippi) as a result of large inequities in the distribution of costs and benefits among stakeholders. Development in that basin was based on the 1944 Pick–Sloan plan, an agreement developed by federal agencies that was intended to benefit all parties in the basin, but which primarily benefited the lower basin states at the expense of the upper basin states. Indian tribes, who legally hold senior water rights in the basin and who paid the highest price through loss of land to flooding for reservoirs and displacement of population, were excluded from the process (Thorson, 1994). Monetary damages in the 1993 flood alone, which brought about the failure of approximately 1000 levees, were estimated at US$16 billion.

The value of a meaningful participatory process in the planning phase of large development projects is perhaps best illustrated in the 'Mackenzie Valley Pipeline Inquiry', which took place in Canada in the 1970s and which challenged Canadian assumptions regarding development in the far north (Berger, 1977, 1988). At the time, there was a controversial proposal to build a 3860 km pipeline from Prudhoe Bay, on the north coast of Alaska, to the southern, interior region of Canada, across the arctic coast, the caribou migration route and the northern Yukon territory. A Canadian Judge, Thomas Berger, was asked by the prime minister, to form a commission to conduct an inquiry by holding public hearings on the subject. The pipeline project was largely viewed as a way to bring northerners into the mainstream economy, and the hearings as little more than a formality. But, in the course of the inquiry, in Ottawa, Judge Berger found a region of conflicting goals, preferences and aspirations, in which organizations both for and against the pipeline claimed to speak for all northerners. So he decided to conduct the inquiry in 'the north', going to 35 communities and hearing testimonies from almost one thousand northerners and 300 experts.

The inquiry brought recognition of the importance of the subsistence economy in a remote region in which the market economy would always be marginal, and that the assumptions that guided the south of Canada would not hold in the far north, even if conventional economic opportunities were to become available. The commission's report, *Northern Frontier, Northern Homeland*, recommended that native land claims issues be resolved first, and that development plans be based on consideration of the northern way of life, thereby creating an opportunity for a vision of progress that included native rights and environmental values. Old problems have not vanished and development activities are still at issue, but the native communities now have a voice in the debate and, as land claims are resolved, take an active role in conservation planning.

The Mississippi case is not unique – it is just one of those with better documented costs. Examples of development projects that became expensive failures are abundant. Within Brazil, the expert panel that reviewed the Hidrovia assessments calls attention to Polonoreste, Carajás, Itaipu, the Trans-Amazonic Highway and the expansion of mechanized soybean cultivation in southern Brazil and Paraguay. Particular mention is made of the Carajás project, which, like the Hidrovia, is a transportation project associated with the expansion of mining and iron ore exports, and where the impacts of induced development have been particularly massive. From the perspective of promoting economic development and poverty alleviation, these are all considered to have resulted in costly failures because of the massive influx of settlers, destruction of natural resources, pollution, land-tenure conflicts and increased concentration of large land holdings (Dunne *et al.*, 1997).

The Berger inquiry may be unique in part because of the scale on which it was conducted. Bridging local, regional and global levels of discourse is a key challenge in an era of globalization and remote control, as decisions are more likely to be influenced by international markets and climatic events such as El Niño than by local conditions. Successes are harder to identify because it depends on how success is defined and who benefits. The development of the Colorado River in the western United States is an example of development that has been perceived by some as 'successful'. However, this was in the past, when the major competing water interests held all of the water rights and little if any consideration was given to impacts on third parties, such as communities left with dry river beds and whose traditional institutional structures for resource management were destroyed. This is changing as the large historical water interests, primarily irrigation and hydroelectric power, are forced to compete with growing urban areas and environmental concerns as well as with legal challenges from Indian tribes. The issue of 'instream flow', that is, whether keeping enough water in the river to support fish and ecosystem integrity is a legitimate use of water or whether it is 'wasteful', reflects an underlying clash between those who value off-stream and in-stream uses of water (National Research Council, 1992). This is not an issue that can be resolved through optimization. As with the Berger inquiry, the end result is a continuing process of conflict resolution and negotiation regarding the distribution of rights and responsibilities.

CONCLUSION

The Hidrovia project is reminiscent of a large number of controversial water development projects, many of which are now being restored at many times the cost of the original development activities. For example, it is estimated that US$2.5 billion is required to restore the Kissimmee River and Lake Okeechobee in the Florida Everglades, with US$276 million being spent just to restore curves, or approximately eight times the cost of the original channelization and straightening (ENR, 1990). Cost–benefit analysis itself was originally developed to support decisions for large and controversial water projects in the early 1930s (Hanley and Spash, 1993; Porter, 1995).

Sparseness of data and complexity of the Pantanal ecosystem both suggest limits to precise predictions of impacts of the Hidrovia project. However, because of its location in the headwaters region of the large international La Plata River Basin, the project has the potential for both local and distant large-scale irreversible impacts on both the hydrological cycle and the scale and extension of the flooding period, on which the Pantanal ecosystem with its exceptional characteristics and level of biodiversity, and its existing traditional economies and their associated land uses and management practices, are closely coupled

Because of irreducible uncertainties, this complexity may be impossible to capture in a technical framework that seeks to establish pathways between all causes and effects of any kind of development project, and it is unlikely that these could ever be compensated for through investments in manufactured capital. It may also lead to the emergence of new kinds of problems and uncertainties that are beyond the realm of past experience and the response capacity of existing institutions. This problem is not one of how to incorporate correctly all of these unknown costs in a cost–benefit analysis, but, rather, one of incorporating multiple perspectives in the decision process, and considering multiple criteria in the decision itself. Regardless of whether or not the Hidrovia project goes forward, the large and regional scale of potential irreversible impacts warrants a more extensive process of public deliberation in the context of an integrated assessment that provides a basis for mutual understanding, if not agreement, between a wide range of interests, and gives a voice to those most affected.

REFERENCES

Alfonsi, R.R. and M.B.P. de Camargo (1986), 'Condições climáticas para a região do Pantanal Mato-grossense EMBRAPA-DDT', in *Anais do 1º Simpósio sobre Recursos Naturais e sòcio-econômicos do Pantanal*, Corumbá, MS: EMBRAPA, Centro de Pesquisa Agropecuária do Pantanal/ Universidade Federal de Mato Grosso do Sul, Brasília (EMBRAPA-CPAP, Documentos, 5), pp. 29–42.

Berger, T.R. (1977, 1988), *Northern Frontier, Northern Homeland – The Report of the Mackenzie Valley Pipeline Inquiry*, revised edn, Vancouver: Douglas & McIntyre Ltd.

Britski, H.A., K.Z. de S. Silimon and B.S. Lopes (1999), *Peixes do Pantanal: Manual de identificação*, Brasilia and Corumbá: Embrapa-SPI, Embrapa-CPAP.

Brown Jr, K.S. (1986), 'Zoogeografia da região do Pantanal Mato-grossense', in *Anais do 1º Simpósio sobre Recursos Naturais e sòcio-econômicos do Pantanal*, Corumbá, MS: EMBRAPA, Centro de Pesquisa Agropecuária do Pantanal/ Universidade Federal de Mato Grosso do Sul, Brasília (EMBRAPA-CPAP, Documentos, 5), pp. 137–78.

Bucher, E.H. and P.C. Huszar (1995), 'Critical Environmental Costs of the Paraguay–Paraná Waterway Project in South America', *Ecological Economics*, **15** (1), 3–9.

Bucher, E.H., A. Bonetto, T.P. Boyle, P. Canevari, G. Castro, P. Huszar and T. Stone (1993), 'Hidrovia: An Initial Environmental Examination of the Paraguay–Paraná

Waterway: Wetlands for the Americas', produced and published by Wetlands for the Americas, with cooperation from the Woods Hole Research Center, Woods Hole, Massachusetts, USA.

Cadavid-Garcia, E.A. (1986), 'Análise técnico-econômica da pecuária bovina do Pantanal. Sub-regiões da Nhecolândia e dos Paiaguás', EMBRAPA-CPAP, Circular técnica, **15**, p. 92.

Catella, A.C., J. Peixer and S.daS. Palmiera (1996), 'Sistema de Controle da Pesca de Mato Grosso do Sul: SCPESCA/MS – I, maio de 1994 a abril de 1995', Corumbá, MS: EMBRAPA-CPAP/SEMADES.

da Fonseca, G.A.B., A.B. Rylands, C.M.R. Costa, R.B. Machado ad Y.L.R. Laite (eds) (1994), *Livro Vermelho dos Mamíferos Brasileiros Ameaçados de extinção*, Belo Horizonte: Fundaçao Biodiversitas.

Davis, S.H. (1997), 'Public Involvement in Environmental Decision-Making – Reflections on the Western European Experience', Research Paper No. 12, Oxford, UK: Centre for the Environment, Ethics and Society (Mansfield College, Oxford University).

Dunne, T., J. Melack, B. Melià, J. Paggi, S.J. de Paggi, T. Panayotou, H. Rattner, E. Salati, I. Klabin, T. Scudder and M. Clemens (eds) (1997), *The Hidrovía Paraguay–Paraná Navigation Project: Report of an Independent Review*, Washington, DC: Environmental Defense Fund (EDF) and Fundação Centro Brasileiro de Referência a Apoio Cultural (CEBRAC).

Engineering News Record (1990), 'River Restoration is Approved', *ENR 224* (8 February).

Galinken, M., S. Guimarães and J.C. Libânio (1994), 'Quem Paga a Conta? Análise Da Viabilidade Econômica', WWF, ICV and CEBRAC, Brasília, DF. Brasil.

Hanley, N. and C.L. Spash (1993), *Cost–Benefit Analysis and the Environment*, Brookfield, US and Aldershot, UK: Edward Elgar.

Hanna, S. (1995), 'Efficiencies of User Participation in Natural Resource Management', in S. Hanna and M. Munasinghe (eds), *Property Rights and the Environment*, Washington, DC: Beijer International Institute of Ecological Economics and The World Bank, pp. 59–68.

Internave Engenharia (1992), 'Hidrovia Paraguai–Paraná. Estudo de viabilidade econômica. Relatório final', Internave Engenharia S.C. Ltda, São Paulo.

Jacobs, M. (1997), 'Environmental Valuation, Deliberative Democracy and Public Decision-Making Institutions', in J. Foster (ed.), *Valuing Nature*, London: Routledge, pp. 211–31.

Lammers, O., D. Moore and K. Treakle (1994), 'Considering the Hidrovia: A Preliminary Report on the Status of the Proposed Paraguay/Paraná Waterway Project', Berkeley, CA: International Rivers Network.

Mauro, R. de A. (1993), 'Abundância e padrão de distribuição de cervo-do-pantanal, *Blastoceros dichotomus* (Illiger,1815), no Pantanal Matogrossense', Dissertação de Mestrado em Ecologia, conservação e manejo de vida silvestre, UFMG, Belo Horizonte MG.

May, Peter H. and O.S. Bonilla (1997), 'The Environmental Effects of Agricultural Trade Liberalization in Latin America: an Interpretation', *Ecological Economics*, **22** (1), 5–18.

Moran, D. and A. de Moraes (1999), 'Contingent Valuation in Brazil: an Estimation of Pollution Damage in the Pantanal', in P.H. May (ed.), *Natural Resource Valuation and Policy in Brazil: Methods and Cases*, New York: Columbia University Press, pp. 143–72.

National Research Council (1992), *Water Transfers in the West: Efficiency, Equity, and the Environment*, Washington, DC: National Academy Press.
O'Connor, M. (1997), 'Environmental Valuation: From the Point of View of Sustainability', in A.K. Dragun and K.M. Jakobsson (eds), *Sustainability and Global Environmental Policy: New Perspectives*, Cheltenham, UK and Lyme, NH, US: Edward Elgar, pp. 149–79.
O'Connor, M. and J. Martinez-Alier (1998), 'Ecological Distribution and Distributed Sustainability', in S. Faucheux, M. O'Connor and J. van der Straaten (eds), *Sustainable Development: Concepts, Rationalities and Strategies*, Dordrecht: Kluwer, pp. 33–56.
Ostrom, E., L. Schroeder and S. Wynne (1993), *Institutional Incentives and Sustainable Development. Infrastructure Policies in Perspective*, Boulder, CO: Westview Press.
Panayotou, T. (1997), 'The Hidrovía Paraguay–Paraná: An Environmental Economist's Perspective', in T. Dunne, J. Melack, B. Melià, J. Paggi, S.J. de Paggi, T. Panayotou, H. Rattner, E. Salati, I. Klabin, T. Scudder and M. Clemens (eds), *The Hidrovía Paraguay–Paraná Navigation Project: Report of an Independent Review*, Washington, DC: Environmental Defense Fund (EDF) and Fundação Centro Brasileiro de Referência a Apoio Cultural (CEBRAC), pp. 169–92.
Ponce, V.M. (1995), 'Hydrologic and Environmental Impact of the Paraná–Paraguay Waterway on the Pantanal of Mato Grosso, Brazil: A Reference Study', San Diego State University.
Porter, T.M. (1995), *Trust in Numbers: The Pursuit of Objectivity in Science and Public Life*, Princeton, NJ: Princeton University Press.
Sagoff, M. (1988), *The Economy of the Earth. Philosophy, Law, and the Environment*, Cambridge: Cambridge University Press.
Thorson, J.E. (1994), *River of Promise, River of Peril: The Politics of Managing the Missouri River*, Lawrence, KS: University Press of Kansas.
Wade, J.S., J.C. Tucker and R.G. Hamann (1993), 'Comparative Analysis of the Florida Everglades and South American Pantanal', Interamerican Dialogue on Water Management, Miami, Florida.
Webler, T., H. Kastenholz and R. Ortwin (1995), 'Public Participation in Impact Assessment: A Social Learning Perspective', *Environmental Impact Assessment Review*, **15**, 443–63.
Wynne, B. (1997), 'Methodology and Institutions – Value as Seen from the Risk Field', in J. Foster (ed.), *Valuing Nature? Economics, Ethics and Environment*, London and New York: Routledge, pp. 135–52.

6. Collaborative planning and co-management: the development plan for Zudañez, Chuquisaca, Bolivia

Claudia E. Natenzon and Héctor A. Poggiese

INTRODUCTION

As is generally known, Latin America is at a crux in the search for its own development path. The reinstatement of political democracy in most of its countries has not in itself been enough in the face of economic adjustment and social fragmentation.

FLACSO Argentina has been developing and applying its own methodology for addressing the formulation of public policies and for elaborating development projects. Its application fosters democratic decision making, and could therefore be considered an example of the exercise of post-normal science (Funtowicz and Ravetz, 1993). In post-normal science, complex problems in which there are high stakes and high uncertainty require the participation of stakeholders in the decision-making process because these decisions involve value judgments that cannot be made by experts alone. Also, diverse perspectives are needed even to define such problems.

The description of a case to which such methodology has been applied in the past few years will enable us to illustrate some of its characteristic features. This project was initiated at the request of a non-profit, non-governmental organization (henceforth NGO): PROAGRO (Promotores Agropecuarios), which has been active in the province of Zudañez (Dept. Chuquisaca, Bolivia) since 1984. This NGO originally directed its actions towards rural development and, more specifically, to the improvement of peasant agricultural production, the main economic activity in the province.

However, five years later, local circumstances forced its members to admit the impossibility of acting solely on the modernization of agricultural techniques. Little by little, they had to deal with other questions related to basic structural issues affecting the population, such as their educational capacity, health, means of transport, cultural values and nutrition. The situation also required them to address political and management issues both at the heart of the local community and in its relations with other levels of public management.

In other words, they found that agricultural modernization was a complex problem that they could not face alone if they wanted to succeed; rather, the situation required that they develop a strategy for collaboration that would then indicate a course of action. A key element was the need to find common interests with traditionally opposed or distant sections located at different levels (local, provincial, departmental, national and even international), with diverse perceptions of reality and distinct cultural backgrounds.

In 1990, the directors of PROAGRO took part in a seminar on Collaborative Planning Methodology conducted by FLACSO lecturers and organized by the Departmental Council for Social Development in Chuquisaca, under the auspices of the Departmental Prefecture and UNESCO. On that occasion a proposal was presented to perform a practical application of FLACSO methodology to the Zudañez province. The proposal was accepted and developed, culminating in the joint elaboration of core strategies for a Development Plan for the Zudañez province in April 1992.

Thus, from its very outset, the project counted on the association of diverse institutions as a model for action: an NGO, PROAGRO; a governmental institution, the Departmental Prefecture of Chuquisaca; and an academic institution, FLACSO. This initial association, and the initiative developed expressly by FLACSO, which consisted of a methodology for institutional action through co-management, served to articulate the roles of other institutions and areas related to the provincial reality. These included the Departmental Federation of Chuquisaca Peasants, the Zudañez Civic Committee, the Corporation for the Development of Chuquisaca (CORDECH), the Ministry of Agricultural Affairs, the Departmental Sanitary Unit, the major university, several educational institutions and other social development NGOs.

MATERIAL STUDIED, AREA DESCRIPTIONS, METHODS, TECHNIQUES

The Case Studied

The Province of Zudañez is part of the Chuquisaca Department, in Bolivia. It is located in the eastern Andean range, with an area of 3108 km^2. According to 1988 data, Zudañez had 37 112 inhabitants. The urban population was less than 50 per cent of the total population (see Table 6.1). The landscape is mountainous, irregular and abrupt, with soils of low productivity and reduced agricultural extensions. Heights range from 2200 to 2800 metres above sea

Table 6.1 Inhabitants of Zudañez main towns

Main towns	Inhabitants
Zudañez (capital)	2 200
Redención Pampa	1 035
Presto	797
Pasopaya	774
Icla	724
Mojocoya	446

Source: CDDS/PROAGRO/FLACSO (1992a).

level. The topography is irregular and consists of high peaks and deep valleys. The climate is temperate, with a mean annual temperature of 15.6°C and annual mean rainfall of 577mm, which occurs mostly in summer, giving rise to a great variety of microclimates. These conditions, which are optimal for productive diversification, are hampered by winter frosts between June and September.

The fluvial system consists of two main rivers: the Guapay or Grande, and the Pilcomayo. The combination of tropical rains and steep slopes generates a high risk of landslides. However, the major hazard for the peasants is the frequent droughts.

According to the Agricultural Census of 1984, only 30 488 hectares were cultivated, less than 10 per cent of the total area. Only 11 049 hectares from the cultivated area were irrigated. Agricultural production included wheat, corn, barley, potatoes, peanuts, green peas, onions, beans and fruits (peaches, apples, grapes and oranges). Zudañez province contributed 28 per cent of the poultry raised in the Chuquesaca department. Livestock (a subsidiary economic activity), consisted of 47 210 sheep, 33 113 goats, 21 769 cows and 6579 pigs.

From a socioeconomic point of view, this province had the lowest indicators in the region, with deficient (or even absent) infrastructure in the areas of health, communication, roads, housing, sanitary installations and, especially, provision of drinking water. The levels of poverty, malnutrition and mortality were high, while the education levels were very low. There was also a housing shortage.

At the time that we worked on this project (1992), the CORDECH revealed the following data for Zudañez: life expectancy of 33 years; infant mortality rate of 220 children per thousand per year; and illiteracy of up to 76 per cent of the population. Given these conditions, population growth was very low in spite of high fertility rates: 1.22 per cent per year. Another contributing factor was the outmigration of young people in search of new job opportunities. The mostly peasant population was distributed among 114 communities of approximately 60 families each.

Zudañez, the capital of the province and the most highly populated city, is 111 kilometres away from Sucre. Its founding was associated with social and economic changes that affected the colonial farms when Bolivia emerged as an independent republic. It was strategically located on the main road from Sucre to Muyupampa, which enabled it to offer transport and travel-related services. It also became a centre of attraction for members of peasant communities, who frequently went there – especially on Sundays – to market their products and to buy other commodities. However, roads were deficient and not fully developed.

In 1992, Zudañez was the focus of the activities developed by many institutions, governmental and non-governmental, religious and lay, national and international (see the list of identified actors in Table 6.2). Their presence indicated the rich social history of the province. Nonetheless, most of them worked on their own projects, with little or no coordination between the different institutions, and without a joint plan for Zudañez (CDDS/ PROAGRO/ FLACSO, 1992a, 1992b).

Methods and Techniques

The FLACSO methodology allows complex management problems to be approached simultaneously in a multisectoral, cross-disciplinary and collaborative fashion. The methodology supports and accompanies the design, start and evaluation of programmes, projects and policies with the collaboration of the broadest possible spectrum of social actors necessary to address the issue (Poggiese, 1994). The 1993 version of the FLACSO Methodology for Integrated Planning and Co-Management was a proposal to go beyond the limits of the traditional planning and production of knowledge for action, through public participation and the expansion of democracy in decision making.

The central idea is to plan during management and manage during planning, by involving actors collectively in a continuous process of modelling the reality that they want to transform and generating conditions conducive to the emergence of new social actors. FLACSO theory and practice, which have evolved in diverse waves over the past two decades, are now being used in projects of regional and local planning and development, and in the elaboration of public choices of great complexity with plurality of stakeholder participation.

Its general characteristics (being interdisciplinary, multisectoral and participatory), facilitate coordination among the different actors, programmes and projects that constantly come and go in any planning process. At present, emphasis is on simultaneity between disciplines, sectors and social levels, which always tends to generate complex and participatory associations. It also increases the importance of the phenomenon of sociopolitical construction of scenarios in which forms of anticipatory management and decision making are practised.

This approach has different principles – sometimes even opposing ones – from those of traditional planning, which had a fragmented and homogenizing view of reality, with proposals prepared in an office without taking into account the historical variables of each particular case and whose technocratic solutions were imposed in a standard and vertical fashion (from higher to lower levels). These characteristics have led to the discrediting of traditional planning in Latin America, since very often its results have remained in beautiful publications without achieving any change in the reality it was intended to modify (Robirosa, 1986; de Mattos, 1986).

In contrast, the concept of planning and management as a single and integrated process is motivated by the need to elaborate viable action strategies. In this way, the methodology is structured as a mechanism that makes the emergence of these types of strategies possible. However, the principal obstacle to obtaining this result is the viability of the use of the proper methodology. In other words, without the methodology, viable strategies are not obtained, but first it is necessary to develop a viable strategy which ensures that the space can accommodate its application.

The construction of the planning scenario as a space for the application of the methodology is in itself a strategy: the political viability of the planning scenario depends on the existence of a political will favourable to its utilization. Thus the methodology contributes to democratization of the decision process, but at the same time it requires a democratic context. The methodology therefore requires certain conditions for its application:

- the political will to accomplish the objective and to associate for that purpose;
- an adequate period of time must be devoted to the preparation of the planning scenario, which also implies an adaptive process to management that involves testing, training and, at the same time, application of the proper methodology in the preparation process;
- in the implementation of the methodology, the planning scenario must be formalized and action strategies must be formulated within it;
- such strategies must be revised after an appropriate period of time.

Experience indicates that there is no necessary relationship between the first two conditions but, if they are not fulfilled, the third becomes merely an academic exercise, with some production of knowledge, but with no better fate than that of other searches and experiences of the social sciences.

Table 6.2 Zudañez identified actors

Acción Cultural Loyola – Institución	Cruz Roja Suiza	Organización Mundial de la Salud
Acción Cultural Loyola – Radio	Dirección de Desarrollo de Comunidades	Organización Panamericana de la Salud
Acción Rural Fé y Alegría	Dirección de Educación Rural	Partidos Políticos
Agrocentral	Dirección de Educación Urbana	Plan de Emergencia Nacional
Alcaldías	Dirección de Saneamiento Ambiental	Plan Internacional de Padrinos
Asociación de Instituciones de Promoción y Educación	Dirección de Telecomunicación Rural	Poder Ejecutivo Nacional
Asociación Nacional de Productores Tuna Cochinilla	Distrito IV° de Salud, Zudañez	Policía de Zudañez
Ayuda Internacional de Los Estados Unidos	Empresa Nacional de Ferrocarriles	Prefectura Departamental de Chuquisaca
Banco Interamericano de Desarrollo	Escuela Normal Rural	Prensa
Banco Mundial	Facultad Latinoamericana de Ciencias Sociales	Programa de las Naciones Unidas para el Desarrollo
Brigada Parlamentaria de Chuquisaca	Fondo de Asistencia al Medio Ambiente	Programa Mundial de Alimentos
Cámara Agropecuaria de Chuquisaca	Fondo de Desarrollo Campesino	Promotores Agropecuarios
Canal de Televisión de Zudañez	Fondo de Inversión Social	Proyectos de Investigación de la Papa y de la Semilla de Papa
Carboneros	Fondo de La Cuenca del Plata	Proyecto Social Cardenal Maurer
Cáritas – Ayuda de La Iglesia Católica	Fondo Internacional de Alimentos	Proyecto Sucre – Ciudad Universitaria
Comité Católico Téveris	Hospital de Zudañez	Registro Civil
Comités Cívicos	Iglesia de Zudañez	Sectas Religiosas

Comunidad Económica Europea	Instituto Geográfico Militar	Servicio Nacional de Caminos
Consejo Departamental de Desarrollo Agropecuario	Instituto Nacional de Estadística	Sindicato Provincial de Maestros
Consejo Departamental de Desarrollo Social	Juzgados Locales	Sindicato Campesino
Consejo Regional de Semillas	MACA – Ministerio de Asuntos Campesinos y Agricultura	Sub Centralías Sindicales Campesinas
Cooperación Técnica Suiza	MACA – Sede Regional/ Sub Inspectorías	Sub Prefectura Provincial de Zudañez
Cooperativa Eléctrica	Ministerio de Educación y Cultura	Supervisión Educativa Provincial
Cooperativas de Productores	Ministerio de Industria y Comercio	Supervisión Educativa Zonal
Cordech – Corporación Regional de Desarrollo de Chuquisaca	Misión Técnica Holanda	Transportistas
Cordech – Gerencia de Ingeniería de Recursos Hídricos	Movimiento Educativo Yachay Wasi	Unidad Sanitaria de Chuquisaca
Cordech – Gerencia de Planificación	Núcleos Educativos Básicos – Directores	Unión de Instituciones del Sur
Cordech – Plan Forestal	Organismo se las UN para la Educación y la Cultura	Universidad Andina
Cordech – Proyecto Norte de Chuquisaca	Organización Internacional del Trabajo	Universidad San Francisco Xavier de Chuquisaca

Source: CDDS/ PROAGRO/FLACSO (1992a, 1992b).

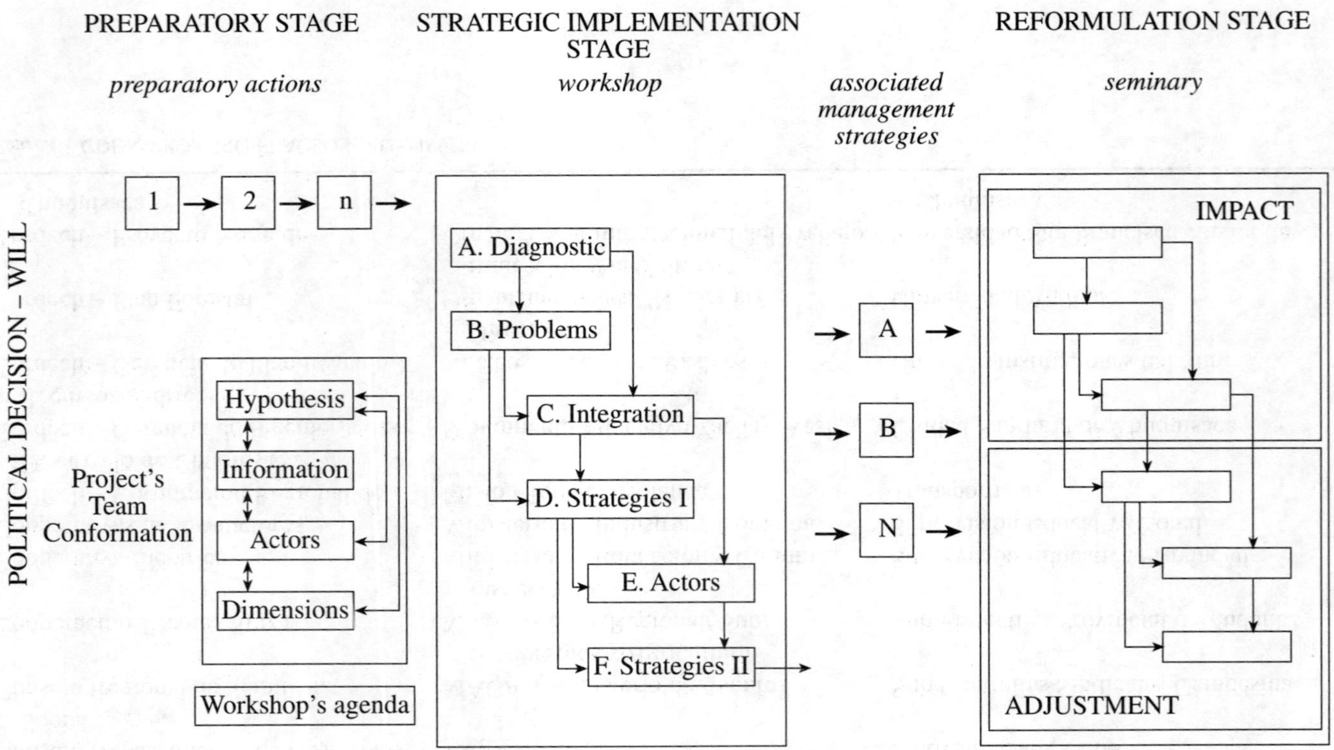

Source: Robirosa (1986), Poggiese (1994).

Figure 6.1 Methodological cycle

In the methodology it is possible to distinguish two components: a three-stage cycle and a particular logical sequence within each stage of the cycle; that is, there are different stages and a distinct form of operational logic in each one of them. The cycle consists of three stages for the formulation of the plan/project: the preparatory stage, the strategic implementation stage and the reformulation stage. Figure 6.1 shows the theoretical relationships between the stages of the cycle and the corresponding sequences.

In the first stage, of preparation, the scenario is only outlined. Its construction is gradual, based on the early interaction among various actors. The 'script' or the argument of each actor is flexible rather than unique. The hypothesis is that the interaction leads to association, that negotiation can broaden the common interest in the entire community, and that the exchange contributes to the increase of knowledge.

In the second, strategic implementation stage, the scenario is more formal, and the rules of the game have been made explicit and agreed upon. Although the result cannot be anticipated, the mechanism by which it will be produced is known: in such a mechanism – the methodology – the rules and procedures are part of the process of agreement and consensus.

In a third stage, of reformulation and adjustment, the association for co-management has materialized, a process of fusion among concepts, method and action is embodied in a group of actors, who, as if they were a single actor, drive and guide the transformation of the decision model and the political culture included in the project.

The planning scenario, prepared under these circumstances, is the basis for the instersubjective reconstruction of the reality in point, a reconstruction that is effected by means of successive approximations and the negotiation of perceptions, objectives and values, where adjustments and reformulations are frequent. This scenario serves simultaneously for decision making, training, negotiation and agreement of/between participants.

RESULTS

For the province of Zudañez, the first and second stages of the cycle, preparation and implementation, took place in 1991/92. This period witnessed the association of political, technical and financing governmental organizations, besides NGOs and peasant organizations. Whenever necessary, meetings were conducted in two languages (Spanish and Kechwa).

The development plan for the Province was formulated as a result of this collaborative design (see Figure 6.2). Major problems in Zudañez were characterized through a series of hypotheses that were then used as basic reference for joint management: a local government without political power and showing no

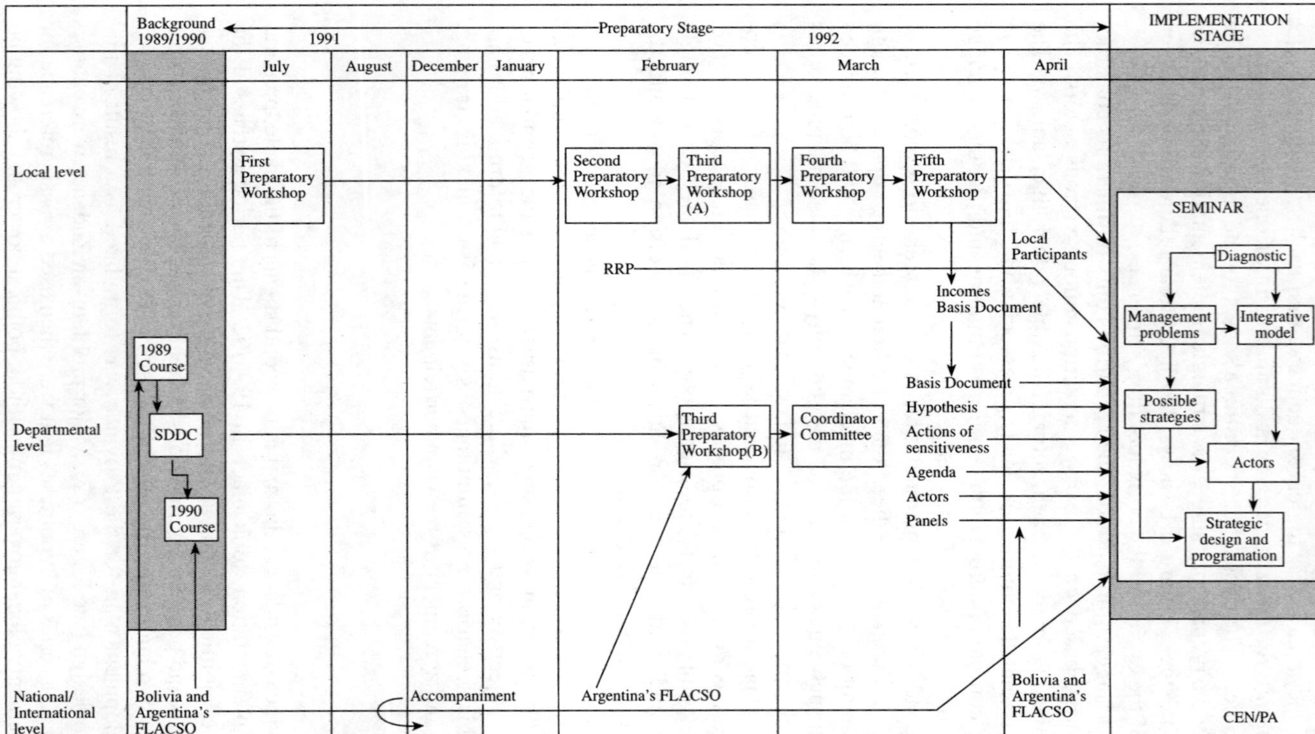

Notes: SDDC (Social Development Departmental Council), RRP (Rapid Rural Poll), FLASCO (Latin American School of Social Sciences).

Figure 6.2 The cycle of FLASCO methodology for the Zundañez development plan

clear reaction in the face of the decentralization process at the national level; a weak economy where agriculture proved hardly productive and farmers' (peasants') nutrition was consequently insecure; deep cultural differences expressed in different languages; a network of scattered settlements and a fragmented rural sphere; and, as a result of insufficient communications, the isolation of the micro region from the rest of the department and of the nation at large.

The integral plan developed during the implementation stage included seven viable strategies to respond to diagnosed problems (CDDS/PROAGRO/FLACSO, 1992b, pp. 79–95). Two strategies were defined with respect to local power:

1. To consolidate the plan's joint management process by setting up a Coordinating Committee. This committee comprised every social actor and guaranteed their interests through participation and consensus; attracted external resources, obtained political support and, at governmental levels, took part in the distribution of resources assigned to Zudañez; coordinated, managed and realized plans and programmes; and promoted other development opportunities.
2. To promote growth and transformation of the peasant organizations into development agents, while permanently enhancing their knowledge and planning/management capacity.

Strategy 3, which concerned the increase in production and sustainability of agricultural development, aimed to consolidate collaborative action through the negotiated construction of innovative alternatives and the strengthening of effective traditional practices so as to ensure the non-degradation of environmental support.

Strategy 4, which concerned marketing, consisted of the development of direct forms of marketing in order to offer products to the market in periods of higher demand, thus consolidating the product specialization of micro regions and the experiences of rural agroindustrialization.

Strategy 5, in the area of nutrition and health, was to articulate group and community resources necessary to guarantee the survival of the population in the short term, while actively waiting for the beginning of productive transformation fostered by the other strategies of the plan.

The aim of strategy 6, in the area of education, was to integrate public (formal education) and non-governmental (alternative education) systems by covering every cycle and including peasant interests.

A final strategy concerned human settlements and the strengthening of the relationship between populated areas and the scattered rural population by means of alternative actions, taking into account that the state resources available were scarce or non-existent.

DISCUSSION AND CONCLUSION

FLACSO Argentina concluded its active role at the end of the implementation stage (1992). The strategy which articulated every action was the first one: the establishment of a Committee for the Coordination of Co-Management, at whose executive head was the Departmental Prefecture, the CORDECH (Corporation for the Development of Chuquisaca), Zudañez's Civic Committee, the Departmental Peasants' Centre, and PROAGRO.

From the methodological angle, the sequence has not completed its third stage yet, probably because of the political changes brought about by the general election in 1993, the problems regarding the financing of the NGO that leads the project, and the changes in the roles of people who are important to the process. Thus the philosophy that pervades joint management has been abandoned in practice.

However, if for a moment we regard it as traditional technical management, the project and its results have meant a crucial step forward for Zudañez Province, to the extent that, in 1994, the Ministry of Human Development – created by the new national government – chose Zudañez as one of nine provinces that would have priority for pilot projects in social development, and it was the only one that was not chosen owing to its critical situation or high risk, but because it already possessed a development plan with specific projects elaborated collaboratively and ready to be implemented.

When co-management mechanisms that enabled the collaborative elaboration of the plan were abandoned, the project took up group actions. In 1995, the situation was assessed against the parameters of the basic dimensions adopted during the implementation stage (Poggiese, 1995):

- reconfiguration of identities – the symbolic confirmation of the multiethnic cultural pluralism continues as long as the plan and its contents (hypotheses, strategies, actions) are taken up at each step of the negotiation;
- reconstruction of the network – the negotiation capacity of the region/province has increased in several aspects; nowadays it has political visibility and organizations with arguments/projects of a larger scope that can be moved from the local to the central level; the plan's philosophy reaches governmental institutions as members of social organizations or NGOs are incorporated in state decision-making levels;
- practical experience of co-management – when joint management was interrupted at a key moment during the implementation stage, the configuration of the new collective actor was blurred, with the effectiveness of negotiations being partly reduced and operated by isolated actors.

Constitutive conditions such as those of the case examined above turn many areas of Latin America into 'losers' in the context of the changes imposed by the process of globalization. Uncertainty is no longer a temporary or circumstantial situation here but a historical and structural feature that is part of its inhabitants' ordinary lives (Natenzon, 1993). In this light, the emergence of instances of post-normal science like that of Zudañez – although rare – aims to handle this uncertainty, acknowledging it and incorporating it explicitly into the formulation of strategies.

It is true that participative democratic practices like this generally require critical situations for decision makers to bring them into the picture, with such practices being abandoned once the crisis is overcome. However, the case set out here (despite the difficulties in communication, the changes in participants, the delays in the times set, even the return to traditional management) demonstrates the existence of tested methods to solve complex problems.

When decisions are to be made, these methods are crucial for the incorporation of every participant involved if the goal is to guarantee the democratic nature of the process while simultaneously managing its turbulence and uncertainty.

ACKNOWLEDGEMENTS

We want to say thanks to Silvio Funtowicz and Sylvia Tognetti, for giving us this opportunity to share our experience.

REFERENCES

CDDS/PROAGRO/FLACSO (1992a), 'Documento Base', *Seminario Taller de Implementación del Plan de Desarrollo de la Provincia Zudañez*, Sucre: PROAGRO.

CDDS/PROAGRO/FLACSO (1992b), 'Plan de desarrollo de la Provincia Zudañez: Estrategias', *Seminario Taller de Implementación del Plan de Desarrollo de la Provincia Zudañez*, Sucre: PROAGRO.

de Mattos, C.A. (1986), 'Paradigmas, modelos y estrategias en la práctica latinoamericana de planificación regional', *Pensamiento Iberoamericano*, 10 (July–December).

Funtowicz, S.O. and J.R.Ravetz (1993), *Epistemología política. Ciencia con la gente*, Buenos Aires: CEAL.

Natenzon, C.E. (1993), 'Gestión asociada y desarrollo rural: una metodología participativa como respuesta a la crisis', *IV° Congreso Internacional*, Mendoza: SOLAR – Sociedad Latinoamericana de Estudios sobre América Latina y el Caribe, p. 10.

Poggiese, H.A. (1994), 'Metodología FLACSO de Planificación – Gestión (Planificación Participativa y Gestión Asociada). Versión 1993', *Documentos e Informes de Investigación*, **163**, Buenos Aires: FLACSO.

Poggiese, H.A. (1995), 'Reconfiguración de identidades, reentramado social, nuevos actores colectivos y modelos de gestión asociada en regiones perdedoras por el impacto de la reestructuración', *Seminario Internacional sobre impactos territoriales de los procesos de reestructuración*, Santiago de Chile: PUC de Chile/Red Iberoamericana de Investigación sobre Impactos Territoriales de la Reestructuración, p. 25.

Robirosa, M. (1986), 'Articulación multidisciplinaria de conocimientos en una metodología integrada para la planificación y gestión ambiental del desarrollo', in E. Leff (ed.), *La problemática del conocimiento y la perspectiva ambiental del desarrollo*, Mexico: Siglo XXI, p. 429.

7. Challenges and opportunities for scientist–stakeholder collaboration in integrated assessment of climate change

Stewart J. Cohen

INTRODUCTION

The Intergovernmental Panel on Climate Change (IPCC) published its Second Assessment Report (SAR) in 1995 (IPCC, 1995). One of its main conclusions was that recent climatic trends cannot be ascribed completely to 'natural' forces. The human influence on the earth's climate is being felt now. This has created a sense of urgency among scientists and stakeholders, particularly on the issue of mitigation of greenhouse gas emissions.

Much of the discussion on policy response in IPCC and the Conference of the Parties (COP) to the United Nations Framework Convention on Climate Change (UNFCCC) is focused on the costs of mitigation options (that is, how to reduce greenhouse gas emissions). Comparatively less information is provided on the benefits of impacts avoided, including adaptation options. This is reflected in IPCC reports (for example, IPCC, 1998, 2001) and the literature on integrated assessment (IA).

Meanwhile, mitigation efforts continue to face challenges. Political support for such efforts is becoming more visible as a result of events associated with the COP-3 meeting in Kyoto in December 1997, but there is still opposition to climate change policy measures in many countries. Emissions are continuing to increase in developed and developing countries (Worldwatch Institute, 2000; UNEP, 1999). Some countries are pursuing voluntary programmes. Several have entered into joint implementation initiatives, now known as 'Activities Implemented Jointly' (AIJ). This set of international development aid initiatives is currently at the pilot stage but is expanding rapidly (Foundation Joint Implementation Network, 2000). Emissions trading has also attracted a great deal of attention (Rolfe, 1998). However, even if Kyoto targets are met, there may be little effect on global temperature or impacts (Parry *et al.*, 1998; Parry and Livermore, 1999).

Since the IPCC and COP have been the focal points for mitigation policy debates, results of IA have attracted considerable attention, and this will certainly continue throughout the coming years. It is appropriate, therefore, to consider whether IA is capturing the full extent of the climate change issue. IA, as a research and learning process, has been the subject of intensive scrutiny and debate since the publication of the IPCC SAR brought integrated assessment models (IAM) into the spotlight (Weyant *et al.*, 1996). Although such models have been under development for a number of years, the policy development process that was launched by the ratification of the UNFCCC has accelerated their application to the climate change issue.

The IPCC considers IA to be a framework for combining knowledge from a wide range of disciplines. Within the SAR and a subsequent special report (IPCC, 1997), the preferred IA methodology has been a modelling approach that enables stakeholders to make informed decisions about mitigation options. These IAMs have played an important role in the analysis of emission reduction (that is, mitigation) options, and the application of such tools has dominated much of the results of IPCC Working Group III. The IPCC SAR included a comparison of 23 IAMs designed to address mitigation (Weyant *et al.*, 1996).

The SAR highlighted the IAMs as the main approach to integrated assessment because of their energy and emission model components, which could enable simulations of different emission paths resulting from various energy policy scenarios. Concerns have been raised (IPCC, 1997) about what was left out of this modelling process, including stakeholder trade-offs in developing countries, and vulnerability concerns related to climate change impacts and adaptation. Using damage functions derived from developed countries may understate the social damage that climate change may cause in developing countries. Morita *et al.* (1997, p. 133) stated that 'it has been argued that simplistic assumptions about the south and a lack of understanding about the southern perspective are inherently imbedded in present IAMs, reflecting what has been described as a lack of procedural equity'. Shukla (1997) noted that socioeconomic dynamics of developing countries are missing from IAMs, including dual economies (traditional and modern), informal activities and land use practices.

Actions that would reduce vulnerability and climate change damages (that is, adaptation) have received considerably less attention (Burton, 1997). This is encouraged by the conventional thinking that impact costs will be less than 2 per cent of GDP in a $2\times CO_2$ scenario[1] for most countries, with the exception of agricultural systems in some developing countries and small island states or other areas vulnerable to sea level rise (see Pearce *et al.*, 1996). Recent analyses in the United States have also suggested relatively low damage costs, depending in part on adaptation assumptions (Mendelsohn and

Neumann, 1999). This is in contrast to the observed increases in total damage costs from extreme events such as floods and windstorms during the 1980s and 1990s (Munich Re Group, 2000). In the United States, this trend is certainly being influenced by urban and regional development patterns, suggesting that current development trends are leading to increased vulnerability (Changnon *et al.*, 2000).

The narrow dimensions of the current debate on climate change may be a consequence of the lack of attention given to the needs of stakeholders who may be affected by the impacts of climate change on land, fresh water and marine resources (Cohen, 1995a, 1995b). Many developing countries may become marginalized in the global dialogue on climate issues if the focus continues to be on greenhouse gas emissions, and not the consequences of failure to control emissions (Hernes *et al.*, 1995). The current disagreement between developed and developing countries over greenhouse gas emission reductions highlights this dilemma, in which developing countries with low per capita subsistence emissions stand to bear the greatest impacts costs, largely because of developed countries' high per capita lifestyle emissions (Jepma and Munasinghe, 1998; Toth, 1999).

Since the publication of the SAR, regional vulnerability issues have been receiving more attention. Recognition of the need for dialogue with stakeholders on regional responses to climate change is influencing the dialogue on IA (for example, IPCC, 1999). This broader dialogue is also considering linkages between climate change and sustainable development (IPCC, 2000). A participatory approach to IA of climate change can contribute to this, as a complement to IAM exercises.

The purpose of this chapter is to explore a more holistic approach to IA of climate change. This approach includes stakeholder participation in the formation of research questions, the generation of new information and the discussion on results and recommendations. This 'learning by doing' approach has been employed in exercises to get stakeholders to identify policy options (Vellinga *et al.*, 1995), but this also assumes understanding of all dimensions of the climate change issue, including the impacts and adaptation dimension. It is suggested that a broad 'scientist–stakeholder collaborative' (s–s collaborative) could be a useful framework for producing an IA of climate change impacts for regions and countries. Such a collaborative could make use of IAMs and other tools, and would also be able to try non-modelling approaches. Some perspectives from the Mackenzie Basin Impact Study (MBIS), a case study from northwest Canada, are included in this discussion.

THREE QUESTIONS FOR INTEGRATED ASSESSMENT OF CLIMATE CHANGE

Impacts research is a complex challenge because it includes physical, biological and socioeconomic aspects. So far, impact assessments have generally been sectoral in dimension. Most assessments in the regional/country context have included several key economic sectors in a parallel sectoral assessment format. They have not explicitly looked at connections between sectors. In principal, IA could do this, and there are some case studies (for example, Rosenberg, 1993; Hulme, 1996; Mortsch and Mills, 1996; Strzepek *et al.*, 1996; Cohen, 1997a, 1997b; Braaf, 1999; JISAO/SMA, 1999; Cohen *et al.*, 2000; Strzepek and Yates, 2000) which have attempted to use various models and other approaches for this purpose. Some of these have included participatory processes. New and continuing case studies from the UNEP Country Studies Program (O'Brien, 2000), the United Kingdom (Mackenzie Hedger *et al.*, 2000), Bangladesh (Huq *et al.*, 1999) and the United States (United States National Assessment, 2000) are also incorporating participatory processes to varying degrees. Rather than relying on a single 'end to end' global model, these case studies have been disaggregated in approach (Parson, 1995) and regional in scale, serving to highlight questions that may be missed by global-scale, mitigation-focused, IA modelling efforts.

What is the Problem with Integrated Assessment?

The main problem with IA of climate change is that it is difficult to determine economic and social costs of impacts, and the benefits of adaptation measures. The idea that adaptation can reduce climate change damage costs originates from experience with current climate variations and extreme events (Burton, 1997; Pielke, 1998; Tol *et al.*, 1998). In the climate change issue, however, IA and IA modelling have been designed to focus primarily on mitigation, not on climate impacts. As a result, stakeholders have generally focused on mitigation alone, without recognizing the costs of inaction or the potential role of proactive adaptation to reduce climate change costs.

This separation of mitigation and adaptation issues is also a separation of emission reduction from vulnerability reduction. The dynamics of the political debates on climate change reflect the consequences of this division. Environmentalists and advocates of sustainable development and proactive mitigation responses have tended to 'leap' from the initial indicator of stress (that is, global temperature increase) to the policy debate over eco-taxes and AIJ. Opponents have done a similar 'leap' but for opposite reasons. This enables them to focus their critical attacks on uncertainties associated with temperature projections, rather than facing broader and more numerous interests associated with potential impacts of scenarios of climate change. Such interests include forestry, parks, water resources, financial services (such as insurance) and aboriginal communities, all of which are affected by current variations in climate. Their futures could follow various paths, depending on changes in technology, institutional arrangements and trading patterns. It is difficult to 'predict' with absolute certainty the role climate change would play, when superimposed on these other changes, so impacts research uses climate model simulations, population projections and other possible futures, as part of assessments of scenarios or plausible pictures of the future.

An IA could construct scenarios of the way regions could evolve over the next 50–100 years, and whether a warmer climate would make a difference. This would tell stakeholders the cost of doing nothing about climate change, thereby providing the context for policy discussions: the 'What Should Be Done' question. This question of policy response needs more contexts than just projections of temperature changes from climate models. Better information on climate change damage may actually be of higher economic value than similar improvements in information on mitigation or atmospheric processes (Nordhaus and Papp, 1997). This is why it is important to raise the profile of the 'What If' and 'So What' questions. The success of future international agreements on climate change will ultimately depend on making this broader discourse a part of the information base being used by regional/national-scale decision makers as they feel their way through this global-scale challenge.

What If?

What if the world becomes warmer because of increased concentrations of greenhouse gases? What would the impacts be for regions and countries? The desired attributes of an assessment of 'what if' should be (a) an interdisciplinary framework, (b) a forward-looking orientation, but one cognizant of scientific uncertainties, (c) a more holistic assessment of the costs of inaction, (d) a focus on places and issues, not disciplines and tools, and (e) a partnership with stakeholders in planning and research. Perhaps there may not be much disagreement regarding the principle that increased interdisciplinarity and stakeholder involvement should be encouraged, but this has not been easy to achieve. Participation from social scientists has not reached a level comparable to those from the natural sciences, while stakeholders face other near-term demands on their time and resources, given the nature of their activities.

There are methodological challenges in providing assessments with these attributes. The use of alternative analytical tools is hindered by lack of data, in part because social and economic data needs are not well defined in the climate change context. This occurs when attempting to incorporate local knowledge, including traditional aboriginal knowledge, into the assessment (see the MacKenzie Basin Impact Study, below).

There are also the 'marketing' aspects of IA, especially identifying the 'risk capital' of the IA community that might attract new partners and shareholders in collaborative research. This is more difficult than it may appear. Stakeholders are naturally suspicious of 'black boxes' and there needs to be some way of improving their transparency. Stakeholders tend to trust local knowledge more than 'science' because the former has been acquired in order to survive, rather than as a product of the curious mind.

So What/What Should be Done?

Does the impacts scenario make a difference to stakeholders' visions of the future? What potential responses to this scenario can be identified? Addressing these two questions in the context of 'what if' would provide similar attributes, including stakeholder ownership through input to the assessment process, a focus on places and issues that is forward-looking, and a dialogue between scientists and stakeholders on the implications of research results. This represents an important opportunity for scientist and stakeholder communities to learn from each other. There are, however, some significant challenges:

- how to overcome the 'leap' of advocates and opponents of proactive measures;
- how to address the 'leap' of sustainable development advocates, who tend to view climate change as a symptom of overuse of energy and other resources, and yet propose alternatives which might increase vulnerabilities to climate change (for example, increased use of renewable resources, densification of urban areas), and
- how to define the role(s) of IA in promoting dialogue.

The latter should include the generation of various adaptation and mitigation scenarios and description of their benefits and costs, compared with the costs of inaction.

IA as a Process

IA is an evolving, non-linear process which can identify problems, raise questions, propose solutions and encourage cross-sectoral learning (Turner and O'Hara, 1996). Such a process requires analytical tools, but, more than that, it is also dependent on the communication skills of its participants. If stakeholders and their knowledge are to be drawn into this process, IA must become less of a 'black box' and more human. This relates both to the use of IAMs and to the personal networks developed by IA participants during an IA exercise. Networking outside one's peer group is a time-consuming process, which generally occurs behind the scenes. It is not 'model development' in the traditional sense, and scientists rarely get the opportunity or the recognition for such activities.

IA is therefore about two kinds of activities: (a) construction or modification of analytical tools (IAMs, other models, non-model approaches) and (b) development of impact research frameworks and networks. IAM construction and IA of regions and countries have not generally involved stakeholder participation, but they have always developed research networks. It may be that, owing to time and resource constraints, many regional and national IAs of climate change impacts have really been framework and network builders, rather than model builders, and would seek out existing analytical tools that could be applied to their particular cases. The case study from Canada (MBIS, below) is an example of both model building (on a small scale), and network building involving researchers (*scientists* from various backgrounds) and people with local knowledge and cultural, financial and/or political investments in the place of interest (*stakeholders*).

SCIENTIST–STAKEHOLDER COLLABORATION

Current practice in IA of climate change can be categorized into nine types of exercises (Table 7.1). Some of these (analogue, education, expert judgment, themes and places) use non-model exercises to combine information, and may be perceived as more accessible to stakeholders, but it is also possible to draw stakeholders into assessments using decision-support models and testing of instruments. A particular s–s collaborative may, in fact, consist of a range of integration exercises. The point is that the issue, rather than a particular analysis tool, should be the guide.

Stakeholders have a role to play in all of these. The non-model exercises do not involve the mathematical 'black boxes', although instrument testing may include the models developed within stakeholder organizations (for example, government departments, hydroelectric utilities). Also participatory approaches must account for the 'mental models' of various interests. Application of the model-based exercises requires considerable discussion with stakeholders in advance of their participation, so that they understand how their input would be used, especially if the technique involves the characterization of goals or preferences. This includes some model-based scenarios, such as population growth. The key is that one or more of these techniques

Table 7.1 Current practice in integrated assessment of climate change impacts and related issues

Type	Description
Analogue and model-based scenarios	(a) assessments of past climatic events and responses as a means of forecasting by analogy, (b) common vision of future climate, economy, institutional arrangements, population, technology and so on
Economic models	cost–benefit analysis, input–output models or other tools which focus on monetary aspects (markets, welfare and so on)
Education	collection of research results into comparative frameworks based on a common protocol, including common climate scenarios
Expert judgment	opinions of experts provided individually or as part of a sample that produces a probabilistic estimate
Decision support models	mathematical models describing performance of systems when constrained by multiple objectives
Integrated assessment models: single sector, 3–4 box and 4-module	system of linked models: (a) within a single sector (such as agriculture); (b) across a 3–4 step continuum from (1) emissions to (2) atmospheric composition to (3) climate/sea level changes [to (4) first-order impacts], and back to (1) impacts affecting emissions; or (c) across 4 modules from (1) pressure, to (2) state, (3) impact and (4) response
Participatory approaches, such as policy exercises, focus groups	assessment of 'lay' knowledge and opinions on trends, scenarios, impacts, policies
Testing of management and policy instruments	assessment of performance of instruments used to manage resources such as harvest quotas, water allocations
Themes and places	issue and/or location serve as an interdisciplinary platform for collection and analysis of information, *and* include models and/or other integrating exercise(s)

Source: Adapted from Cohen (1997b).

could become part of an IA, if an s–s collaborative is established during the planning stages of the assessment.

A Research and Consulting Framework

At the initial stage of an IA of climate change, or other concerns related to sustainable development, the project leader organizes a steering committee composed of scientists and stakeholders with an interest in the issue, because of the topic, or the study area, or both (Cohen *et al.*, 1998b). Government (national, regional, local) and non-governmental (private sector, environmental and other non-government organizations or NGOs, communities) stakeholders need to be part of this (Figure 7.1).

The steering committee would have several tasks as part of its terms of reference. First, it would define critical issues and, if necessary, critical regions within the study area, that the IA should focus on. These might differ from those that would be defined by scientists alone. Second, it would play a role in identifying scenarios for the IA, including baseline economic and population scenarios, which provided context for the climate change impact assessment. Third, it would review and rank proposals for sectoral and cross-sectoral research activities within the IA, using a broad range of criteria. Such activities would have to show that they could address the study's critical issues. Good science, by itself, would not be enough for a high ranking. Finally, it would facilitate communication between (a) scientists and stakeholders, in which research is designed and performed within a policy or decision-making context ('vertical' integration), and (b) scientists of various disciplines, in which the impacts of climate change on a place could be assessed in an interdisciplinary manner ('horizontal' integration). This kind of communication does not necessarily happen on its own.

Scale is an important component of the integration challenge. The s–s collaborative is built on the goal of including those synergies that gives each region a unique relationship with climate and climate change. These synergies can be missed in continental or global-scale aggregation of physical, biological and social processes. Regional stakeholders must therefore be brought in at the earliest stage of the assessment process; that is, during the first iteration of developing the assessment programme.

There is a growing interest in applying participatory approaches that have generally been used in studies of rural development or the collection of traditional ecological knowledge (TEK), but rarely applied in a climate change context (Table 7.2). An example is participatory rural appraisal (PRA) which is widely practised because it engages stakeholders in their places of residence and work, rather than in some other setting (Pretty *et al.*, 1995). There is also an approach from the business community called 'Appreciative Inquiry', which is

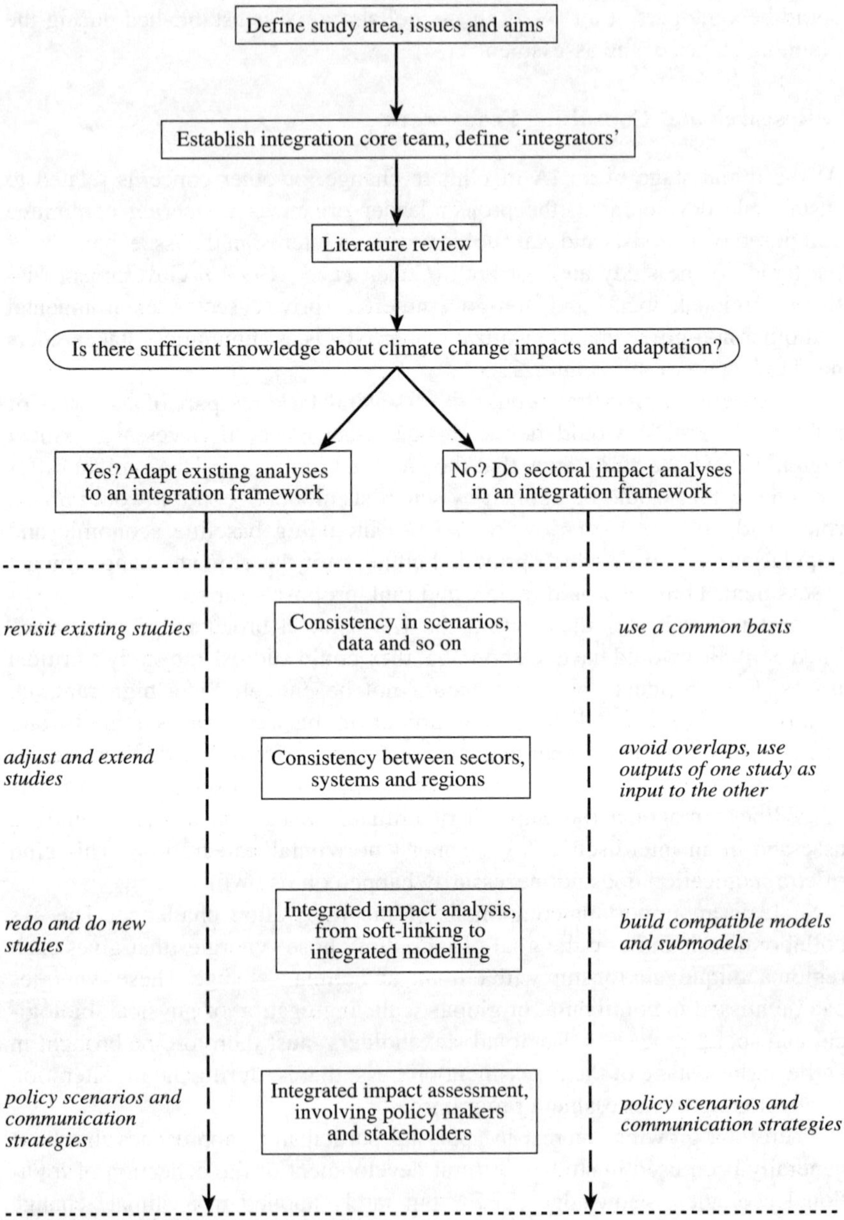

Source: Adapted from Cohen *et al.* (1998b).

Figure 7.1 A framework for integration

Table 7.2 Examples of participatory approaches

	Participatory rural appraisal (PRA)	Participatory action research (PAR)	Appreciative inquiry
Application	rural development	traditional/local knowledge	business
Orientation	practical	academic with community control	practical
Purpose	related to development project; project-oriented	Research-oriented; lengthy process	focus on performance of organization
Process	vision exercise	interviews; answers affected by choice of questions and respondents	vision exercise

directed at identifying what works in an organization, and how to do more of what works (Hammond, 1996). This is meant to help communities visualize a desired future and communicate that vision to decision makers.

An example of applying these approaches is a project to collect aboriginal observations of climate change in a remote community in northern Canada (IISD, 1999, 2000). Another way of doing this is through Participatory Action Research (Ryan and Robinson, 1992; Johnson, 1992), which was initiated for MBIS, but not completed (see below).

IAMs and other models can be used to help stakeholders visualize different futures, as part of an exercise in mutual learning (Rotmans and van Asselt, 1996). This idea is being applied in the ULYSSES project (Kasemir *et al.*, 1997) and in a study on sustainability in British Columbia, Canada (Rothman *et al.*, this volume). Focus groups are part of the former and will likely be used in the latter as well, but there should be opportunities for individual participation. Climate change could become an explicit part of these exercises, and this would help to bring the climate change and sustainable development research agendas closer together (Cohen *et al.*, 1998a).

It is also possible to use the results of first-order impact studies in this context. An example is a case study of the Columbia River Basin, in which stakeholders in water management and water-dependent sectors were asked to react to a scenario of climate-related changes in natural streamflow (Cohen *et al.*, 2000). This approach combines some aspects of PAR and PRA, in that it involves interviews, but is meant to be practical rather than academic, and is aimed at measuring expert judgment rather than community or public opinion. In this case study, questions focused on potential responses to the streamflow scenario by actors in flood control, hydroelectricity production and sales, fish habitat protection and irrigation.

Advantages

The s–s collaborative represents an opportunity for stakeholders to acquire some ownership of the IA. It encourages the development of interdisciplinary approaches to research, and provides common ground for linking scientific expertise ('what if') with stakeholders' knowledge ('so what' and 'what should be done'). There is also the potential for the creation of new data bases and scientist–stakeholder networks that would have value long after the completion of the IA. Most important for analytical purposes, this approach is more likely to be able to describe the *indirect* implications of climate change, which may turn out to be more costly than direct impacts.

Having both hierarchical (vertical) and egalitarian (horizontal) relationships among the members of the collaborative is an important feature of this partnership. Just as a doctor and patient are partners in a patient's health, or an accountant and client are partners in long-term financial planning, so do professional researchers and stakeholders with local knowledge become partners in IA of climate change. In each case, the two dimensions are present. The vertical dimension is where the policy issues are defined (and if necessary, redefined). The horizontal dimension is the platform for technical information exchange that often involves other professionals as well as stakeholders.

Successful collaboratives could lead to post-assessment capacity-building activities. This would make it easier for local interests to stay informed about current research projects and to consider initiating new programmes from within the region rather than waiting for external bodies to do so.

Constraints

By necessity, this approach would involve the recruitment of a diverse group of interested parties. Some of these would participate on a voluntary and/or part-time basis, and their locations would probably be widely scattered. This group might be difficult to manage and coordinate, unless financial resources could be made available to engage these individuals directly as consultants or 'members of the Board'. It may also be difficult to attract regional stakeholders if the IA is initiated and managed from outside the study area. However, stakeholder participation can grow over time, as long as the first steps are taken to build the collaborative (see next section).

There are several considerations of a technical nature that also need to be considered. First, time and resource constraints may create a dependence on existing data sets generated outside the IA. These may be difficult to adapt to the analytical tools being considered for the IA. Second, the wide range of available geographic information systems (GIS) has led to problems in data transfer between systems. A common GIS platform might be appropriate for a collaborative, but this would need to be decided upon at the earliest possible time. This could affect selection of integration exercises for the IA. Finally, requirements to maintain communication among the various parties will require a full-time secretariat for the duration of the assessment. This secretariat would also have to maintain an archive that could be transferred to a permanent location following completion of the assessment.

AN EXAMPLE OF A SCIENTIST–STAKEHOLDER COLLABORATION ON CLIMATE CHANGE: MACKENZIE BASIN IMPACT STUDY (MBIS)

A lengthy description of this case study is available in Cohen (1993, 1994, 1996, 1997a, 1997b, 1997c). A sketch of the MBIS integrating framework is shown in Figure 7.2.

Within this process, several types of integration exercises were used, including models, stakeholder consultation and thematic discussions. Several examples of the participatory process are summarized below.

Adaptation to Current Conditions

Community response to floods was examined in two remote communities within the region (Newton, 1997). Residents and regional authorities were interviewed, and observations of individual and community responses to recent flood events were recorded. Results showed that responses varied both with the physical nature of flooding and with the social networks that developed in each community. Changes in road access had a profound effect on the nature of community response (Table 7.3).

There was also an attempt to use PAR to obtain aboriginal knowledge (TEK) on impacts of past climatic events. Residents of a community along the shore of Great Slave Lake were to have been interviewed in their language, and the researcher would have been living for one or two years in the

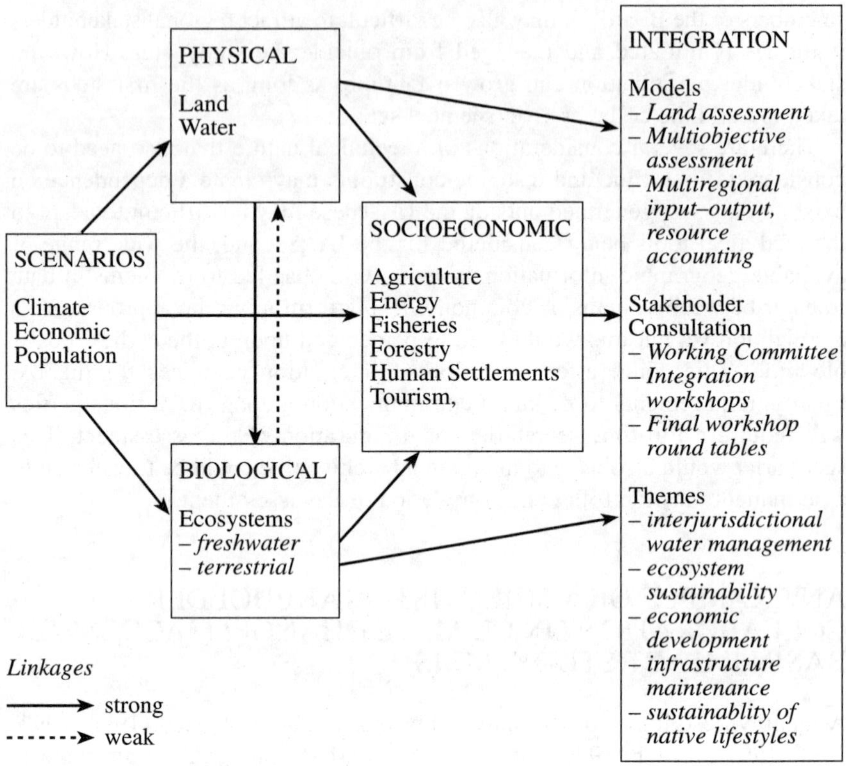

Note: Scenarios were generated for use by physical system and biological system studies. The studies within the physical component were not able to use results from the biological component, so this linkage was weak. The socioeconomic component used results from the physical and biological components, as well as the climate scenario information where appropriate. Integration exercises were based on outputs from these varied sectoral studies.

Source: Cohen, 1997b.

Figure 7.2 Research framework for MBIS

community (Bielawski, 1994; Bielawski and Masuzumi, 1994). This project was never completed owing to the high costs of the PAR approach, including supporting the researcher during the entire period (Cohen, 1997c). For this method to be applied in developing-country settings, support for the investigators could represent an important financial obstacle. Perhaps a linkage with rural development activities would make this feasible.

Table 7.3 Comparison of flood response activities in Aklavik and Fort Liard at three operational levels

	Operational Level					
	Individual		Community		Government	
Response Activities	AK	FL	AK	FL	AK	FL
1. Move belongings to high ground	●	+	●	●	●	●
2. Secure personal belongings	+	+	●	●	●	●
3. Watch children	+	+	●	●	●	●
4. Take an inventory of belongings	+	≈	●	●	●	●
5. Ensure adequate supply of food	+	≈	≈	≈	●	●
6. Have boats & canoes ready	+	≈	+	≈	●	●
7. Conserve water	+	≈	≈	≈	●	●
8. Care for sick & elderly	+	+	+	+	+	≈
9. Monitor ice & water levels	+	+	+	+	+	+
10. Broadcast information	+	≈	+	+	+	+
11. Supply additional resources	●	●	+	+	+	+
12. Establish operations centre	●	●	+	+	+	≈
13. Establish evacuation procedures	●	●	+	+	+	≈
14. Organize reception services	●	●	+	+	+	≈

Note: AK = Aklavik; FL = Fort Liard; + = activity occurs; ≈ = activity does *not* occur; ● = not an area of responsibility or possible action; Aklavik does not have all-season road access and is located in a low-lying area (Newton, 1997).

Perceptions/Opinions of Future Scenarios

Two exercises dealt with individual perceptions of aboriginal responses to future scenarios. The first asked for a listing of physical and biological impacts, and how aboriginal people would be affected if they continued to pursue a traditional aboriginal lifestyle, or if they became more active in the formal wage economy (similar to the dual economy situation described by Shukla, 1997). Results showed that perceptions of impact and vulnerability were influenced by visions of future lifestyles (Aharonian, 1994). The second exercise used input–output modelling and a community survey to look at responses to a potential benefit of warming – an opportunity for expanded activity in the formal wage economy (because of the longer summer) that would force people to relocate from their traditional community if they wanted the employment. Results showed a willingness to accept the opportunity, but there were concerns about social impacts on the community of relocation or creation of commuter workers who would be absent for extended periods (Lonergan *et al.*, 1995; Lonergan and Kavanagh, 1997).

Theoretical Responses within a Model Exercise

Two sectoral exercises looked at potential impacts and adaptation responses through models of sectoral impacts. The first concerned agriculture. Could the region take advantage of a longer growing season to expand wheat production? Results showed that this was possible (given the constraints of the model), but only if expanded irrigation services would be made available (Brklacich *et al.*, 1996, 1997). The side-effects of this were unknown. The second case was a forestry study which showed that commercial yields of softwood lumber would decline because of changing growth potential for these species combined with increased fire frequency. This would offset improvements for hardwood species (Hartley and Marshall, 1997; Rothman and Herbert, 1997). The land assessment framework used a technique known as Analytic Hierarchy Process (AHP) in order to assess stakeholder preferences between pairs of goals (Yin and Cohen, 1994). Results of this exercise were used as input to the land assessment framework, along with the results of the sectoral studies. The integrated scenario assessment indicated that agriculture production would be able to achieve its goals, but there would be shortfalls in softwood (spruce) production and a substantial increase in erosion (Table 7.4). The framework did not assess impacts on water supply.

These changes in potential represented a new vision for stakeholders, and the new trade-offs meant that various renewable resource management issues would have to be reassessed. New opportunities might not necessarily be pursued because of impacts these could have on current land uses, and the policy instruments that regulate them. A new dialogue would need to begin. It was not clear how effective proactive adaptation would be under these circumstances.

Stakeholder Round Tables

Stakeholders were asked to react to the various research results through thematic round table discussions. Information on all of the round tables can be found in Cohen (1997a, 1997b, 1997c).

One of these themes was infrastructure maintenance. Engineers suggested that physical infrastructure, such as roads, airstrips and pipelines, could be repaired or designed differently to meet changing climatic conditions, but there would certainly be increased costs in consequence. It was also suggested that the notion of infrastructure should include education and insurance mechanisms, emergency response, and social and cultural institutions that pool risk and support people in times of stress (Zdan, 1997).

Interjurisdictional water management was considered by a group of stakeholders representing different levels of government, as well as aboriginal

Table 7.4 *Results of land assessment model simulation for base case and climate change impacts scenario, using the GISS climate model and results from MBIS agriculture and forestry studies (Yin* et al.*, 2000)*

		Wheat (t)	Barley (t)	Oats (t)	Hay (t)	Canola (t)	Spruce (m^3)	Pine (m^3)	Deciduous (m^3)	Net return ($)	Soil erosion (t)	Habitat value (bird)
Basic scenario	Goal target	432	767	231	1 517	350	1 198	409	952	102 015	43 511	6 663
	Deviation	0	0	0	0	0	0	0	0	0	0	0
GISS scenario	Goal target	648	1 151	347	2 276	525	1 115	429	808	153 022	43 511	6 663
	Deviation	0	0	0	0	0	–154	0	0	0	+10 715	0

Note: All values are in thousands.

organizations. Recent attempts to manipulate water levels in a freshwater delta were then re-examined in light of observed warming and drying trends in the region. The climate change scenario would lead to further reductions in water levels, and the discussion focused on new legislation that would provide a framework for joint management (Mortsch, 1997). Additional work would be needed to identify a useful set of adaptation strategies that might be considered.

In another thematic context, ecosystem sustainability, it was not clear whether current institutions in the region would be capable of coping with a scenario of simultaneous changes to renewable resources and dependent communities, superimposed on other non-climate stresses affecting the region. During the last fev years in northern Canada, co-management processes have been developing for aboriginal and non-aboriginal (and government) stakeholders concerned with wildlife and water resources. This has been part of a larger trend of devolution of responsibility from central to regional authorities in Canada, a trend that is taking place for reasons other than climate change. However, regional stakeholders see these processes as their best approach to coping with climate change. Within the ecosystem sustainability round table, however, it was noted that climate change would be a new experience for everyone, and that all regional stakeholders would have to learn more about this phenomenon of global change (Irlbacher, 1997).

POST-MBIS ACTIVITIES: WHAT IS THE LEGACY OF THIS PROCESS?

The s–s collaborative operating within MBIS incorporated two kinds of relationships: (a) scientists and stakeholders as partners in setting the research agenda based on policy issues, and (b) scientists leading the individual research activities, with stakeholders providing input (data, responses to surveys, information on sites, issues, infrastructure and so on). This two-dimensional hierarchy was developed because stakeholders were very interested in the overall direction of the research, but they looked to scientists (of various disciplines) to design and lead specific research activities. Stakeholders wanted to provide input, so they did play an important role at this level, too, but they did not serve as principal investigators of any research activities. Perhaps in the future, the working-level arrangement could evolve into a different kind of partnership, similar to that at the 'steering committee' level.

At the MBIS Final Workshop, held in May 1996 (Cohen, 1997a, 1997c), regional stakeholders were asked if the climate change impact scenarios made a difference to their visions of the future. Most of them said 'yes' or 'yes in the long term'. Their views on possible responses to the scenarios included reactive and proactive adaptation, as well as intervention in policy debates at other levels (national, international). Two examples of the latter were (a) participation by the Inuit Circumpolar Conference (an organization that represents Inuit people from Canada, Alaska, Russia and Greenland) at the COP-2 session in 1996 (ECO Newsletter, 1996), and (b) positions taken by the Northwest Territories government during ministerial discussions on climate change within Canada before the 1997 COP-3 session in Kyoto (GNWT, 1997).

The disaggregated approach followed in MBIS presented challenges to successful integration. An advantage was that it did not depend on any single integration exercise. The disadvantage was that there were difficulties in coordinating the various activities (for example, different geographic information system (GIS) formats, and mistiming of outputs from first-order exercises which delayed or prevented their use in higher-order studies), so some opportunities were missed (Cohen, 1997b). This process could be improved in a number of ways, such as ensuring at the outset that a common GIS platform be specified, and selecting integration exercises on the basis of additional criteria (besides a good fit with the rest of the programme, a sound research plan and so on), including commitments to assist in communication between study participants.

These problems were recognized by the collaborative and reflected in the recommendations that emerged from MBIS:

- production of plain language reports;
- establishment of a regionally based structure to serve as an information source on climate change and other global-scale issues;
- support for community-based monitoring programmes to augment those of central authorities; and
- encouragement of efforts to facilitate collaboration between research projects initiated in different regions.

A response from the international research community was the initiation of similar regional assessments in the Bering Sea and Barents Sea regions by the International Arctic Science Committee (Weller and Anderson, 1998; Lange *et al.*, 1999). Each of these is fashioned as an s–s collaborative as well, but customized to meet the unique requirements of these multinational regions.

Within northern Canada, the Yukon Territorial Government and Yukon College established a 'Northern Climate Exchange' office at Yukon College. This serves to meet the second recommendation above, with the important feature that funding for this is shared by both levels of government and the College (Yukon Government and Yukon College, 1998; Northern Climate

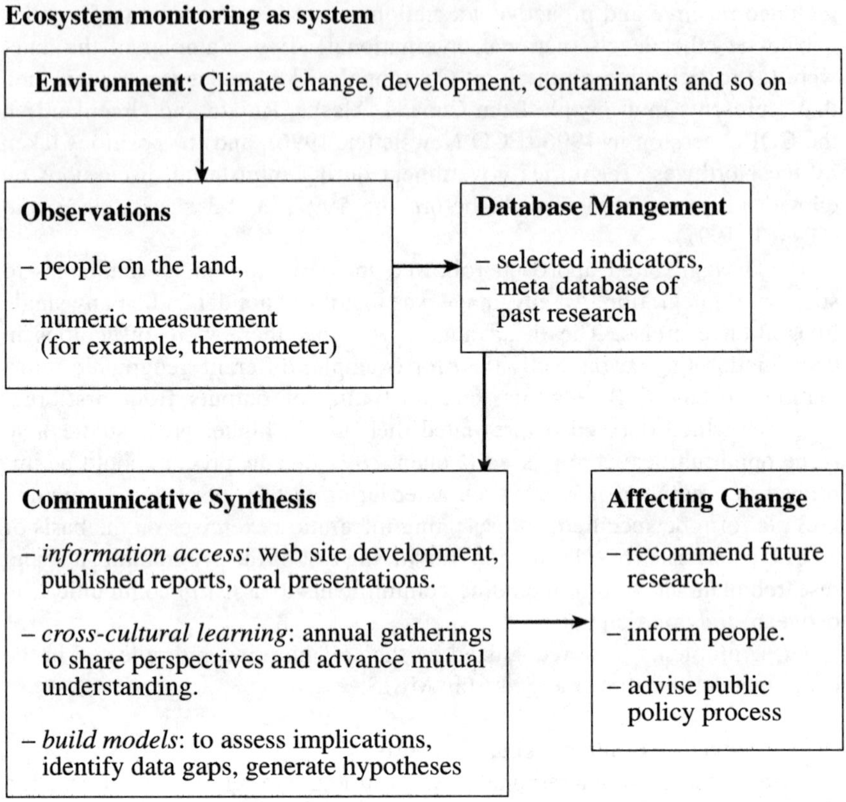

Source: Adapted from Eamer and Kofinas (1998).

Figure 7.3 Role of community-based monitoring in integrated assessment and capacity building

Exchange, 2000). As a direct response to the s–s collaborative, this venture exhibits the influence of a research activity on the formation of social capital, in this case, a common property institution in a local academic setting (Berkes and Folke, 1993). It further feeds into the expressed desire by Arctic stakeholders to create a network of regional institutions under an electronic umbrella known as the University of the Arctic (Young *et al.*, 1998). Such a structure would not be dependent on any individual research study, and would become a fixture of the region over the long term.

Coincident with the Bering Sea study and ancillary activities in Alaska has been the establishment of a community-based monitoring programme in northern Yukon. This serves to engage aboriginal stakeholders in knowledge gathering in partnership with other levels of government (Eamer and Kofinas, 1998). MBIS was not the reason for starting this programme, but it mutually reinforces the effort at building regional capacity to participate in climate change research in a meaningful way, rather than waiting for outside intervention. Community-based monitoring can provide stakeholders with access to information, ownership of information and an opportunity to advise the public policy process (Figure 7.3).

CONCLUSION

A scientist–stakeholder collaborative is offered as an alternative integrating model that can be applied in the context of climate change impacts and adaptation. This can complement continental/global-scale integrated assessment modelling efforts that largely focus on emission limitation.

The collaborative can help in capacity building, providing the foundation for creating a common property institution that focuses on climate change (or global change) stewardship. The Northern Climate Exchange and community-based monitoring are small but important examples. Integration tools of various kinds aid the integration process, but the key is that there is ownership of the issue by stakeholders. This would go beyond those with interests only in fossil fuels or deforestation, and incorporate the wider community of regional stakeholders in sustainable development. Mutual learning could result from this effort, leading to a richer form of integration than could be achieved by models alone (Rotmans and van Asselt, 1996; Rothman and Robinson, 1997; Rothman *et al.*, this volume).

The practical challenge for regional studies in both developed and developing countries is to identify *regional champions* of this process, and attract needed support from both regional and external (international) sources. This raises the question of eligibility of such a process for inclusion in programmes funded by the Global Environmental Facility, or within a joint implementation programme. Since this process focuses on impacts and adaptation, there would need to be a different metric other than emission reductions (or reduction in the rate of growth of emissions), since adaptation and vulnerability issues would have to be part of the way success would be measured.

The regional champion of the collaborative process would have to guide it through its formative stages of consultation, formulation of research questions, selection of research activities and communication. This individual, however, is not 'the boss'. Indeed, there is no boss, and there are no promises/guarantees that this process will achieve integration, or that the results of this exercise will influence decision making within the region/country, or at the international level. What can be said, however, is that it provides an opportunity for building capacity, for bringing in local knowledge and for bringing in narratives (qualitative knowledge), since the process is not restricted to only those kinds of information that can be quantitatively modelled. This process can be customized for the region/country of interest, since the research agenda would be set by the collaborative, within the framework of the global climate change challenge itself.

ACKNOWLEDGEMENTS

The Mackenzie Basin Impact Study (MBIS) was a broad collaborative research effort involving scientists and stakeholders from governments, universities, aboriginal organizations and the private sector. Their contributions are sincerely appreciated. Opinions expressed in this chapter are those of the author, and do not necessarily reflect the views of Environment Canada.

NOTE

1. A doubling of atmospheric CO_2 concentration since the pre-industrial era of the early 19th century.

REFERENCES

Aharonian, D. (1994), 'Land use and climate change: An assessment of climate–society interactions in Aklavik NT', in S.J. Cohen (ed.), 410–20.

Berkes, F. and C. Folke (1993), 'A systems perspective on the interrelationships between natural, human-made and cultural capital', *Ecological Economics*, **5** (1), 1–8.

Bielawski, E. (1994), 'Lessons from Lutsel k'e', in S.J. Cohen (ed.), 74–6.

Bielawski, E. and B. Masuzumi (1994), 'Dene knowledge on climate: Cooperative research in Lutsel k'e, Northwest Territories', in R. Riewe and J. Oakes (eds), *Biological Implications of Global Change: Northern Perspectives*, Edmonton: Canadian Circumpolar Institute, 99–103.

Braaf, R.R. (1999), 'Improving impact assessment methods: climate change and the health of indigenous Australians', *Global Environmental Change*, **9**, 95–104.

Brklacich, M., P. Curran and D. Brunt (1996), 'The application of agricultural land rating and crop models to CO_2 and climate change issues in Northern regions: the Mackenzie Basin case study', *Agricultural and Food Science in Finland*, **5**, 351–65.

Brklacich, M., P. Curran, D. Brunt and D. McNabb (1997), 'CO_2-induced climatic change and agricultural potential in the Mackenzie Basin case', in S.J. Cohen (ed.), 242–6.

Burton, I. (1997), 'Vulnerability and adaptive response in the context of climate and climate change', *Climatic Change*, **36**, 185–96.

Changnon, S.A., R.A. Pielke Jr., D. Changnon, R.T. Sylves and R. Pulwarty (2000), 'Human factors explain increased losses from weather and climate extremes', *Bulletin of the American Meteorological Society*, **81** (3), 437–42.

Cohen, S.J. (ed.) (1993), *Mackenzie Basin Impact Study Interim Report*, 1, Downsview, Ontario: Environment Canada.

Cohen, S.J. (ed.) (1994), *Mackenzie Basin Impact Study Interim Report*, 2, Downsview, Ontario: Environment Canada.

Cohen, S.J. (1995a), 'An interdisciplinary assessment of climate change on northern ecosystems: The Mackenzie Basin Impact Study', in D.L. Peterson and D.R. Johnson (eds), *Human Ecology and Climate Change: People and Resources in the Far North*, Bristol, USA: Taylor and Francis, 301–16.

Cohen, S.J. (1995b), 'Mackenzie Basin Impact Study: broadening the climate change debate', *Ecodecision*, **17**, 34–7.

Cohen, S.J. (1996), 'Integrated regional assessment of global climatic change: lessons from the Mackenzie Basin Impact Study (MBIS)', *Global and Planetary Change*, **11**, 179–85.

Cohen, S.J. (ed.) (1997a), *Mackenzie Basin Impact Study (MBIS) Final Report*, Downsview, Ontario: Environment Canada, MBIS web site [http://www.msc-smc.ec.gc.ca/airg/pubs/mbisfinal.htm].

Cohen, S.J. (1997b), 'Scientist–stakeholder collaboration in integrated assessment of climate change: lessons from a case study of Northwest Canada', *Environmental Modeling & Assessment*, **2**, 281–93.

Cohen, S.J. (1997c), 'What if and so what in northwest Canada: Could climate change make a difference to the future of the Mackenzie Basin?', *Arctic*, **50** (4), 293–307.

Cohen, S., D. Demeritt, J. Robinson and D. Rothman (1998a), 'Climate change and sustainable development: Towards dialogue', *Global Environmental Change*, **8** (4), 341–71.

Cohen, S.J., R. Tol and A. Magalhaes (1998b), 'Integration', in UNEP, ch. 4.

Cohen, S.J., K. Miller, A. Hamlet and W. Avis (2000), 'Implications of climate change for the Columbia River Basin', *Water International*, **25** (2), 253–72.

Eamer. J. and G. Kofinas (1998), Personal communication, web site for Arctic Borderlands Ecological Knowledge Co-operative and Sustainability of Arctic Communities under Global Change [http://www.taiga.net/index.html].

ECO Newsletter (1996), 'Voice of Inuit Denied, and Inuit Statement', in COP2 – Geneva NGO Newsletter, numbers 6 & 7, 17 & 18 July, Climate Action Network; web site: [http://www.igc.apc.org/climate/Eco.html].

Foundation Joint Implementation Network (2000), *Joint Implementation Quarterly*, **6** (2), Foundation JIN, Groningen; web site: [http://www.jiqweb.org].

Government of the Northwest Territories (GNWT) (1997), 'Statement by the Honourable Stephen Kakfwi, Minister of Resources, Wildlife and Economic Development', news release, 19 November.

Hammond, S.A. (1996), *The Thin Book of Appreciative Inquiry*, Dallas, Texas: CSS Publishing Co.

Hartley, I. and P. Marshall (1997), 'Modeling forest dynamics in the Mackenzie Basin under a changing climate', in S.J. Cohen (ed.), 146–56.

Hernes, H., A. Dalfelt, T. Berntsen, B. Haltsmark, L.O. Naess, R. Selrod and A.

Aaheim (1995), 'Climate Strategy for Africa', CICERO Report 1995:3, Center for International Climate and Environmental Research, Oslo.

Hulme, M. (ed.) (1996), *Climate Change and Southern Africa: An Exploration of Some Potential Impacts and Implications in the SADC Regions,* World Wide Fund for Nature and Climate Research Unit, Norwich.

Huq, S., Z. Karim, M. Asaduzzaman and F. Mahtab (eds) (1999), *Vulnerability and Adaptation to Climate Change for Bangladesh*, Dordrecht: Kluwer.

Intergovernmental Panel on Climate Change (IPCC) (1995), 'The 1995 Second Assessment Report. Synthesis Report and Summaries for Policymakers', World Meteorological Organization, Geneva.

Intergovernmental Panel on Climate Change (IPCC) (1997), *Climate Change and Integrated Assessment Models (IAMs) – Bridging the Gaps*, ed. O.K. Cameron, K. Fukuwatari and T. Morita, Proceedings of the IPCC Asia–Pacific Workshop on Integrated Assessment Models, United Nations University, Japan: 10–12 March 1997. Center for Global Environmental Research, Tsukuba Japan.

Intergovernmental Panel on Climate Change (IPCC) (1998), *The Regional Impacts of Climate Change – An Assessment of Vulnerability*, ed. R.T. Watson, M.C. Zinyowera and R.H. Moss, a special report to Working Group II, New York: Cambridge University Press.

Intergovernmental Panel on Climate Change (IPCC) (1999), *Development and Climate Change in Africa: Opportunities for Integrated Assessment*, ed. M. Kok and B. Heij, Report of the IPCC Workshop on Integrated Assessment of Climate Change in Africa, 22–25 November, 1998, Kadoma Zimbabwe; Dutch National Research Programme on Global Air Pollution and Climate Change (NRP), Bilthoven, Netherlands.

Intergovernmental Panel on Climate Change (IPCC) (2000), *Climate Change and its Linkages with Development, Equity and Sustainability*, ed. M. Munasinghe and R. Swart, proceedings of the IPCC Expert Meeting held in Colombo, Sri Lanka, 27–29 April, 1999; World Meteorological Organization, Geneva.

Intergovernmental Panel on Climate Change (IPCC) (2001), Climate Change 2001: *Impacts, Adaptation and Vulnerability*, ed. J. McCarthy, O. Canziani, N. Leary, D. Kokken and K. White, contribution of Working Group II to the Third Assessment Report of the Intergovernmental Panel on Climate Change, New York: Cambridge University Press.

International Institute for Sustainable Development (IISD) (1999), 'Inuit Observations on Climate Change', Trip Report 1, 15–21 June, Sachs Harbour Northwest Territories. International Institute for Sustainable Development, Winnipeg [http://www.iisd.ca].

International Institute for Sustainable Development (IISD) (2000), 'Inuit Observations on Climate Change', Trip Report 3, 14–21 February, Sachs Harbour Northwest Territories, International Institute for Sustainable Development, Winnipeg [http://www.iisd.ca].

Irlbacher, S. (1997), 'Sustainability of Ecosystems', in S.J. Cohen (ed.), 50–54.

Jepma, C.J. and M. Munasinghe (1998), *Climate Change Policy: Facts, Issues and Analyses*, Cambridge: Cambridge University Press.

JISAO/SMA Climate Impacts Group (1999), 'Impacts of Climate Variability and Change: Pacific Northwest', JISAO/SMA Climate Impacts Group, University of Washington, Seattle, JISAO Contribution 715.

Johnson, M. (ed.) (1992), 'Lore: Capturing Traditional Environmental Knowledge',

Dene Cultural Institute, Hay River, and International Development Research Centre, Ottawa.

Kasemir, B. and 16 others (1997), 'Focus groups in integrated assessment: The ULYSSES pilot experience', ULYSSES working paper WP-97-4; ULYSSES web site [http://zit1.zit.tudarmstadt.de/ulysses].

Kerr, J.A. (1997), 'Future water levels and flows for Great Slave and Great Bear Lakes, Mackenzie River and Mackenzie Delta', in S.J. Cohen (ed.), 73–91.

Lange, M.A., S.J. Cohen and P. Kuhry (1999), 'Integrated global change impact studies in the Arctic: the role of stakeholders', *Polar Research*, **18** (2), 389–96; Barents Sea Impact Study web sites: [http://www.urova.fi/~arktinen/basis.htm], [http://basis.uni-muenster.de].

Lonergan, S. and B. Kavanagh (1997), 'Global environmental change and the dual economy of the North', in S.J. Cohen (ed.), 298–306.

Lonergan, S., B. Kavanagh, R. Cox, R. DiFrancesco, L. Nayally and G. Hardisty (1995), 'Two economies: the implications of climate change in Canada's North for a First Nations community', Centre for Sustainable Regional Development, University of Victoria, and The Pedzeh Ki First Nation; submitted to Mackenzie Basin Impact Study, Environment Canada, Downsview, Ontario.

Mackenzie Hedger, M., M. Gawith, I. Brown, R. Connell and T. Downing (eds) (2000), *Climate Change: Assessing the Impacts – Identifying Responses. The first three years of the UK Climate Impacts Programme (UKCIP)*, Oxford: UKCIP Technical Report and Department for Environment Transport Regions; web site: [http://www.ecu.ox.ac.uk/ukcip.htm].

Mendelsohn, R. and J.E. Neumann (eds) (1999), *The Impact of Climate Change on the United States Economy*, Cambridge: Cambridge University Press.

Morita, T., P.R. Shukla and O.K. Cameron (1997), 'Epistemological gaps between Integrated Assessment Models [IAMs] and developing countries', in IPCC, 127–38.

Mortsch, L. (1997), 'Interjurisdictional water management', in S.J. Cohen (ed.), 46–9.

Mortsch, L. and B. Mills (eds) (1996), *Great Lakes – St. Lawrence Basin Project. Progress Report One*, Downsview, Ontario: Environment Canada.

Munich Re Group (2000), *Annual Review of Natural Catastrophes 1999. Munich Re Topics, 7th Year – 2000*, Munich: Munich Re.

Newton, J. (1997), 'Coping with floods: An analogue for dealing with the transition to a modified climate in the northern sector of the Mackenzie Basin', in S.J. Cohen (ed.), 219–24.

Nordhaus, W.D. and D. Papp (1997), 'What is the value of scientific knowledge? An application to global warming using the PRICE model', *The Energy Journal*, **28** (1), 1–45.

Northern Climate Exchange (2000), 'Northern Climate Exchange Workshop: Taking Action on Climate Change in the Yukon', Yukon College, Whitehorse, 15–17 May; web site: [http://www.taiga.net/nce/may2000workshop.html].

O'Brien, K. (ed.) (2000), 'Developing Strategies for Climate Change: The UNEP Country Studies on Climate Change Impacts and Adaptations Assessment', United Nations Environment Programme, and Center for International Climate and Environmental Research (CICERO), Oslo; CICERO Report 2000:2.

Parry, M. and M. Livermore (eds) (1999), 'A new assessment of the global effects of climate change', *Global Environmental Change*, **9**, Supplementary Issue.

Parry, M., N. Arnell, M. Hulme, R. Nicholls and M. Livermore (1998), 'Adapting to the inevitable', *Nature*, **395**, 741.

Parson, E.A. (1995), 'Integrated assessment and environmental policy making: In pursuit of usefulness', *Energy Policy*, **23**, 463–75.

Pearce, D.W., W.R. Cline, A.N. Achanta, S. Fankhauser, R.K. Pachauri, R.S.J. Tol and P. Vellinga (1996), 'The Social Costs of Climate Change: Greenhouse Damage and the Benefits of Control', in J.P.Bruce, H. Lee and E.F. Haites (eds), *Climate Change 1995: Economic and Social Dimensions of Climate Change*, Contribution of Working Group III to the Second Assessment Report of the Intergovernmental Panel on Climate Change, Cambridge: Cambridge University Press, 179–224.

Pielke, R., Jr (1998), 'Rethinking the role of adaptation in climate policy', *Global Environmental Change*, **8** (2), 159–70.

Pretty, J., I. Guijt, I. Scoones and J. Thompson (1995), 'A Trainers Guide for Participatory Learning and Action', International Institute for Environment and Development, London.

Rolfe, C. (1998), 'Turning Down the Heat: Emissions Trading and Canadian Implementation of the Kyoto Protocol', West Coast Environmental Law Research Foundation, Vancouver.

Rosenberg, N.J. (ed.) (1993), *Towards an Integrated Impact Assessment of Climate Change: The MINK Study*; reprinted from *Climatic Change*, **24** (1–2), Dordrecht: Kluwer.

Rothman, D.S. and D. Herbert (1997), 'The socio-economic implications of climate change in the forest sector of the Mackenzie Basin', in S.J. Cohen (ed.), 225–41.

Rothman, D.S. and J.B. Robinson (1996), 'Growing pains: a conceptual framework for considering integrated assessments', *Environmental Monitoring and Assessment*, **46**, 23–43.

Rotmans, J. and M. van Asselt (1996), 'Integrated assessment: a growing child on its way to maturity', *Climatic Change*, **34**, 327–36.

Ryan, J. and M.P. Robinson (1992), 'Implementing participatory action research in the Canadian North: a case study of the Gwich'in language and cultural project', *Culture*, **X** (2), 57–71.

Shukla, P.R. (1997), 'Socio-economic dynamics of developing countries: Some ignored dimensions in integrated assessment', in IPCC, 165–82.

Strzepek, K.M. and D.N. Yates (2000), 'Responses and thresholds of the Egyptian economy to climate change impacts on the water resources of the Nile River', *Climatic Change*, **46** (3), 339–56.

Strzepek, K.M., D.N. Yates and D.E.D. El Quosy (1996), 'Vulnerability Assessment of Water Resources in Egypt to Climatic Change in the Nile Basin', *Climate Research*, **6** (2), 89–95.

Tol, R., S. Fankhauser and J. Smith (1998), 'The scope for adaptation to climate change: what can we learn from the impacts literature?', *Global Environmental Change*, **8** (2), 109–23.

Toth, F.L. (ed.) (1999), *Fair Weather? Equity Concerns in Climate Change*, London: Earthscan Publications.

Turner, R.S. and F.M. O'Hara, Jr. (1996), 'Integrated Assessment of Climate Change: Characterizing Key Policy Issues', Report of a DOE Workshop on the Integrated Assessment of Climate Change, Washington, June 1994; U.S. Department of Energy, contract number DE-AC05-84OR21400.

United Nations Environment Programme (UNEP) (1998), *Handbook on Methods for Climate Change Impact Assessment and Adaptation Strategies*, ed. J.F. Feenstra, I.

Burton, J.B. Smith and R.S.J. Tol, Version 2.0, October; Nairobi: United Nations Environment Programme and Amsterdam: Institute for Environmental Studies (IVM), Vrije Universiteit; web site: [http://www.vu.nl/ivm/handbook].

United Nations Environment Programme (UNEP) (1999), *Global Environment Outlook 2000*, Nairobi: United Nations Environment Programme and London: Earthscan Publications.

United States National Assessment (2000), 'United States National Assessment of the Potential Consequences of Climate Variability and Change', web site: [http://www.nacc.usgcrp.gov/].

Vellinga, P., H. Hisschemoller, J.H.G. Klabbers, M.M. Berk, R.J. Swart and A.P. van Ulden (1995), 'Climate change, policy options and research implications', in S. Zwerver, R.S.A.R. van Rompaey, M.T.J. Kok and M.M. Berk (eds), *Climate Change Research: Evaluation and Policy Implications*, Amsterdam: Elsevier, 119–34.

Weller, G. and P.A. Anderson (1998), 'Implications of global changes in Alaska and the Bering Sea Region', proceedings of a Workshop, June 1997, Center for Global Change and Arctic System Research, University of Alaska, Fairbanks, Alaska, USA; Bering Sea Impact Study web site: [http://www.besis.uaf.edu].

Weyant, J., O. Davidson, H. Dowlatabadi, J. Edmonds, M. Grubb, R. Richels, J. Rotmans, P. Shukla, R. Tol, W. Cline and S. Fankhauser (1996), 'Integrated assessment of climate change: An overview and comparison of approaches and results', in J.P. Bruce, H. Lee and E.F. Haites (eds), *Climate Change 1995 – Economic and Social Dimensions,* Intergovernmental Panel on Climate Change, Cambridge: Cambridge University Press, 367–96.

Worldwatch Institute (2000), *Vital Signs 2000*, Washington: Worldwatch Institute.

Yin, Y. and S.J. Cohen (1994), 'Identifying regional goals and policy concerns associated with global climate change', *Global Environmental Change*, **4** (3), 246–60.

Yin, Y., S. Cohen and G.H. Huang (2000), 'Global climate change and regional sustainable development: the case of the MacKenzie Basin in Canada', *Integrated Assessment*, **1** (1), 21–36.

Young, O., R. Langlais and O. Snellman (eds) (1998), 'The University of the Arctic – With Shared Voices: Launching the University of the Arctic', A Report from the Circumpolar Universities Association Working Group on the University of the Arctic to the Arctic Council, Circumpolar Universities Association, University of Lapland, Rovaniemi, Finland.

Yukon Government and Yukon College (1998), 'Northern Climate Exchange – Building the Foundation', project proposal submitted to the Government of Canada, October.

Zdan, T. (1997), 'Maintenance of infrastructure', in S.J. Cohen (ed.), 59–61.

8. Signs of life: linking indicators and models in the context of QUEST

Dale S. Rothman, John B. Robinson and Dave Biggs

OVERVIEW

In recent years there has been a big push to develop indicators reflecting, not just environmental, but also social and economic, aspects of sustainable development. These are considered important both for assessing the current situation and for monitoring progress towards future goals. Examples include the State of the Environment reporting at the provincial and federal levels in Canada, and the international work being coordinated by the Environment Department of the World Bank (British Columbia Ministry of Environment, 1995; Environment Canada, 1995; World Bank, 1995; Serageldin, 1996).

While being very useful in some ways, sets of indicators suffer, in that they are static in nature and lack interactivity. They provide a snapshot, but do not show the dynamic relationships between indicators. They are not capable, therefore, of illustrating how the circumstances may change in the future.

At the same time, there have been numerous efforts to develop models to aid in the policy-making processes surrounding local, national and international efforts to address issues pertaining to sustainable development. Much of this effort can be traced back to the World Model developed by Jay Forrester and presented in the Club of Rome's 1972 report, *The Limits to Growth* (Meadows *et al.*, 1972). Models are specifically designed to consider the relationships between the parts of a system and their intended use is to understand better the holistic workings of the system being modelled. The choice of how to represent and model a system, and the overall effectiveness of the model, depend heavily upon the choice of the set of indicators to be followed.

It is not surprising, therefore, that the need to link indicators and models of sustainability more explicitly has been a key focus of a number of recent studies (Swart *et al.*, 1995; Balaton Group, 1996; Gallopin, 1996; Lonergan *et al.*, 1996). In this chapter, we discuss how the relationship between indicators, models and users has been approached in the development and use of a novel tool, QUEST (the Quite Useful Ecosystem Scenario Tool) developed at the Sustainable Development Research Institute in the University of British Columbia.

A NEW APPROACH

Introduction and Use

QUEST is a microcomputer-based scenario generation and evaluation system, which is intended to encourage thinking about sustainability in a regional context. It was pioneered in the Lower Fraser Basin QUEST model (LFB–QUEST), and the approach has generated active interest in many countries (Biggs *et al.*, 2000). This version is currently being updated and expanded to the spatial scale of the entire Georgia Basin, for use in exploring alternative scenarios for reconciling ecological, social and economic goals in the Georgia Basin (Robinson and van Bers, 1998). QUEST projects have also been developed in several urban-centred regions in Latin America and Asia, and others are under way in other regions in Europe and Asia. The most advanced of these is NW England QUEST, which is being developed in an active partnership with the Manchester component of the EU-funded VISIONS project (Rotmans *et al.*, 2000).

Through QUEST, single users or groups of users can explore different possible future scenarios in terms of their social, economic and environmental characteristics and consequences.[1] QUEST illustrates 'real-world' situations and provides a reasonable summary of socioeconomic and ecological data from recent surveys and research. The goal is to acquaint users with the complex realities of decision making, specifically the uncertainties involved, necessary trade-offs, and role of subjective values. Thus the information it provides must reflect the issues and uncertainties inherent in trying to understand complex human and natural systems at the regional scale.

QUEST, however, does not simply present these scenarios as static illustrations. Instead it actively involves the user in their creation and evaluation in the form of a computer game. The idea for QUEST grew out of the Sustainable Society Project (Robinson *et al.*, 1996), which produced detailed scenarios of a sustainable future for Canada, in part using a large-scale input–output model of the Canadian economy. Project participants realized that the main learning occurred in the process of constructing and running alternative scenarios. This led to the idea of developing a game tool that would allow the interested public to construct and evaluate their own scenarios. Thus an essential feature in designing QUEST was to ensure that it would be interactive and enjoyable to use.

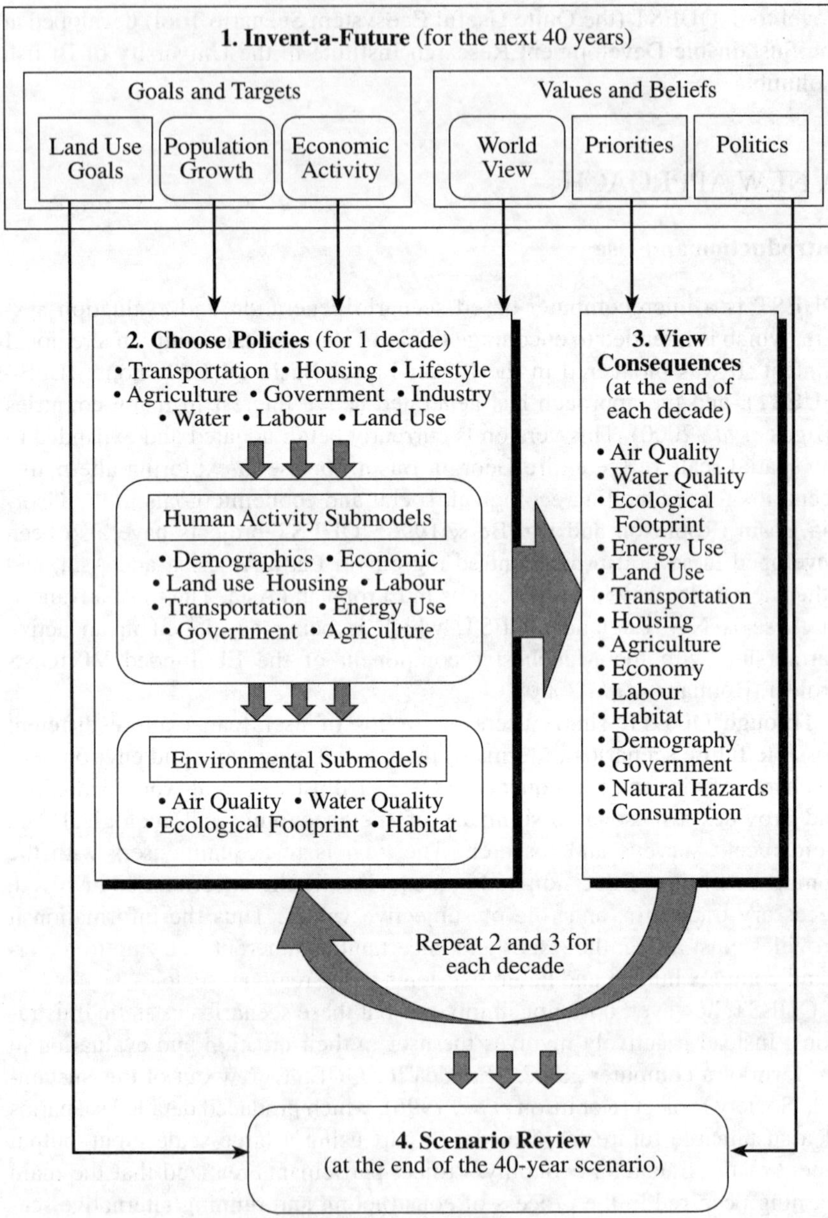

Figure 8.1 Conceptual framework of QUEST

In running QUEST, the user first 'invents a future'[2] (see Figure 8.1) that is, sketches a general picture of a desired or expected future by providing information about their values and beliefs about how the world works (see box),

WORLD-VIEWS AND ALTERNATIVE VALUES

We use the term '*world-view*' to describe a set of major assumptions about how the world works with regard to three broad variables: resilience of the ecosystem, future of technological development, and flexibility of individuals and social institutions. The user chooses whether each of these should be set to a high, medium or low value. This allows the user to represent differing opinions reflecting uncertainties in knowledge within the world described by QUEST. The choice of world-view affects the dynamic relationships within the model. For example, a high setting for social adaptability will increase the speed at which changes in behaviour can occur, while a low setting for environmental resilience will increase the ecological impacts of various policies. By comparing scenarios under different assumptions, the user can get a sense of the robustness of policies and the importance of recognizing uncertainties as to how the world works. (Note: the current versions of QUEST do not allow for major discontinuities or surprises; future versions are expected to incorporate these possibilities.)

Alternative values play multiple roles in QUEST. At the beginning of the game, the user must specify a desired set of values. These are meant to express differing opinions as to how the world should work in terms of policy emphasis and also as to what is of most importance in judging the *success or failure* of a scenario. Since the process of creating a future may involve conflicts, forcing users to make trade-offs, the policy decisions made while iterating through the series of time periods may or may not be consistent with the initially specified values. The degree of (in)consistency is reported to the user. Thus the user's performance is evaluated, not only for the achievement of goals, but also for consistency between their expressed values and the results of their policy choices. More specifically related to indicators, the user's expressed values are reflected in the way indicators are presented and in how aggregate indicators are calculated, as described in later sections of this chapter.

and by setting the broad outline of the scenario to be explored. These include their goals for the general state of the region's population, economy and broad patterns of land use at the end of the scenario period. QUEST then interpolates to create the population and economic growth paths to reach these goals. The user then adds flesh to this skeleton by 'choosing policies' to develop the full scenario. This involves a series of decisions in such areas as transport, housing and land use. The user must make these at each time step during the scenario period. At the end of each period, the user 'views consequences'. This module reports on the ecological, economic and social consequences of the user's decisions, providing feedback to the user during the process of generating the scenario.[3] A list of specific indicators representing these consequences is shown in Table 8.1. These results may influence the user to alter the decisions made in the 'choose policies' module for the next decade. In this way, QUEST allows for *sequential decision making*, where the user sees consequences and can change policies in a step-by-step fashion. The information produced in the 'invent a future' module shapes the development of the actual scenario, as well as the calculations of the consequences and the evaluation of the 'performance' of the user.

The Philosophy behind QUEST

The underlying design approach employed by QUEST is based upon the backcasting techniques developed by Robinson (1988, 1990, 1992). In contrast to predictive, or forecasting, approaches, backcasting attempts to explore the feasibility and consistency of normatively defined 'desirable' futures. It involves a visioning exercise which forces the user to focus on the steps required to reach a scenario instead of concentrating on which scenario is the most likely. This is a deliberate response to the problems associated with predictive forecasting methods, which are not only usually highly inaccurate (Ascher, 1978, 1989), but also tend to be used to legitimize policy decisions made for other reasons (Baumgartner and Midttun, 1987).

By encouraging users to consider different, user-defined futures, QUEST attempts to overcome some of the problems inherent in using traditional predictive models in a complex, uncertain and very human world. It is intended to promote sensitivity to the challenges and trade-offs involved in decision making regarding sustainability. The goal is to provide heuristics that make sense of the real world; not to present solutions optimized around a projected future. In this way, QUEST is designed to reflect the recognition that it is not useful to think in terms of 'base case' or 'business as usual' futures; instead there exists a wide range of alternative future paths, each of which is dependent upon a series of often irreversible decisions.[4] The user is invited to reflect on the desirability of the consequences and

Table 8.1 Specific indicators in LFB-QUEST

Population, Land Use and Housing	
Total population	Population by subregion
Population by age category (under 20, 20–60, over 60)	Population density in developed land
Overall population density	Population by density classification (low, high)
Population density by subregion	Share of population in other dwelling types
Share of population in single family dwellings	Area of agricultural land
Area of natural land	Area of high-density land
Area of low-density land	Yard space per capita
Floor space per capita	
Economy	
Agricultural intensity	GDP per capita
Total output per capita	Net exports by sector
Net revenue by sector	Employment by sector
Total person hours worked	Male workforce, percentage
Female workforce, percentage	Participation rate
Unemployment rate	Average income
Transport	
Modal shares by category (car, bus, walk/bike)	Commuter trips per capita
Automobile km per capita	Vehicle occupancy
Ecology and Environment	
Local vehicle emissions	Greenhouse gas vehicle emissions
Local point source emissions	Greenhouse gas point source emissions
Local air emissions	Greenhouse gas emissions
Emergency room visits	Total ecological footprint
Ecological footprint per capita	Habitat by species group
Energy Use	
Total energy use	Energy use per capita
Personal energy use per capita	Industry energy use per capita
Government and Social Services	
Deficit	Education per capita
Health care per capita	Social services per capita

trade-offs associated with alternative policy choices, rather than upon predicting the future.

A second defining characteristic of the QUEST approach is a focus on learning through scenario construction rather than on scenario results. Previous experience in modelling sustainable society futures (Robinson *et al.*, 1996) led to the realization that it was the act of creating scenarios, which involved complex discussion and negotiation of inputs based on consideration of trade-offs and potential consequences, that led to real learning about the issues involved. While the results of such scenario analysis could be published, it was not realistic to reproduce the scenario-generation process for a larger audience, particularly using the large-scale, complex and rather opaque models customarily used. This led to the view that much simpler modelling tools, which could be distributed more widely and allow users to reproduce the experience of creating, testing and learning from scenarios, would be useful.

Finally, the commercial success of computer-based simulation games that address such complex topics as urban planning (SIMCITY®) or geophysics (SIMEARTH™) suggests that such topics, if presented in user-friendly ways, can interest the general citizenry. Since, arguably, political decisions on sustainability issues are driven more by public pressure than by the direct impact of expert analysis on senior decision makers, QUEST has been designed to appeal to the interested citizen. This has resulted in an attempt to make it 'fun to use' as well as to achieve the more traditional modelling goal of being 'true to life', an approach that one colleague has referred to as 'ontologically schizophrenic'.[5]

The result of these factors has been the development of a simulation tool that is neither purely a game nor purely a model. It is like a computer game in that it is user-friendly and speaks to issues that users care about, and it is like a computer model in that it contains actual data and shows real-world effects and consequences.

Many existing indicator systems tend to be focused more heavily on environmental than on economic or social indicators. Even more importantly, they tend to be accessible only in the essentially static form of tables, charts and figures. A principal goal of QUEST is to make ecological, social and economic indicators interactive (by showing the interrelationships among variables) and dynamic (by allowing indicators to be combined in the form of scenarios in the future), and to put them in a framework that allows the user to make up his or her own mind about what it all means. This has required giving some thought to the distinction between general and specific indicators and aggregation issues, the selection of indicators, the dynamic calculation of indicator values, and their presentation. Each of these issues is addressed in the following sections of this chapter.

SPECIFIC VERSUS GENERAL INDICATORS AND ISSUES OF AGGREGATION

In trying to model any issue as complex as sustainability, it is unlikely that any single indicator or small set of indicators can provide a full picture of progress towards or movement away from sustainability. At the same time, long laundry lists of indicators have not proved useful, as users find themselves in the position of not being able to see the forests for the trees. This is compounded by the lack of a truly operational definition of the concept of sustainability.

Lonergan *et al.* (1996) suggest that it is best to group specific indicators into 'indicator classes'. Most attempts to flesh out a working definition of sustainability have focused on the ecological, economic and increasingly social aspects of sustainability (Serageldin, 1996; Robinson and Tinker, 1997). Thus obvious choices for indicator classes are environmental, economic and social.

Specific indicators are those that can be measured directly, such as emissions and concentrations of particular air pollutants, total population, levels of unemployment, and land area in agricultural production. At the level of the indicator classes, it is possible to conceive of broader indicators, or more properly indices, which 'aggregate' the specific indicators. Thus we can consider measures of ecological, economic and social 'health'.[6] These are abstract and provide a general picture, but lack the detailed information of the indicators that make up the classes. For clarity, we will refer to these two categories as *specific* and *general* indicators.

This indicator structure can be pictured as an overlapping hierarchy, as shown in Figure 8.2.[7] The general indicators are shaded and the specific indicators are solid circles (a list of the specific indicators for LFB-QUEST is shown in Table 8.1). Also an overall 'sustainability index' is shown, although this implies an even higher level of aggregation (see Prescott-Allen, 1995, for one attempt to create such an indicator).

The relationship between specific and general indicators raises several issues. First, the specific indicators provide the information that is inherent in the general indicators, but how is this aggregation to be accomplished? How does one aggregate across indicators that use different units of measurement, and is it appropriate to aggregate across indicators that are considered incommensurable? Secondly, certain specific indicators, such as levels of unemployment, may fit more than one of the general indicators, for example economic and social health. In Figure 8.2, the specific indicators are shown as being of differing size, reflecting their differing levels of importance, that is, the weight they receive in calculating or representing the general indicators. As the figure also indicates, specific indicators can be part of more than one general indicator. We

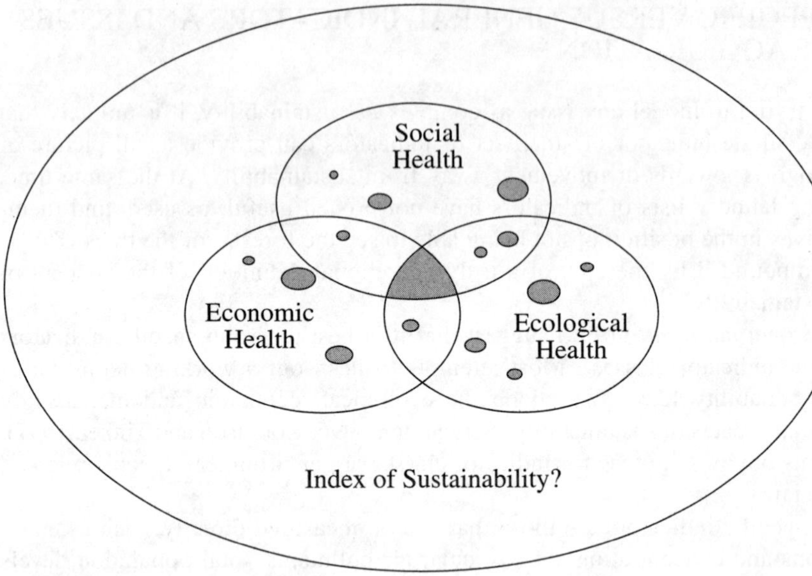

Figure 8.2 Linking specific and general indicators

cannot show it in the figure, but, in these cases, their size (importance) may be different for the different general indicators.

These issues are inherently subjective in nature, and we make this explicit in QUEST. The user is presented with a list of all of the specific indicators and is asked to select and rank indicators for specific aggregations. These choices provide the information base for the general indicators. Our objectives are to let users express their values by indicating what is most important to them, and also to show how different perspectives can influence the values of indicators. Possibilities for comparing indicators using different measures include deviations from a target value or changes from current values (Hammond *et al.*, 1995).

At this point, we have chosen to use a visual aggregation of the indicators in each category, as shown in Figure 8.3. For each of the categories – Ecological Health, Economic Health and Social Well-Being – the user selects three most important specific indicators, specifies whether increases from the 1990 levels are desirable or undesirable, and attaches a relative weight to each. The results of these are shown on the front page of the 'newspaper' shown at the end of each decade of the scenario, the thickness of the bar indicating the relative weight, with movements to the right indicating improvements, and movements to the left indicating a turn for the worse. This approach meets the definition of what Gallopin (1996, p. 106) calls a 'profile' that provides 'information not

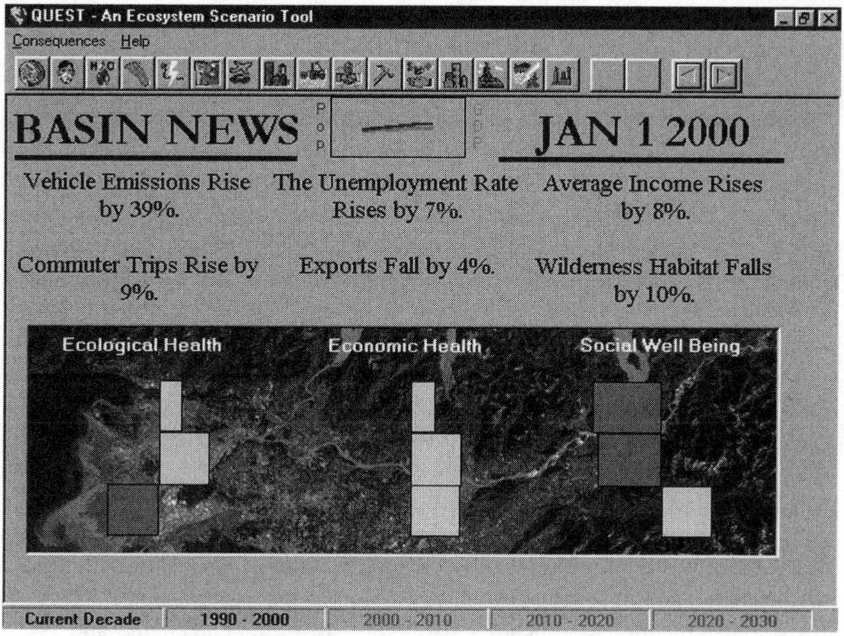

Figure 8.3 The QUEST consequences: screen clicking on any icon or headline brings up further information

only on the values of the individual variables included, but also a Gestalt view of the whole'.

SELECTING INDICATORS

As described above, social, environmental and economic health are used as general indicators in QUEST. These arise out of the overall concerns of sustainability. The values of the general indicators are calculated from the specific indicators. Therefore the choice of specific indicators must meet the requirement that they provide the information needed to calculate the general indicators. Also they must be calculable within the modelling procedures used in QUEST. Finally, for the purpose of manageability and to maintain the clarity of the learning process, it is useful to limit the overall number of indicators and to group these into broader categories (Lonergan *et al.*, 1996).

Along with these pragmatic considerations, an important design criterion of QUEST is that it be relevant to users by making connections to their everyday lives. The selection of indicators plays an important role in this process. Thus they should correspond to common, everyday concerns experienced by the users and represent some of the more attention-grabbing, exceptional events that arise in the course of striving for sustainability.

A sense of what is relevant and credible, both in terms of decision making and for typical residents of the region being studied, comes, in part, from looking at indicators and issues posited by government organizations and politically active groups in this region. Insight into relevant and credible indicators can also be gained by examining broader policy initiatives and discussion at national and international level about sustainability. Similarly, academic sources (journals, experts and research projects) provide broad-scale ideas about what is interesting and believable, as well as shedding light on the basic understanding of key relationships. Users' responses to prototypes of the game also provide valuable information.

A major source of data for LFB-QUEST was the Fraser Basin Ecosystem Study (BEST) (Fraser Basin Management Program, 1995). This research programme has examined many of the most important environmental, social and economic issues in the Lower Fraser Basin. Also much of the research in BEST has involved close relationships between local, regional and municipal governments, and in some cases other public groups.

We also considered indicators used by government agencies and NGO groups to deal with environmental consequences. We pay particular attention to groups and organizations in the Lower Fraser Basin, such as the Greater Vancouver Region District (GVRD), the Fraser River Estuary Management Program (FREMP) and the Fraser Basin Management Program (FBMP), as they reflect current local thinking about sustainability. Broader regional, national and international efforts were also explored (see, for example, Hammond *et al.*, 1995; Lonergan *et al.*, 1996; British Columbia Ministry of Environment, Lands, and Parks, 1995; and Environment Canada, 1995). The set of indicators chosen is shown in Table 8.1. This set ultimately relied on the judgment of the developers, but is open to inspection by users, whose input has influenced the development of other versions of QUEST.

CALCULATING INDICATOR VALUES

The calculation of the specific indicators is perhaps the most recognizable aspect of QUEST from a formal modelling perspective. In designing this part of QUEST, we have focused on three criteria: credibility, the ability to reflect uncertainty, and transparency. Credibility was addressed in much the same way as the selection of indicators: the structural relationships and algorithms for performing calculations were developed with reliance on the best available current research and direct consultation with members of the academic, policy and broader communities with understanding of the issues involved. In many cases, relevant research was done at scales or levels of detail which were inappropriate for QUEST. Since we were considering a broad set of issues, it was necessary to strike a balance between having very detailed representation of each system component, such as transport and air pollution, representing the relationships between these components, and maintaining the overall accessibility of QUEST.

How to represent uncertainty, both in our understanding of real systems and in our ability to simulate them, has been a principal concern for formal models since their first use. A common practice is to perform sensitivity analyses by varying a single parameter or a subset of parameters and observing the changes in particular results. Sensitivity analyses are generally presented as an addendum to the main results or, in the case of broader uses of a model, for example use by persons other than the modellers themselves, provided as an *option* available to the user.

With QUEST, we have chosen to make this an *explicit* and *required* part of using the model. In sketching out the scenario to be explored, the users must specify their world-view, that is, their general presumptions about how the world *does* work in such areas as resilience of the ecosystem, dynamics of technological development and flexibility of individuals and social institutions. The choice of world-view affects the actual relationships within the model: the world that the user specifies becomes the world in which the user's scenario is played out. This forces an explicit recognition on the part of the user that there are uncertainties about these variables, that other settings than the ones chosen for them are possible, and that changing these settings may change the results significantly. In this way, uncertainty is an inherent property of the scenario construction. By comparing scenarios under different assumptions, users can get a sense of the robustness of their policy choices relative to different possible world-views.[8]

Recall that the presentation of the general indicators also relies on the users and, in particular, on their ranking of what is of most importance to them. This is one aspect of what we refer to as reflecting the *values* of the users. By providing these mandatory and optional elements as well as a detailed description of the structure of the models, it is hoped that the 'black box' has been converted into a clear 'glass box' and the 'workings of the machine' have been made transparent.

PRESENTATION OF INDICATORS

Finally, it is important to consider how indicators are presented. Any tool such as QUEST can provide an abundance of information for the user, often inhibiting rather than enhancing understanding. In designing QUEST, we followed a philosophy based upon the following principles: show users what they are most concerned with, show them what else they should know, make all indicators accessible, allow the user to trace back reasons why specific changes have occurred, show more than 'traditional' indicators, and leave the final evaluation in the hands of the user.

In presenting the consequences to the user, approachability and relevance play a central role. Those indicators users indicate as being of most interest to them are specifically flagged, as are those that show significant change or which drive other significant consequences.[9] At the same time, all of the indicators are available to the user. Using the analogy of a newspaper (see Figure 8.3), there are headlines announcing important events, special sections on those matters of most interest to the user, and an index allowing the user to look up other topics.

Allowing the user to see how indicators are calculated has been one of the more challenging aspects of developing QUEST. LFB-QUEST contains detailed documentation, including flowcharts, detailed equations and text descriptions, which provide users with a number of tools to help them to understand the models. However, it does not contain an auto-tracing system for the indicators. Current efforts are being directed at hot linking indicators, graphs and maps to the documentation sections providing detailed information on model calculations. Users will also be able to view customized screens, highlighting the specific calculations involved in whatever they are looking at, as well as tips on key policy drivers that they might want to consider if they are unhappy with the progress of the indicator(s).

Users are also presented with some 'non-traditional' indicators. One of these is the degree of coherence between their values, as expressed in the 'invent a future' module, and their policies, as expressed in the 'choose policies' module. During scenario generation, the user will be making and modifying policy choices in several sequential time steps. The decisions made in each time step will likely be influenced by the consequences shown at the end of each of the previous time steps.

Finally, determination of the ultimate 'success' or 'failure' of a scenario is left in the hands of the user. There is no single score or 'grade' provided by QUEST.[10]

FINAL THOUGHTS

The development of QUEST represents the culmination of many years of trying to come to grips with the problems associated with the way energy and environment/economy models are designed and used by analysts and policy makers. The concept is of a game tool that embodies state-of-the-art understanding of how ecological, social and economic systems interact, in a framework which makes indicators interactive and dynamic but speaks to real-world concerns of users and allows them to make up their own minds about the consequences of their choices instead of trying to predict the most likely future. This represents, we believe, a novel approach to modelling, to indicators, and to the use of science in decision making. The further development and use of QUEST will ultimately establish the usefulness and effectiveness of our approach, but there are certain lessons we can draw at this stage.

First, the values of models and sets of indicators are mutually enhanced by creating specific links between the two. As suggested above, we see this as eventually leading to 'sustainability game and information systems' that link an expanded sustainability database for a given region to the game tools which make it interactive and dynamic, and connected to the concerns of citizens in that region. Figure 8.4 illustrates how this is being pursued in the Georgia Basin in the form of the Georgia Basin Digital Library (GBDL). Such a system could be used in schools, in public processes of various kinds, as a training tool for government employees, or even as a stand-alone game.

Second, it is important not to fool ourselves and others about our ability to predict the behaviour of natural and human systems. Models are better seen as tools that allow exploration and understanding of key relationships than as forecasting engines. It is the insights generated by playing with the model that are critical, not the absolute values of the outputs. This conclusion has important implications for the design of models, their appropriate degree of complexity, and the extent to which they speak directly to users' concerns.

Third, no model is useful if it is not used. To establish credibility with, and relevance for, users, both modellers and developers of sets of indicators must move beyond dictating to, or merely convincing, eventual users, to actively involving them in the development of the tools (Rothman and Robinson, 1997).

Finally, we have a more speculative comment. In our work, we have become convinced that the difference between games and models is not merely, as is sometimes suggested by modellers, that games are simple (and thus less accurate) models. Instead, we have discovered that adding the design criterion 'fun to use' to the traditional criterion 'true to life' does not merely constrain the modelling process. It actually changes the nature of the design process itself, in ways we are not yet fully able to understand. Determining how complex natural and human processes can be rendered in comprehensible terms and related to common concerns is not, it turns out, primarily a process of simplification. Instead, it seems to involve an active recasting of the relationships. It seems to us that QUEST does not just

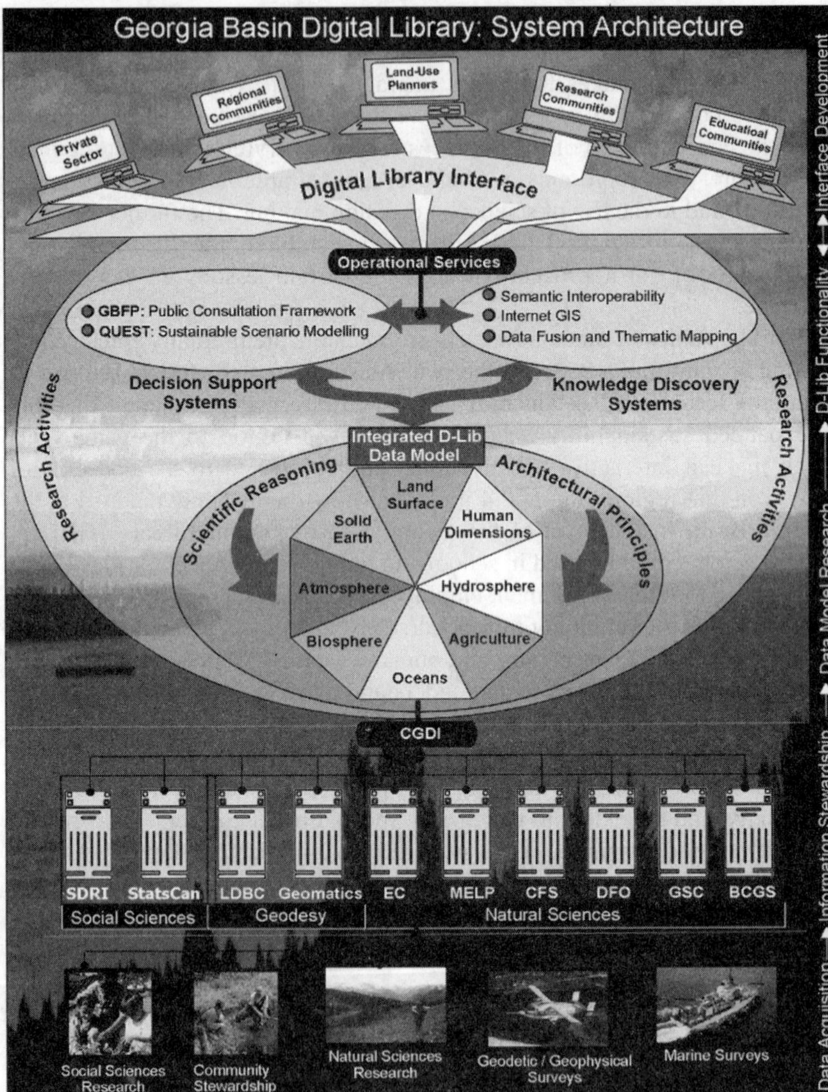

Note: This is an initiative to promote the integration of natural science and socioeconomic information for purposes of sustainability modelling, community consultation and land-use planning in the Georgia Basin region of south-western British Columbia.

Figure 8.4 Conceptual framework of the Georgia Basin Digital Library Network

embody simpler and more aggregate relationships than a more complex and traditional model would contain. Instead it embodies a different framing of the issues. In this sense, it provides an illustration of the difference between what Newby (1994) describes as science-driven and problem-driven approaches to understanding the relationship between human and natural systems. Like Newby, we prefer the latter.

ACKNOWLEDGEMENTS

The authors would like to acknowledge the hard work of a large number of colleagues, including graduate students, who have worked on the various versions of the QUEST modelling system: building QUEST is truly a team effort. We should also like to acknowledge the financial support of the Social Sciences and Humanities Research Council of Canada, without whose funding there would be no QUEST.

NOTES

1. Throughout the remainder of the chapter, we will write as if we are assuming a single user. However, our expectation and experience to date suggests that the use of QUEST will involve a number of users, who will discuss and decide upon the choices to be made in developing the scenario.
2. The working names of the three key modules of QUEST are shown in inverted commas.
3. The consequences are calculated in a series of linked submodels. As opposed to many simulation models, these are more akin to accounting models than to dynamic system models.
4. For more on the need for multiple-base cases in environment/economy modelling, see Hourcade and Robinson (1996) and Rothman and Robinson (1997).
5. We should like to thank Silvio Funtowicz for this succinct and expressive phrase.
6. We acknowledge that the use of the term 'health' to represent this abstract quantity is somewhat problematic, but it is in common parlance: for example, the International Society for Ecosystem Health.
7. It was pointed out by Gilberto Gallopin that a strict hierarchy might not be appropriate, as certain higher-level indicators are not merely aggregations of lower level ones. For more on this, see Gallopin (1996).
8. This is, of course, limited in LFB-QUEST by the fact that it does not include major discontinuities or surprises, as noted earlier.
9. A compromise was obviously made here in our basic philosophy of keeping the assumptions of the modellers out of the model as much as possible.
10. QUEST allows the user to complete their scenario no matter how bad things may get. This is in contrast to a game such as SimHealth© where, if users' actions are too much at variance with their stated intentions, they get voted out of office and the game ends.

REFERENCES

Ascher, W. (1978), *Forecasting: An Appraisal for Policy-makers and Planners*, Baltimore: Johns Hopkins University Press.

Ascher, W. (1989), 'Beyond Accuracy', *International Journal of Forecasting*, **5** (4), 469–84.

Balaton Group (1996), 'Indicators and Information Systems for Sustainable Development', Bilthoven, The Balaton Group.

Baumgartner, T.M. and A. Midttun (eds) (1987), *The Politics of Energy Forecasting: A Comparative Study of Energy Forecasting in Western Europe and North America*, New York: Clarendon Press.

Biggs, B., J.B. Robinson, C. Tague and M. Walsh (2000), 'Tools for Linking Choices and Consequences', in M. Healey (ed.), *Sustainability Issues and Choices in the Lower Fraser Basin: Resolving the Dissonance*, Vancouver: UBC Press.

British Columbia Ministry of Environment, Lands and Parks (1995), 'State of the Environment for British Columbia', Victoria, BC, British Columbia Ministry of Environment, Lands and Parks.

Environment Canada (1995), 'State of the Environment Report', Environment Canada, Ottawa, Ontario.

Fraser Basin Management Program (1995), 'State of the Fraser Basin : Assessing Progress Towards Sustainability', FBMP, Vancouver.

Gallopin, G. (1996), 'Environmental and Sustainability Indicators and the Concept of Situational Indicators: A Systems Approach', *Environmental Modeling and Assessment*, **1** (3), 101–17.

Hammond, A., A. Adriaanse, E. Rodenburg, D. Bryant and R. Woodwood (1995), 'Environmental Indicators: A Systematic Approach to Measuring and Reporting on Environmental Policy Performance in the Context of Sustainable Development', World Resources Institute, Washington, DC.

Hourcade, J.-C. and J.B. Robinson (1996), 'Mitigating Factors. Assessing the Costs of reducing GHG Emissions', *Energy Policy*, **24** (10/11), 863.

Lonergan, S., J. Ruitenbeek and K. Gustavson (1996), 'Selection and Modelling of Sustainability Indicators for the Fraser River Basin: Final Report', Occasional Paper Series, Environment Canada, State of the Environmental Directorate and Pacific and Yukon Region, Victoria, Canada.

Meadows, D.H., D.L. Meadows, J. Randers and W.W.I. Behrens (1972), *The Limits to Growth: A Report for The Club of Rome's Project on The Predicament of Mankind*, New York: Universe Books, Publishers.

Newby, H. (1994), 'Global Environmental Change and the Social Sciences: Retrospect and Prospect', in *Collaboration between the Natural and Social Sciences in GEC Research*, Riswijk, The Netherlands: Dutch Advisory Council for Research on Spatial Planning, Nature and the Environment (RMNO).

Prescott-Allen, R. (1995), 'Barometer of Sustainability: A Method of Assessing Progress Toward Sustainable Societies', contribution to the IUCN/IDRC Project on Monitoring and Assessing Progress Toward Sustainability, Victoria, BC.

Robinson, J.B. (1988), 'Unlearning and Backcasting: Rethinking Some of the Questions We Ask About the Future', *Technological Forecasting and Social Change*, **33** (4), 325–38.

Robinson, J.B. (1990), 'Futures Under Glass: A Recipe for People Who Hate to Predict', *Futures* **22** (9), 820–43.

Robinson, J.B. (1992), 'Of Maps and Territories: The Use and Abuse of Socio-Economic Modelling in Support of Decision-Making', *Technological Forecasting and Social Change*, **42** (4), 147–64.

Robinson, J.B. and J. Tinker (1997), 'Reconciling Ecological, Economic, and Social Imperatives: A New Conceptual Framework', in T. Schrecker (ed.), *Surviving Globalism: Social and Environmental Dimensions*, London: Macmillan, pp. 71–94.

Robinson, J.B. and C. van Bers (1998), 'Reconciling Ecological Carrying Capacity and Human Well-being: Exploring alternative futures for the Georgia Basin, B.C.', project proposal, Vancouver, BC, Canada, Sustainable Development Research Institute.

Robinson, J.B., D. Biggs, G. Francis, R. Legge, S. Lerner, D.S. Slocombe and C. van Bers (1996), *Life in 2030: Exploring a Sustainable Future for Canada*, Vancouver, BC: UBC Press.

Rothman, D. and J. Robinson (1997), 'Growing Pains: A Conceptual Framework for Considering Integrated Assessments', *Environmental Monitoring and Assessment*, **46** (1–2), 23–43.

Rotmans, J., M.B.A.van Asselt, C. Anastasi, S.C.H. Greuw, J. Mellors, S. Peters, D. Rothman and N. Rijkens (2000), 'Visions for a sustainable Europe', *Futures*, **32** (9/10), 809–31.

Serageldin, I. (1996), 'Sustainability and the Wealth of Nations: First Steps in an Ongoing Journey'. Environmentally Sustainable Development Studies and Monograph Series, The World Bank, Washington, DC.

Swart, R.J., J.A. Bakkes, L.W. Niessen, J. Rotmans, H.J.M. de Vries and R. Waterings (1995), 'Scanning the Global Environment: A Framework and Methodology for Integrated Environmental Reporting and Assessment', RIVM/UNEP, Nairobi.

World Bank (1995), 'Monitoring Environmental Progress: A Report on Work in Progress', Environmentally Sustainable Development Series, The World Bank, Washington, DC.

PART III

Perspectives in Ecological Economic Modelling

9. Integrated modelling and evaluation of spatial and dynamic–evolutionary processes in environment–economy systems

Jeroen C.J.M. van den Bergh

INTRODUCTION

Integrated economic–ecological modelling includes a variety of approaches. Whatever approach is adopted, it always involves a particular set of choices in terms of description of spatial and temporal dimensions. We will consider these here from the perspective of formal modelling and evaluation, and in a policy context determined by sustainable development of economic–ecological systems. To clarify this context, a classification of various interpretations of sustainable development, along with modelling implications, is presented in the next section. In subsequent sections attention is devoted to the integration of concepts and models, alternative theoretical perspectives, thermodynamic elements in models, spatial aspects of sustainable development, (co)evolutionary modelling, and evaluation of spatial and dynamic indicators. Two examples illustrate some of the issues discussed. They deal with the structure of materials flows and materials balance production functions in a multisectoral context; and the integration of dynamic–spatial analysis and evaluation of a regional economic–ecological system.

INTERPRETING AND MODELLING SUSTAINABLE DEVELOPMENT

The concept of sustainable development has over a rather short period of time become commonplace in environmental economics, after the Brundtland Commission brought it to the attention of a large audience (WCED 1987). The following perspectives can be distinguished.

1. Sustainability as 'intergenerational equity' is the main starting point in economic growth theory, which is characterized by a very aggregate and abstract perception of growth and development. It has been translated into the criterion of non-decreasing welfare over generations, which comes down to non-decreasing welfare over time in single-generation models, or non-decreasing welfare over generations in discrete-generations models. This represents a very strict criterion, as it regards any temporary decrease as a sign of unsustainable development.
2. A different starting point is that of maintaining total capital intact, known as weak sustainability (Pearce *et al.*, 1990). It allows for substitution between man-made and natural capital. This has been expressed as focusing attention on equal opportunities for present and future generations, which are assumed to be shaped by the total capital endowment. Although having different starting points, the previous perspective and this one can lead to similar conclusions. Common and Perrings (1992) refer in this context to economic Solow/Hartwick sustainability (Hartwick 1977, Solow, 1986; see also Gutés, 1996).
3. Strong sustainability is a third starting point. It requires that different types of capital (economic, ecological, social) are each independently maintained in physical/biological terms. The motivation for this standpoint can be either the recognition that natural resources are essential (and thus complementary to other) inputs in economic production, consumption or welfare, or the acknowledgment of environmental integrity and rights in nature. In either case it is understood that environmental components may be unique and that environmental processes may be irreversible (over relevant time horizons). Very strong sustainability (as supported by the 'Deep Ecology' movement) would then imply that every component or subsystem of the natural environment is preserved. A somewhat weaker version of strong sustainability could focus on ecosystems and environmental assets that are critical in the sense of providing unique services (such as life support) or non-use values. Alternatively, a weaker version can be regarded in terms of a minimum amount of certain environmental assets that should be maintained, so that such assets are partly complementary to economic assets and partly substitutable by these. It is evident that different interpretations of strong sustainability are possible. Furthermore, although weak and strong sustainability are usually mentioned in one and the same breath, their formalization differs completely (see, further, Ayres *et al.*, 2000).
4. Daly (1991) has forcefully argued in favour of the idea of a steady state, in which population and economic stocks are maintained at a constant level. With regard to man-made economic stocks of capital, 'constancy' is perhaps a somewhat misleading qualification since their quality (value)

may be improved. In the context of the steady-state economy the main social aim of development is minimizing the human impact on the natural environment. This is realized by maximum reduction of material and energetic throughput of the economy. This means an entirely different development objective than posed by standard economics, while still leaving open opportunities for improvement in living conditions and welfare. An alternative viewpoint on this objective is in terms of optimal scale of the economy, which Daly has argued should complement the standard economic concept of optimal allocation (Daly, 1987, 1992). In terms of policy implications, the steady-state perspective is very close to the strong sustainability perspective.

5. Many ecologists support the idea that environmental sustainability is mainly a matter of stability, resilience and biotic diversity. Common and Perrings (1992) refer to this as ecological Holling sustainability (see Holling, 1986). Traditional economic models neither address fluctuations and cycles nor incorporate any real ecosystem structure, as a result of which they are unable to deal with stability and uncertainty in a way consistent with ecological theory. Integrated ecological economic models incorporating ecosystem descriptions, and possibly (co)evolutionary models, seem appropriate to address these issues.

It should be noted that these perspectives or starting points are not necessarily in disagreement with each other. It can be that they give rise to similar or identical conclusions at a general level or in specific cases. However, more important is that they can lead to different and possibly conflicting conclusions. For this reason a choice between them is ultimately inevitable. Such a choice will always remain open to debate, as it is subjective and ethical. Scientists can contribute to this debate by studying the implications of the various perspectives. In particular, integrated models can be used for this purpose. As a result, the choice between perspectives on sustainable development can be based on both starting points and consequences.

INTEGRATION OF MODELS

The concept of model integration can be technically or mathematically operationalized in different ways. Some models or methods combine optimization of an objective function with a description of a system. The system can then be represented by a set of constraints or equations, which can take different forms: linear or nonlinear, static or dynamic, and deterministic or stochastic. Constraints can also represent spatial relations or interactions. Modelling a complex economic–ecological system can involve integration or linking of separate models or techniques. The result is a non-analytical, numerical and consequently less powerful approach, due to linking of various nonlinear, spatial and dynamic submodels. Nevertheless, this allows for simulating complex economic–ecological systems in a much more realistic way than with partial analytical–theoretical models.

The linking of models is restricted by the model type. If economic and ecological models fit in a (general) systems frame, they may be blended in a single model structure, where compartments or modules may represent the original models, and certain outputs of one module serve as input for another. However, often it is not easy to link models directly. For instance, if both the economic and ecological systems are represented in the form of programming or optimization models, one should decide what to do: look for a new, aggregate objective; adopt a multi-objective or conflict analysis framework; or, when possible, derive multiple sets of optimality conditions and solve these simultaneously. In many cases, however, economic models have an optimization or programming format and ecosystem models have a descriptive format. Then direct technical integration is feasible. In cases where formats differ, a transformation to other model types is necessary, sometimes requiring aggregating components and relationships. This will usually lead to a loss of information, and be unattractive from a monodisciplinary perspective.

Three other aspects of integration may present some difficulties: units of measurement, temporal scale and spatial aggregation. First, monetary units dominate in economic models and theories, and physical units in ecological ones. Of course, both types of theories also employ functional units, such as number of commodities, number of actors and population size. Direct coupling of the three types of units can be difficult when no clear theoretical and empirical basis for this is available. Examples are the relationships between physical–ecological variables (water level, nutrients, soil quality, temperature, toxic pollutants and so on) and the monetary value of output as indicated by production functions in agriculture and fisheries, or related to health. Traditionally, environmental economists have approached the transformation between value and other units from the perspective of optimal individual behaviour and revealed preferences, allowing them to transform physical changes into monetary terms (Freeman, 1993). Recently, much attention has been given to stated preference methods. In contrast, integrated models focus on relationships between physical and functional units, and mixing physic and monetary units. Both methods go along with restrictive assumptions and data problems. The transformation and linking of different units remains one of the most important and difficult aspects of environmental and ecological economics.

A COMPARISON OF THEORIES AND MODELS APPLIED IN ECOLOGICAL ECONOMICS

Integrated models should be based on some theoretical starting point. Classifying theories and models can be done in many ways. For instance, Costanza *et al.* (1993) distinguish theories and models on the basis of whether they optimize

- generality: characterized by simple theoretical or conceptual models that aggregate, caricature and exaggerate;
- precision: characterized by statistical, short-term, partial, static or linear models with one element examined in much detail; and
- realism: characterized by causal, non-linear, dynamic–evolutionary and complex models.

These three criteria are usually conflicting, so that a trade-off between them is inevitable. In Table 9.1, twelve theoretical perspectives, discussed in detail in van den Bergh (1996), are tentatively linked to the latter categorization. In addition, four other criteria are included in the table, namely whether the approach is of a formal type, whether thermodynamic considerations have an impact, whether short-term dynamics are included (for example, dynamic materials balance, accumulation, regeneration, delays) and whether long-run dynamics are included (for example, 'development', structural shifts in sectoral composition, cycles, 'qualitative change', evolutionary patterns). These criteria are relevant to assessing what type of basis and orientation the approaches have.

Integrated modelling involves economists or ecologists transferring theories and models from one discipline to another and transforming them for their specific purpose. This requires activities such as reduction, simplification or summarization. The outcomes may not always be very acceptable within the original fields of science. More extensive discussions of this issue, with epistemological considerations, can be found, among others, in Vedeld (1994) and Turner *et al.* (1997).

INCORPORATING THERMODYNAMIC INSIGHTS IN MODELS

In the context of integrated economic–ecological analysis the relevance of thermodynamics is often discussed (see the special issue of *Ecological Economics*, **22** (3), 1997). It can be linked to discussions about substitution, limits to recycling and technical progress, and dynamic issues such as economic

Table 9.1 Characteristics of theoretical perspectives

Theory	Generality	Realism	Precision	Formal rigid	Thermo-dynamics	Short-run dynamics	Long-run dynamics
Equilibrium–neoclassical	x		x	x		x	
Neoaustrian–temporal	x	x		x	x	x	x
Ecological–evolutionary		x			x	x	x
Evolutionary–technological		x		x	x	x	x
Physico–economic	x	x		x	x	x	
Biophysical–energy	x	x		x	x	x	
Systems–ecological		x	x	x	x	x	
Ecological engineering		x	x		x	x	
Human ecology	x	x				x	
Socio-biological	x						x
Historical–institutional		x					x
Ethical–utopian	x						x

Source: van den Bergh (1996).

growth and evolution. For overviews of applications in economics, see Ayres (1978), Ruth (1993) and van den Bergh (1996, 1999).

A point stressed by Georgescu-Roegen (1971a) in the context of production, matter and energy – and much referred to by others – is the distinction between stocks, flows, funds and actors. A fund differs from a stock in that the allocation over time of the services it generates is restricted by time and the speed at which it can generate these services. A stock, on the other hand, may at any time be emptied or, alternatively, used up as slowly as desired. The exploitation of a stock, furthermore, gives rise to a flow of the same quality in terms of units of measurement (for example, matter, products, individuals of a population). Actors are specific funds, which include capital and labour, and may be defined as operating to transform flows. In other words, they are performing tasks for which energy and materials are required. The main difference between an actor, on the one hand, and materials and energy flows, on the other hand, is that the actor both enters and leaves the process in the same quality (except for some physical deterioration and depreciation after being a long period in use), whereas the materials and energy flows change quality (for example, from a raw or pure material into an integrated element of some commodity or compound material). The flows are thus transformed into different qualities by the actors, which are funds. To complete the picture, the entropy law implies that the actor requires maintenance afterwards (food, rest, leisure) and possibly compensation for decay (investment) in order to regain its original state. Materials end up as either (integrated) elements of the product or as waste output. These different categories of inputs allow for a more precise treatment of the notion of substitution between production factors. A distinction can be made between direct or ex-ante substitution within a category (the replacement of one type of material by another) and indirect or ex-post substitution (the saving on materials use by longer working hours, or more capital or labour input; or by technological progress) (see van den Bergh, 1999). This distinction allows us to formulate production functions with environmental variables and satisfying materials balance conditions (see Georgescu-Roegen, 1971b; Gross and Veendorp, 1990; and van den Bergh and Nijkamp, 1994a; for related issues, see Smith and Weber, 1989; and and the examples at the end of this chapter).

The entropy law has been used to show that materials will become more and more dispersed (Georgescu-Roegen, 1971a). This can be regarded as an increase in 'materials entropy', meaning that too much dispersion (or too low concentrations) of materials complicate their recycling and make it economically unprofitable. Thermodynamics provides information about technical limits: a lower bound of energy or work required to operate a system, maximum efficiency of a combustion engine at various combustion temperatures, or maximum heat exchange of an ecosystem with its environment. Some authors have gone further, and relate energy contents or maintenance flows to value (for different perspectives on this, see various articles in Daly and Umaña, 1981). Berry *et al.* (1978, p. 133) conclude that 'when conditions of economic cost minimization are stated in terms of prices and convex production functions, thermodynamic optimality adds no new insights'. A similar, though more general, conclusion is drawn by Young (1991). He points out that production relationships based on diminishing returns may be a concrete outcome of applying the entropy law to economic production systems. Daly has often stressed (for example, 1991, 1992) that the entropy law is a formalized expression of the general or absolute scarcity that mankind and its economy are subjected to. Similarly, in Georgescu-Roegen's jargon, the entropy law is the 'taproot' of economic scarcity.

Unlike traditional environmental economics, ecological economics has devoted much attention to thermodynamics. Nevertheless, it is not yet clear whether this actually means that thermodynamics is useful and can be integrated in relevant analyses. It can be used to derive conditions for specifying production functions in theoretical and empirical work, or to temper optimism about economic growth and technological progress. The reading of many of the above-mentioned writings leaves the feeling that the entropy law may provide in any case a consistency check on both economic and ecological theories, and allow for a common ground upon which to base integration of these (see also Ruth, 1993). In order to be successful in this respect, economists need to devote more attention to the economic analysis of materials and energy flows through economic systems, and integrate physical units and insights into economic theories and methods (for efforts in this direction, see Starreveld and van Ierland, 1994; Ayres and Ayres, 1996; Kandelaars and van den Bergh, 1996; Rose and Casler, 1996).

SPATIAL ASPECTS OF ECOLOGICAL ECONOMICS AND SUSTAINABLE DEVELOPMENT

The spatial dimension of sustainable development has, as opposed to the global context, received little attention. The importance of the spatial element arises from a reciprocal relationship: (1) local processes have global impacts and (2) global trends give rise to local effects. For example, the loss of ecosystems in some regions may have a large impact on global climatological conditions and geochemical cycles. Overgrazing and deforestation may lead to large-scale soil erosion, downstream sedimentation, flooding and salinization. Furthermore, environmental processes do not affect all regions uniformly and smoothly, but may have important different consequences on a regional scale. The specific regional environmental and economic structure determines the sensitivity of a region to external environmental and economic forces.

The integrated study of economic and natural systems on a global scale is complicated because of the variety of economies, ecosystems and political interests. Performing this at a regional level has a number of advantages. First, it allows one to analyse less complex systems with fewer components and interactions. In addition, the use of indicators can be more easily accomplished at such a meso level. Aggregation of information into global-scale indicators may lead to a significant loss of information. This is illustrated in a study of a region in the Netherlands characterized by conflicts between agriculture and nature protection (van den Bergh *et al.*, 2001). The results show the influence of different spatial and subindicator aggregation schemes on the evaluation outcome. A third advantage is the easier access to regional than to global data, and avoidance of some of the problems of data incomparability that will occur with a global scale of analysis. Fourth, a study region may be chosen such that it coincides with an administrative region, thus guaranteeing a uniform policy. Finally, a regional scale allows for easier identification of the source of environmental problems.

Regional sustainable development is a concept which has received only a little attention (an early treatment, focusing on international trade issues, is Daly, 1989). This is somewhat strange in view of the large literature that did evolve on (general or global) sustainable development. It would seem that the regional concept is linked to even more subjective and ethical issues than is the global concept, and perhaps this is why it has been neglected. The most obvious, immediate choice of disaggregation starting from a global sustainable development concept is a distinction between developed and developing regions of the world. Here the ethical dimension of defining regional sustainable development becomes immediately clear.

Two regional characteristics are responsible for the difference between sustainable development and regional sustainable development (RSD): (1) cross-boundary flows of environmental and economic goods (or materials) and (2) external determinants of regional development. A realization of regional sustainable development can therefore be regarded as based on two elements, namely the sustainable provision of natural resources in the region, and a sustainable interaction with other regions. The latter means that imports and exports are not related to unsustainable patterns of production and consumption in other regions.

In order to discuss the sustainable development of a region, it has to be made clear what the problem is and how solutions can be found. The problem of unsustainable development of a region is linked to the fact that the size of a regional population and economy are not checked sufficiently by the region's carrying capacity. Therefore overshooting may occur. Sometimes this is acceptable if at a higher spatial level sustainability is ensured by balancing and compensating measures. A second reason for unsustainable development of a region is the existence of negative externalities associated with regional development, cross-boundary pollution and global phenomena (for example, climate change), from which regional control is separated. Cross-boundary physical flows, both trade and pollution, cause the regional carrying capacity to be exceeded, temporarily or permanently, which can do permanent damage to the regional environment. This has negative consequences for the carrying capacity itself and thus for the long-run performance of the regional economy (van den Bergh and Nijkamp, 1994b, 1995). Consequently, regional sustainable development has to fulfil two goals: (1) it should ensure an acceptable level of welfare for the regional population, which can be sustained in the future; and (2) it should not be in conflict with sustainable development at a supraregional level.

In the light of this, spatial sustainability can perhaps only be dealt with to its full extent in a multiregional setting. The following important elements of spatial sustainability might then be addressed.

1. Imports can cause unsustainable patterns in the importing region when the commodities generate consumption externalities.
2. Although imports seem to increase the region's 'carrying capacity', they can in fact lead to overshooting of critical thresholds of regional ecosystems.
3. Imports can cause a region to become a sink for flows of materials and nutrients that are not internationally recycled owing to high costs. Ultimately, this can give rise to cross-boundary pollution through air and groundwater.
4. Imports in one region can cause unsustainable patterns in the region of origin, when the imports are based on unsustainable production techniques.
5. Environmental sustainability of one region is linked to that of other regions via the sustainability of the global environment.

Some of these impacts can be referred to as 'importing sustainability' or 'exporting unsustainability'. This classification should not be interpreted as a statement against trade. Trade in itself is not necessarily harmful for the environment, as long as it is based on sustainable production. Of course, that is not the case for most current trade. Under the same condition, trade can even aid in reducing environmental pressure, by allocating production in space in such a way that the resulting spatial pattern of environmental pressure (resource use, pollution and other disturbances) is adapted to the spatial pattern of 'ecologically sensitive' ecosystems. This can be interpreted as making use of 'ecological comparative advantages'.

Such issues can be addressed by combining information about the spatial distribution of production, consumption, pollution, resource extraction and ecosystems. Recently, a very aggregate indicator, the 'Ecological Footprint', has been proposed by Wackernagel and Rees (1996, 1997) for this purpose. Despite its quickly rising popularity, it is not yet clear that this concept reflects anything close to spatial sustainability (see van den Bergh and Verbruggen, 1999). In the first place, it represents not actual but hypothetical land use (notably for energy generation). Second, it does not make a clear distinction between unsustainable and sustainable land use. Third, it does not consider spatial variation of sensitive ecosystems. Fourth, it cannot be used to compare regions of very different size and with very different geographical and physical characteristics. Finally, comparing a region's footprint with its available land area implies an anti-trade assumption. Indeed, it is not clear why in general land use inside a region should be preferred to imports (that is, land use outside a region).

A region or country with much available (fertile or ecologically productive) land per capita (such as Canada) has in the traditional economic sense a comparative advantage which can be used to trade with regions or countries where land is relatively more scarce (such as Belgium). Comparing them on the basis of the footprint denies the uneven pattern of population density across space, regions (note especially cities versus countryside) and countries. All in all, the footprint indicator in its present format is unable to address the rich mechanisms that explain the spatial distribution of people and activities on the planet. In fact, what is needed is not a static, blueprint type of indicator, but spatially disaggregated modelling and indicators that take production and consumption externalities into account, and match these spatially with ecosystem characteristics. Aggregation, although inevitable to some extent, leads to a loss of information. Scientists should avoid as much as possible presenting results or indicators that embody a strong ethical choice, since this will confuse 'end-users' who usually assume a large degree of objectivity of results of scientific studies.

DYNAMIC MODELS OF (CO)EVOLUTION

Ever since sustainable development has been studied by economists and ecologists, it has been stressed that it is inherently dynamic, and that attention should therefore be devoted to growth, structural change, irreversible change and so on. This can be regarded as an unambiguous plea for dynamic analysis and modelling. Neoclassical economics has mainly focused in this context on exogenous growth theory and recently also endogenous growth theory (for diverse approaches, see Solow, 1974; Hartwick, 1977; Pezzey, 1989; Gradus and Smulders, 1993; Howarth and Norgaard, 1995; Toman *et al.*, 1995). As opposed to this stream of literature, dynamic modelling on a less aggregate, regional or ecosystem level is more heterogeneous in approach and style (for surveys, see Braat and van Lierop, 1987; van den Bergh, 1996).

Recently, sustainable development has also been studied from the perspective of evolutionary economics (see van den Bergh and Gowdy, 2000). The basic idea is that changes in economic reality come so quickly that it is impossible to have some stable, stationary or equilibrium state of the economic system. Evolutionary economics regards economic processes as inherently accidental, cumulative and irreversible. The method is based on Darwinian, Lamarckian and Schumpeterian evolutionary theories, as well as on recent developments in evolutionary biology. One important direction is that linked to behaviour and game theory in economics (Maynard Smith, 1982; Weibull, 1995), while another addresses non-gradual changes leading to 'punctuated equilibria' (Gould, 1982). All in all, the Darwinian, gradual and adaptive, approach dominates in evolutionary economics. It should be noted that in biology this approach had already been replaced a long time ago by a broader perspective on evolution and adaptation (see Gould and Lewontin, 1979). Evolutionary models in economics and environmental economics covers a large variety of approaches (see Hodgson, 1993; Nelson, 1995). The key words – qualitative change, structural change, uncertainty (noise, luck), diversity, mutations, selection and adaptation – are essential in most contributions (see Ayres, 1994; Boulding, 1978; Clark *et al.*, 1995; Faber and Proops, 1990; Gowdy, 1994; Hodgson, 1993; Norgaard, 1994).

Ayres (1994) and Ruth (1996) argue for an evolutionary approach that is based on physics, in particular thermodynamics, and information theory. Ayres presents an interesting combination of insights from physics, geology, chemistry, biology and economics. He formulates an economy-wide model that can be interpreted as a rare alternative for the general equilibrium market-based model of standard economics. This alternative formulation includes satisficing behaviour, pairwise exchange of goods, associated pairwise prices and irreversibility of transactions. The same idea has independently been incorporated in the famous numerical 'sugarscape' model (Epstein and Axtell, 1996). These together lead to a path-dependent development of the economy as a whole. Ruth (1996) states that drawing analogies from either biology or physics has hampered progress and a scientific approach in evolutionary economics. He argues that we should focus on 'non-analogy-based applications of concepts from physics', focusing on non-linear systems models and information theory indicators. Whether it is possible to work entirely without analogies is not made clear. This seems to assume that we know what is reality, and therefore what is a 'realistic' approach.

The two most important differential characteristics of evolutionary models compared with neoclassical models are non-determinism and non-average behaviour (microdiversity). On the basis of these characteristics Allen (1998) makes a distinction between three types of models: deterministic (characterized by determinism and average behaviour), self-organizing (non-deterministic and average behaviour) and evolutionary (non-deterministic and micro-diversity). Self-organizing systems can show qualitative change only on the level of collective structure (spatiotemporal organization of molecules), whereas the evolutionary type can also change qualitatively on the lowest micro level.

When modelling evolutionary processes in a broad sense, various options are open.

1. 'Evolutionary technology models': in much of the evolutionary economics literature, and also in the modern growth theory literature, technological change is considered to be crucial for economic progress and growth in developed and developing economies. Evolutionary approaches regard technological change as an evolutionary process (Nelson and Winter, 1982; Dosi *et al.*, 1988), dating back to ideas of Schumpeter. Such approaches aim at breaking open the black box of technology invention and temporal and spatial diffusion of innovations, using crucial information about patents for inventions and detailed statistics on changes in technologies used in specific sectors. In the context of environmental economics, Faber and Proops (1990) have related long-run interactions between invention, innovation and technical progress to pollution and resource use, using a Neoaustrian approach (see also Faber *et al.*, 1987). This approach is similar to neoclassical economics in its assumption of rational behaviour, but it differs from it in its treatment of irreversibility and uncertainty. These models devote more attention to substantial and detailed issues of technological invention, innovation and diffusion than modern growth theory models.
2. 'Evolutionary resource models': a few studies have considered the economics of evolutionary environmental systems or ecosystems. The main question here is what type of management is adequate or economically optimal when dealing with control of environmental systems characterized by both mechanistic and evolutionary processes. For instance, in agriculture the use of pesticides has a short-run mechanistic effect via killing pests, and a long-run effect via changing the genotypic structure of the pest population, possibly resulting in a reduced genotypic diversity, that is, domination by pest-resistant genes. This is studied by Munro (1994), with a deterministic modelling approach, resulting in a (difficult) optimal control problem with two state variables.
3. 'Integrated dynamic models': these focus on long-run interactions between economic and environmental systems, rather than on evolution of one subsystem independent of the other. Economic development is made

dependent, then, on both economic and environmental factors, which change over time and interact. The economy is here regarded as an open system with respect to physical and biological processes. Integrated models have been applied on a global scale (Meadows *et al*., 1972, 1982, 1992; Barney, 1980), as well as on a regional scale (Zuchetto and Jansson, 1985; Braat and van Lierop, 1987; Giaoutzi and Nijkamp, 1993; van den Bergh, 1996).

4. 'Coevolutionary models': Coevolution of environmental and economic systems regards the evolution of one system as essentially interrelated with that of the other (Norgaard, 1984, 1994; Gowdy, 1994). This can be regarded as a mix of the evolutionary and the previous integrated models. The idea of coevolution comes from biology, and is based on joint evolution of interacting species in an ecosystem (predator–prey, parasite–host, mutualism, commensalism and so on). In fact, the interdependence between ecosystem evolution and species evolution can be considered as an expression of the coevolutionary process. Coevolution of economic and environmental systems can be regarded in a similar way – as an analogy (for a critical view on this, see Ruth, 1996) – and can be based on the hierarchical and spatial structure of economy–environment systems with multiple feedback mechanisms. Clark *et al.* (1995) illustrate such evolutionary dynamics in two case studies of Senegal and Crete (Greece). Janssen (1996) discusses elements of evolution in the context of integrated assessment of climate change and policies. The main lesson from the perspective of coevolution is that environmental policy and management should aim for preservation of biological diversity. The temptation here is obviously to extend this conclusion to cover also diversity in economic systems.

Evolutionary models are not supposed to be predictive, which is often regarded as a weakness. Nevertheless, if evolution is 'for real' no other model type has much predictive power either. Evolutionary modelling serves other purposes than prediction. It can, for instance, be used to examine stability of systems, convergent trends and probabilistic behaviour, using analytical models, dynamic simulation, scenario analysis and Monte-Carlo techniques. At best, evolutionary approaches offer a critique on neoclassical analysis, notably on the standard approach to average out variety. In a way, standard growth theory deals with a rather short-term, stable economic regime characterized by homogeneous firms, whereas evolutionary theory deals with a longer time-frame in which microdiversity has an essential impact. In this sense the two fields are rather complementary: growth theory should be regarded as only appropriate for relatively short periods of time under strict conditions; evolutionary theories are essential when following economies over longer periods of time.

EVALUATION METHODS AND SPATIAL AND DYNAMIC INDICATORS

Integrated models possibly generate a large number of economic, physical, biological, welfare and environmental quality indicators. Aggregation of these in order to arrive at clear conclusions is often inevitable. For this purpose some evaluation procedure is needed. Various methods have been developed and applied to the context of environmental and ecological economics issues (Janssen, 1992; Munda, 1995; van den Bergh, 1996; and Janssen and Munda, 1999).

An evaluation method can support the ranking of alternative decisions regarding management, policy, development scenarios or projects. This can lead to a complete ranking, the best alternative, a set of acceptable alternatives or an incomplete ranking. In general, multiple criteria are relevant in the evaluation procedure. Each of these should be comprehensive and measurable. 'Comprehensive' means that the criterion's value is sufficiently indicative of the degree to which a specific objective is met. 'Measurable' means that it is consistent with a particular measurement scale that allows ordering of the alternatives (management strategies, policies, scenarios, projects) for a particular objective. The ratio, interval ordinal and binary scales qualify as suitable scales of measurement, as they make it possible to order alternatives.

There is a wide range of multicriteria evaluation methods, for continuous and discrete alternatives, based on graphical methods, on aggregation procedures, on ranking of importance of criteria (lexicographic methods) and so on (see Nijkamp *et al.*, 1990; Janssen, 1992). In practical applications two types of input are required for a multicriteria analysis: a table with effects scores for each alternative and criterion (or indicator); and a set of weights. Sensitivity analysis can focus on either of these (see the Greek islands example, below). Multicriteria evaluation can be regarded as a general method of welfare analysis, and as such allows for a good alternative to traditional, neoclassical cost–benefit analysis of social welfare and policy instruments (see Munda, 1997).

Many ecological–economic analyses are based on dynamic and spatial models that generate temporal and spatial patterns for various indicator variables. Comparison thus involves three dimensions: space, time and indicators. Only cost–benefit analysis includes an explicit standard procedure to integrate the different types of effect, as only those in monetary terms are considered, as well as the time pattern for each type of effect, namely via discounting. In multicriteria analysis the time or spatial pattern of effects can be included by specifying evaluation criteria that reflect the different spans of the effects. Via this route short- and long-term effects can be included in a single effects table and decision rule. Not all multicriteria methods are, however, suitable for dealing with spatial and temporal issues (see Nijkamp *et al.*, 1990). Dynamic indicators can be aggregated in various ways. One approach is to discount each indicator pattern according to a specific procedure; even when only monetized values are included, varying discount rates can be used for separate variables, each measured in monetary terms (which is done in the Krutilla–Fisher algorithm; see Porter, 1982). Alternatively, one may regard indicator values at each point in space and time, as separate attributes in the multicriteria evaluation procedure, and assign weights to each of these. Again, this is also possible when dealing only with monetized values. This approach will not be very attractive in general, as it requires the choice of too many weights, especially when temporal and spatial dimensions are considered simultaneously. Still other approaches can focus on average values over time or space for indicators, or on final values. It should be noted that any weighting or discounting should take account of both time or spatial discounting and uncertainty discounting aspects. Finally, uncertainty, which is often crucial in ecological economics, requires a special treatment in multicriteria analysis. For discussion of this, see Munda (1995).

EXAMPLES

Introduction

Two examples of integrated analyses are presented, one theoretical and one applied. Each focuses on a particular combination of elements discussed in the previous sections.

The first example integrates elements from growth theory with a multisectoral economic structure and a materials flow model. The sectors include manufacturing of final goods and of investment (capital) goods, non-renewable and renewable resource-based activities, and abatement and recycling. The materials flow model is based on dynamic mass balance conditions, which are integrated in the multisectoral production structure. The model allows for a detailed analysis of limits to growth and sustainable development. It differs from most theoretical economic models in that it offers a much more elaborate economic structure. Evidently, the analysis has to proceed via numerical simulation of scenarios (see van den Bergh and Nijkamp, 1994a). The alternative is a very simple model that is analytically tractable (Kamien and Schwartz, 1982; Toman *et al.*, 1995; Faucheux *et al.*, 1996). Van den Bergh and Hofkes (1998) offer a wide range of approaches to formal modelling of sustainable development that shows the potential for less simplistic descriptions of reality.

The second example is probably most in line with what many ecological economists regard as integrated modelling. It provides a systems modelling study linking dynamic and spatial models into one comprehensive model (van den Bergh and Nijkamp, 1994c). Scenario analysis and multicriteria evaluation are used to examine which policy options aimed at a sustainable regional development are most attractive. Although the approach of explicitly linking empirical ecological and economic models seems straightforward, there are only a few studies that have actually tried to do this in an applied context. An important reason for this is probably that this approach requires significant inputs from various disciplines.

Long-run Materials Flow Patterns in an Integrated Multisector Economy–Ecology Model

The model is designed with the aim to study the long-term relationship between an economy and its natural environment. The approach is based on two main elements: (1) reciprocal interactions between, on the one hand, population growth, investment, allocation of inputs and outputs, technology and productivity, and, on the other hand, declining environmental quality, pollution and resource exhaustion; and (2) a more realistic and consistent representation of the interdependence between various environmental effects, from extraction to emission, by using a materials balance (MB) perspective on economic processes. The model includes production functions that are consistent with MB. The model is multisectoral, including economic processes of extraction, production of commodities and investment goods, waste abatement and recycling. Environmental processes of resource regeneration and waste assimilation are linked through the economic and environmental sphere. Disaggregation leads to economic categories of investment goods, and private and public consumption, and to environmental categories of non-renewable resources, renewable resources, slowly renewable resources and environmental pollution. The model allows for endogenous development of resource-efficient technology. Feedback mechanisms are included that take account of the effect of sustainability conditions and societal values on both technology formation and allocation of investment goods over the various economic sectors. The model is specified, calibrated and subsequently used for simulation of scenarios. Finally, some sensitivity analysis results are discussed.

What are the implications of production combined with MB for long-term development? Here this question will be answered by analysing a multisectoral integrated macro model. The model describes two phenomena: (1) the material flows (and processes based upon these flows) in the economy, the natural environment and their interdependencies; and (2) the feedback mechanisms from economy, environment and value systems to economic actions and policies. The latter occurs over a long-term horizon.

The material flow is shown in Figure 9.1. It describes an economy with six sectors. The model has a supply orientation reflecting a long-term horizon. It includes economic and materials balance conditions, economic activity and production functions. These production functions satisfy materials balance conditions, as discussed in van den Bergh and Nijkamp (1994a). Economic activities include resource extraction, production, waste treatment (abatement), recycling, research and development of environmental technology, and environmental cleaning. Some of these activities are taken to be competitive for economic (financial) means, and can to some extent be stimulated by government policies.

In Figure 9.2 the economic–environmental relationships represented in the model are displayed. They include flows as well as impacts upon processes. An environmental quality indicator related to stocks of resources and pollution is used as a state variable for codetermination of the level of natural processes of regeneration and assimilation. Environmental quality is also assumed to have an impact upon the efficiency of final goods production (for example, agriculture) and the quality of extracted renewable resources (for example, the stock of fish). It is important to note that changes in non-economic variables (technology and population) are also included.

The description of the economic activities module is based upon production and activity functions for six sectors: final goods production; investment goods production; waste treatment; recycling activity; renewable resource extraction; and non-renewable resource extraction. The functions satisfy, where necessary, materials balance conditions, and may include a mix of environmental and economic production factors, available resource materials (in inventory), environmental quality and the technological progress indicator.

The first economic sector is an aggregate of all final goods-producing sectors (including relevant types of agriculture). Output (Q) is produced with capital (K_Q). It requires resource inputs $c_Q(T_{rd})$ per unit of output. A higher overall environmental quality (E) positively affects the productive efficiency. The availability of resources (R_{sup}) in inventory (that is, supply of resource materials) imposes an upper limit on the output level of production. Therefore we have the output function as in (9.1). It is in agreement with the third type of materials balance production function (MBPF) formulation as given in van den Bergh and Nijkamp (1994a). For an updated account of formal expressions of mass balance production functions, see van den Bergh (1999).

$$Q = MIN\left\{ F_Q(K_Q, E), \frac{R_{\mathrm{sup}}}{c_Q(T_{rd})} \right\}. \tag{9.1}$$

It is clear that output Q cannot exceed resource input and that some material loss in production is inevitable. This means that $c_Q(T_{rd}) > 1$. Techno-

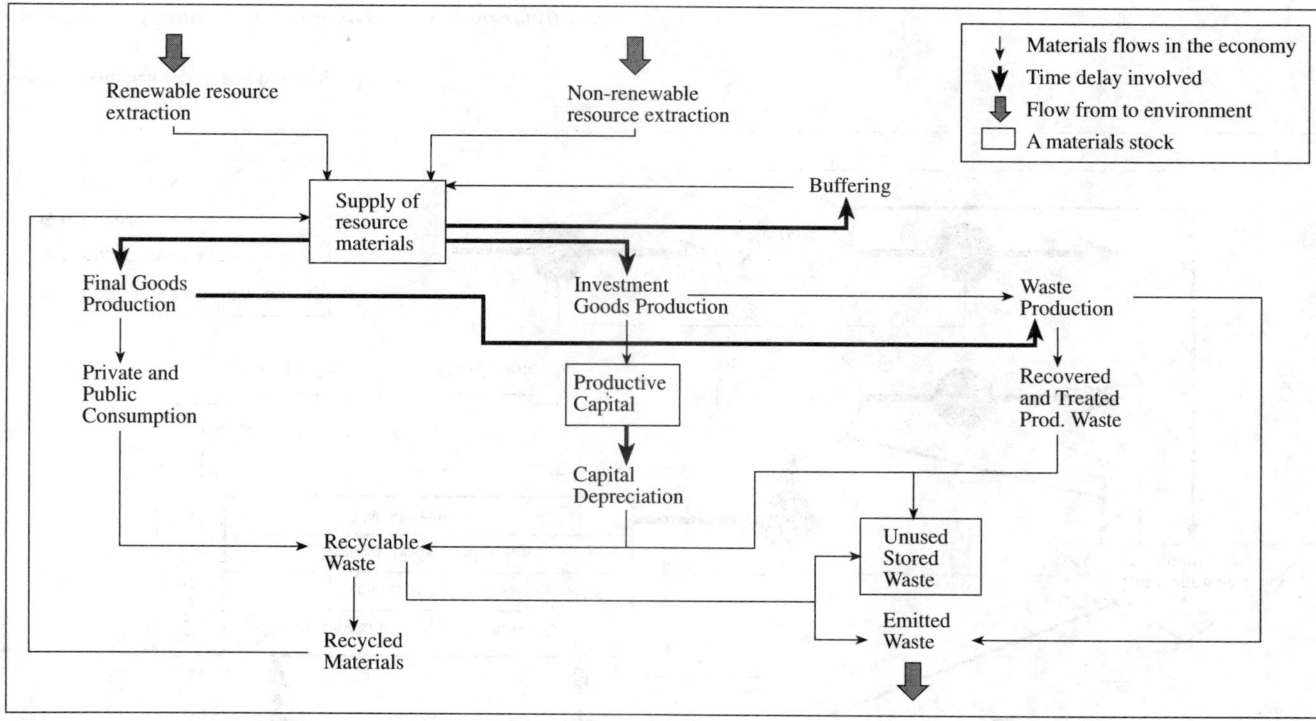

Source: van den Bergh and Nijkamp (1994a).

Figure 9.1 Materials flow diagram of the economy

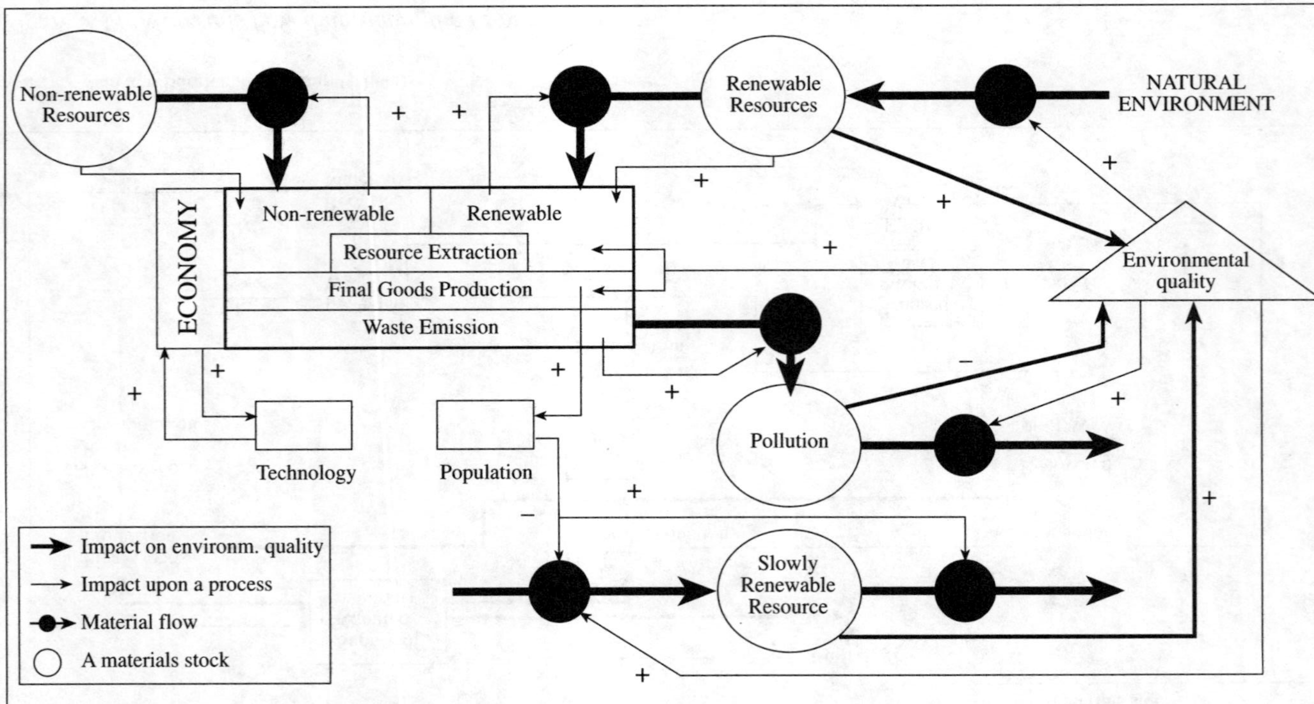

Source: van den Bergh and Nijkamp (1994a).

Figure 9.2 Economy–environment flows and relationships

logical change is assumed to generate more efficiency in terms of a lower ratio of resource input to Q, so that for all $x \geq 0$ $dc_Q(x)/dx < 0$.

A second activity is capital goods formation (I). This may be interpreted as the production of machines and new technology. The level of output is directly related to the amount of capital in this sector (K_I). An upper limit to the output level is set by taking the ration of the supply (inventory) of resource materials (R_{sup}) less the amount required for the first (Q) production process to the per unit of output required input in this sector; thereby it is assumed that Q production is more important than I production for general welfare, and is therefore given priority for resource use; $c_I(T_{rd})$ is, like $c_Q(T_{rd})$, made dependent on the state of technology T_{rd}. Again, (9.2) is of the third type of MBPF (van den Bergh and Nijkamp, 1994a).

$$I = MIN\left\{F_I(K_I), \frac{R_{\text{sup}} - c_Q(T_{rd}) * Q}{c_I(T_{rd})}\right\}. \tag{9.2}$$

Next, we consider two other economic sectors that are related to environmentally beneficial activities. Both sectors use capital. One process represented in (9.3) treats production waste in such a way that not all of it is directly carried to the natural environment. The amount of waste treated (R_{wa}) is determined by the level of waste arising directly from the two 'real' production processes ($W_{Q,I}$), the amount of capital used (K_{wa}) and the state of technology (T_{rd}). The latter two affect positively the effectiveness coefficient (f_{wa}) of abatement.

$$R_{wa} = f_{wa}(T_{rd}, K_{wa}) * W_{Q,I}. \tag{9.3}$$

A second process represented in (9.4) is concerned with recycling of materials. Its output R_{rec} is determined by the waste flow suitable for recycling (W_{rec}) and the state of technology, which positively affect the effectiveness coefficient (f_{rec}) of recycling.

$$R_{rec} = f_{rec}(T_{rd}, K_{rec}) * W_{rec}. \tag{9.4}$$

The functions f_{wa} and f_{rec} have values between 0 and 1, so that abated (recycled) waste does not exceed production waste (waste amenable for recycling): $R_{wa} < W_Q$ ($R_{rec} < W_{rec}$); all first partial derivatives are positive. Both (9.3) and (9.4) are special cases of the last type of general MBPF, as mentioned in van den Bergh and Nijkamp (1994a).

Finally, two-resource based economic activities remain to be described: renewable and non-renewable resource extraction (R_N and R_S, respectively), both using capital (K_N and K_S, respectively). The production functions, given in (9.5) and (9.6), are based on the relevant stocks or resources; in the case of renewable exploitation, the environmental quality is also significant since it determines the part of the stock that is of sufficient quality (for example, clean water, or healthy, non-toxic resources, normal size fish).

$$R_N = MIN\{F_N(K_N, N, E), R_{N,perc}\}. \tag{9.5}$$

$$R_S = MIN\{F_S(K_S, S), R_{S,perc}\}. \tag{9.6}$$

Results of scenario analysis based on this multisector model, which includes mass balance conditions and other economic model equations, are presented in van den Bergh and Nijkamp (1994a).

Integration of Methods in an Ecological–Economic Study of an Island Region

In this section some flavour is given of an application of a combination of methods, in particular integrated dynamic modelling and multicriteria evaluation, to study regional sustainable development of an island region, the Sporades, in Greece. The islands in this region are characterized by a potential conflict between environmental conservation and rapid growth of tourism. A dynamic model was used to depict the development of the economies of three main islands and their interactions with the terrestrial and marine environment. For more details on the study context, see Giaoutzi and Nijkamp (1993).

The Northern Sporades are a complex of islands located in the Aegean Sea close to central Greece. They constitute an area where socioeconomic objectives conflict with environmental conservation objectives. This area embraces the inhabited islands of Skiathos, Skopelos and Allonisos, and some uninhabited islands. For the purpose of the present study, a nearby, fairly undeveloped area on the mainland, Pillion, was included in the analysis as well, because of spillover effects that may result from quick economic development induced by tourism on the islands. The population levels in 1985 of Skiathos, Skopelos, Allonisos and Pillion were 5064, 4226, 1621 and 600, respectively. There exists a rich vegetation on the islands, including pine forests and different types of Mediterranean scrubland (indicated by the French names maquis and garrigue). Both flora and fauna include many interesting, and some unique, species. The marine environment is also rich in species, such as corals, different types of fish, dolphins and the Mediterranean monk seal (*Monachus monachus*). This latter species is very valuable from a conservation point of view: it is unique in the world, threatened and highly valued by tourists (laymen) and biologists (experts). In addition, the monk seal is a critical part of the marine ecosystem, in which it is situated at the top of the foodchain. However, the existence of this species is threatened by sea water pollution, fishing and tourism in the area. The number of seals has gone down and stabilized in recent years to the present level of approximately 40. A marine park was established in September 1986 to protect the marine system. The implications are that visits of tourists are limited to certain parts of the marine area. In addition, fishing is being controlled by rules, fishing zones, fishing periods and type of nets. Besides tourism and fishing, a third type of negative impact of human activity on the marine system is occurring, namely through flows of pollution and waste generated by the island population, tourists and economic activities.

The model of the island region focuses on the interaction of land-based and marine-based activities, considering marine park policies in a wider economic, coastal zone perspective. The past directions of development of the three main islands Skiathos, Skopelos and Allonisos have been greatly influenced by the pattern of tourism. However, the development stages of the three islands differ significantly. The island economies are rather small. The following economic sectors can be distinguished: local services, fishery, agriculture, public sector, construction and two tourism-based sectors (accommodation and services). Trade and transport are arranged by mainland firms, leaving no special benefits for the local population other than via the local services. This sectoral disaggregation is based on a combination of considerations: labour market operation, interdependencies between activities, and economic–environmental relationships. The model is descriptive and used for dynamic simulation based on well-chosen development and policy scenarios. A complete account of the general model structure, scenarios and evaluation is given in van den Bergh (1996, ch. 11). For technical details, the reader is referred to van den Bergh and Nijkamp (1994c).

In Figure 9.3, the overall structure of the model is shown, which is designed according to interactive modular components. On this highest modular level, descriptions are given of the three main island economies, the socio-economic relationships with the outside world, the influence on the nearby area of Pillion, and the impact of the mainland on the marine system. The three main islands in the region are treated separately, for three reasons. First, their development levels differ. Second, only the Allonisos module includes a terrestrial submodule with a description of land use and natural vegetation cover. Finally, Allonisos receives special attention in the study from the policy perspective. The economy and people modules are set up for each of the islands.

One important economic–environmental interaction occurs through the fisheries (Figure 9.4). Vessels from three islands and the mainland generate a certain amount of fishing effort, which is one determinant of total fish catch. There are two other determinants. One is the sum of the sizes of the four

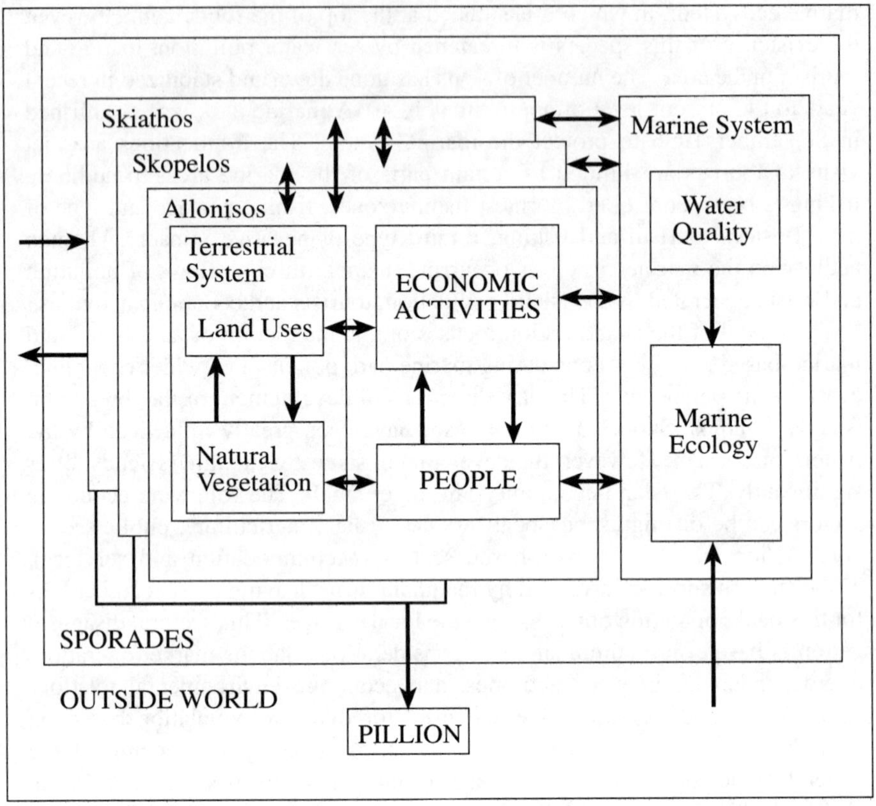

Source: van den Bergh and Nijkamp (1994c).

Figure 9.3 Structure of the economic–environmental model

stocks of fish and lobster species being subjected to fishing. The other is the constraint on catch to realize sustainable fishing patterns, operationalized by restrictions on fishing nets, periods and zones.

Many scenario simulation results are available. Figure 9.5 gives an example of time patterns of an amenity index under various scenarios. More details about scenarios, and time patterns for a number of other indicators can be found in van den Bergh (1996, ch. 11). In addition to this a multicriteria analysis and a geographic information systems (GIS) analysis were performed, which can serve as input for a decision support system for sustainable development planning of the Greek Sporades Islands.

The multicriteria analysis can generate a ranking of policies or scenarios under different preference structures of decision makers (such as policy mak-

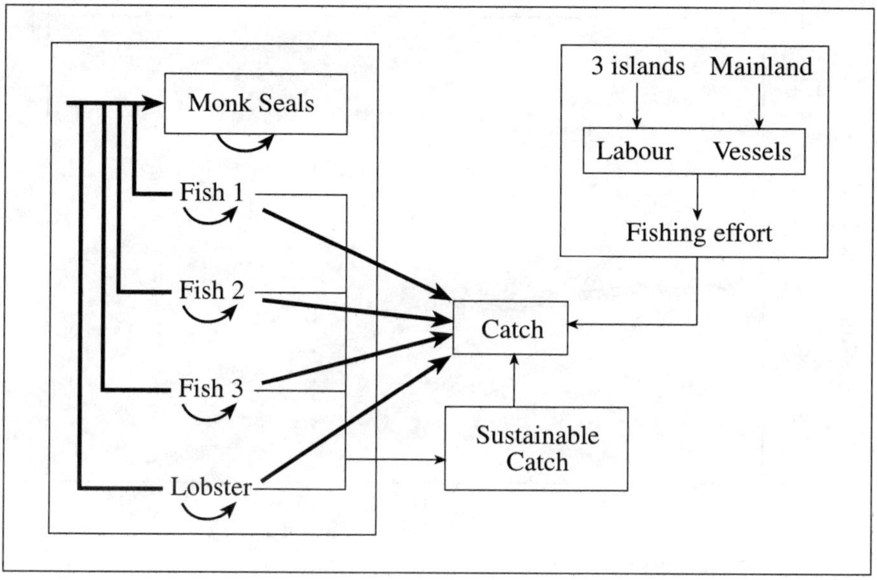

Note: Fat arrows denote flows of fish in the ecological system or to the economy.

Source: van den Bergh and Nijkamp (1994c).

Figure 9.4 Submodule fisheries

ers or politicians). A set of weights can be applied to aggregate the various indicators into 'compound criteria'. In the present case this was done in such a way that two indicators resulted, one representing the goal of socioeconomic development (SED), and the other reflecting the goal of ecological development (ED). Figure 9.6 includes a histogram, showing for each scenario what the relative score is in terms of each of the compound criteria. One can immediately detect (visually) which scenarios are dominated by others, that is, perform worse on each criterion; for instance, SEG and SF are dominated by MP. Of course, if one scenario dominates all others a trivial problem, given the initial aggregation, is to be solved. In general, however, a subset of scenarios will remain which have to be evaluated by further aggregation. Accordingly, the evaluation procedure can be continued by aggregating the compound indicator applying higher-level weights. Given two criteria, it is possible, furthermore, to represent graphically the impact of changing weights on scenario ranking, and immediately detect indifference ('turning' or 'break-even') points. Finally, sensitivity of the disaggregated effects (of all indicators) entering the first, lower-level aggregation procedure can be exam-

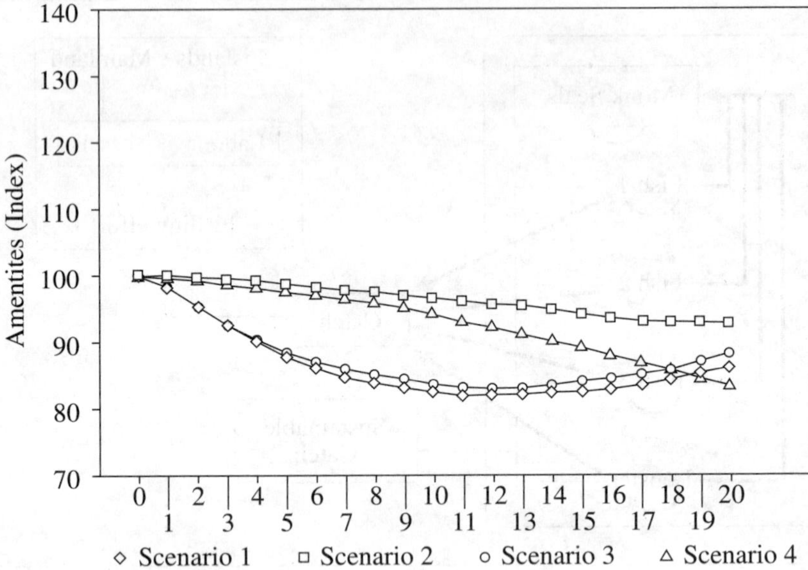

Source: van den Bergh and Nijkamp (1994c).

Figure 9.5 Amenities index under various scenarios

ined by performing a Monte Carlo experiment, allowing for a range of values around the initial points used, and generating probabilistic rankings (given specific weights). In this way one can check which scenario rankings are robust or reliable.

The six development alternatives in Figure 9.6 were unspecified in terms of spatial details; that is, they do not (or hardly) discriminate in a geographical sense. Therefore five spatially different policies (called 'land use alternatives') were considered, that focused on the growth of urban areas on the island of Allonisos (for details, see Despotakis, 1991). These five distinct policies can be combined with the above-mentioned individual six development alternatives, which leads altogether to 30 different combined alternatives. These were suitable for a spatial evaluation. Various judgment criteria can be used to evaluate the alternative land use maps associated with these alternatives, for instance, based on land use suitable for tourism, nature, landscape and transport. The GIS maps can of course also be translated into numerical information, so that also multicriteria analysis of spatial scenario outcomes can be performed.[1]

Summarizing this case study shows that one can realize decision support for coastal zone management, based on tools of dynamic modeling, multi-

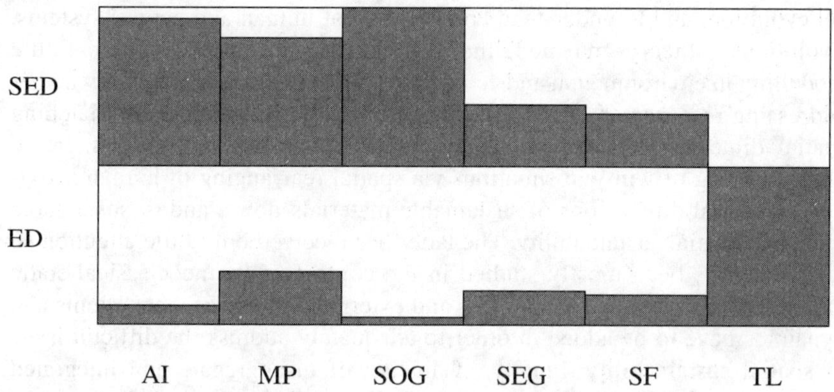

Notes: SED = Socio-economic development; ED = Ecological development; AI = Agricultural Incentive; SEG = Steady Growth; MP = Marine Park: SOG = Strong Growth; SF = Sustainable Fishing; TL = Tourist Limits.

Source: van den Bergh (1996, ch. 11).

Figure 9.6 Histogram of compound development criteria (horizontally scenarios; vertically compound criteria)

criteria analysis and geographical information evaluation. This may increase awareness of current frictions and future incompatibilities in economic development, environmental sustainability, land use shifts and marine park policies.

CONCLUSIONS

This chapter has discussed a broad range of concepts, ideas and methods underlying integrated modelling for sustainable development. Clearly, many interesting and relevant issues have not been addressed due to space limits. The selection of topics is also a bit personal. The area of integrated modelling is so wide and includes so many diverse approaches that anyone trying to oversee it is limited by his or her own research past experience.

Both at fundamental and applied levels of integrated modelling much work remains to be done. Especially the translation of different interpretations of sustainable development into formal, operational models needs further research. The application of thermodynamics in formal models can be focused on the role of the entropy law for long-run economic change. This might be combined with evolutionary or 'self-organization' modelling including elements from information theory and physics. Biological evolutionary theory is useful to depict the influence of human activities on the direction of biological evolution, and to understand co-evolution of human and natural systems. Evolutionary theory and modelling can become an integral part of future modelling in environmental and ecological economics, irrespective of whether addressing resource or ecosystem management or climate change. Matching spatial dimensions of economic and environmental systems will increase understanding of win-win situations via spatial rearranging of human activities, of spatial dimensions of sustainable materials flows, and of sustainable trade and spatial sustainability. The latter has received only little attention so far. Trade has been mostly studied in the context of the neoclassical static model with comparative advantages and externalities. Space, ecosystems and dynamics have to be added in order to adequately address the difficult issue of spatial sustainability. Finally, evaluation of disaggregate and integrated model output will mean that a range of indicators measured in different units have to be aggregated. Multicriteria evaluation methods are useful then. They need to pay attention to aggregating or weighting three dimensions, namely time, space, and indicators. Incorporating all these issues together suggests that the development of integrated modelling will increasingly be dominated by large, multidisciplinary research teams.

ACKNOWLEDGEMENTS

Dale Rothman and Jack Ruitenbeek provided helpful comments.

NOTE

1. The multicriteria analysis discussed here was performed by Ron Janssen and Marjan van Herwijnen, Institute for Environmental Studies, Free University, Amsterdam. For more details, see van den Bergh (1996, ch. 11).

REFERENCES

Allen, P. (1998), 'Evolutionary Complex Systems and Sustainable Development', in J.C.J.M. van den Bergh and M.W. Hofkes (eds), *Modelling of Sustainable Development between Theory and Practice*, Dordrecht: Kluwer Academic Publishers, pp. 67–99.

Ayres, R.U. (1978), *Resources, Environment and Economics: Applications of the Materials/Energy Balance Principle*, New York: Wiley-Interscience.

Ayres, R.U. (1994), *Information, Entropy and Progress: A New Evolutionary Paradigm*, American Institute of Physics, New York: AIP Press.

Ayres, R.U. and L.W. Ayres (1996), *Industrial Ecology: Towards Closing the Materials Cycle*, Cheltenham, UK and Brookfield, US: Edward Elgar.

Ayres, R.U., J.C.J.M. van den Bergh and J.M. Gowdy (2000), 'Strong versus Weak Sustainability: Economics, Natural Sciences, and Consilience', *Environmental Ethics*, **23** (1), 155–68.

Barney, G.O. (ed.) (1980), *The Global 2000 Report to the President of the U.S., Entering the Twenty-first Century*, 2 vols, Harmondsworth: Penguin Books.

van den Bergh, J.C.J.M. (1996), *Ecological Economics and Sustainable Development: Theory, Methods and Applications*, Cheltenham, UK and Brookfield, US: Edward Elgar.

van den Bergh, J.C.J.M. (1999), 'Materials, Capital, Direct/indirect Substitution, and Mass Balance Production Functions', *Land Economics*, **75** (4), 547–61.

van den Bergh, J.C.J.M. and J.M. Gowdy (2000), 'Evolutionary Theories in Environmental and Resource Economics: Approaches and Applications', *Environmental and Resource Economics*, **17** (1), 37–57.

van den Bergh, J.C.J.M. and M.W. Hofkes (eds) (1998), *Modelling of Sustainable Development between Theory and Practice*, Dordrecht: Kluwer Academic Publishers.

van den Bergh, J.C.J.M. and P. Nijkamp (1994a), 'Dynamic Macro Modelling and Materials Balance: Economic–environmental Integration for Sustainable Development', *Economic Modelling*, **11**, 283–307.

van den Bergh, J.C.J.M. and P. Nijkamp (eds) (1994b), 'Sustainability, Resources and Region', *The Annals of Regional Science*, **28** (1), special issue.

van den Bergh, J.C.J.M. and P. Nijkamp (1994c), 'An Integrated Model for Economic Development and Natural Environment: An Application to the Greek Sporades Islands', *The Annals of Operations Research*, **54**, 143–74.

van den Bergh, J.C.J.M. and P. Nijkamp (1995), 'Growth, Trade and Sustainability in the Spatial Economy', *Studies in Regional Science*, **25** (2), 67–87.

van den Bergh, J.C.J.M. and H. Verbruggen (1999), 'Spatial Sustainability, Trade and Indicators: An Evaluation of the "Ecological Footprint"', *Ecological Economics*, **29** (1), 63–74.

van den Bergh, J.C.J.M., A. Barendregt, A. Gilbert, M. van Herwijnen, P. van Horssen, P. Kandelaars and C. Lorenz (2001), 'Spatial Economic–hydroecological Modelling and Evaluation of Land Use Impacts in the Vecht Wetlands Area', *Integrated Environmental Modelling and Assessment*, **6** (2), 87–100.

Berry, R.S., P. Salamon and G. Heal (1978), 'On a Relation between Economic and Thermodynamic Optima', *Resources and Energy*, **1**, 125–37.

Boulding, K.E. (1978), *Ecodynamics: A New Theory of Societal Evolution*, Beverly Hills: Sage Publications.

Braat, L.C. and W.F.J. van Lierop (eds) (1987), *Economic–Ecological Modelling*, Amsterdam: North-Holland.

Clark, N., F. Perez-Trejo and P. Allen (1995), *Evolutionary Dynamics and Sustainable Development: A Systems Approach*, Aldershot, UK and Brookfield, US: Edward Elgar.

Common, M. and C. Perrings (1992), 'Towards an Ecological Economics of Sustainability', *Ecological Economics*, **6**, 7–34.

Costanza, R., L. Wainger, C. Folke and K.-G. Mäler (1993), 'Modeling Complex Ecological Economic Systems', *BioScience*, **43**, 545–55.

Daly, H.E. (1987), 'The Economic Growth Debate: What Some Have Learned, but Many Have Not', *Journal of Environmental Economics and Management*, **14**, 323–36.

Daly, H.E. (1989), 'Sustainable Development of Regions', unpublished mimeo.

Daly, H.E. (1991), *Steady-State Economics*, 2nd edn, Washington DC: Island Press.
Daly, H.E. (1992), 'Is the Entropy Law Relevant to the Economics of Natural Resource Scarcity? – Yes, of Course It Is!', *Journal of Environmental Economics and Management*, **23**, 91–5.
Daly, H.E. and A.F. Umaña (eds) (1981), *Energy, Economics and the Environment*, AAAS Selected Symposia Series, Boulder, Col.: Westview Press.
Despotakis, V.K. (1991), 'Sustainable Development Planning Using Geographical Information Systems', PhD dissertation, Free University, Amsterdam.
Dosi, G., C. Freeman, R. Nelson, G. Silverberg and L. Soete (eds) (1988), *Technical Change and Economic Theory*, London: Pinter Publishers.
Epstein, C. and R. Axtell (1996), *Growing Artificial Societies: Social Science from the Bottom Up*, Boston, MA: MIT Press.
Faber, M. and J.L.R. Proops (1990), *Evolution, Time, Production and the Environment*, Heidelberg: Springer-Verlag.
Faber, M., H. Niemes and G. Stephan (1987), *Entropy, Environment and Resources: An Essay in Physico-Economics*, Heidelberg: Springer-Verlag.
Faucheux, S., D.W. Pearce and J.L.R. Proops (1996), *Models of Sustainable Development*, Cheltenham, UK and Brookfield, US: Edward Elgar Publishers.
Freeman, A.M. (1993), *The Measurement of Environmental and Resource Values: Theory and Methods*, Baltimore: Resources for the Future.
Georgescu-Roegen, N. (1971a), *The Entropy Law and the Economic Process*, Cambridge, MA: Harvard University Press.
Georgescu-Roegen, N. (1971b), 'Process Analysis and the Neoclassical Theory of Production', *Energy and Economic Myths*, New York: Pergamon.
Giaoutzi, M. and P. Nijkamp (1993), *Decisions Support Models for Regional Sustainable Development*, Aldershot: Avebury.
Gould, S.J. (1982), 'The Meaning of Punctuated Equilibrium and Its Role in Validating a Hierarchical Approach to Macroevolution', in R. Milkman (ed.), *Perspectives on Evolution*, Sunderland MA: Sinauer Associates.
Gould, S.J. and R.C. Lewontin (1979), 'The Spandrels of San Marco and the Panglossian Paradigm: A Critique of the Adaptationist Programme', *Proceedings of the Royal Society of London B*, **205**, 581–98.
Gowdy, J. (1994), *Coevolutionary Economics: The Economy, Society and the Environment*, Dordrecht: Kluwer Academic Publishers.
Gradus, R. and S. Smulders (1993), 'The Trade-off between Environmental Care and Long-term Growth: Pollution in Three Prototype Growth Models', *Journal of Economics*, **58**, 25–52.
Gross, L.S. and E.C.H. Veendorp (1990), 'Growth with Exhaustible Resources and a Materials-balance Production Function', *Natural Resource Modeling*, **4**, 77–94.
Gutés, M.C. (1996), 'The Concept of Weak Sustainability', *Ecological Economics*, **17**, 147–56.
Hartwick, J.M. (1977), 'Intergenerational Equity and the Investing of Rents from Exhaustible Resources', *American Economic Review*, **67**, 972–4.
Hodgson, G.M. (1993), *Economics and Evolution: Bringing back Life into Economics*, Cambridge: Polity Press, Ann Arbor: University of Michigan Press.
Hodgson, G.M. (1995), 'Introduction', *Economics and Biology*, The International Library of Critical Writings in Economics, vol. 50, Aldershot, UK and Brookfield, US: Edward Elgar.
Holling, C.S. (1986), 'The Resilience of Terrestrial Ecosystems: Local Surprise and

Global Change', in W.C. Clark and R.E. Munn (eds), *Sustainable Development of the Biosphere*, Cambridge: Cambridge University Press, pp. 292–317.

Howarth, R.B. and R.B. Norgaard (1995), 'Intergenerational Choices under Global Environmental Change', in D.W. Bromley (ed.), *The Handbook of Environmental Economics*, Oxford: Blackwell, pp. 111–38.

Janssen, M. (1996), *Meeting Targets: Tools to Support Integrated Assessment Modelling of Global Change*, PhD dissertation, University of Maastricht, Maastricht.

Janssen, R. (1992), *Multiobjective Decision Support for Environmental Management*, Dordrecht: Kluwer Academic Publishers.

Janssen, R. and G. Munda (1999), 'Multicriteria Methods for Quantitative, Qualitative and Fuzzy Evaluation Problems', in J.C.J.M. van den Bergh (ed.), *Handbook of Environmental and Resource Economics*, Cheltenham, UK and Northampton, MA, USA: Edward Elgar, pp. 837–52.

Kamien, M.I. and N.L. Schwartz (1982), 'The Role of Common Property Resources in Optimal Planning Models with Exhaustible Resources', in V.K. Smith and J.V. Krutilla (eds), *Explorations in Natural Resource Economics*, Baltimore, MD: Johns Hopkins University Press.

Kandelaars, P.P.A.A.H. and J.C.J.M. van den Bergh (1996), 'Materials-product Chain Analysis: Theory and an Application to Zinc and Pvc Gutters', *Environmental and Resource Economics*, **8**, 97–118.

Maynard Smith, J. (1982), *Evolutionary Game Theory*, Cambridge: Cambridge University Press.

Meadows, D.H., D.L. Meadows and J. Randers (1992), *Beyond the Limits: Confronting Global Collapse; Envisioning a Sustainable Future*, Post Mills: Chelsea Green Publishing Co.

Meadows, D.H., J. Richardson and G. Bruckmann (1982), *Groping in the Dark: The First Decade of Global Modeling*, New York: Wiley.

Meadows, D.H., D.L. Meadows, J. Randers and W.W. Behrens (1972), *The Limits to Growth*, New York: Universe Books.

Munda, G. (1995), *Multicriteria Evaluation in a Fuzzy Environment*, Heidelberg: Physica-Verlag.

Munda, G. (1997), 'Multicriteria Evaluation as a Multidimensional Approach to Welfare Measurement', in J.C.J.M. van den Bergh and J. van der Straaten (eds), *Economy and Ecosystems in Change: Analytical and Historical Approaches*, Cheltenham, UK and Lyme, US: Edward Elgar, pp. 96–115.

Munro, A. (1994), 'Economics and Biological Evolution', *Environmental and Resource Economics*, **9**, 429–49.

Nelson, R. and S. Winter (1982), *An Evolutionary Theory of Economic Change*, Cambridge, MA: The Belknap Press of Harvard University Press.

Nelson, R.R. (1995), 'Recent Evolutionary Theorizing about Economic Change', *Journal of Economic Literature*, **33**, 48–90.

Nijkamp, P., P. Rietveld and H. Voogd (1990), *Multicriteria Evaluation in Physical Planning*, Amsterdam: North-Holland.

Norgaard, R.B. (1984), 'Coevolutionary Development Potential', *Land Economics*, **60**, 160–73.

Norgaard, R.B. (1994), *Development Betrayed: The End of Progress and a Coevolutionary Revisioning of the Future*, London and New York: Routledge.

Pearce, D.W., E.B. Barbier and A. Markandya (1990), *Sustainable Development: Economics and Environment in the Third World*, Aldershot, UK and Brookfield, US: Edward Elgar.

Pezzey, J. (1989), 'Economic Analysis of Sustainable Growth and Sustainable Development', Environmental Department Working paper no. 15, Environmental Department, The World Bank; reprinted as J. Pezzey (1992), 'Sustainable Development Concepts: An Economic Analysis', World Bank Environment Paper 2, Washington, DC.

Porter, R. (1982), 'The New Approach to Wilderness Appraisal through Cost–benefit Analysis', *Journal of Environmental Economics and Management*, **11**, 59–80.

Rose, A. and S. Casler (1996), 'Input–output Structural Decomposition Analysis: A Critical Appraisal', *Economic Systems Research*, **8**, 33–62.

Ruth, M. (1993), *Integrating Economics, Ecology and Thermodynamics*, Dordrecht: Kluwer Academic Publishers.

Ruth, M. (1996), 'Evolutionary Economics at the Crossroads of Biology and Physics', *Journal of Social and Evolutionary Systems*, **19**, 125–44.

Smith, J.B. and S. Weber (1989), 'Contemporaneous Externalities: Rational Expectations and Equilibrium Production Functions in Natural Resource Models', *Journal of Environmental Economics and Management*, **17**, 155–70.

Solow, R.M. (1974), 'Intergenerational Equity and Exhaustible Resources', *Review of Economic Studies*, **41**, 29–45.

Solow, R.M. (1986), 'On the Intergenerational Allocation of Natural Resources', *Scandinavian Journal of Economics*, **88**, 141–9.

Starreveld, P.F. and E.C. van Ierland (1994), 'Recycling of Plastics: A Material Balance Optimisation Model', *Environmental and Resource Economics*, **4**, 251–64.

Toman, M.A., J. Pezzey and J. Krautkraemer (1995), 'Neoclassical Economic Growth Theory and "Sustainability"', in D. Bromley (ed.), *Handbook of Environmental Economics*, Oxford: Blackwell, pp. 139–65.

Turner, R.K., C. Perrings and C. Folke (1997), 'Ecological Economics: Paradigm or Perspective', in: J.C.J.M. van den Bergh and J. van der Straaten (eds), *Economy and Ecosystems in Change: Analytical and Historical Approaches*, Cheltenham, UK and Lyme, US: Edward Elgar, pp. 25–49.

Vedeld, P.O. (1994), 'The Environment and Interdisciplinarity. Ecological and Neoclassical Economical Approaches to the Use of Natural Resources', *Ecological Economics*, **10** (1), 1–13.

Wackernagel, M. and W. Rees (1996), *Our Ecological Footprint: Reducing Human Impact on the Earth*, The New Catalyst Bioregional series vol. 9, Gabriola Island, BC and Philadelphia, PA: New Society Publishers.

Wackernagel, M. and W. Rees (1997), 'Perceptual and Structural Barriers to Investing in Natural Capital: Economics from an Ecological Footprint Perspective', *Ecological Economics*, **20** (1), 3–24.

WCED (1987), *Our Common Future*, Oxford and New York: World Commission on Environment and Development, Oxford University Press.

Weibull, J.W. (1995), *Evolutionary Game Theory*, Cambridge, MA: MIT Press.

Young, J.T. (1991), 'Is the Entropy Law Relevant to the Economics of Natural Resource Scarcity?', *Journal of Environmental Economics and Management*, **21**, 169–79.

Zuchetto, J. and A.M. Jansson (1985), *Resources and Society: A Systems Ecology Study of the Island of Gotland, Sweden*, New York: Springer-Verlag.

10. Non-equilibrium theory of African arid ecosystems: designing for monitoring and evaluation

Maryam Niamir-Fuller

INTRODUCTION

Looking back at the history of development in arid and semi-arid Africa in the last three decades, one is struck by the extent to which the different interventions have been labelled as failures by reviewers, researchers and development representatives. This disappointment has even led donor countries and organizations in the late 1980s strategically to reduce their involvement in African arid lands – a phenomenon described as 'benign neglect', or 'leave them alone and they'll be better off' (Swift, 1993). The reasons for such failures have been reviewed extensively elsewhere (see, for example, pastoral development literature), but their underlying problem was the adoption of inappropriate paradigms by scientists and development workers on the relation between man and environment.

Basic ecological data on arid ecosystems are still scarce, and there are important gaps in global coverage (for example, hardly any work has been done in the drylands of Latin America, and relatively minimal work in Africa). The lack of data reflects a lack of political concern by funding organizations, researchers and experts who view arid ecosystems as marginal areas – marginal in terms of their value for economic growth, ecological biodiversity, social quality and political strength. However, arid ecosystems are gradually emerging as important sources of drought-adapted mechanisms (species and processes), and their impact on global climate (dust cycles, carbon sinks and so on) is only now being re-evaluated. In addition, increasing human population in developing countries is prompting governments and development organizations to re-evaluate the economic potential of arid lands. Efforts such as the Desert Biome Project in Utah, USA, one of the elements of the International Council of Scientific Unions (ICSU)-initiated International Biome Project (IBP), which included desert ecosystem modelling, material cycling, dynamics of interactions between ecosystem elements and so on, are some of the more recent attempts to gain knowledge about a little-known ecosystem.

Rainfall is so variable and unpredictable in the arid lands that it poses tremendous constraints on management of natural resources, on integrated assessments of the environment, and on monitoring and evaluation of these resources and production systems. This chapter reviews some of the theoretical background, and points out some guidelines for monitoring and evaluating ecosystem function, structure and health in arid and semi-arid environments. It addresses a practical world where political decisions are taken that affect ecosystem health. Its objective is to translate theoretical advances in ecological theory into appropriate policies and development activities. The discussion is confined in spatial scale to dryland ecosystems and, even more specifically, to African drylands, although lessons and implications can be derived for other drylands around the world.

The time-scale adopted for the discussion is not geological or molecular time, but the time-scale relevant to an African pastoralist (and the researchers and development workers dependent upon him), that is, two to three generations.

NON-EQUILIBRIUM VERSUS EQUILIBRIUM ECOLOGICAL THEORY IN ARID LANDS OF AFRICA

Arid and semi-arid ecosystems of Africa (hereafter called 'drylands') occur mainly in the North Africa–Sahara–Sahel belt, but also in eastern Africa (Somalia to northern Kenya and Uganda) and southern Africa's inland and coastal deserts (Kalahari, Namibia and so on). Using Thornthwaite's moisture index of the ratio of precipitation to potential evapotranspiration (UNEP, 1991), almost 6000 million hectares of land worldwide can be classified as semi-arid or drier. More than a third of this occurs in Africa, and comprises about 60 per cent of that continent. These ecosystems are characterized by low net primary productivity, and high variability in ecosystem productivity, both spatially and temporally. The drylands have long been the home of mostly mobile populations – whether pastoralist or hunter-gatherer – because production systems have had to adapt to an especially harsh and unpredictable environment.

There has been increasing recognition in recent years that classical equilibrium theory is not able adequately to account for empirical data emerging from arid ecosystems. The main anomalies lie in:

- non-systematic interactions between biota;
- unpredictability in patterns of succession, evolutionary change and species composition;

- unpredictable effects of externalities in ecosystem dynamics.

In parallel with trends in other scientific fields, there is a changing intellectual climate for ideas related to nonlinear dynamics among ecologists. The 'non-equilibrium ecological theory' (Walker *et. al.*, 1981; Westoby *et al.*, 1989; Ellis and Swift, 1988; Friedel, 1991; Behnke and Scoones, 1991; Swallow, 1993) recognizes three characteristics of arid ecosystems: ecological variability, unpredictability and resilience. According to this view, arid ecosystems, such as in Africa, may never achieve equilibrium because of the high degree of uncertainty caused by climatic variability. This implies therefore that ecosystem structure and function is not internally driven (that is, not influenced by internal processes of competition and feedback among biotic components), nor is it self-organizing or teleological. Grazing and other biotic factors may not be as important in determining ecosystem structure and function as abiotic factors. All ecosystems fall somewhere in the continuum from equilibrial to non-equilibrial. The latter applies better to arid lands and is characterized by weak biotic coupling, independence of species, abiotic limitations, density independence and large stochastic effects.

The term 'non-equilibrium' is intended to liberate and extend the scope of ecological theory from the equilibrium paradigm that has dominated it since the 1970s (Immanuel Noy-Meir, personal communication). It does not necessarily imply that there is no equilibrium in ecological community dynamics; rather that there is no one single equilibrium point, as implied by classical theory. Arid ecosystems can be considered as 'emergent complex systems' where the dialectics between hegemony and fragmentation (Funtowicz and Ravetz, 1994) is driven, in the absence of equilibriating forces, by external factors, preeminent of which are climatic variability and man (widening the system boundary would naturally incorporate these as internal factors).

Non-equilibrium theory does not imply that the ecosystem is chaotic, because it does recognize causality (e.g. pressure-state-response approach) and patterns in vegetation dynamics (e.g. state and transition models). The concept of non-equilibrium ecological systems encompasses four possibilities (Noy-Meir, personal communication):[1]

1. there may be several equilibrium states between which the system 'jumps' across thresholds as a result of positive feedbacks ('multiple equilibrium', 'catastophe theory');
2. the system may never get close to any equilibrium because the fluctuations or 'jump' caused by external and internal forces are faster than the stabilization by negative feedbacks;
3. the intrinsic dynamics of the system may not tend towards an equilib-

rium point, but towards a stable 'limit cycle' or 'strange attractor', or may even be chaotic;

4. any combination of the above.

Scale, both spatial and temporal, affects the choice of terminology. A system that appears to be in equilibrium may in fact be in non-equilibrium on larger or smaller scales. The theories of patch dynamics, for example, depend on what geographical scale is adopted: a single patch may be at non-equilibrium, but may show long-term equilibrium when considered on the scale of a large collection of patches.

Total annual rainfall in arid lands varies greatly from year to year. In some areas a coefficient of variability as high as 50 per cent has been recorded. Intra-annual rainfall, measured in terms of monthly variability, is also very high. Equally importantly, spatial distribution of the rainfall can be very high, and is largely unpredictable (Noy-Meir, 1973). This results in resources that are very 'patchy'; that is, the ecosystem is extremely heterogeneous and composed of myriad 'micro-niches' that are important determinants of its structure and function (De Angelis and Waterhouse, 1987). The productivity of these resources is hard to track, let alone to predict.

Non-equilibrium ecological theorists question the usefulness of principles such as climax and succession in describing arid ecosystems. Since the 'climax' community is impossible to determine, the 'desired vegetation community' is a better management objective to work towards. If equilibrium is either unattainable or is achieved for only very short periods of time, then the pathway to it (whether it be autogenic or allogenic succession[2]) is not always constant, progressive or replicable. Vegetation can shift between ecological states even in the absence of anthropic disturbance, because of the primary factor of rainfall (Sharp *et al.*, 1990; Laycock, 1991). In its stead, some theorists are proposing the concept of 'state and transition' (Westoby *et al.*, 1989; Walker, 1993) as a methodological tool to describe vegetation dynamics (Iglesias and Kothmann, 1997).

Consequently, the range management tools of carrying capacity and stocking rate, calculated on the basis of both climax and succession theories, are useful only in providing a generalized description of the ecosystem, averaged over space and time (de Leeuw and Tothill, 1993). They do not take into account yearly variability, or spatial heterogeneity at the micro level ('patches' or niches). Spatial distribution of grazing pressure may be more important in determining ecosystem response than how many animals are grazed or how intensively the area is grazed (Milchunas and Lauenroth, 1993). It is precisely the two factors of space and time, rather than a static average of primary productivity, that determine sustainable carrying capacity, a fact which traditional pastoral managers were well aware of, and adjusted to, through their tools of mobility and 'tracking' (Niamir, 1990; Scoones, 1995).[3]

Xerophytic plants in these areas have evolved traits adaptive to the variable climate and to grazing pressure since before Neolithic times, thus ensuring a high degree of resilience (Stiles, 1995). Seen on the larger scale, in both time and space, the dual elements man and nature were kept in a dynamic 'balance' by man's mobility: nomadism as a system has survived thousands of years. In the short, medium and long terms, however, there have been booms and busts in the system which have caused bounty and famine. The periodic crashes were not a symptom of a destructive conflict, but of a dynamic adaptation by man to the variability of the environment. Ecosystem resilience in the context of non-equilibrium ecological theory can be defined, not as the resistance to disturbance and speed of return to a stable state of equilibrium (Pimm, 1984), but rather as the magnitude of disturbance that can be absorbed before the system loses its capacity to respond to and buffer the effects of climatic variability (Holling, 1986). The resilience of the arid ecosystem is highlighted by the fact that, when periodic booms and busts result in periodic land degradation, the ecosystem has a tremendous capacity to 'spring back' following a return to normal rainfall, as long as the soil structure and function have not been impaired.

Permanent land degradation, as a possible symptom of destructive conflict between the opposing forces (that is, resulting in a collapse of the very system) is now occurring because of various anthropic factors (primarily population increase, sedentarization and fundamental changes in the political system) compounded by the effects of droughts. Interannual variations in biomass and annual plant density in arid lands, however, should not be confused with long-term human-induced degradation. Dryland plants and animals are more resilient to droughts and flooding than has been appreciated so far, but we still do not know the exact threshold of tolerance to disturbances such as deficits in soil moisture, soil temperature extremes, soil compaction and salinity (Stafford-Smith and Morton, 1990). The Sahara–Sahel desert margin, once considered a good indicator of permanent land degradation, or desertification,[4] is now known to be constantly contracting and expanding year by year (Tucker *et al.*, 1991), and therefore its usefulness as an indicator separating 'normal' variation from permanent degradation is being questioned.

Since the beginning of the 20th century there have been major changes in global climatic patterns. Although precipitation in North America and Australia has remained constant, temperature has dropped in Asian deserts but has increased elsewhere. Precipitation in the Sahel–Sudan zone of Africa has decreased markedly (Williams and Balling, 1995). Depending on the author, there can be many different explanations for these changes (El Niño oscillation in ocean surface temperatures, greenhouse effect, reduced forest cover and so on). Whatever the reason, it is important to remember that decreasing total precipitation also means an increasing coefficient of variability, and therefore greater stress on the entire system and its ability to avoid destructive conflicts.

Notwithstanding the apparent difficulties of evaluating the degree of permanence of land degradation, there are various system errors, mistakes and other signs of autolysis that have prompted many to fear an eventual collapse of the arid lands: for example, the more than 50km of degraded soils around boreholes in the Sahel and the disappearance of perennial grasses and large old trees. Unfortunately, the responses to these fears are so varied that it will be difficult to achieve a meaningful consensus in the near future. The environmental lobby would have one believe that arid lands should be evacuated by man. Somewhere in the middle are most governments and politicians who continue to push for settlement and sedentarization of pastoralists (with a hidden agenda for greater administrative control from the centre). At the other end of the scale, researchers and arid lands experts are gradually achieving a consensus among themselves that nomadism and mobility should be encouraged. Pastoralists themselves are divided among the last two categories. Participatory ecological economic assessment techniques should be applied to African pastoral lands in order to facilitate the process of negotiation and consensus building.

INTEGRATED ASSESSMENT, NON-EQUILIBRIUM ECOLOGICAL THEORY AND MONITORING

Integrated Assessment (IA) is a process developing policy responses to issues with environmental implications (Gough, 1996). The term is open to several interpretations and definitions; however, in the working definition adopted by participants in the first UNEP/SCOPE project workshop, it was recognized to be applicable in situations that are characterized by high uncertainties and conflict over possible courses of action, and as a tool to help articulate and move toward a 'shared' vision of a sustainable development. It is a cyclic, iterative and adaptive process that allows decision makers to identify cause-and-effect chains and to characterize complex systems by developing modelling frameworks, which are then used for experimentation, assessment, evaluation and decision making. IA combines knowledge from diverse scientific disciplines, from the social and the ecological sides, to develop a procedural framework for decision making and conflict resolution. The key to successful IA is the involvement of all stakeholders as integral parts of the procedure.

Tools used by researchers have included integrated assessment models, simulation gaming, scenario analysis, data sets and qualitative analysis (Rotmans and van Asselt, 1996). Models, therefore, are only one kind of tool used in IA. Since decision making takes place in the context of an integrated management, monitoring and governance structure (Kay, 1996), suitable indicators and monitoring programmes must be integrated within the IA process to ensure the functioning of the feedback loops and iterative adjustments. IA is a possible framework for achieving consensus among stakeholders, but that cannot happen within a static, one-time application of data or models. It requires continual monitoring and adjustment of data, variables, indicators and parameters, to be used both in the modelling and scoping phase in the consensus-building phase.

It is necessary to achieve a proper perspective when applying these concepts to developing worlds. It must be recognized that traditional societies normally function within a framework where consensus building is the primary tool for decision making, and that a holistic world-view where social and ecological elements are equally represented provides the basic database. They are already one step ahead of researchers in the process of IA. Researchers are not only stakeholders as the local people are, but must understand, adapt to and use the customary IA process.

There are many forms of inherent uncertainties in non-equilibrium ecological systems that pose difficulties for decision makers. These include parameter variability, process uncertainty and data quality. The presence of 'nonlinearities, and spatial and temporal lags, significantly reduce the ability of traditional reductionist science to provide the insights that are necessary to make proper decisions' about the management of complex systems (Costanza and Ruth, 1996). A more synoptic, holistic and integrated process is required to capture not only the environmental uncertainties but also the anthropic ones.

Commonly held objectives for monitoring in the African arid lands are:

- to provide early warning of long-term degradation;
- to assist with the tracking and management decisions taken by land users in the short and medium term;
- to provide necessary information for a better understanding of ecological dynamics.

A monitoring programme will need a participative set of human goals, a conceptual model of the system, a set of indicators, a methodology for data collection and analysis, and a participative process for synthesizing and prioritizing indicators, and for feeding the results into management and governance (Gallopin, 1996). A monitoring programme must be relevant to and support decisions, it must ensure participation by all stakeholders, adequately consider different scales and levels of decision making, allow overall integration of the system, and be adaptive, flexible and cost-effective.

Indicators are the backbone of monitoring programmes. A holistic treatment of indicators would need to cover scale issues on both the socioeconomic side (family, neighbourhood, clan, tribe, district, nation and so on) and the ecological side (species, patches, communities on the ecological side). Indicators should also address all thematic issues relevant to the problem, using an appropriate analytical framework, such as the pressure–state–impact–response approach (OECD, 1991). Different indicators are required on different scales. Indicators may be quantitative or qualitative, depending on the nature of the parameter, availability and ease of data collection, and potential end use. One can consider two types of indicators: specific indicators that are signs of specific changes or dangers; the idea of the 'most critical factor'; and aggregation of a series of indicators to show low, medium and high potential for change or threats.

Both types of indicators, however, pose problems in non-equilibrium ecological situations because, by definition, the relative importance of factors and the relationships between the factors are variable. For example, soil compaction might be a very good indicator of soil degradation and long-term system disintegration, but only in normal and bad rainfall years. A successive series of very good rainfall years would reduce soil compaction, thus making it insensitive to soil degradation. An example of aggregation of several indicators can also show how the relationship between parameters can vary according to climatic variability. A good aggregate index of land degradation is to combine the two indicators of (a) portion of human population sedentarized, and (b) portion of livestock sedentarized. A high rating on this index would show potentially high threat to land degradation in arid lands because mobility and tracking have been curtailed. However, in a drought year, one would have a very high proportion of livestock sedentarized (most are dead, and the rest congregate around water points) and a high proportion of humans who are sedentarized, as they join refugee camps for famine relief, or join relatives in villages and urban areas. The high rating on this index in drought years would not indicate long-term land degradation, because the rangelands would have been essentially evacuated, allowing natural regeneration to take place.

ECOLOGICAL INDICATORS AND MONITORING IN NON-EQUILIBRIUM ECOSYSTEMS

Non-equilibrium theory's contribution to the debate is in the fact that it turns the focus onto the tremendous variability and unpredictability in natural resource function and structure. How can indicators be designed accordingly? Aggregated indices either have to be modified each time to fit different climatic regimes, or would have to be based only on those indicators that are not affected by the variability. It would be easier to find indicators that are insensitive to variability within the environmental side of the equation than on the social side. However, it is questionable, from the non-equilibrium point of view, whether one would want such insensitive variables. After all, the main challenge is to track variability, not to ignore it.

Indicators that track variability (that is, range as opposed to average) appear more appropriate in capturing the complexity and uncertainty of arid lands. Table 10.1 provides a comparison of different indicators that could be used in equilibrium versus non-equilibrium situations. The main differences between the two types of systems are as follows.

1. Non-equilibrium systems require more frequent measurements and monitoring; the high degree of variability of rainfall in time needs greater frequency of sampling to provide better confidence limits to mean values; in addition, greater frequency of measurements focuses the attention on the amount of deviation from the mean, and allows such deviations to be predicted with more accuracy.
2. More sampling to cover spatial variability; the high degree of patchiness of resources in arid lands (for example, patches of very high-quality riparian areas or oases, next to patches of very poor or low-quality biomass) requires a larger sampling frame.
3. More reliance on ground truthing rather than remote sensing; digitalized remote sensing from satellite imagery is usually of too low a resolution to pick up most of the finely distributed patches of vegetation; average values of biomass over several pixels will invariably be lower than the actual combined biomass of these patches. Local land users, such as herders, take advantage of these patches, and have been shown to be able to sustain higher stocking rates per hectare, because of their mobility and patch tracking, than conservative per hectare stocking rates applied on western-style ranches. Remote sensing, however, has the value of providing data easily over time. Technological progress in obtaining very high-resolution imagery will help to increase the usefulness and perhaps accessibility of remote-sensing tools.
4. More emphasis on monitoring soil and climatic factors; in the past, the emphasis has been on monitoring vegetation as a quick and easy indicator of system function and health. In non-equilibrium ecosystems, vegetation variability is high and influenced by climatic and soil factors. It is very difficult to evaluate short-term changes meaningfully; the emphasis has to be on monitoring long-term trends.[5]

Table 10.1 A comparison of ecosystemic indicators for pastoral areas in arid lands of Africa

Framework	Parameter	Equilibrium indicators	Non-equilibrium indicators
Pressure	external factors	• quantity of rainfall • stocking rate • incidence of fire	• coefficient of variability (CV) in rainfall • quantity of rainfall • dispersion, frequency and duration of grazing • frequency of fire • land use (%)
State	primary production (quantity)	• average biomass (carrying capacity) • total density	• min./max. range of biomass • interannual CV of biomass • patch frequency • CV of patch average biomass • density of key species
	primary production (quality)	• species composition • average nutritive value	same, except measured per patch, and for interannual CV
Impact	condition	compare species composition to 'climax'	compare key species composition to 'desired' community
Response	trend	density of increaser and decreaser species	• direct measurement of soil indicators • number of transitions linking number of states of vegetation change • increaser & decreaser expressed in terms of phenological and morphological types rather than species
	long-term land degradation	• soil cover • woody stratum density • perennial herb stratum density • soil erosion	• soil compaction • soil infiltration rate • soil erosion • climatic variability

All this implies more cost. More frequent and intensive sampling, more ground truthing, more monitoring of soil conditions, all require greater investment of financial and human resources. But in the last decade of the twentieth century, the level of investment in international development, let alone in scientific research in developing countries, has decreased drastically. Costs can be better managed if the monitoring system is more decentralized and involves the local land users and their organizations. A decentralized monitoring system has the following elements:

- reliance on traditional/locally recognized indicators of environmental change, in addition to 'scientific' indicators;
- reliance on local scouts and monitors, and training in collection of scientific indicators, if necessary;
- institutional links between information gatherers and decision makers at the local level;
- institutional links and transfer of information between local systems and district, regional and national systems of monitoring.

Not only can the cost be reduced with a decentralized system, but the very objective of monitoring – a tool to influence decision making – can be better achieved. This, incidentally, assumes that the other conditions for local-level land management and decision making have also been met, such as devolution of responsibility, local control over land and land use, and land tenure security (Niamir, 1997).

INDICATORS AND MONITORING ON THE SOCIAL SIDE: IMPLICATIONS FOR ECONOMIC EVALUATION OF GRAZING SYSTEMS IN ARID ECOSYSTEMS

Equilibrium theory, as applied in Africa's semi-arid and arid lands, invariably led evaluators to underestimate the ecological value of traditional grazing systems. The status and health of African arid lands was compared to an externally defined 'climax' vegetation. The climax vegetation of the more humid forest-tall grass savannas of the Sudan transition zone is considered to be a forest, which grazing and fire have 'degraded' into a savanna landscape. But the non-equilibrium systems in more arid lands, such as the grass steppe and short grass bushland, were also thought to have forest as their climax vegetation (hence the many reforestation efforts, including the 'green belt programme' where savanna-type trees were used unsuccessfully to stop the presumed advance of the desert). Both grazing and fire have been important anthropic factors for thousands of years, and many plant species have evolved traits adaptive to both influences. Experiments in both equilibrium and non-equilibrium systems with enclosures (Senegal and Sudan), or areas where fire has been banned for decades (Zimbabwe and Kenya), have not resulted in a return of the forest. If anything, they have resulted in severe bush encroachment and loss of productivity of the land.

Non-equilibrium theory, on the other hand, maintains that the mobility of traditional extensive grazing systems in Africa was the key factor in ensuring ecological sustainability. Mobility itself is a mechanism adaptive to the variability and unpredictability of the ecosystem.

Vegetation condition was the main indicator of ecosystem health. Monitoring of vegetation showed short-term trends of biomass loss in the 1970s and 1980s, and led evaluators to blame pastoralists for overgrazing. However, it is now agreed that the vegetation change was mainly the result of the severe droughts of 1970–73 and 1982–4, the general desiccation of the climate during those two decades, and fundamental changes in pastoral land use systems. Grazing was undoubtedly a compounding factor, but the pastoral system had developed many traits that allowed it to adapt to such booms and busts (see, for example, Bovin and Manger, 1990). More important anthropic factors leading to the current crisis in pastoralism were sedentarization, indiscriminate creation of water points, conversion of rangeland into cropland, and population increase.

The concept of economic irrationality has long been applied to nomads and their so-called 'cattle complex'.[6] Fortunately, many studies since the 1970s have shown that a nomad will sell his livestock if the price is right, and if it does not interfere with his long-term survival/adaptation strategies (Niamir, 1990).[7]

The economic–ecological evaluation of pastoral production in arid and semi-arid areas of Africa also includes the 'meat versus milk controversy'. In the past, pastoral livestock production was evaluated according to only one, exportable, product: meat. The contribution of other products to subsistence production (milk, hides, draught power, manure) was not a priority issue for governments interested in expanding exports. Since pastoral production is primarily a subsistence activity, surplus meat available for sale and export is always a small percentage of total production (usually 4–7 per cent offtake rate in pastoral systems, compared to 15 per cent in American ranches). Early evaluators ignored the importance of subsistence production, and branded pastoral production as inefficient and outdated.

Another controversy is that linked to the 'Tragedy of the Commons' concept. Privatization of land resources has failed to improve the livelihoods of the majority of pastoralists in arid Africa. If anything, it has aggravated the problem through land shortages and conflicts. Because of the high degree of ecosystemic variability, private production in African arid lands cannot be sustainable, unless the scale of the private ranch is very large. This, however, requires heavy capital investment, something that is outside the reach of the majority of pastoralists. Communal production of livestock is another way of achieving the necessary scale. In situations where it has been allowed to develop, such as in Zimbabwe (Scoones, in press) and Morocco (Bourbouze, in press), it has shown itself to be a viable and sustainable form of land use. The key issues to consider for communal land use are allocation of land rights to specific social entities (such as clan or village) on an inclusive rather than exclusive basis; distinction between primary, secondary and tertiary access holders; development of appropriate sets of rules and regulations; and the creation of procedures that facilitate negotiation between social entities for access to resources, bearing in mind that negotiation requires not only more disaggregated information, but also more frequent renewal of data.

A major stumbling block for appropriate pastoral development in the past has been the negative stereotypes and biases against extensive livestock production. These biases, imported from more humid, agriculturally based economies, consider extensive livestock production an inferior activity and form of land use (in terms of productivity, efficiency and consumer demand). For example, the set of sustainability indicators developed by CIAT/UNEP (see review by Tognetti, 1997) for Latin America is biased towards crop cultivation. All indicators related to livestock are negative ones (such as methane emissions and overgrazing) or ignore livestock altogether (for example, agriculture land need, but not pastureland need). And yet extensive livestock production is a major land use in most of the savannas and drylands of Latin America (for example, caatinga and cerrado of Brazil, Patagonia of Argentina, the Andes of Peru and Chile, and drylands of Mexico).

Only in the 1990s was attention refocused on the ecological viability and economic efficiency of pastoral systems.[8] Increasing livestock numbers, one of the CIAT/UNEP indicators, does not necessarily lead to land degradation, especially if mobility (in physical and economic terms) is maintained (Behnke and Scoones, 1991). With the crisis facing pastoralists in the last few decades (for example, per capita livestock has dropped dramatically since the turn of the 20th century) there has also been a tendency towards increasing income gaps between a small number of nomadic elite, and a majority of marginal producers (NOPA, 1992). This income disparity (a spread measure rather than average income per capita) should be adequately monitored, since policy makers often assign a lower value to externalities when those they affect are the poor and marginal (O'Connor and Martinez-Alier, 1996).

Appropriate social indicators of the viability of pastoral production and livelihood systems, therefore, must consider a host of interrelated factors, ranging from production parameters to land tenure security, within the overall context of uncertainty and variability in the ecosystem. Given that monitoring is a tool for decision making, it is equally important to ensure that the list of priority indicators is developed within a participatory process. There may be several lists, each suited to different purposes. The pastoralist's own set of indigenous indicators, linked directly to his/her world-view and goals, should be the starting point for the selection of indicators, and for the development of a decentralized monitoring programme. Early warning indicators for climatic variability and land degradation used by many pastoralists are scientifically correct and sensitive to long-term variability (Niamir, 1990). In addition, a decentralized monitoring system based on indigenous indicators will help to establish the 'proprietorship' and usefulness of the monitoring exercise for daily decision making, negotiation of resource access rights, and conflict resolution.

Pastoral production and livelihood systems in Africa have yet to be modelled effectively. Most models in the past have taken environment as an invariable constant (or varying only between bad, normal and good years), and have focused on only a few economic products. Notable exceptions are early work in the 1970s by the University of Arizona's Anthropology Department using data from Bedouin communities, and Dahl and Hjort's work (Sweden) on the minimal production package required for long-term survival. Recently, some researchers (for example, at the NREL (Natural Resources Ecology Laboratory) of Colorado State University and the International Livestock Research Institute, ILRI/IFPRI) are incorporating different variations of non-equilibrium ecological theory into integrated models of the pastoral system.

CONCLUSIONS

Non-equilibrium ecological theory of arid lands has prompted a critical look at our long-held assumptions about ecosystem dynamics, and the management tools that are based on such assumptions. It is too early to expect non-equilibrium theory to replace these classical tools (stocking rate, for example) with more appropriate ones because more work needs to be done to understand the underlying patterns and causes of variability in arid systems.

Anthropological work in the last few decades, together with a greater understanding of non-equilibrium systems, has helped us to appreciate how pastoral systems function, to understand the impact of their long-term strategies on short-term production, and to avoid underestimating their true economic value, both to self-sufficiency and to the national gross domestic product.

They have also pointed out that extensive, mobile forms of pastoral production are more suitable and sustainable in arid lands than sedentary livestock production and cultivation.

This chapter has tried to show some of the theoretical and practical differences between equilibrium and non-equilibrium systems, and to draw implications for better monitoring and evaluation. If we select indicators based on already available data, we cannot expect to change anything. Changes in the theoretical view of arid lands should naturally lead to changes in the types of indicators used to model and monitor the system. The next step, better management, needs a greater fundamental understanding of the processes in arid systems, if a management system better than that of traditional pastoralists is to be found.

Non-equilibrium ecologists can effectively borrow from the discipline of economics, although they have rarely done so in the context of arid lands. A complex systems approach to economics recognizes that in reality equilibrium is never achieved (Costanza *et al.*, 1993), and that partial equilibrium analysis (where a subsystem is analysed with the underlying assumption that there are no feedback loops from other subsystems) is inadequate in capturing the 'whole is greater than the sum' interactions. Modelling of non-equilibrium ecological systems could integrate some of the methodological principles and concepts now being developed within interdisciplinary fields such as ecological economics. It should incorporate the elements of uncertainty, non-equilibrium, long-term loops and feedbacks. The application of the evolutionary game theory to non-equilibrium systems may prove to be more appropriate than the high-generality models of the past.

'Sustainable development' is the key concept that prompted the development of ecological economics. There has been much debate about its exact definition since it was first proposed by the Brundtland Report in 1987 (see for example Dourojeanni, 1994). Definitions range from 'development without growth beyond environmental carrying capacity' (Goodland and Daly, 1994), to 'non-decreasing per capita well-being over time' (Pearce *et al.*, 1996), to a complex definition incorporating the 'four attributes of productive capacity, ecological integrity, social health, and cultural identity' (Altieri *et al.*, 1994). However, they are all based on equilibrium theory, as they assume that a constant per capita level of consumption/production (whether higher or lower than today's) can be sustained without endangering future capacity. Yet, in arid ecosystems, yearly variability is a fundamental attribute of the productive capacity of the ecosystem. It is difficult to envisage sustaining a constant level of production, in the short and medium term, unless there is very high subsidy of the production system and investment in technologies (as in the western United States), both of which are impossible in the foreseeable future in Africa. The appropriate process for assessing sustainable development should begin with the derivation of the definition of sustainable development through a consensus of stakeholders.

Sustainable development in arid systems requires fundamental changes in the way the system is evaluated and monitored. The variability and uncertainty in arid systems require modification of research frameworks, monitoring programmes and processes of indicator selection, whether one subscribes to non-equilibrium or multiple equilibrium theory. More attention needs to be given to the two issues of scale and time.

Management-oriented decision making and monitoring programmes need to be decentralized and participatory in order to account for variability in time, and heterogeneity in space and scale. Indicators therefore need to be disaggregated, and to concentrate on range rather than average values. In addition, the list of indicators needs to be reviewed constantly in order to account for changes in the relative importance of factors, and changes in the relationship between factors, both resulting from climatic and systemic variability.

ACKNOWLEDGEMENTS

Many thanks go to Sylvia Tognetti for constructive comments and to Immanuel Noy-Meir for clarifying definitions.

NOTES

1. 'Disequilibrium' refers to a stage in the dynamic process: it is used to mean that a system is out of equilibrium (perhaps temporarily).
2. The driving force in autogenic succession is primarily internal processes of competition, while in allogenic succession they are external forces such as climate, as defined by F.E. Clements and later expanded by A.W. Sampson (1919).
3. The term 'opportunism' has been used to describe how pastoralists adjust their mobility to fit ecological variability and take the best opportunity of available resources (Behnke and Scoones, 1991). However, it unfortunately has a negative connotation when applied to people, and is closely linked to G. Hardin's 'Tragedy of the Commons' theory (Ostrom *et al.*, 1992). In this chapter, the word 'tracking' is used instead, to describe how the ecosystem is constantly monitored and livestock behaviour and use of range resources is adjusted to the ecological variations.
4. The term 'desertification' has its own controversies. There are many different definitions, depending on the particular stakeholder. The Convention to Combat Desertification has attempted to resolve this controversy, but unfortunately has only succeeded in adding to it. In this chapter, the definition used by Warren and Agnew (1988) is preferred because of its clarity. 'Desertification' refers to the process of degradation that creates desert-like features. Therefore desertification is only one type of land degradation. The Sahelian zone of Africa is seeing both desertification and other forms of land degradation (such as bush encroachment, waterlogging from excessive irrigation and gully erosion).
5. The recent attempts to establish a global network of terrestrial monitoring sites (GCOS,

1997) may prove helpful, if variability and uncertainty are adequately taken into account in designing the system. However, of the more than 3000 sites in existence globally, very few are located in Africa and Asia. There is still a need for an appropriate international agency to take on a coordinating role.

6. The term was originally used to describe East African Nilotes (Dinka, Nuer and so on) for whom a beautiful bull has the same value as does a beautiful BMW to western man). According to this view, the nomad will hold on to all his cattle even when he sees the range capacity degrading.
7. For example, the larger the herd, the more chances that a core group of females will survive a drought and be able to regenerate the herd quickly.
8. For example, see the advocacy work being done by the Overseas Development Institute (ODI)'s Pastoral Development Network, UNSO (UN office to combat desertification), Institute for Development Studies (IDS) (Sussex) and the International Institute for Environment and Development (IIED) (London).

REFERENCES

Altieri, M., A. Yurjevic, J.-M. von der Weid and J. Sanchez (1994), 'Assessing the sustainability of NGO-led agroecological interventions in Latin America', proceedings of SCOPE workshop, ISEE, Costa Rica.

Behnke, R.H. and I. Scoones (1991), *Rethinking Range Ecology: Implications for Range Management in Africa*, London: ODI/IIED.

Bourbouze, A. (in press), 'Les organisations pastorales et la gestion de la mobilité chez les éleveurs du Nord de l'Afrique', in M. Niamir-Fuller (ed.), *Managing Mobility in African Rangelands*, Beijer Institute, FAO.

Bovin, M. and L. Manger (eds) (1990), *Adaptive Strategies in African Arid Lands*, Uppsala: Scandinavian Institute of African Studies.

Costanza, R. and M. Ruth (1996), 'Dynamic systems modeling for scoping and consensus building', paper presented at the conference of the European chapter of the ISEE, Paris.

Costanza, R.L. Wainger, C. Folke and K.-G. Maler (1993), 'Modeling of complex ecological economic systems', *Bioscience*, **43** (8), 545–55.

De Angelis, D. and J. Waterhouse (1987), 'Equilibrium and non-equilibrium concepts in ecological models', *Ecological Monographs*, **57**, 1–21.

de Leeuw, P.N. and J.C. Tothill (1993), 'The concept of rangeland carrying capacity in sub-saharan Africa – myth or reality', in R.H.Behnke, I. Scoones and C. Kerven (eds), *Range Ecology at Disequilibrium*, London: ODI/IIED.

Dourojeanni, M.J. (1994), 'Creating the institutional setting for sustainability', proceedings of SCOPE workshop, ISEE, Costa Rica.

Ellis, J.E. and D.M. Swift (1988), 'Stability of African pastoral ecosystems: alternate paradigms and implications for development', *J. Range Manage*, **41**, 450–59.

Friedel, M.H. (1991), 'Range condition assessment and the concepts of thresholds: a viewpoint', *J. Range Manage*, **44**, 422–6.

Funtowicz, S.O. and J.R. Ravetz (1994), 'Emergent complex systems' *Futures*, **26** (6), 568–82.

Gallopin, G.C. (1996), 'Environmental and sustainability indicators and the concept of situational indicators. A systems approach', *Environmental Modeling and Assessment*, pre-press issue.

Goodland, R. and H. Daly (1994), 'The universality of environmental sustainability', proceedings of SCOPE workshop, ISEE, Costa Rica.

Gough, C. (1996), EC-JRC-ISIS, mimeo.

Holling, C.S. (1986), 'The resilience of terrestrial ecosystems: local surprise and global change', in W.C. Clark and R.E. Munn (eds), *Sustainable Development of the Biosphere*, Cambridge: Cambridge University Press.

Iglesias, R.M.R. and M.M. Kothmann (1997), 'Structure and causes of vegetation change in state and transition model applications', *J. Range Management*, **50** (4), 399–408.

Kay, J. (1996), 'The ecosystem approach and monitoring', paper presented at the SCOPE/UNEP workshop on Integrated Adaptive Ecological Economic Modeling and Assessment, Boston University, August.

Laycock, W.A. (1991), 'Stable states and thresholds or range condition on North American rangelands: a viewpoint', *J. Range Manage*, **44** (5), 427–33.

Milchunas, D.G. and W.K. Lauenroth (1993), 'Quantitative effects of grazing on vegetation and soils over a global range of environments', *Ecological Monographs*, **63** (4), 327–66.

Niamir, M. (1990), 'Herder's decision-making in arid and semi-arid Africa', FAO Community Forestry Note, no.4, Rome.

Niamir, M. (1997), 'The resilience of pastoral herding in Sahelian Africa', in F. Berkes and C. Folke (eds), *Linking Social and Ecological Systems: Institutional Learning for Resilience*, Cambridge: Cambridge University Press.

NOPA (1992), *Pastoralists at a Crossroads*, UNICEF/UNSO project on Nomadic Pastoralists of Africa, UNSO, New York.

Noy-Meir, I. (1973), 'Desert ecosystems: environment and producers', Dept of Botany, Hebrew University, Jerusalem.

O'Connor, M. and J. Martinez-Alier (1996), 'Ecological distribution and distributed sustainability', in S. Faucheux, M. O'Connor and J. van der Straaten (eds), *Sustainable Development: Concepts, Rationalities and Strategies*, Dordrecht: Kluwer.

OECD (1991), *The State of the Environment*, Paris: OECD.

Ostrom, E., J. Walker and R. Gardner (1992), 'Covenants with and without a sword: self-governance is possible', *Amer. Pol. Sci. Review*, **86** (2), 404–17.

Pearce, D., K. Hamilton and G. Atkinson (1996), 'Measuring sustainable development: progress on indicators', *Environment and Development Economics*, **1** (1), 85–102.

Pimm, S.L. (1984), 'The complexity and stability of ecosystems', *Nature*, **307**, 321–6.

Rotmans, J. and M. van Asselt (1996), 'An integrated talk: what the heck is "Integrated Assessment"?', paper presented at the second SCOPE/UNEP Workshop on Integrated Adaptive Ecological Economic Modeling and Assessment, Boston University, August.

Scoones, I. (ed.) (1995), *Living with Uncertainty: New Directions for Pastoral Development in Africa*, London: Intermediate Technology Publications.

Scoones, I. (in press), 'Ecological dynamics and grazing resource tenure: a case study from Zimbabwe', in M. Niamir-Fuller (ed.), *Managing Mobility in African Rangelands*, Beijer Institute, FAO.

Sharp, L.A., K. Sanders and N. Rimbey (1990), 'Forty years of change in a shadscale stand in Idaho', *Rangelands*, **12** (6), 313–28.

Stafford-Smith, D.M. and S.R. Morton (1990), 'A framework for the ecology of arid Australia', *J. of Arid Environments*, **18**, 255–78.

Stiles, D. (1995), 'Desertification is not a myth', *Desertification Control Bulletin*, **26**, 29–36.

Swallow, B. (1993), 'The role of mobility within the risk management strategies of pastoralists and agropastoralists', workshop on New Directions in African Range Management and Policy, ODI/IIED/Commonwealth Secretariat, Woburn, UK.

Swift, J. (1993), 'Pastoral policies', in M. Niamir-Fuller (ed.), *Pastoral Development in Africa; proceedings of the first technical consultation on donor and international development agencies*, Paris: UNSO/UNDP.

Tognetti, S.S. (1997), 'Integrated ecological and economic models and indicators for sustainable development – a preliminary literature review', draft, paper for SCOPE/UNEP project on IA and EE modeling and assessment, University of Maryland.

Tucker, C.J., H.E. Dregne and W.W. Newcomb (1991), 'Expansion and contraction of the Sahara Desert from 1980 to 1990', *Science*, **253**, 299–301.

UNEP (1991), *Status of Desertification and Implementation of the United Nations Plan of Action to Combat Desertification*, III/3, Nairobi: UNEP/GCSS.

Walker, B.H. (1993), 'Stability in rangelands: ecology and economics', *Proceedings of the XVII International Grassland Congress*, Palmerston North, Hamilton, Lincoln, NZ.

Walker, B.H., D. Ludwig, C.S. Holling and R.M. Peterman (1981), 'Stability of semi-arid savanna grazing systems', *Journal of Ecology*, **69**, 473–98.

Westoby, M., B. Walker and I. Noy-Meir (1989), 'Opportunistic management for rangelands not at equilibrium', *J. Range Manage*, **42**, 265–74.

Williams, M.A.J. and R.C. Balling (1995), 'Interactions of desertification and climate: an overview', *Desertification Control Bulletin*, **26**, 8–16.

11. Linking the environment with production activities: an extended input–output model to assess the impacts of production on deforestation

Maria J. Willumsen

INTRODUCTION

Public opinion, governments and world organizations have become increasingly concerned about the links between economic activity and environment quality. International investment spending has also become increasingly sensitive to long-run environmental impacts, potential changes in government policies, the potential reactions of environmentally conscious consumers and their implications for the overall risk to capital. These concerns have been particularly significant in the case of the Brazilian Carajás region. While there has been considerable interest on the part of transnational firms in investment in the region, much of that investment has not been realized, in part because of uncertainty over the environmental impacts (direct and indirect) of that investment.

In 1967, US Steel discovered the world's second largest deposit of strategic minerals (iron, manganese, copper, tin, nickel, aluminium and others) in the Carajás highlands of Park, Brazil, at the eastern end of the Brazilian Amazon region. The mine was later sold to the Campania Vale do Rio Dose (CVRD), at the time a state-owned steel company, which, soon after its acquisition, planned the construction of a US$3.5 billion project composed of (a) urban and mining infrastructure in the Carajás area, (b) a large capacity (300 000 dwt) and modern deep-water harbour, located at São Luis, 560 miles away from the mines; and (c) a railroad connecting the mines to the harbour, providing cheap transportation for minerals, essential to secure CVRD international competitiveness. This project was called Projeto Ferro Carajás, or simply Projeto Carajás, PC (the Carajás Project), and its construction began in the early 1980s.

The Carajás project brought significant growth to the eastern Amazon region, and many of the changes resulting from this growth were unintended.

Between 1985 and 1987, thirteen independent pig iron firms received government authorization to operate. The first of these firms began operations in 1988. There are currently eight plants in operation, with a total production capacity of about 1 million tons per year. Five other plants received authorization to operate, but could not meet the deadline for their installation and had their licences rescinded in 1990. Another plant was ordered to close for not complying with the current environmental legislation.

Environmental assessments of the Carajás iron ore project focused mainly on its direct effect within the area under the control of CVRD. While these analyses were careful, and the resulting mitigating measures generally effective, they did not extend beyond the immediate project area. As a result, they failed to anticipate much of the substantial induced development caused by the project which, through the Carajás railway and road investments, greatly improved physical access to extensive parts of the region. This and other factors led to intensified immigration by loggers, ranchers, prospectors, small farmers, land speculators, urban settlers and other groups, which had significant environmental and social impacts, including rapid deforestation.[1]

After 1987, the international community began to express strong concern over the impacts of the Carajás project, especially the pig iron industry's impact, on the region's deforestation. The Carajás metallurgical complex became the 'culprit' of the Amazon's deforestation. The industry's environmental reputation played a major role in the failure to complete the planned metallurgical complex. Foreign capital shied away from financing activities related to the expansion of the industrial complex. Moreover, the Brazilian government, through the Greater Carajás Programme, prohibited the expansion of pig iron production by firms that could not prove self-sufficiency of charcoal production originating from cultivated forests. Since reforestation has not yet been tested in the region on a commercial scale, pig iron production continues to be restricted and continues to rely primarily on charcoal produced from agriculture and lumber industry residues. Iron ore production continues primarily to be exported, precluding the emergence of inter-industry linkages and the diversification of the regional economy in ways that would support the region's economic growth.

The processes of settlement and economic growth were accompanied by deforestation of large areas in the region. In the 1980s, deforestation reached alarming proportions. Data collected by Brazil's National Institute for Space Research (INPE, 1992, 1993, 1994, 1995, 1996) reported that the total surface area deforested between 1978 and 1987 increased sharply. An area of 54 600km^2 had been deforested in the Legal Amazon in 1978, while in 1988 the area of deforestation reached 280 000km^2. An average of 12 500km^2 per year of forest was being lost in this region alone. Annual rates of gross deforestation seem to have reached their peak in the second half of the 1980s, and have tapered off since then. The pace of deforestation in the area closest to the Carajás project fell to an annual average of 6200km^2 between 1988 and 1997. Despite this improvement, the rate of deforestation is still alarmingly high.

The purpose of this study is to perform an integrated assessment of the environmental consequences of production on the region by examining the economic interaction among productive sectors and macroeconomic and environmental conditions. A two-region extended input–output (I–O) model is constructed to assess the economic interactions among productive sectors, and the direct and indirect demand for commodities that result in deforestation. The model's design was driven by the objective of evaluating the macroeconomic and deforestation effects of expanding and diversifying the production of metals and agricultural products within the region most directly affected by the Carajás railway. Simulations of alternative external demand shocks (changes in regional exports and investment) were performed to evaluate the impacts of these sectors' growth on regional macroeconomic variables and the rate of deforestation.

LITERATURE REVIEW

In the last two decades, researchers have examined the relationship between government actions, economic activities and deforestation in a variety of frameworks. A number of analyses have explored policy issues, while others have centred on specific activities and/or regions. Several studies have examined the effects of Brazilian government policies on the deforestation of the Amazon region. This body of literature includes studies of the role of infrastructure, subsidies and other incentives (Hecht, 1982; Mahar and Schreider, 1994), development projects (Bunker, 1985; Fearnside, 1989; Binswanger, 1989; Hall, 1989; Mahar, 1989; Cagnin, 1993; Moran, 1993; Almeida and Campari, 1995) and property rights (Angelsen, 1995; Reis, 1996; Deacon, 1999) in determining deforestation. All these studies, however, tend to contain very little formal analysis of the determinants of deforestation.

Another stream of work, more closely related to this study, deals with the identification of factors leading to deforestation in the Brazilian Amazon region. Most of theses studies encompass econometric analysis. Their major focus is on population, although a number of them have considered a few variables other than population in their analysis of deforestation. The common result of these studies reveals population as the most important factor determining deforestation (Palo *et al.*, 1987; Rudel, 1989; Reis and Gusman, 1992; Cropper and Griffiths, 1994; Deacon, 1994; Pimentel *et al.*, 1997). Another characteristic of these studies is their failure to formalize deforestation dynamics and their implications for causal linkages.

Similar studies have been conducted for different areas of the world, generating similar results (Palo *et al.*,1987; Panayotou and Sungsuwan, 1989; Sagawe, 1991; Southgate *et al.*, 1991; Amelung and Diehl, 1992; Brown and Pearce, 1994; Cropper and Griffiths, 1994; Mahar and Schreider, 1994; Thiele and Wiebelt, 1994; von Amsberg, 1994; Jones and O'Neill, 1995; Barraclough and Ghimire, 1995; Keyfiz, 1996; Bawa and Dayanandan, 1997; Koop and Tole, 1997; Nelson and Hellerstein, 1997; Pimentel *et al.*, 1997; Amacher *et al.*, 1998; Deininger and Minten, 1999; Menotti, 1999; Sambrook *et al.*, 1999).

Pfaff (1999) was the first researcher to deal formally with deforestation dynamics. He analysed the effects of a large number of factors on deforestation. The main distinction of Pfaff's study, however, is his treatment of population as an endogenous variable. The results obtained from his model are quite interesting. Despite confirming the importance of population as the sole explanatory variable for deforestation, his results show that this effect disappears with the inclusion of other factors such as transport costs, distance, soil quality, credit and so on. Moreover, contrary to the results from the literature, he also finds a nonlinear effect of population on deforestation.

Pfaff's main claim is that common factors drive both population and deforestation, as migrants choose economic activities and location simultaneously. His work, therefore, highlights the importance of economic activities in the process of deforestation. Very few works have explored the role of economic activities in deforestation. Sierra and Stallings (1998), for instance, have examined the role of production structure on pollution, while Angelsen (1999) has analysed the role played by agriculture on deforestation. Despite the insights brought about by these studies, all of them fail to examine fully the linkages between production and deforestation.

The methodology chosen for this study – input–output analysis – is designed to overcome the limitations of the previous studies, as it is designed to capture a wide range of interactions among different economic sectors and between these sectors and other aspects of society, including the environment. Input–output models are very useful for visualizing complex interactions, fulfilling the criteria of usefulness from the perspective of supporting the government decision-making process. These models have been widely used in economic analysis. One of the main virtues of this analytical framework is its flexibility, which permits integration of several dimensions of a social system, allowing a better understanding of the complex interactions among these systems and their consequences for the environment (for example, Isard *et al.*, 1968; Isard, 1971; Leontief, 1970; Converse, 1971; Lee, 1982; Chen, 1973; Hordijk, 1980; Hannon *et al.*, 1983; Espinosa and Smith, 1995; Wajsman, 1995; Gibson, 1996; Alfsen, 1997; Lee and Roland-Holst, 1997; Lopez, 1997).

Unfortunately, input–output analysis has not yet been utilized to study deforestation. This work aims at providing an analytical framework with which to capture the induced impacts of economic activities on deforestation.

MODEL DESCRIPTION

The core model is an extended fixed-price interregional I–O model that represents the basic economic interactions among production sectors and between the broader Carajás Region ('Region') and the more immediately affected Carajás area ('Corridor'). Figure 11.1 depicts the study area. The model's structure is very simple and designed to allow a clear exposition of the existing relationship between production and environmental degradation.

Production output in the model is disaggregated into 47 sectors: eight agriculture sectors, three mining sectors, 22 manufacturing sectors, a construction sector, two public utilities (electricity and water), and eleven service sectors. The regions trade goods and services with one another and with the rest of Brazil and the rest of the world. The interregional export equations link the two regions' economies. The variables appearing in the equations are defined as follows:

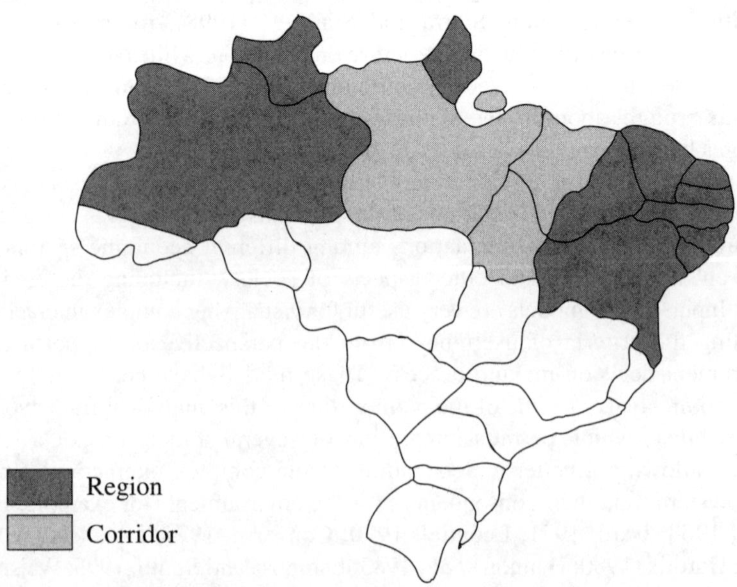

Figure 11.1 Brazil study area

X_i^h, output of industry '*I*' in region '*h*';
I_i^h, investment spending;
E_i^{hk}, exports of goods '*I*' from region '*h*' to region '*k*';
G_i^h, government spending;
E_i^{hB}, exports of goods '*I*' from region '*h*' to rest of Brazil;
E_i^{hW}, exports of goods '*I*' from region '*h*' to rest of the world;
T^h, transfer payments to households;
C_i^{hk}, consumption of goods '*I*' produced in region '*h*' and consumed in '*k*';
Y^k, household disposable income in region '*k*'.

The parameters of the model are defined as:

a_{ij}^{hk}, intermediate input requirement good *I* produced in *h* purchased by industry *j* in region *k*;
λ_i^h, labour value added per unit of output in region '*h*' for industry '*I*';
κ_i^h, capital value added per unit of output in region '*h*' for industry '*I*';
τ_i^h, indirect tax rate for good '*I*' in region '*h*';
π^h, personal tax rate for households in region '*h*';
δ_i^h, share of capital income generated in industry '*I*' and retained by region '*h*';
β_i^{hk}, propensity to consume good '*I*' produced in region '*h*' by households in region '*k*';
Y^k, household disposable income in region 'k'.

The following set of equations describes the core model:

$$X_i^h = \sum_j a_{ij}^{hh} X_j^h + E_i^{hk} + E_i^{hB} + E_i^{hW} + G_i^h + I_i^h + C_i^h, \qquad (11.1)$$

where *h* = {Carajás Region, Carajás Corridor}.

Industry output is demand determined in each sector according to the following equations. The endogenous expenditure components are interregional exports and household consumption. The interregional export equations are

$$E_i^{hk} = \sum_j a_{ij}^{hk} X_j^k + \beta_i^{hk} Y^k, \qquad (11.2)$$

where *h* = {Carajás Region, Carajás Corridor}; *k* = {Carajás Region, Carajás Corridor}; and $h \neq k$. Intraregional household consumer expenditures are determined by a set of simple expenditure functions:

$$C_i^h = \beta_i^{hh} Y^h. \qquad (11.3)$$

The household disposable income and regional GDP, respectively, are given by the following identities:

$$Y^h = (1 \bullet \pi^h)\left(\sum_i \lambda_i^h X_i^h + \sum_i \delta_i^h \kappa_i^h X_i^h\right) + T^h \tag{11.4}$$

and

$$GDP^h \equiv \sum_i \lambda_i^h X_i^h + \sum_i \kappa_i^h X_i^h + \sum_i \tau_i^h X_i^h \tag{11.5}$$

determines the regions' GDP.

The first extension to the core model is the addition of a set of equations that reflect deforestation activity. The production of charcoal requires wood inputs that are available from four sources (extractive forestry; forest management; land clearing for agriculture and livestock; and illegal deforestation). Rezende and Sampaio (1994) as well as Valle and Nascimento (1994) estimated the amount of charcoal that can be produced from each type of activity. For each hectare of land area under forestry management (extractive forest management) approximately 10m^3 of charcoal could be produced. The forestry sector (extractive forestry) produces wood for charcoal production as a by-product of its own activities.[2] For every US$1 million of sales from logging, enough wood by-product is produced to allow the production of 8400m^3 of charcoal. The third source of material input for charcoal production originates from the clearing of land for the expansion of agricultural goods and livestock production. Each hectare of land area cleared for agriculture or livestock generates the material wood inputs necessary to support the production of 160m^3 of charcoal production. If the material inputs necessary to produce the amount of charcoal demanded is not sufficient, then the fourth source of wood input is illegal deforestation. Approximately 100 000m^3 of charcoal are produced for every US$1 million of charcoal industry sales.

The amount of charcoal (in million m^3) that can be produced from legal sources of wood inputs is given by

$$\begin{aligned} CHCAP = {} & 10 \bullet AREAMGT + 0.0084444 \bullet (X_{xv} / e) \\ & + 160 \bullet (DAGR + DLIV), \end{aligned} \tag{11.6}$$

where *CHCAP* represents charcoal capacity; *AREAMGT* represents the land area under forestry management in million hectares; X_{xv} is total output in extractive forestry sector; '*e*' represents the exchange rate in 1993; *DAGR* is land cleared to support expansion of agriculture (in million ha.) and *DLIV* is land cleared to support expansion of livestock production (in million ha.). No wood for charcoal is currently produced under managed areas (*AREAMGT* = 0), but it remains a potentially important future source if necessary.

Historical data on land use patterns and agricultural and livestock output in the Corridor (FIBGE, 1994, 1995) suggest that 7km^2 of land is required to produce US$1 million of agricultural output, while 63.1km^2 are needed to produce US$1 million of output in the livestock industry. The same data reveal that farmers and ranchers keep a considerable amount of idle land relative to the area of land actually utilized in production (Miller, 1994). For each km^2 used in production, another 0.62 km^2 are left idle. As output in agriculture and livestock expands, more land is cleared and inputs for charcoal production are generated as part of this process. In the absence of changes in land productivity and the ratio of idle to utilized land area, the land cleared to support expansion of agricultural and livestock production is given by the following functions:

$$DAGR = 11.34 \bullet (X^t_{AG} \bullet X^{t\bullet 1}_{AG}) / e, \tag{11.7}$$

$$DLIV = 102.222 \bullet (X^t_{LS} \bullet X^{t\bullet 1}_{LS}) / e. \tag{11.8}$$

The amount of charcoal that cannot be produced from these legal sources of material inputs is given by the identity:

$$CHGAP = (X_c / e) \bullet CHCAP, \tag{11.9}$$

where X_c is the actual output of the charcoal industry and *CHGAP* the output gap of charcoal ($CHGAP \geq 0$). Approximately 110km^2 of forest is consumed for every million cubic metres of charcoal produced, and approximately 0.9km^2 of forest area is consumed for every US$1million of output produced in the timber industry.

The deforestation identity (km^2) is given by

$$DEF = 0.89 \bullet (X_{xv} / e) + DAGR + DLIV + 109.649 \bullet CHGAP \tag{11.10}$$

Additional land area must be cleared as economic activity in the logging and agricultural sectors expands without a concomitant increase in land productivity. Similarly, economic growth leads to an increase in the demand for charcoal and, unless the material inputs necessary for charcoal production are available from the clearing of land, forest management and by-products from the logging industry, additional forest must be cleared to satisfy the demand for charcoal.

A set of six simulation exercises was conducted to gauge the responsiveness of regional economies and regional deforestation to exogenous changes in final demand for metal products. These exercises were designed to represent the expansion of the Metallurgic Pole in the Carajás areas as proposed in the region's Master Plan (NATRON, 1988; *Plano Diretor de Desenvolvimento Integrado do Corredor da Estrada de Ferro Carajás,* 1989). Three simulations were made to examine the effect of changes in regional exports (Sim1, Sim2 and Sim3). The other three simulations (Sim4, Sim5 and Sim6) look at the impact from an exogenous increase in investment spending in these sectors.

SIMULATION RESULTS

The first simulation conducted to analyse the effect of changes in regional exports (Sim1) examines the impact of an *across-the-board*, 10 per cent increase in exports to the rest of Brazil and the rest of the world. The results exhibited in Table 11.1 show that the two regions are differently affected by an equal expansion in exports: gross regional product (regionally generated value added) increases by 2.3 per cent in the Carajás Region (Region) while it expands by 3.5 per cent in the Carajás Corridor (Corridor). Since the Corridor is a more export-oriented economy than the Region, one would expect a larger relative impact on this area.[3] Household income increases by 2.1 per cent in the Region and by 3.4 per cent in the Corridor. Other variables (such as consumption, labour and capital incomes, disposable income and savings) also exhibit a similar behaviour.

The expansion in total production in the Corridor is caused basically by the expansion of wood extraction (forestry), soybean production, livestock, iron ore mining and pig iron production. In the Region, the leading sectors were soybean production, extraction of other metallic minerals and steel production. Again the multiplier effects are proportionally higher in the Corridor than in the Region for all sectors (Table 11.2).

In terms of deforestation, the baseline simulation (Table 11.3) shows that nearly 17 400km^2 of land area is deforested per year in the Region and the Corridor combined. This area is consistent with the pace of deforestation witnessed in the late 1980s and early 1990s. In both the Region and the Corridor the greatest amount of deforestation results from agricultural activities. The production of livestock accounts for between 70 and 80 per cent of the total area deforested. The residual by-products from these activities are more than sufficient to meet the needs of charcoal production activities that take place. This result is very sensitive, however, to the pace of economic growth in the agriculture and livestock sectors. The clearing of land originates from an expansion of economic activity in these sectors, rather than from the level of activity itself. That is, it is the growth of output that leads to additional clearing of land. Once production in these sectors stabilizes, there

Table 11.1 Summary of simulation results

	Change from Baseline (%)					
	Sim1	Sim2	Sim3	Sim4	Sim5	Sim6
Region						
Total production	2.3	1.9	0.4	3.8	3.1	0.7
GDP	2.2	1.9	0.4	3.7	3.1	0.6
Consumption	2.1	1.8	0.3	3.6	3.0	0.6
Household income	2.1	1.8	0.3	3.6	3.0	0.6
Labour	1.6	1.3	0.3	3.1	2.6	0.5
Capital	2.6	2.2	0.4	4.1	3.5	0.7
Transfers	0.0	0.0	0.0	0.0	0.0	0.0
Direct taxes	2.1	1.8	0.3	3.6	3.0	0.6
Disposable income	2.1	1.8	0.3	3.6	3.0	0.6
Savings	2.1	1.8	0.3	3.6	3.0	0.6
Savings rate	0.0	0.0	0.0	0.0	0.0	0.0
Corridor						
Total production	3.5	0.3	3.2	3.9	0.5	3.4
GDP	3.7	0.3	3.4	3.3	0.5	2.9
Consumption	3.4	0.3	3.1	3.2	0.4	2.8
Household income	3.4	0.3	3.1	3.2	0.4	2.8
Labour	2.4	0.3	2.2	3.0	0.4	2.6
Capital	4.5	0.3	4.2	3.4	0.5	3.0
Transfers	0.0	0.0	0.0	0.0	0.0	0.0
Direct taxes	3.4	0.3	3.2	3.2	0.4	2.8
Disposable income	3.4	0.3	3.2	3.2	0.4	2.8
Savings	3.4	0.3	3.2	3.2	0.4	2.8
Savings rate	0.0	0.0	0.0	0.0	0.0	0.0

is no further need to clear land (provided that land productivity does not decline).

The baseline simulation corresponds to 1993; in the early part of the 1990s the level and pace of economic growth in these sectors slowed considerably from the rates observed in the early to mid-1980s. In the absence of any growth in agricultural and livestock production, nearly 2800km^2 of forest would have needed to be cleared in order to meet the needs of charcoal production in the baseline simulation. That rate of deforestation represents approximately half the rate most recently observed. This last result highlights the need to find/develop either alternative energy sources to charcoal or a

Table 11.2 Industry output, selected industries

	Change from Baseline (%)					
	Sim1	Sim2	Sim3	Sim4	Sim5	Sim6
Region						
Extractive – forestry	4.3	4.0	0.3	2.9	2.5	0.4
Charcoal	2.8	2.6	0.3	4.5	2.8	1.7
Soybean	8.9	8.8	0.1	0.5	0.4	0.1
Other agriculture	3.2	2.7	0.6	3.2	2.5	0.7
Livestock	4.7	4.4	0.3	2.5	2.0	0.4
Extractive – forest management	2.8	2.6	0.3	4.5	2.8	1.7
Reforestation	2.9	2.5	0.5	4.2	3.6	0.6
Extractive – iron ore	2.9	2.5	0.5	4.2	3.6	0.6
Extractive – other metallic minerals	5.9	5.6	0.3	2.4	1.9	0.5
Alloys	3.1	2.6	0.5	4.3	3.8	0.6
Pig iron	2.9	2.5	0.5	4.2	3.6	0.6
Steel	5.2	4.9	0.3	2.9	2.5	0.4
Lumber	3.0	2.7	0.3	5.3	4.9	0.4
Furniture	2.0	1.4	0.6	4.2	3.4	0.7
Total industry output	2.3	1.9	0.4	3.8	3.1	0.7
Corridor						
Extractive – forestry	6.2	0.6	5.7	2.1	0.8	1.3
Charcoal	3.9	0.3	3.6	3.1	0.5	2.6
Soybean	8.6	0.1	8.6	0.7	0.1	0.6
Other agriculture	6.9	0.2	6.7	1.5	0.3	1.2
Livestock	7.5	0.2	7.4	1.2	0.3	0.9
Extractive – forest management	3.9	0.3	3.6	3.1	0.5	2.6
Reforestation	10.0	0.0	10.0	0.0	0.0	0.0
Extractive – iron ore	10.0	0.0	10.0	0.0	0.0	0.0
Extractive – other metallic minerals	4.3	0.6	3.7	4.2	2.8	1.4
Alloys	2.6	0.9	1.7	4.5	104	3.1
Pig iron	10.0	0.0	10.0	0.0	0.0	0.0
Steel	3.1	1.0	2.1	4.7	0.8	3.9
Lumber	2.9	0.2	2.7	6.2	0.2	5.9
Furniture	2.7	0.2	2.4	4.7	0.4	4.3
Total industry output	3.5	0.3	3.2	3.9	0.5	3.4

renewable supply of wood for charcoal once the region's agricultural and livestock sectors stabilize.

When the economies experience a 'balanced' increase in export demand (Sim 1 in Tables 11.3 and 11.4), the resulting stimulus to the logging, agriculture and livestock sectors leads to an increase in the amount of land area cleared by these activities. The wood by-products from this land-clearing process is then sufficient to meet the input requirements of charcoal production, even though the production (and export) of pig iron also increases by almost the same percentage. This result is obtained for both the Region and the Corridor. In the Corridor, the production capacity of charcoal from wood by-products increases by approximately 75 per cent, while the actual demand for charcoal increases by nearly 8 per cent. This result is due, in large measure, to the composition of the Corridor's exports, which is highly skewed towards agricultural products and minerals and the manufacture of mineral-related products (mainly metals).

Exports of agricultural products, minerals and related manufactures accounted for almost half of the Region's total exports, while accounting for approximately two-thirds of total exports from the Corridor. Exports of agricultural products alone accounted for one-third of the Region's exports and 40 per cent of the Corridor's exports. Consequently, an increase in exports is largely directed towards exports of agricultural products, leading to an expansion of land under cultivation and deforestation. The residual by-products from the expansion of agriculture more than satisfy the input needs of the charcoal sector even in the face of increased production of pig iron.

An across-the-board increase in exports has a significant impact on deforestation. A 10 per cent increase in exports (Sim1), in both Region and Corridor, from their 1993 levels results in an additional 28 400km^2 of area deforested in the Region and an additional 19 900km^2 of area deforested in the Corridor (Table 11.4). This suggests that, for every additional US$1 million (at constant 1993 prices) of exports, 43km^2 of forest is lost in the Region. By the same token, an increase in exports of US$1 million leads to the loss of 39km^2 of forest in the Corridor.

Alternative simulations (Sim2 and Sim3) illustrate the economic interrelationship between the two regions. Sim2 simulates the exogenous growth of external demand in the Region only. Under this simulation the Region's GDP rises by 1.9 per cent, while household income rises by 1.8 per cent (Table 11.1), showing that an increase in exports only in the Region has a lower impact than an across-the-board expansion in exports. This outcome implies the existence of economic interaction between the two regions, as part of the impact from changes in the Region leaks to the Corridor. The mechanism for this leakage is interregional trade. Since the Region buys goods from the Corridor, the resulting economic stimulus in the Region leads to increased

Table 11.3 Deforestation activity (sq. km unless otherwise indicated)

	Baseline	Sim1	Sim2	Sim3	Sim4	Sim5	Sim6
Region							
Land cleared by logging activity	332.6	346.8	345.9	333.5	342.3	340.9	334.0
Land cleared for agriculture	1 923.0	5 233.6	4 911.7	2 244.9	3 984.3	3 574.0	2 333.3
Land cleared for livestock	9 391.8	34 494.0	32 947.2	10 938.7	22 432.0	20 070.8	11 753.0
Land cleared to meet charcoal needs	0.0	0.0	0.0	0.0	0.0	0.0	0.0
Total area deforested per year	11 647.4	40 074.5	38 204.8	13 517.1	26 758.5	23 985.7	14 420.2
Corridor							
Land cleared by logging activity	638.4	678.1	642.0	674.6	651.5	643.2	646.7
Land cleared for agriculture	1 003.5	3 568.1	1 104.4	3 467.2	1 682.9	1 161.5	124.9
Land cleared for livestock	4 066.3	21 410.6	4 482.0	20 995.0	6 883.9	4 742.3	6 208.0
Land cleared to meet charcoal needs	0.0	0.0	0.0	0.0	0.0	0.0	0.0
Total area deforested per year	5 708.3	25 656.8	6 228.4	25 136.7	9 218.3	6 547.0	8 379.6
Region plus Corridor per year	17 355.6	65 731.3	44 433.2	38 653.8	35 976.8	31 532.8	22 799.7
Charcoal production potential[1]							
Region (million cubic metres)	103.4	362.6	345.5	120.5	241.2	215.9	128.72
Corridor (million cubic metres)	46.76	228.4	50.5	223.4	78.7	54.4	71.1
Charcoal production less potential[2]							
Region (million cubic metres)	–97.04	–356.0	–339.0	–114.1	–234.5	–209.3	–122.2
Corridor (million cubic metres)	–27.08	–207.9	–31.7	–203.3	–58.4	–34.6	–50.9
Land cleared to accommodate charcoal production							
Region (square kilometres)	0.0	0.0	0.0	0.0	0.0	0.0	0.0
Corridor (square kilometres)	0.0	0.0	0.0	0.0	0.0	0.0	0.0

Notes:
1. From logging and lumber mill by-product and land cleared to accommodate agricultural sector expansion.
2. Negative values imply excess capacity.

Table 11.4 Deforestation activity (absolute change from baseline)

	Sim1	Sim2	Sim3	Sim4	Sim5	Sim6
Region						
Land cleared by logging activity	14.3	13.3	0.9	9.7	8.3	1.4
Land cleared for agriculture	3 310.6	2 988.7	321.9	2 061.3	1 651.0	410.3
Land cleared for livestock	25 102.3	23 555.4	1 546.9	13 040.2	10 679.0	2 361.2
Land cleared to meet charcoal needs	0.0	0.0	0.0	0.0	0.0	0.0
Total area deforested per year	28 427.1	26 557.4	1 869.7	15 111.2	12 338.4	2 772.8
Corridor						
Land cleared by logging activity	39.7	3.5	36.2	13.1	4.8	8.3
Land cleared for agriculture	2 564.6	100.9	2 463.7	679.4	158.0	521.3
Land cleared for livestock	17 344.3	415.7	16 928.6	2 817.6	675.9	2 141.7
Land cleared to meet charcoal needs	0.0	0.0	0.0	0.0	0.0	0.0
Total area deforested per year	19 948.6	520.1	19 428.4	3 510.0	838.8	2 674.3
Region plus Corridor per year	48 375.7	27 077.6	21 298.1	18 621.2	13 177.1	54 444.1
Charcoal production potential[1]						
Region (million cubic meters)	259.1	242.1	17.0	137.7	112.5	25.3
Corridor (million cubic meters)	181.6	4.7	176.9	31.9	7.6	24.3

Notes:
1. From logging and lumber mill by-product and land cleared to accommodate agricultural sector expansion.
2. Negative values imply excess capacity.

economic activity in the Corridor. The Region's propensity to import from the Corridor is not strong, however, and gross regional product in the Corridor rises by only 0.3 per cent (Sim3, Table 11.1).

The economic stimulus to the Region increases the pace of deforestation, as production in the 'forest-consuming sectors' increases. This result is shown in Table 11.4, column Sim2. A 10 per cent increase in the Region's exports results in an additional loss of 26 600km^2 of forest. The stimulus to economic activity in the Corridor also increases the area of land under cultivation and logging activity, and results in an additional 1500km^2 of area deforested.

When only the Corridor witnesses a 10 per cent increase in exogenous exports (Table 11.1, Sim3), gross regional product in the Corridor increases by 3.4 per cent and household income grows 3.1 percent. GDP in the Region rises by 0.4 per cent while the increase in household income is only 0.3 per cent. Again the impact of an expansion in exports in one region only (Corridor) generates lower impact than a balanced increase in exports (Sim1). It is also interesting to note that changes in exports in only one region generate distinct impacts, whether this change takes place in the Corridor or in the Region. The Region benefits more from changes in the Corridor than the Corridor does from increases in exports in the Region (comparing Sim2 with Sim3).

The increase in production in the Corridor's logging, agriculture and livestock leads to an increase in the area deforested. This increase in exports results in an additional 19 400km^2 of forest area lost in the Corridor, as can be observed in Table 11.4 (Sim3). The Corridor's purchases of goods from the Region positively stimulates economic activity in the Region's forest-consuming sectors. An additional 1900km^2 is lost in the Region as a result of export-led expansion in the Corridor economy (Table 11.4, Sim3).

The remaining multiplier simulations look at the impact from an exogenous increase in investment spending. Although the results are qualitatively similar to the results from an increase in exports, the economic and deforestation effects are different because of differences in the composition of investment spending. Changes in investment demand have less of an impact (direct and indirect) on the forest-consuming sectors than the impact that results from a change in exports. The effects are also different in the Corridor because investment goods are less likely to be produced within the Corridor itself. Consequently, increases in investment demand have less of a stimulative, short run macroeconomic impact in the Corridor (Sim4, Sim5 and Sim6 in Tables 11.3 and 11.4).

The Region's economy is more greatly affected by investment spending than by exports. A comparison between Sim4 and Sim1 in Table 11.4 shows that the macroeconomic stimulus from an across-the-board 10 per cent increase in investment is greater than the stimulus from export growth. The deforestation impacts of investment growth, however, are smaller (Tables 11.3 and 11.4). Accordingly, the Region's GDP increases by 3.7 per cent as a result of a 10 per cent increase in investments in both the Region's and the Corridor's investment (Sim4 in Table 11.1). Household income increases by 3.6 per cent under the same stimulus. This increase in investment spending leads to 15 100km^2 of forest being cleared in the Region (Sim4 in Table 11.4).

GDP in the Corridor increases by 3.3 per cent under this simulation, measurably lower than the 3.7 per cent growth under a 10 per cent increase in exports. Household income increases by 3.2 per cent as a result of the increase in investment demand, while an additional 3500km^2 of forest is cleared (Sim4, Table 11.4).

Sim5 represents a 10 per cent increase in investment spending in the Region alone, while Sim6 represents the same percentage increase in investment spending only in the Corridor. The pattern of effects is similar to the simulations involving exports. As can be observed in Table 11.1, an economic stimulus to the Corridor only has a much larger effect on the Region than the same stimulus in the Region has on the Corridor. In addition, economic (Table 11.1) and deforestation (Tables 11.3 and 11.4) impacts are smaller when only one region is growing than when both regions are growing. Finally, the effects on deforestation occur as the forest-consuming sectors adjust to a higher level of production, but once the new 'equilibrium' production level is reached, the effects on deforestation are significantly muted.

CONCLUSIONS

The simulation exercises performed with the model presented in this chapter reveal the existence of interaction between production and deforestation, as the growth of output leads to additional clearing of land. The simulations also demonstrate that farming, ranching and logging are the root causes of deforestation, and that the production of charcoal is made possible by the use of residual by-products of these activities.[4] When the regional economies expand (especially when their agriculture and livestock sectors expand), sufficient wood by-products are generated to meet the input requirements of charcoal production.

However, since the demand for charcoal production comes mainly from the need to supply the pig iron industry with a low-cost source of energy, pig iron production can become an important cause of deforestation. The results obtained with the model, however, indicate that at the present stage the production of pig iron and the resulting demand for charcoal are not the root causes of the region's deforestation. The simulations also show that, in the absence of both land-clearing activities to satisfy the expansion of agriculture and the cultivation of wood to meet charcoal production needs, the annual rate of deforestation that would result from the energy needs of pig iron production would be equivalent to approximately 50 per cent of the rate witnessed during the early 1990s. That is, maintaining or increasing pig iron production without growth of output in forest-consuming sectors, an increase in the productivity of land in these activities, or without an effort to grow the inputs needed to produce charcoal, would lead to continued deforestation of natural areas at about half the rate currently observed.

The model also indicates the existence of economic interactions between the two regions. An increase in final demand in one region affects both regions. When both regions grow owing to an across-the-board increase in exports, the impacts on the Corridor are much larger than the ones observed in the Region. A balanced increase in investment spending in both regions, however, generates a higher impact on the Region than on the Corridor. Finally, when the stimulus takes place in only one economy (Region or Corridor), the Region always experiences larger beneficial impacts than does the Corridor.

The analysis presented here does not directly incorporate the dynamic element of population growth and endogenous investment demand, or the presence of agglomeration economies that would further stimulate regional growth. For this reason, the results obtained with this model must be interpreted with caution. An important extension of the model presented here will be the incorporation of a labour market and the interregional migration of people. With these elements a more dynamic view of the process is obtained, since households are also consumers of charcoal and agricultural products.

Despite the simplicity of the current model, the results reveal the potential of this analytical framework to perform an integrated assessment of several dimensions of a social system, and to obtain a better understanding of the complex interactions among these systems and their consequences on the environment. The results also demonstrate the validity of this analytical framework as a tool for policy analysis. The extensions proposed above will enhance the model's capabilities to provide a more accurate evaluation of the environmental impacts generated by the dynamics of complex economic and social systems.

ACKNOWLEDGEMENTS

The author thanks the anonymous referees for their helpful comments.

NOTES

1. Almeida and Campari (1995) provide an extensive description of population and economic shifts in this area during the 1980s and explore the factors determining the decision of settlers to deforest the land.
2. The forestry sector represents the continuing practice of wood extraction which does not consider the risk of forest depletion. The forest management sector represents a new practice that takes into consideration the forest capacity and its ability for recovery.
3. The ratio of exports to GDP is 0.22 in the Region and 0.62 in the Corridor.
4. Certainly, the ability to sell wood from land cleared for agricultural use reduces the effective cost of forest clearing and thereby encourages more land-intensive farming and ranching techniques. Such cost reductions, however, are minor and not likely to be a major factor in the optimal land-clearing decision.

REFERENCES

Alfsen, K.H. (1997), 'Environmental Economics Based on General Equilibrium Models: the Norwegian Experience', *Swiss Journal of Economics and Statistics*, **127** (2), 228–44.

Almeida, A.O. and J. Campari (1995), *Sustainable Settlement in the Brazilian Amazon*, New York: Oxford University Press.

Amacher, G.S., W. Cruz, D. Grebner and W.F. Hyde (1998), 'Environmental Motivations for Migration: Population Pressure, Poverty, and Deforestation in the Philippines', *Land Economics*, **74** (1), 83–98.

Amelung, R. and M. Diehl (1992), 'Deforestation of Tropical Rain Forests: Economic Causes and Impact on Development', *Kieler Studien*, 241, J.C.B.Mohr, Tübingen.

Angelsen, A. (1995), 'Shifting Cultivation and 'Deforestation': a Study from Indonesia', *World Development*, **23** (10), 1713–29.

Angelsen, A. (1999), 'Agricultural Expansion and Deforestation: Modeling the impact of population, market forces and property rights', *Journal of Development Economics*, **58** (1), 185–218.

Barraclough, S.L. and K.B. Ghimire (1995), *Forests and Livelihoods: The Social Dynamics of Deforestation in Developing Countries*, New York: St Martin's Press.

Bawa, K.S. and S. Dayanandan (1997), 'Socioeconomic Factors and Tropical Deforestation', *Nature*, **386** (6), 1045–68.

Binswanger, H. (1989), 'Brazilian Policies that Encourage Deforestation in the Amazon', Environment Department Working Papers, no. 16, World Bank, Washington, DC.

Brown, K. and D.W. Pearce (1994), *The Causes of Tropical Deforestation: the Economic and Statistical Analysis of Factors Giving Rise to the Loss of Tropical Forests*, Vancouver: University of British Columbia Press.

Bunker, S.G. (1985), *Underdeveloping the Amazon: Extraction, Unequal Exchange, and the Failure of the Modern State*, Urbana-Champaign: University of Illinois Press.

Cagnin, J.U. (1993), 'Impacto Ambiental do Projeto Ferro Carajas', in SEPLAN (ed.), *Anais do Seminario Impacto dos Grandes Projetos Financiados pelo BIRD no Brasil*, Brasilia: SEPLAN.

Chen, K. (1973), 'Input–Output Economic Analysis of Environmental Impacts', *IEEE Transactions on Systems, Man and Cybernetics*, SMC-3, no. 6, 539–47.

Companhia Vale do Rio Doce (1981), *Plano Preliminar de Desenvolvimento da Amazônia Oriental*, Rio de Janeiro: Companhia Vale do Rio Doce.

Companhia Vale do Rio Doce (1992a), *Cenários do Mercado Internacional de Gusa no Ano 2000*, Rio de Janeiro: Companhia Vale do Rio Doce, SUFER-GITEV.

Companhia Vale do Rio Doce (1992b), *Informações Básicas Acerca da Produção de Ferro-Gusa na Área do Programa Grande Carajás*, Rio de Janeiro: Companhia Vale do Rio Doce.

Converse, A.O. (1971), 'On the Extension of Input–Output Analysis to Account for Environmental Externalities', *American Economic Review*, **61** (1), 197–8.

Cropper, M. and C. Griffiths (1994), 'The Interaction of Population Growth and Environmental Quality', *American Economic Review*, **84** (2), 250–54.

Deacon, R.T. (1994), 'Deforestation and the Rule of Law in a Cross-section of Countries', *Land Economics*, **70** (4), 655–83.

Deacon, R.T. (1999), 'Deforestation and Ownership: Evidence from Historical Accounts and Contemporary Data', *Land Economics*, **75** (3), 481–504.

Deininger, K.W. and B. Minten (1999), 'Poverty, Policies and Deforestation: The Case of Mexico', *Economic Development and Cultural Change*, **47** (2), 238–59.

Espinosa. J.A. and V.K. Smith (1995), 'Measuring the Environmental Consequences of Trade Policy: a Nonmarket CGE Analysis', *American Journal of Agricultural Economics*, **77** (3), 611–29.

Fearnside, P.M. (1989), 'Deforestation in Brazilian Amazonia: the Rates and Causes of Forest Destruction, Amazonia: The Future in the Balance', *The Ecologist*, **19** (6), 913–26.

FIBGE (1994), *Economic Census of 1990*, Rio de Janeiro: Fundação Instituto Brasileiro de Geografia e Estatística.

FIBGE 1995), *Agriculture Survey of 1993*, Rio de Janeiro: Fundação Instituto Brasileiro de Geografia e Estatística.

Gibson, B.(1996), 'The Environmental Consequences of Stagnation in Nicaragua', *World Development*, **24** (2), 325–39.

Hall, A.L. (1989), *Developing Amazonia: Deforestation and Social Conflict in Brazil's Carajas Programme*, Manchester and New York: Manchester University Press.

Hannon, B., R. Costanza and R. Herendeen (1983), *Measures of Energy Cost and Value in Ecosystems*, Urbana-Champaign: University of Illinois Press.

Hecht, S. (1982), 'Cattle Ranching Development in the Eastern Amazon: Evaluation of a Development Policy', PhD Dissertation, University of California, Berkeley

Hordijk, L. (1980), 'Economic Structure and the Environment', in Institute for Environmental Studies (ed.), *Production and Energy Consumption in the Netherlands 1973/1985*, Amsterdam: Free University, Institute for Environmental Studies.

INPE-Instituto de Pesquisas Espaciais (1992, 1993, 1994, 1995, 1996), *Deforestation in the Brazilian Amazon*, Sao Jose dos Campos: Instituto de Pesquisas Espaciais (INPE).

Instituto Brasileiro de Siderurgia (1992), *Anuário Estatístico da Indústria Siderúrgica Brasileira: 1992.* Rio de Janeiro: Instituto Brasileiro de Siderurgia.

Instituto Brasileiro de Siderurgia (1993), *A Siderurgia em Numeros: 1993*, Rio de Janeiro: Instituto Brasileiro de Siderurgia.

International Iron and Steel Institute (1993), 'Steel Statistics of Developing Countries', Brussels.

Isard, W. (1971), *Ecologic–Economic Analysis for Regional Planning*', New York: The Free Press.

Isard, W. *et al.* (1968), 'On the Linkage of Socio-Economic and Ecological Systems', *Papers of the Regional Science Association*, **21** (2), 79–99.

Johnson, M. and J. Bennet (1981), 'Regional Environmental and Economic Impact Evaluation', *Regional Science and Urban Economics*, **11** (2), 215–30.

Jones, D.W. and R.V. O'Neill (1995), 'Development Policies, Urban Unemployment and Deforestation: the Role of Infrastructure and Tax Policy in a Two-sector Model', *Journal of Regional Science*, **35** (1), 23–32.

Keyfiz, N. (1996), 'Population Growth, Development and the Environment', *Population Studies*, **50** (3), 335–59.

Koop, G. and L. Tole (1997), 'Measuring Differential Forest Outcomes: a Tale of Two Countries', *World Development*, **25** (12), 2043–56.

Lee, H. and D. Roland-Holst (1997), 'The Environment and Welfare Implications of Trade and Tax Policy', *Journal of Development Economics*, **52** (1), 65–82.

Lee, K. (1982), 'A Generalized Input-Output Model of an Economy with Environmental Protection', *Review of Economics and Statistics*, **64** (3), 466–73.

Leontief, W. (1970), 'Environmental Repercussions and the Economic Structure: An Input–Output Approach', *Review of Economics and Statistics*, **52** (3), 262–71.

Lopez, R. (1997), ' Environmental Externalities in Traditional Agriculture and the Impact of Trade Liberalization: the Case of Ghana', *The Journal of Development Economics*, **53** (1), 17–39.

Mahar, D. (1989), 'Government Policies and Deforestation in Brazil's Amazon Region', (mimeo), World Bank Washington DC.

Mahar, D. and R. Shreider (1994), 'Incentives for Tropical Deforestation. Some Examples from Latin America', in K. Brown and D.W. Pearce (eds), *The Causes of Tropical Deforestation*, Vancouver: University of British Columbia Press, pp. 231–53.

Menotti, V. (1999), 'Forest Destruction and Globalization', *The Ecologist*, **29** (3), 578–93.

Miller, C. (1994), 'Patterns of Land Use in the Carajás Area', Washington, DC: World Bank (ENVLW), preliminary report (mimeo).

Moran, E. (1993), 'Deforestation and Land Use in the Brazilian Amazon', *Human Ecology*, **21** (1), 76–95.

NATRON (1988), *Bases para o Relatório Final do Plano Diretor de Desenvolvimento Integrado do Corredor da Estrada de Ferro Carajás*, vols 1 and 2, Brasilia: NATRON.

Nelson, G.C. and D. Hellerstein (1997), 'Do Roads Cause Deforestation? Using Satellite Images in Econometric Analysis of Land Use', *American Journal of Agricultural Economics*, **79** (1), 63–84.

Palo, M., J. Salmi and G. Merely (1987), 'Deforestation in the Tropics: Pilot Scenarios Based on Quantitative Analyses', in M. Palo and J. Salmi (eds), *Deforestation or Development in the Third World?*, Helsinki: Finnish Forest Research Institute.

Panayotou, S. and S. Sungsuwan (1989), 'An Econometric Study of the Causes of Tropical Deforestation: The Case of Northeast Thailand', Discussion Paper No. 284, Harvard Institute of International Development Cambridge, MA.

Pearce, D., E. Barber and A. Marchantia (1990), *Sustainable Development: Economics and Environment in the Third World*, Aldershot, UK and Brookfield, VT, US: Edward Elgar.

Pearce, D. and R.K. Turner (1990), *Economics of Natural Resources and the Environment*, New York: Harvester Wheatsheaf.

Person, A. and M. Munasinghe (1995), 'Natural Resource Management and Economy Wide Policies in Costa Rica: A Computable General Equilibrium (CGE) Modeling Approach', *The World Bank Economic Review*, **9** (2), 259–85.

Pfaff, A. (1999), 'What Drives Deforestation in the Brazilian Amazon? Evidence from Satellite and Socioeconomic Data', *Journal of Environmental Economics and Management*, **37** (1), 26–44.

Pimentel, D. *et al.* (1997), 'Impact of Population Growth on Food Supplies and Environment', *Population and Environment*, **19** (1), 139–52.

Reis, E. (1996), 'Os Impactos do Pólo Siderúrgico de Carajás no Desflorestamento da Amazônia Brasileira', *A Economia Brasileira em Perspectiva–1996*, vol 2, Rio de Janeiro: IPEA, pp. 691–717.

Reis, E. and R. Guzman (1992), 'An Econometric Model of Amazon Deforestation', IPEA Working Paper no. 28, Rio de Janeiro.

Rezende, M.E. and R.S. Sampaio (1994), 'Estudo de Alternativas Energéticas para o Polo Siderúrgico do Programa Grande Carajás – Componente Siderúrgico', Washington, DC: World Bank (ENVLW), preliminary report (mimeo).

Rezende, M.E. *et al.* (1993), 'Produção Comercial de Carvão Vegetal para a Siderurgia', Washington, DC: World Bank (ENVLW), preliminary report (mimeo).

Rudel, T.K. (1989), 'Population, Development, and Tropical Deforestation: A Cross-National Study', *Rural Sociology*, **54** (3), 621–33.

Sagawe, T. (1991), 'Deforestation and the behavior of households in the Dominican Republic', *Geography*, **76** (33), 769–85.

Sambrook, R. *et al.* (1999), 'Population Pressure, Deforestation, and Land Degradation: A Case Study of the Dominican Republic', *The Professional Geographer*, **51** (1), 25–41.

Sawyer, D. and M. Willumsen (1995), 'Estudo de Alternativas Energéticas para o Pólo Metalúrgico do Programa Grande Carajás, Componente Regional', Washington, DC: World Bank (ENVLW), preliminary report (mimeo).

SEPLAN/Programa Grande Carajás (1989), *Plano Diretor do Corredor da Estrada de Ferro Carajás*, Brasilia, D.F. SEPLAN/PGC.

Sierra, R. and J. Stallings (1998), 'The Dynamics and Social Organization of Tropical Deforestation in Northwest Ecuador, 1983–1995', *Human Ecology: An Interdisciplinary Journal*, **26** (1), 135–61.

Southgate, D., R. Serra and L. Brown (1991), 'The Causes of Tropical Deforestation in Ecuador. A Statistical Analysis', *World Development*, **19** (9), 1863–81.

Thiele, R. and M. Wiebelt (1994), 'Policies to Reduce Tropical Deforestation and Degradation: A Computable General Equilibrium Analysis for Cameroon', *Quarterly Journal of International Agriculture*, **33** (2), 162–78.

Valle, L., C. Cardoso and M.B. Nascimento (1994), 'Estudo de Alternativas Energéticas para o Polo Metalúrgico do Programa Grande Carajás, Componente Recursos Florestais', Washington, DC: World Bank (ENVLW), preliminary report (mimeo).

Von Amsberg, J. (1994), 'Economic Parameters of Deforestation', Working Paper no. 1350, World Bank, Washington, DC.

Wajsman, N. (1995), 'The Use of Computable General Equilibrium Models in Evaluating Environmental Policy', *Journal of Environmental Management*, **44** (2), 127–43.

12. Dynamic modelling of energy use and emissions: the case of US iron and steel

Matthias Ruth

INTRODUCTION

Integrated assessment models of climate change are increasingly used to explore implications of interrelationships among social, economic, technological and policy changes for likely emissions of greenhouse gases (Rotmans and Dowlatabadi, 1998). Researchers developing such models face the formidable tasks of collecting and analysing data, and describing interactions among climatic, socioeconomic, technological and policy variables (Risbey *et al.*, 1996) such that these descriptions are (a) consistent with past and present observations, (b) consistent internally and with economic theory, and (c) consistent through time as the models are used to explore likely future scenarios.

Key challenges for the improvement of existing integrated assessment models lie in developing better descriptions of technologies and co-benefits of technology change, investment decision making and baselines against which to compare alternative investment and policy scenarios. Effectively addressing these challenges to integrated assessment models is important because worldwide industry accounts for approximately 43 per cent of carbon emissions into the atmosphere (Price *et al.*, 1999a; Hendriks *et al.*, 1999).

Early integrated assessment models have, by necessity, aggregated many countries into a small number of regions, and their economic activities into a small number of sectors (for example, Nordhaus, 1994; Edmonds *et al.*, 1995; Yang *et al.*, 1996; Rotmans and de Vries, 1997). Recent advances in theory, computational methods and the proliferation of socioeconomic and technological data have made it possible to increase the resolution of integrated assessment models and to address the needs identified above. The purpose of increasing the resolution of integrated assessment models is to investigate more accurately technology innovation and its diffusion within and among regions and sectors more precisely to estimate greenhouse gas emissions from the production of goods and services, and thus better to meet the needs of policy makers to explore the effects of alternative policies on individual sectors of the economy.

Additional efforts have been launched to improve the representation of technologies and technical change in integrated assessment models with the dual goal of increasing the accuracy of models and providing systems representations that are more closely aligned with the world-view of decision makers in industry (Ruth *et al.*, 2000). It is hoped that the more closely the models reflect constraints and opportunities identified by industry decision makers, the more the decision makers will take part in, and 'buy into', integrated assessment. Becoming part of the modelling and assessment process will mean opportunities for data sharing, learning and consensus building by members of the modelling, assessment, industry decision making, and policy making communities.

The scientific literature is replete with calls for research to advance integrated assessment models so that a consensus on likely policy and technology implications for industrial greenhouse gas emissions can be generated. For example, Risbey *et al.* (1996) address many of the challenges faced by integrated assessment models, including the need to avoid specifying energy efficiency improvements as occurring autonomously, and to promote methodological pluralism to avoid 'anchoring' models so that they conform to 'established, reasonable results' (ibid., p. 390). Azar and Dowlatabadi (1999, p. 538), in an extensive review of the treatment of technical change in assessments of climate policy, conclude by calling assessments which do not have a realistic representation of technological innovation and diffusion of 'questionable value'. Jacobi and Wing (1999) and Sands *et al.* (1999) emphasize the need for more detailed representations of capital vintage structures in integrated assessment models. Dowd and Newman (1999) summarize consensus among more than 100 leading international experts in the development and application of engineering–economic and microeconomic analyses and technologies and policies, highlighting the needs for consistent international data regarding industrial technologies, less aggregated analytical outputs that can support environmental policy and investment decisions, an increased presence of engineering–economic analysis disciplines in data collection and modelling efforts, and web-based sharing of research, knowledge and data. Establishing links between detailed information on sector-specific technology trends and integrated assessment models is especially important as these models become more regionally and sectorally disaggregated. Initial efforts have begun to develop methodologies to foster these linkages (Mongia and Sathaye, 1998a, 1998b; Roy *et al.*, 1999; Schumacher and Sathaye 1999a, 1999b, 1999c, 1999d, 1999e).

Recent engineering and policy analyses have highlighted that changes in industrial carbon emissions are a function of several interrelated factors (see, for example, Repetto and Austin, 1997):

- level of economic activity and the institutional arrangements that guide it;
- industrial mix and structure of an economy;
- materials intensity of products;
- fuel mix within each industry;
- energy efficiency of industrial processes.

Each of these factors has been extensively researched, either separately or in interaction with each other. For example, Ruth (1998a) investigates changes in industrial carbon emissions in the light of changes in industrial mix and structure, with a specific focus on five US metals industries. Ruth (1998b) addresses management and investment implications of environmental policy, changing market dynamics, and globalization for industrial materials and energy use. Broader implications of dematerialization for industrial output and carbon emissions are reviewed in Cleveland and Ruth (1999), and methodologies for modelling dynamic interdependencies between technology change, resource use and emissions are presented in Ruth (1993) and Hannon and Ruth (2000). Driving forces of industrial energy use, including the industrial mix, structure of economies, materials intensity, fuel mix and energy efficiency of industrial processes, are described in Price *et al.* (1998, 1999a). Further analyses of materials intensity and energy efficiency of industrial processes are provided in Khrushch *et al.* (1999), Martin *et al.* (1999, 2000), Schumacher and Sathaye (1999a, 1999b, 1999c,1999d, 1999e), Worrell (1994) and Worrell *et al.* (1999).

This chapter will present one example of the way the dynamics of technology change, energy use and carbon emissions profiles may be analysed and modelled in ways that explicitly draw on expertise of decision makers in industry and government agencies, and provide feedback into their decision making. While the example is limited to the US iron and steel industry, the approach is widely applicable, and indeed has been chosen for several other industries (see, for example, Ruth and Dell'Anno, 1997; Ruth *et al.*, 2000).

The US iron and steel industry accounts for approximately 2.3 per cent of all energy used in the USA, or 21 million BTU (British Thermal Units) per ton of product (OTA, 1993). Iron and steel production is a significant contributor of carbon emissions because the industry relies heavily on fossil fuels as an energy source, and on limestone for the purification of iron oxides. Several major changes occurred in the industry and its economic environment that led to reductions in its energy use and emissions. Significant advances in existing technologies, the emergence of entirely new processes since World War II and toughened environmental standards prompted the adoption of new technologies, and changes in the mix of materials and fuels (Adams, 1995; Ruth, 1995). Changes in the structure of the economy, most notably a move towards increased importance of the service sector, a reorientation of manufacturing from infrastructure to consumer goods and increased competition from foreign producers, have all altered the US market for steel (Ruth, 1998a). Given the technological, regulatory and economic parameters within which the US iron and steel industry operates, what are likely development paths for the industry if new, global climate change policies are introduced into the picture? This chapter addresses this question and focuses on the industry's material, energy and carbon emissions profiles. The arguments of this chapter are supported by the results of a dynamic computer model (Ruth and Hannon, 1997) of the industry that has been developed over the course of more than three years.[1]

To represent the industry's dynamics with sufficient detail to be meaningful for decision makers in industry, and to portray at the same time industrial behaviour at a level that is sufficiently aggregate to facilitate industrial and environmental policy decision making, the graphical programming language STELLA (High Performance Systems, Inc., 1999) was used to develop, and link with each other, modules of individual industry components. The graphical features of STELLA enable non-modellers readily to assess the contents of each module and to judge whether interrelationships are properly captured. Without this transparency, the various individuals involved in the modelling process would have been less able to see how their contributions to the model were accommodated, and their willingness to share information freely would have been significantly hampered. Moreover, the easy-to-use model environment provided a neutral platform for dialogue that quickly engaged the participants in the modelling effort. Rather than debate each other's assumptions and data, efforts were concentrated on where and how to make use of those assumptions and data, and on identifying how the model results changed if alternative specifications had been used. STELLA's user interface further enabled non-modellers readily to play out the industry's dynamics that may result from different model specifications.

Further to foster agreement about the information used to quantify each model component, only published data were used for model specification and, where possible, preference was given to data collected and reported by the industry itself. At various stages of the model development process, representatives from industry, government and science were brought together in a workshop setting to investigate, and comment on, the model.

DYNAMIC MODELLING OF TECHNOLOGY CHANGE IN US IRON AND STEEL PRODUCTION

Model Structure and Specification

To assess impacts of energy taxes and the cost of carbon on the US iron and steel industry, a dynamic computer model was developed that captured the main production stages and technologies (Figure 12.1). In the US, steel is produced by means of two different processes. Basic oxygen furnaces (BOF) produce steel primarily from pig iron, which in turn is produced in blast furnaces (BF) from ores. Electric arc furnaces (EAF) produce steel primarily from scrap.

Engineering information was used to specify material and energy efficiencies of individual technologies at any point in time, limits to those efficiencies, and conversion factors. Time series analysis was used to quantify change in technologies and production rates. The choice between different functional forms and which variables to include as regressors was guided by conventional hypothesis test statistics and, within the context of the dynamic computer model, by a battery of sensitivity and robustness analyses. Special attention was given to regression diagnostics used to detect sources of inefficiency and bias in regression equations. Specifically, statistical tests were carried out for the presence of serial correlation, heteroscedasticity and unit roots, applying Lagrange multiplier tests (Breusch and Pagan, 1979; Godfrey, 1978) and unit root analysis (Dickey and Fuller, 1981). All statistical analyses used to quantify the model meet the respective test criteria at the 95 per cent confidence level. When running the resulting model over historic time and comparing model output to actual observations, mean absolute error rates of less then 2 per cent were observed.

The structure of the computer model is shown in Figure 12.2. Forecasts of future steel production rates and energy prices drive the model for the years 1994 to 2020. Changes in material and energy efficiencies, technology mix and fuel mix are determined endogenously. As the technology mix changes, the differences in material and energy use that are associated with differences between the BOF and EAF routes of steel production determine the industry's overall material, energy and emissions profiles. Specifically, BOF production determines pig iron demand and – given changes in BF and coke oven (CO) efficiencies – production of coking coal and limestone use. Changes in relative production shares of BOF and EAF also determine the rate at which electricity can be self-generated in the industry. Electricity that is not self-generated is purchased from the US electricity sector and generated, by assumption, at the national average efficiencies and fuel mix. Changes in efficiencies and fuel mix of *purchased* electricity are exogenous

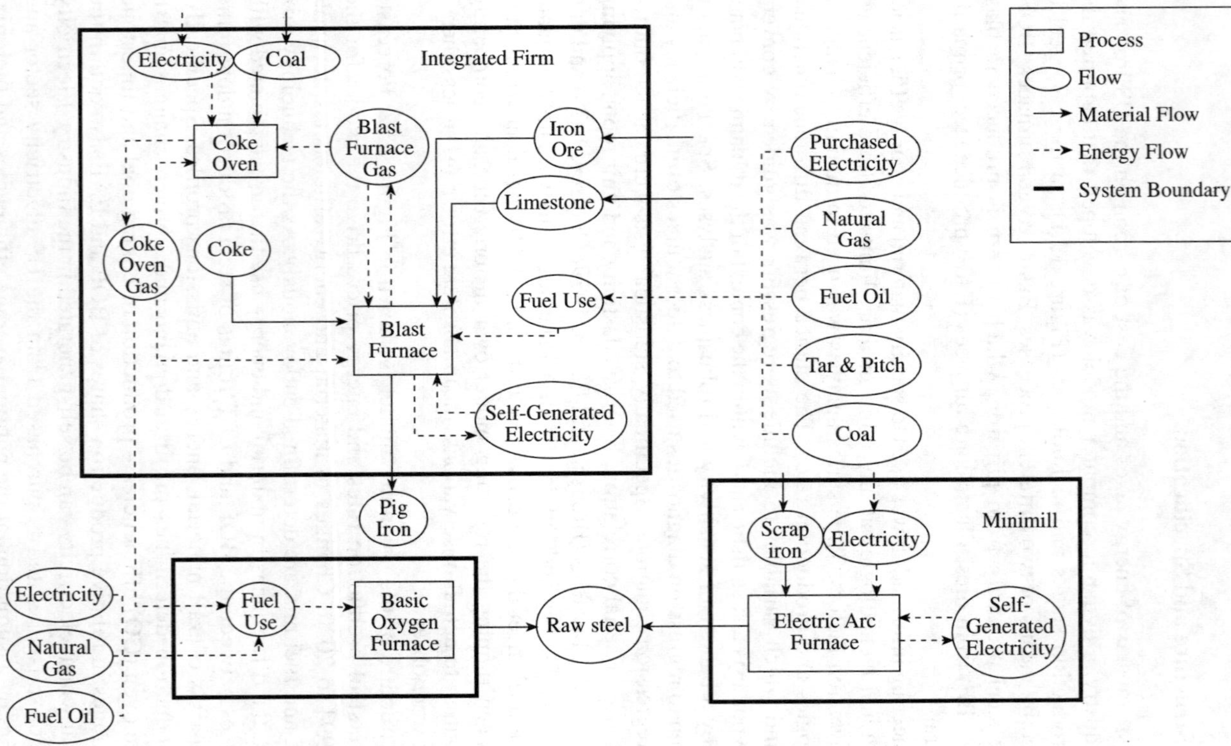

Figure 12.1 *Steel production processes*

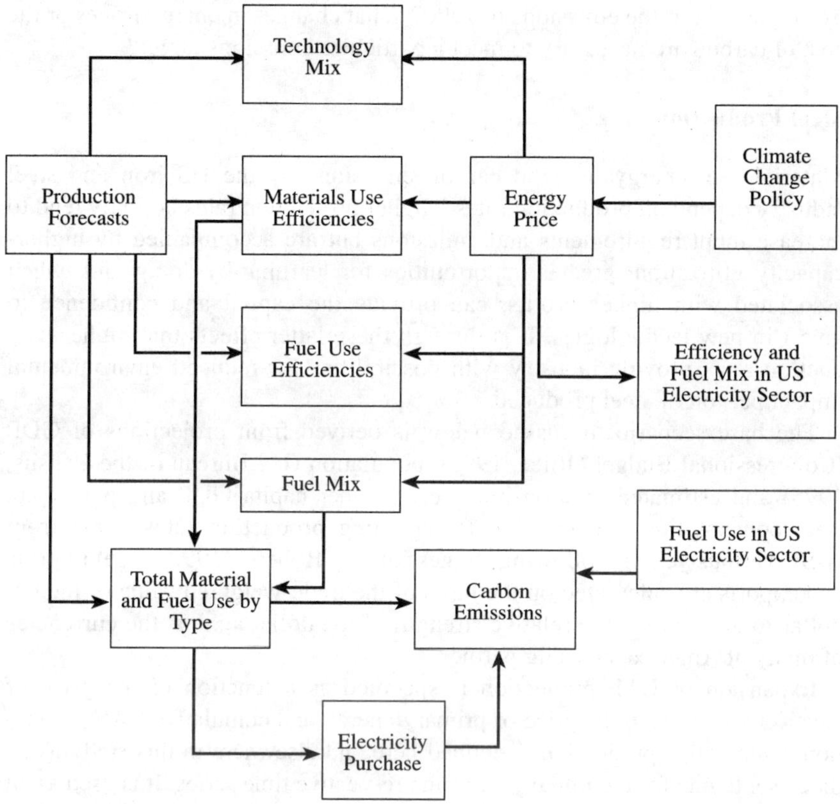

Figure 12.2 Model structure

to the model and follow projections by EIA (1998). Carbon emissions are calculated for direct combustion of fossil fuels, indirect fossil fuel use through the demand for electricity, and the use of limestone for removal of impurities in iron ores.

The model can also be run to 'backcast' market, policy and technology conditions that meet, for example, specific carbon emissions goals. In backcasting mode, the model would answer questions such as the following. Which rates of technology change are required at an individual production stage so that future carbon emissions per ton of raw steel product will not exceed the 1990 levels? What combinations of efficiency improvements or rates of fuel switching at individual production stages will lead to the highest emissions reductions? Which rates of expansion of electric arc technology will be required to cut carbon emissions from coal and coke in the year 2020 by 30 per cent of the emissions in 1990? What changes in energy prices or the cost of carbon are necessary to meet a particular emissions target?

Steel Production

Material use, energy use and carbon emissions by the US iron and steel industry depend on production rates. Higher production rates not only tend to increase input requirements and emissions but are accompanied by higher-capacity utilization, greater opportunities for learning-by-doing and, when associated with higher profits, can provide the capital and confidence to invest in new technologies. It is through these latter effects that higher production rates provide industry with possibilities for reduced environmental impact per ton of steel produced.

The base scenario discussed below is derived from projections of GDP (Congressional Budget Office, 1998), population (US Bureau of the Census, 1996) and estimated relationships between per capita GDP and per capita steel consumption. Historical data regarding production rates come from AISI (various years). Following suggestions by Roberts (1990), steel imports and exports are calculated on the basis of the trade-weighted value of the US dollar to account for the relative strength of the dollar against the currencies of many of America's trading partners.

Expansion of EAF production is specified as a function of the price of electricity relative to the price of primary energy and cumulative EAF production. Cumulative production is defined here and elsewhere in this study as an index set to one for the initial year of the respective time series. It is used as an indicator of experience (Ruth, 1993). A maximum market share of electric arc furnaces of 80 per cent was assumed. The mathematical specification of the expansion path towards that maximum has been chosen such that rapid movement towards that maximum is possible early on, and that with increased market share of electric arc technology future expansion rates become increasingly difficult. By definition, the maximum of 80 per cent will only be approached asymptotically as cumulative production goes towards infinity. For the time-frame modelled here, very similar market shares are reached by the year 2020, whether that ultimate maximum is set at 70 per cent, 80 per cent or 90 per cent.

The split between EAF and BOF influences the industry's energy profile. More than 99 per cent of energy input into EAF is in the form of electricity. The efficiency with which the energy is used depends on cumulative production. As with the equations guiding expansion of electric arc production, cumulative production rates by each technology were used as an indicator of the experience associated with operating that technology.

For each technology, efficiency is measured in BTU per ton output because physical efficiency measures are more robust indicators of energy requirements than measures based on monetary values (Patterson, 1996). The use of purely physical measures is in contrast to many industry and government studies which measure industrial energy efficiency as the ratio of energy use per dollar value of shipments. The use of monetary-based efficiency measures allows for a more proper aggregation of output with different physical and chemical characteristics. However, this model deals with output of raw steel only – not with semi-finished or finished steel products – and thus considers a physically and chemically fairly homogeneous product. Furthermore, in an industry in which energy is a major contributor to the costs of the product, major changes in energy price are likely to affect product price, and thus reduce the ratio of energy use to dollar value of shipments. As a consequence, if efficiency is measured in BTU per dollar value of shipments, energy price increases may appear as efficiency-increasing, even if no change in technology or energy use took place.

Pig Iron Production

In the model six sources are considered for the supply of energy necessary for pig iron production. Blast furnace gas and coke oven gas are self-generated by-products of BFs and COs, respectively. Their availability depends on the production rates of these furnaces. Fuel oil, coal, natural gas and electricity are used in pig iron production alongside blast furnace and coke oven gas. Fuel oil use has historically been decreasing. Its decline has been driven to a significant extent by changes in its relative price. Similarly, the price of coal relative to the average fossil fuel price significantly influenced the choice of coal as an energy source. In the model, the share of energy supplied by natural gas is set as the remainder that is not supplied by the other five energy sources whose contributions are estimated by means of a seemingly unrelated regression model.

Coke Production

Coal use efficiencies in US coke production remained virtually constant over the last three decades. Coal consumption per ton of coke depends primarily on the rate of coke production. Increased production rates frequently lead to higher efficiencies because of reduced heat losses per ton of product. This relationship is confirmed by the regression analysis and used to quantify the model.

Electricity Generation

To reflect the industry's fuel requirements and carbon emissions properly, the model includes fuel requirements by the US electricity sector to supply electricity for iron and steel production. The respective module uses actual data and forecasts of fuel mix in the electricity sector that are reported in the *Annual Energy Outlook* up to the year 2020 (EIA, 1998).

Carbon Emissions

Carbon emissions accrue from burning fossil fuels and from using limestone to reduce the impurity content of pig iron produced in BFs. Burning of fossil fuels and calcination of limestone means oxidizing the carbon that is contained in these inputs. That carbon is ultimately emitted into the atmosphere as carbon oxides. Aside from reducing fuel and limestone use, very limited opportunities exist to reduce carbon oxide emissions. Furthermore, since emissions often occur from technologies which are not perfectly isolated from their environment – for example, furnace doors do not always close properly; sufficient ventilation and aeration is required for proper chemical reactions – the effort of tracing carbon flows is significantly streamlined by concentrating on the carbon content of the fuels that are used, instead of trying to measure emissions from a multitude of 'leaks'.

Table 12.1 Carbon content of fuels

Fuel type	Metric tons of carbon per billion BTU (1994 value)
Coal	25.61
Coal (electricity generation)	25.71
Natural gas	14.47
Residual fuel oil	21.49
Oil (electricity generation)	19.95
Liquid petroleum gas	17.02
Distillate fuel oil	19.95

Source: EIA (1994).

In the model, carbon emissions are calculated by multiplying the carbon content per BTU of a fuel with the industry's use of the respective fuel. Fixed carbon coefficients are applied (Table 12.1). To avoid double-counting, only the carbon content of purchased fuels and of fuels used to generate purchased electricity are taken into account. For the decarbonization of limestone we assume average emissions of 0.0205 metric tons of carbon per ton of steel (Gielen, 1997).

MODEL RESULTS

Base Scenario

For the base scenario of our model we assume future growth of GDP at an annual rate of 1.9 per cent and a trade-weighted value of the dollar, measured as an index, fixed at 78. The former is based on Congressional Budget Office forecasts (Congressional Budget Office, 1998). The latter is the mean value for the years 1970–96 (Federal Reserve Board Dallas, 1998). Under these assumptions, raw steel production rates increase by only 1.1 per cent for the years 1997–2020. At these lower production rates, fossil fuel use declines. Our base case results assume a penultimate market share of 80 per cent for EAF output and an S-shaped asymptotic approach towards that maximum. Concomitant with an increase in EAF production are technology changes that increase electricity use. However, since much of the electricity is produced from fossil fuels, total carbon emissions decline more slowly than total energy use (Table 12.2).

Market-based Climate Change Policies

To investigate impacts of market-based climate change policies on carbon emissions and energy use, we assume that policies are implemented in the year 2000. A plethora of different policy options are available in the model itself. However, for illustrative purposes we will concentrate here only on a $100 charge per ton of carbon and on an energy tax of 77 per cent per BTU. The cost of carbon increase may be caused, for example, by introducing a permit or tax. An increase in the cost of carbon by $100 per ton is consistent with several recent policy proposals. The energy tax rate of 77 per cent has been chosen to generate the same cumulative present value of tax revenues over the time-frame 2000–2020 as the carbon cost (Table 12.2).

Implementation of climate change policies provides incentives for industry to reduce energy requirements per ton of steel, though the rate at which policy-induced efficiency improvements occur declines over time (Figure 12.3). Trends in carbon emissions per ton of steel mirror those of energy efficiency improvements (Figure 12.4). Expansion of EAF production will be hastened by cost of carbon and energy tax increases because of the EAF's significantly smaller energy requirements per ton of steel relative to the BOF route.

An increased share of production by EAFs has marked effects on carbon emissions and carbon per ton of output. As EAF production is expanded, a shift towards cleaner processes takes place. Declines in pig iron production and BOF output, in turn, are associated with higher energy requirements and

Table 12.2 Summary of model results for base case, energy tax and cost of carbon scenarios

	Base Scenario	77% Energy Tax	$100 per ton Carbon
Total energy use (% change from 1994 levels to 2020)	–26.79	–32.46	–31.54
BOF production (% change from 1994 levels to 2020)	–16.52	–32.23	–29.95
BF energy use per ton of product (% change from 1994 levels to 2020)	–31.42	–27.68	–28.17
Years lost in improvement in energy use per ton of product from BF (policy scenario v. base scenario in 2020)		3	2
EAF production (% change from 1994 levels to 2020)	+38.96	+59.68	+59.68
EAF energy use per ton of product (% change from 1994 levels to 2020)	–25.63	–27.58	–27.39
EAF share of production in 2020 (%)	51.90	60.95	59.63
Years gained in improvement in energy use per ton of product from EAF (policy scenario v. base scenario in 2020)		2	2
Total carbon emissions (% change from 1994 levels to 2020)	–21.10	–26.10	–25.97
Cumulative present value of energy expenditures, 2000–2020 (billion 1994$, 5% discount rate)	37.44	63.89	63.42
Cumulative present value of payments, 2000–2020 (billion 1994$, 5% discount rate)		27.81	27.88
Energy expenditure in 2020 (billion 1994$)	0.89	1.56	1.59
Policy-induced payments in 2020 (billion 1994$)		0.68	0.69

carbon emissions per ton of product. If furnaces are operated at lower capacity, heat loss per ton of furnace charge is high, and thus efficiency is low. That furnaces are operated at low output rates during a recession, rather than

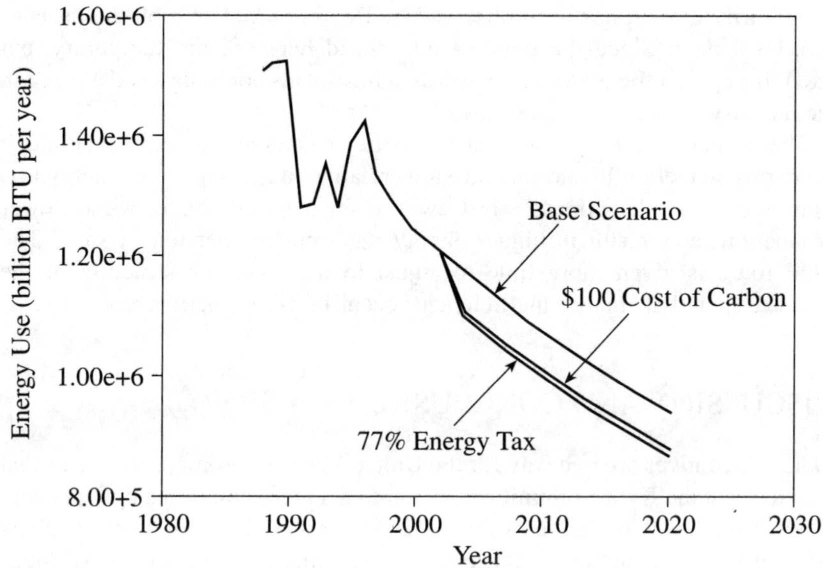

Figure 12.3 Energy use under alternative scenarios

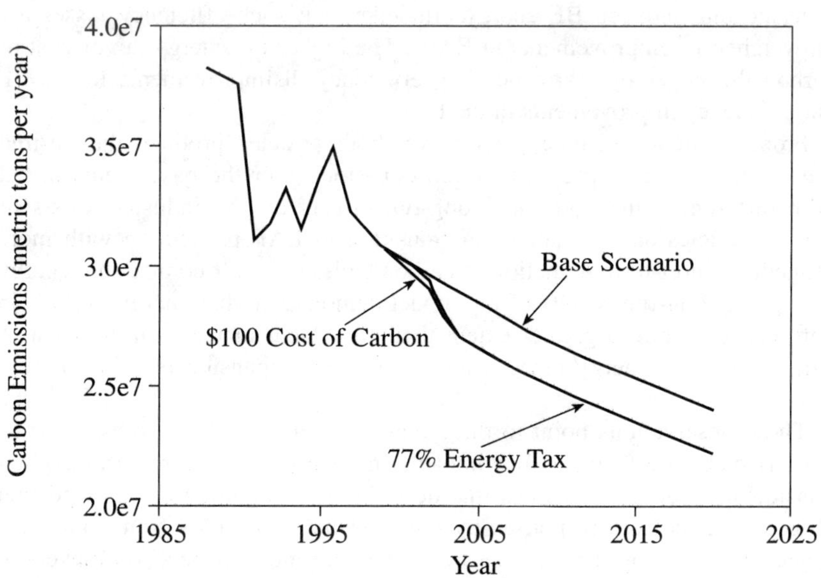

Figure 12.4 Carbon emissions under alternative scenarios

temporarily closed, has been observed by Boyd *et al.* (1993) on the basis of firm-level data. Since the policies introduced here are not temporary, but fixed throughout the 2000–2020 period, adjustments continue to take place in the industry.

The introduction of a cost of carbon policy causes an immediate, although short-run, reduction in carbon emissions relative to a comparable energy tax. This is due to a less drastic shift away from the BOF route, where lower production rates result in higher energy requirements per ton of steel. The BOF route is given more time to adjust to the changing structure of the industry such that smaller inefficiencies occur in its production processes.

DISCUSSION AND CONCLUSION

Market incentives are one way for the United States to promote strategies that help to meet the Kyoto summit obligation to decrease emissions by 7 per cent below 1990 levels in the years 2008–12. The iron and steel industry is a key element in this reduction, because it is a large single end user of fossil fuels. The above analysis shows that implementation of energy taxes or increases in the cost of carbon significantly alter the technology mix, energy profiles and emissions in the US iron and steel industry. A shift is expected away from BOF to EAF production of steel. Reductions in output from BF are likely to translate into reduced BF energy efficiency, but such efficiency losses are outweighed by improvements in EAFs. The higher the energy tax or cost of carbon the larger the corresponding efficiency disimprovements in the BF and efficiency improvements in the EAF.

From a climate change perspective, both policies produce the desired reductions in energy use and carbon emissions over the base scenario, but with differences in short- and long-run effects on the industry. Costs of carbon policies cause a smoother transition to EAF production with more immediate short-term reduction in carbon emissions over comparable energy taxes. The long-run results of the model demonstrate that energy taxes help curb energy use to a greater extent than equivalent increases in the cost of carbon, because energy taxes stimulate a larger expansion in EAF production.

These observations point to three main conclusions. First, to assess market-based climate change policy impacts on US iron and steel requires explicit consideration of the dynamics that describe its technology change and fuel choice. Intermediate responses by the industry may differ from long-term trajectories, making it necessary for policy and industry decision makers to take the entire time profile of industry behaviour into account rather than focus on short-term trends.

Second, responses of individual establishments will vary between basic oxygen and electric arc producers. Effectiveness of the policies depends on the technical details of the production processes, as the example of efficiency declines with lower furnace charge illustrates. These technical issues need to be taken into account in the choice among policies.

Third, because of large sunk investments in the industry, significant changes in overall energy use and emissions are difficult to achieve if the only incentives are through energy price signals. Using the price signal to affect technology change in the US iron and steel industry means application of a blunt instrument for cutting emissions. In contrast, combinations of market-based and investment-led policies may allow for a more surgical approach to overcome past technology lock-in and to induce changes that will hurt the industry less than a purely market-based approach.

Current expansions of the model concentrate on investigating, together with decision makers in industry and policy, when, where and how much to apply investment-led industrial policies in order to foster adoption of new, highly energy-efficient technologies. Choosing a transparent modelling approach will help facilitate this dialogue among key stakeholder groups. The modelling effort will remain dynamic, not only because it captures the time-varying behaviour of the industry, but because it fosters dynamic exchange among stakeholder groups and between stakeholders and the model. By engaging scientists, engineers, modellers and decision makers in industry and policy, the dynamic modelling process further opens the door for integrated assessment actively to inform environmental investment and policy making.

ACKNOWLEDGEMENTS

This project was made possible by the financial support from the US Environmental Protection Agency under Grant Number X 825828-01-0. Valuable research assistance was provided by Brynhildur Davidsdottir and Anthony Amato. Special thanks also go to John 'Skip' Laitner, Lynn Price, Nathan Martin, Steven Bernow, Peter May, Robert Costanza and the participants of the US EPA Technology Workshop on Iron and Steel for their comments on the model and earlier drafts of this chapter. The usual disclaimers apply.

NOTE

1. To request a copy of the model, send an e-mail to Matthias_Ruth@umail.umd.edu.

REFERENCES

AISI (various years), *Annual Statistical Report*, Washington, DC; American Iron and Steel Institute.

Azar, C. and H. Dowlatabadi (1999), 'A Review of Technical Change in Assessment of Climate Policy', *Annual Review of Energy and the Environment*, **24**, 513–44.

Boyd, G., S.H. Karlson, M. Neifer and M. Ross (1993), 'Energy Intensity Improvements in Steel Minimills', *Contemporary Policy Issues*, **11**, 88–100.

Breusch, T.S. and A. Pagan (1979), 'A Simple Test for Heteroscedasticity and Random Coefficient Variation', *Econometrica*, **47**, 1287–94.

Bureau of the Census (1996), http://census.gov/population/projections/nation/npaltsrs.txt.

Cleveland, C.J. and M. Ruth (1999), 'Indicators of Dematerialization and the Materials Intensity of Use', *Journal of Industrial Ecology*, **2**, 15–50.

Congressional Budget Office (1998), http://www.cbo.gov/showdoc.cfm?index=31&sequence=2.

Dickey, D. and W. Fuller (1981), 'Likelihood Ratio Statistics for Autoregressive Time Series with a Unit Root', *Econometrica*, **49**, 291–324.

Dowd, J. and J. Newman (1999), *Challenges and Opportunities for Advancing Engineering–Economic Policy Analysis: Highlights of the IEA International Workshop on Technologies to Reduce Greenhouse Gas Emissions, May 5–7, Washington, DC*, Paris: International Energy Agency.

Edmonds, J.A., H.M. Pitcher, D. Barns, R. Baron and M.A. Wise (1995), 'Modeling Future Greenhouse Gas Emissions, The Second Generation Model Description', in L.R. Klein and F.-C. Lo (eds), *Modelling Global Change*, Tokyo: United Nations University Press, pp. 295–340.

EIA (1998), *Annual Energy Outlook*, Washington, DC: Energy Information Administration.

Federal Reserve Board Dallas (1998), http://www.dallasfed.org/econdata/ findata.html.

Gielen, D.J. (1997), 'Long-Term Energy and Material Strategies for Reduction of Industrial CO_2 Emissions', *1997 ACEEE Summer Study on Energy Efficiency in Industry*, Washington, DC: American Council for an Energy-Efficient Economy, pp. 349–59.

Godfrey, L.G. (1978), 'Testing against General Autoregressive and Moving Average Error Models when the Regressors include Lagged Dependent Variables', *Econometrica*, **46**, 1293–1302.

Hannon, B. and M. Ruth (2000), *Dynamic Modeling*, New York: Springer-Verlag.

Hendriks, C.A., E. Worrell, L. Price, N. Martin and L.O. Meida (1999), 'The Reduction of Greenhouse Gas Emissions from the Cement Industry', IEA Greenhouse Gas R&D Programme, Cheltenham, United Kingdom (Report PH3/7), May.

High Performance Systems, Inc. (1999), 'STELLA Manual and Users Guide', Hanover, New Hampshire.

Jacobi, H.D. and I. Sue Wing (1999), 'Adjustment Time, Capital Malleability and Policy Cost', *The Energy Journal*, special issue, 73–92.

Khrushch, M., E. Worrell, L. Price, N. Martin and D. Einstein (1999), 'Carbon Emissions Reduction Potential in the U.S. Chemicals and Pulp and Paper Industries by Applying CHP Technologies', *Proceedings of the 1999 ACEEE Summer Study on Energy Efficiency in Industry*, Washington, DC: American Council for an Energy-Efficient Economy, pp. 515–28.

Martin, N., E. Worrell and L. Price (1999), 'Energy Efficiency and Carbon Dioxide

Emissions Reduction Opportunities in the U.S. Cement Industry', (LBNL-44182), Lawrence Berkeley National Laboratory, Berkeley, CA, July.
Martin, N., N. Anglani, D. Einstein, M. Khrushch, E. Worrell and L. Price (2000), 'Opportunities to Improve Energy Efficiency and Reduce Greenhouse Gas Emissions in the U.S. Pulp and Paper Industry', Lawrence Berkeley National Laboratory, Berkeley, CA.
Mongia, P. and J. Sathaye (1998a), 'Productivity Trends in India's Energy Intensive Industries: A Growth Accounting Analysis', (LBNL-41838), Lawrence Berkeley National Laboratory, Berkeley, CA.
Mongia, P. and J. Sathaye (1998b), 'Productivity Growth and Technical Change in India's Energy Intensive Industries: A Survey', (LBNL-41840), Lawrence Berkeley National Laboratory, Berkeley, CA.
Nordhaus, W.W. (1994) *Managing the Global Commons: The Economics of Climate Change*, Cambridge, MA: MIT Press.
OTA (1993), *Industrial Energy Efficiency*, Washington, DC: Office of Technology Assessment, Government Printing Office.
Patterson, M. (1996), 'What is energy efficiency?', *Energy Policy*, **24**, 377–90.
Price, L., E. Worrell and M. Khrushch (1999a), 'Sectoral Trends and Driving Forces of Global Energy Use and Greenhouse Gas Emissions: Focus on Industry and Buildings', (LBNL-43746), Lawrence Berkeley National Laboratory, Berkeley, CA.
Price, L., L. Michaelis, E. Worrell and M. Khrushch (1998), 'Sectoral Trends and Driving Forces of Global Energy Use and Greenhouse Gas Emissions', *Mitigation and Adaptation Strategies for Global Change*, **3**, 263–319.
Repetto, R. and D. Austin (1997), *The Costs of Climate Protection: A Guide for the Perplexed*, Washington, DC: World Resources Institute.
Risbey, J., M. Kindlikar and A. Patwardhan (1996), 'Assessing Integrated Assessments', *Climatic Change*, **34**, 369–95.
Roberts, Marc C. (1990), 'Predicting Metal Consumption: The Case of US Steel', *Resources Policy*, March, 56–73.
Rotmans, J. and B. de Vries (1997), *Perspectives on Global Change: The TARGETS Approach*, Cambridge: Cambridge University Press.
Rotmans, J. and H. Dowlatabadi (1998), 'Integrated Assessment Modeling', in S. Rayner and E. Malone (eds) *Human Choice and Climate Change*, Vol. 3, The Tools for Policy Analysis, Colombus, OH: Batelle Press, pp. 281–375.
Roy, J., J. Sathaye, A. Sanstad, P. Mongia and K. Schumacher (1999), 'Productivity Trends in India's Energy Intensive Industries', *The Energy Journal*, **20** (3).
Ruth, M. (1993), *Integrating Economics, Ecology and Thermodynamics*, Dordrecht: Kluwer Academic Publishers.
Ruth, M. (1998a), 'Energy Use and CO_2 Emissions in a Dematerializing Economy: Examples from Five US Metals Sectors', *Resources Policy*, **24**, 1–18.
Ruth, M. (1998b), 'Mensch and Mesh: Perspectives on Industrial Ecology', *Journal of Industrial Ecology*, **24**, 13–22.
Ruth, M. and P. Dell'Anno (1997), 'An Industrial Ecology of the US Glass Industry', *Resources Policy*, **23**, 109–24.
Ruth, M. and B. Hannon (1997), *Modeling Dynamic Economic Systems*, New York: Springer-Verlag.
Ruth, M., B. Davidsdottir and S. Laitner (2000), 'Impacts of Energy and Carbon Taxes on the US Pulp and Paper Industry', *Energy Policy*, **28**, 259–70.
Sands, R.D., J.A. Edmonds and C.N. MacCracken (1999), 'SGM 2000: Model De-

scription and Theory', draft, Washington, DC: Pacific Northwest National Laboratory.
Schumacher, K. and J. Sathaye (1999a), 'India's Iron and Steel Industry: Productivity, Energy Efficiency and Carbon Emissions', (LBNL-41844), Lawrence Berkeley National Laboratory, Berkeley, CA.
Schumacher, K. and J. Sathaye (1999b), 'India's Cement Industry: Productivity, Energy Efficiency and Carbon Emissions', (LBNL-41842), Lawrence Berkeley National Laboratory, Berkeley, CA.
Schumacher, K. and J. Sathaye (1999c), 'India's Pulp and Paper Industry: Productivity and Energy Efficiency', (LBNL-41843), Lawrence Berkeley National Laboratory, Berkeley, CA.
Schumacher, K. and J. Sathaye (1999d), 'India's Aluminum Industry: Productivity, Energy Efficiency and Carbon Emissions', (LBNL-41845), Lawrence Berkeley National Laboratory, Berkeley, CA.
Schumacher, K. and J. Sathaye (1999e), 'India's Fertilizer Industry: Productivity and Energy Efficiency', (LBNL-41846), Lawrence Berkeley National Laboratory, Berkeley, CA.
Worrell, E. (1994), 'Potentials for Improved Use of Industrial Energy and Materials', PhD thesis, Utrecht University, Utrecht, The Netherlands.
Worrell, E., N. Martin and L. Price (1999), 'Energy Efficiency and Carbon Emissions Reduction Opportunities in the U.S. Iron and Steel Sector', (LBNL-41724), Lawrence Berkeley National Laboratory, Berkeley, CA, July.
Yang, Z., R.S. Echaus, A.D. Ellerman and H.D. Jacobi (1996), 'The MIT Emissions Prediction and Policy Assessment (EPPA) Model', MIT Joint Program on the Science and Policy of Global Change, Report No. 6, Cambridge, MA.

Index